Contents

Acknowledgements

Acknowledgements

We would like to thank everybody who contributed to the Survey and the production of this report. We were supported by our specialist colleagues in ONS who were responsible for sampling, fieldwork, coding and editing. Our thanks also go to colleagues who supported us with administrative duties. Particular thanks are due to the interviewers who worked on the 1996 survey, and to all those members of the public who gave their time and co-operation.

1 Introduction

Development and content of the survey

The General Household Survey (GHS) is a continuous survey which has been running since 1971[1] and is based each year on a sample of the general population resident in private (that is, non-institutional) households in Great Britain. Since the 1988 survey, the fieldwork has been conducted on a financial rather than calendar year basis, so for the 1996 survey inverviews were carried out from April 1996 to March 1997. During this period, interviews were obtained with 17043 people aged 16 and over, either in person or occasionally by proxy, in 9158 households throughout the country[2]. Since the 1994 survey, interviews have been conducted using computer-assisted personal interviewing (CAPI) on laptop computers and the BLAISE software. This has had the effect of reducing costs, the amount of missing data at individual questions, the amount of office-based coding and editing and output timetables.

Since 1971, the GHS has included questions on population and fertility, family and household information, housing, health, employment and education. In so doing, it provides a unique opportunity to examine the inter-relationship between these important areas of social policy and to monitor changes in their associations over time. The survey is widely used by central government as a source of background information for decisions on resource allocation, in developing household projection techniques and national population projections. It is also widely used by a wide range of health professionals, and by researchers and secondary analysts with an interest in social policy and demographic issues.

The GHS provides valuable information about particular social groups, such as lone parents, although it is often necessary to aggregate data over a number of years in order to obtain large enough subsamples for analysis. The survey also helps to fill in some of the gaps in information about social changes between decennial population censuses.

The GHS was designed as a 'modular' survey and, as a result, other subjects are covered periodically and new topics are introduced from time to time. The 1996 survey repeated questions from earlier years on smoking, drinking, sport and leisure activities, burglary, mobility and movers out of owner occupation. A new section on young carers, quality of life indicators and a shortened section on activities of daily living were also included.

The report

This report on the 1996 survey is the twenty-sixth annual report of results from the GHS. In addition to the latest information available on a wide range of topics, the report provides data on a number of trends and changes measured by the GHS since it began. The main analysis presented in Chapters 2-13 are followed, as usual, by a number of appendices. These include a glossary of definitions and terms used throughout the report and useful notes on how these have changed over time (Appendix A); information about the sample design and response (B); a section on sampling errors (C); the household and individual questionnaires used in 1996, excluding self-completion forms and prompt cards (D) and a list of the main topics covered by the survey since 1971 (E).

The availability of unpublished data

Unpublished GHS data can be made available to researchers, for a charge, if resources are available, and provided that confidentiality of informants is preserved. Any work based on the GHS data is the responsibility of the individuals concerned, but ONS should be given the opportunity to comment in advance on any report or paper using GHS data, whether prepared for publication or for a lecture, conference or seminar.

In addition, copies of GHS datasets are available for specific research projects, subject to similar conditions, through the Data Archive at the University of Essex[3].

Notes and references

1. A list of published reports from the survey, including details of the report of preliminary findings from the 1996 survey published in November 1997, is given at the end of this report.
2. See Appendix B 'Sample design and response' for full details of the sample design and size since 1971.
3. For further information, contact:
   Data Archive
   University of Essex
   Wivenhoe Park
   Colchester
   Essex
   CO4 3SQ
   Tel: 01206 872 001
   Fax: 01206 872 003
   e-mail: archive@essex.ac.uk

Notes to Tables

1. **Harmonised outputs:** where appropriate, tables including marital status, living arrangements, ethnic groups, tenure, economic activity, accommodation type, length of residence and general health have adopted the harmonised output categories described in the publication *'Harmonised Concepts and Questions for Government Social Surveys'* London: ONS (1996). However, where data from the 1996 survey has been combined with data from earlier years to provide sufficient sample size for analysis and where long established time series are shown, harmonised outputs have not generally been used.

2. **Classification variables:** variables such as age and income, are not presented in a standard form throughout the report partly because the groupings of interest depend on the subject matter of the chapter, and partly because many of the trend series were started when the results used in the report had to be extracted from tabulations prepared to meet different departmental requirements.

3. **Non-response and missing information:** the information from a household which co-operates in the survey may be incomplete, either because of a partial refusal (eg to income), or because information was collected by proxy and certain questions omitted because considered inappropriate for proxy interviews (eg marriage and income data), or because a particular item was missed because of lack of understanding or an error.

Household and individuals who did not co-operate at all are omitted from all the analyses; those who omitted whole sections (eg marriages) because they were partial refusals or interviewed by proxy are omitted from the analyses of that section. In 1996 the 'no answers' arising from omission of particular items have been excluded from the base numbers shown in the tables and from the bases used in percentaging. The number of 'no answers' is generally less than 0.5% of the total and at the level of precision used on GHS the percentages for valid answers are not materially affected by the treatment of 'no answers'.

Socio-economic group and income variables are the most common variables which have too many missing answers to ignore.

4. **Base numbers:** Very small bases have been avoided wherever possible because of the relatively high sampling errors that attach to small numbers. Often where the numbers are not large enough to justify the use of all categories, classifications have been condensed; however, an item within a classification is occasionally shown separately, even though the base is small, because to combine it with another large category would detract from the value of the larger category. In general, percentage distributions are shown if the base is 50 or more. Where the base is 20-49, the percentages are shown in square brackets.

For some analysis several years data have been combined to increase the sample size to enable appropriate analysis.

5. **Percentages:** A percentage may be quoted in the text for a single category that is identifiable in the tables only by summing two or more component percentages. In order to avoid rounding errors, the percentage has been recalculated for the single category and therefore may differ by one percentage point from the sum of the percentages derived from the tables.

The row or column percentages may add to 99% or 101% because of rounding.

6. **Conventions:** The following conventions have been used within tables:

.. data not available
- category not applicable
0 less than 0.5% or no observations
[] the numbers in square brackets are percentages on a base of 20-49. See note 4.

7. **Statistical significance:** Unless otherwise stated, changes and differences mentioned in the text have been found to be statistically significant at the 95% confidence level.

8. **Mean:** Throughout the report the arithmetic term 'mean' is used rather than 'average'. The mean is a measure of the central tendency for continuous variables, calculated as the sum of all scores in a distribution, divided by the total number of scores.

2 Households, families and people

Household size and composition

Trends over time

The average (mean) size of households in 1996 was 2.43.

Since the GHS started in 1971, there has been a gradual decline in the average size of households:

- in the 1970s and 1980s, the average household size declined steadily from 2.91 in 1971 to 2.51 in 1989;
- in the early 1990s, the average household size continued to decline but at a slower rate.

Over the past two decades, there has been considerable change in the types of household in which people live. Overall households have been getting smaller and there has been:

- an increase in one person households (from 17% in 1971 to 28% in 1995). In 1996, 27% of households consisted of one person living alone of which, 59% were aged 60 or over;
- a decrease in the proportion of households consisting of a married or cohabiting couple with dependent children from 31% in 1979 to 25% in 1991. There has been little further change in the 1990s. In 1996, 23% of households consisted of a married couple with dependent children and 3% consisted of a cohabiting couple with dependent children;
- an increase in households consisting of a lone parent with dependent children (from 4% in 1979 to 7% in 1993). Since then there has been no change.

Tables 2.1-2.3 Figures 2A-2B

Families with dependent children

Trends over time

- Since 1971, there has been a marked decrease in the proportion of all families with dependent children who were married or cohabiting couple families (from 92% in 1971 to 78% in 1993) . Over the same period, there was an increase in lone parent families (from 8% in 1971 to 22% in 1993). Since 1993, there has been no significant change.

In 1996, families headed by a lone parent formed 21% of all families with dependent children, the majority of lone parents being lone mothers.

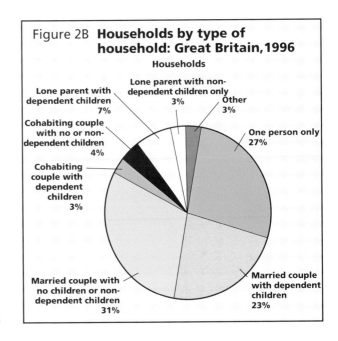

Figure 2B **Households by type of household: Great Britain, 1996**

Figure 2A **Mean household size: Great Britain, 1971-1996**

The proportion of all families with dependent children headed by:

- a single lone mother increased from 1% in 1971 to 7% in 1996;
- a divorced lone mother increased from 2% in 1971 to 6% in 1996;
- a separated lone mother increased from 2% in 1971 to 5% in 1996.

The proportion of lone father families has remained at 1% -2% since 1971.   **Table 2.4 Figure 2C**

Number of dependent children

In families with dependent children, the average (mean) number of dependent children decreased from 2.0 in 1971 to 1.8 in the early 1980s. Since then it has remained stable. Since the early 1970s, the average number of dependent children per lone parent family has been consistently smaller than in families headed by a married or cohabiting couple (on average 1.7 compared with 1.9 in 1996).   **Table 2.5**

Income

In 1996, usual gross weekly household income was considerably lower among lone parent families than among either married or cohabiting couple families. For example:

- 33% of families with a lone mother and 27% with a lone father had a gross weekly income of £100 or less compared with 3% of married and 6% of cohabiting couple families;

- conversely, 5% of families with a lone mother had a weekly income in excess of £500 compared with 48% of married and 31% of cohabiting couple families. Similarly, families with a lone father were less likely than married couple families to have an income in excess of £500 (19% compared with 48%).   **Table 2.8**

Step families

The General Household Survey focuses on step families in which there is at least one dependent child from a previous marriage or relationship of one or both of the partners. Only respondents aged 16-59 were asked questions about step children.

In 1996, 8% of families with dependent children, where the head of family was aged under 60, contained one or more step children;

- in 84% of step families there was a stepfather (a couple and at least one child from a previous relationship of the woman);
- in 12% there was a stepmother (a couple and at least one child from a previous relationship of the man);
- in 4% there was both a stepmother and stepfather (a couple and children from both partners' previous relationships).   **Table 2.9**

People

Since the GHS started in 1971, changes in the characteristics of the sample have reflected the gradual ageing of the

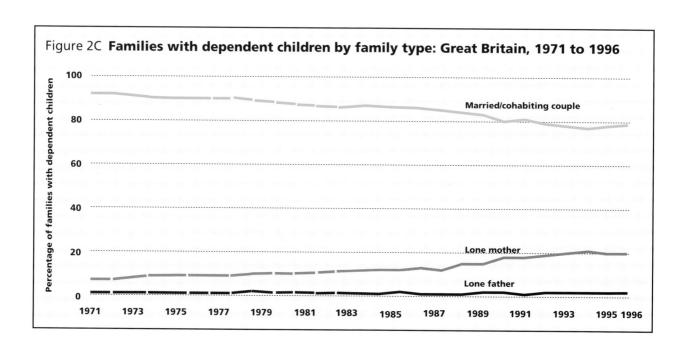

Figure 2C **Families with dependent children by family type: Great Britain, 1971 to 1996**

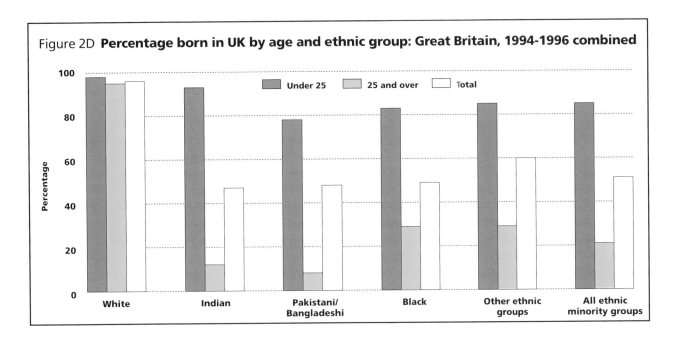

Figure 2D **Percentage born in UK by age and ethnic group: Great Britain, 1994-1996 combined**

population. The proportion of people aged 75 and over increased from 4% in 1971 to 7% in 1996. Women accounted for 58% of this age group.   **Tables 2.10-2.11**

Living alone

The proportion of people living alone increased from 9% in 1973 to 14% in 1991, since then there has been little change. The group most likely to be living alone (58%) were elderly women, particularly those over 75.

The increase in the proportion living alone mainly occurred among two age groups:

- people aged 25-44 (from 2% in 1973 to 8% in 1996). Men in this age group were nearly twice as likely as women to live alone (11% compared with 6%);
- people aged 75 and over (from 40% in 1973 to 47% in 1983). Since then the proportion has fluctuated between 47% and 51%. In 1996, 47% of people living alone were aged 75 and over.   **Tables 2.12-2.13**

Ethnic group

The majority (94%) of respondents described themselves as White. Ninety six per cent of those who described themselves as White were born in the UK.

Patterns of immigration can be seen in the way proportions of each ethnic minority group who were born in the UK differ by age . Based on the data for the combined years 1994-1996:

- among those aged under 25, 93% describing themselves as Indian, 83% describing themselves as Black and 78% describing themselves as Pakistani/Bangladeshi were born in the UK;
- among those aged 25 and over, 29% of those who described themselves as Black were born in the UK, compared with only 12% who described themselves as Indian and 8% who described themselves as Pakistani/Bangladeshi.   **Table 2.14-2.15 Figure 2D**

The average (mean) household size differed among ethnic groups. Based on data for the combined years 1994-1996, Pakistani and Bangladeshi households were on average the largest (4.5 persons). They were nearly twice as large as White households (2.4 persons) and larger than both Indian and Black households (3.7 and 2.5 persons respectively).   **Table 2.16**

The age profile of different ethnic groups varied considerably. Among the Pakistani/Bangladeshi population there was a particularly high proportion of children aged under 16 (41% compared with 31% of the Indian, 25% of the Black and 22% of the White population).

Among all ethnic minority groups, the proportion of people aged 65 and over was lower than among the White population (3% of Pakistani/Bangladeshi, 4% of Indian, 7% of Black compared with 16% of the White population). **Table 2.17**

Table 2.1 Household size: 1971 to 1996

(a) Households and (b) Persons   Great Britain

Number of persons in household (all ages)	1971	1975	1979	1981	1983	1985	1989	1991	1993	1995	1996
					Percentage of households of each size						
(a) Households	%	%	%	%	%	%	%	%	%	%	%
1	17	20	23	22	23	24	25	26	27	28	27
2	31	32	32	31	32	33	34	34	35	35	34
3	19	18	17	17	17	17	17	17	16	16	16
4	18	17	17	18	18	17	16	16	15	15	15
5	8	8	7	7	7	6	6	6	5	5	5
6 or more	6	5	4	4	3	2	2	2	2	2	2
Base = 100%	11988	12097	11490	12006	10068	9993	10085	9955	9852	9758	9158
Average (mean) household size	2.91	2.78	2.67	2.70	2.64	2.56	2.51	2.48	2.44	2.40	2.43
					Percentage of persons in households of each size						
(b) Persons	%	%	%	%	%	%	%	%	%	%	%
1	6	7	9	8	9	10	10	11	11	12	11
2	22	23	24	23	24	26	27	27	28	29	28
3	20	19	19	19	19	20	21	20	19	20	20
4	25	25	26	27	27	27	26	25	25	24	25
5	15	14	13	14	13	12	11	11	10	10	10
6 or more	13	11	9	9	7	6	5	5	6	5	6
Base = 100%	34849	33579	30716	32410	26587	25555	25269	24657	24079	23385	22274

Table 2.2 Household type: 1971 to 1996

(a) Households and (b) Persons   Great Britain

Household type	1971	1975	1979	1981	1983	1985	1989	1991	1993	1995	1996
					Percentage of households of each type						
(a) Households	%	%	%	%	%	%	%	%	%	%	%
1 adult aged 16-59	5	6	7	7	7	8	9	10	10	12	11
2 adults aged 16-59	14	14	14	13	13	15	16	16	16	17	15
Youngest person aged 0-4	18	15	13	13	14	13	13	14	14	13	13
Youngest person aged 5-15	21	22	22	22	19	18	17	16	16	16	17
3 or more adults	13	11	11	13	13	12	13	12	11	10	11
2 adults, 1 or both aged 60 or over	17	17	17	17	18	17	16	16	17	16	16
1 adult aged 60 or over	12	15	16	15	16	16	16	16	17	15	16
Base = 100%	11934	12090	11490	12006	10068	9993	10085	9955	9852	9758	9158
					Percentage of persons in each type of household						
(b) Persons	%	%	%	%	%	%	%	%	%	%	%
1 adult aged 16-59	2	2	3	3	3	3	4	4	4	5	5
2 adults aged 16-59	10	10	11	10	10	12	13	13	13	14	13
Youngest person aged 0-4	27	23	20	21	21	21	21	22	22	20	21
Youngest person aged 5-15	31	34	34	33	30	28	26	25	25	26	27
3 or more adults	15	13	14	16	17	17	17	16	15	15	15
2 adults, 1 or both aged 60 or over	11	12	12	12	13	13	13	13	14	14	13
1 adult aged 60 or over	4	5	6	6	6	6	7	7	7	6	7
Base = 100%	34720	33561	30716	32410	26587	25555	25269	24657	24079	23385	22274

Table 2.3 **Type of household: 1979 to 1996**

(a) Households and (b) Persons   *Great Britain*

Household type	1979	1981	1983	1985	1989	1991	1993	1995	1996
	Percentage of households of each type								
(a) Households	%	%	%	%	%	%	%	%	%
1 person only	23	22	23	24	25	26	27	28	27
2 or more unrelated adults	3	3	3	4	3	3	3	2	3
Married/cohabiting couple									
with dependent children	31	32	30	28	26	25	24	24	25
with non-dependent children only	7	8	8	8	9	8	7	6	6
no children	27	26	27	27	27	28	28	29	28
Married couple									
with dependent children	..	..	..	..	.	..	..	..	23
with non-dependent children	..	..	..	..	.	..	..	..	6
no children	..	..	..	..	.	..	..	..	25
Cohabiting couple									
with dependent children	..	..	..	..	.	..	..	..	3
with non-dependent children	..	..	..	..	.	..	..	..	0
no children	..	..	..	..	.	..	..	..	4
Lone parent									
with dependent children	4	4	5	4	5	6	7	7	7
with non-dependent children only	4	4	4	4	4	4	3	3	3
Two or more families	1	1	1	1	1	1	1	1	1
Base = 100%	*11454*	*11982*	*10031*	*9993*	*10085*	*9955*	*9852*	*9738*	*9138*
	Percentage of persons in each type of household								
(b) Persons	%	%	%	%	%	%	%	%	%
1 person only	9	8	9	10	10	11	11	12	11
2 or more unrelated adults	2	3	3	3	3	2	3	2	3
Married/cohabiting couple									
with dependent children	49	49	47	45	42	41	41	40	42
with non-dependent children only	9	10	11	11	12	11	9	9	9
no children	20	19	21	21	22	23	23	25	24
Married couple									
with dependent children	..	..	..	..	.	..	..	..	37
with non-dependent children	..	..	..	..	.	..	..	..	9
no children	..	..	..	..	.	..	..	..	21
Cohabiting couple									
with dependent children	..	..	..	..	.	..	..	..	4
with non-dependent children	..	..	..	..	.	..	..	..	0
no children	..	..	..	..	.	..	..	..	3
Lone parent									
with dependent children	5	5	5	5	6	7	8	8	8
with non-dependent children only	3	3	3	4	3	3	3	3	3
Two or more families	2	2	2	1	2	2	2	1	1
Base = 100%	*30546*	*32310*	*26425*	*25454*	*25269*	*24657*	*24079*	*23325*	*22190*

See Appendix A for the definition of a household.

Table 2.4 Family type, and marital status of lone mothers: 1971 to 1996

Families with dependent children* *Great Britain*

Family type	1971	1975	1979	1981	1983	1985	1989	1991	1993	1995	1996
	%	%	%	%	%	%	%	%	%	%	%
Married/cohabiting couple†	92	90	88	87	86	86	83	81	78	78	79
Lone mother	7	9	10	11	12	12	15	18	20	20	20
single	1	1	2	2	3	3	5	6	8	8	7
widowed	2	2	2	2	2	1	1	1	1	1	1
divorced	2	3	4	4	5	5	6	6	7	7	6
separated	2	2	3	2	2	3	3	4	4	5	5
Lone father	1	1	2	2	1	2	2	1	2	2	2
All lone parents	8	10	12	13	14	14	17	19	22	22	21
Base = 100%	*4864*	*4776*	*4203*	*4445*	*3538*	*3348*	*3223*	*3143*	*3145*	*3022*	*2975*

* Dependent children are persons under 16, or aged 16-18 and in full-time education, in the family unit, and living in the household.
† Including married women whose husbands were not defined as resident in the household.

Table 2.5 Average (mean) number of dependent children by family type: 1971 to 1996

Families with dependent children* *Great Britain*

Family type	Average (mean) number of children										
	1971	1975	1979	1981	1983	1985	1989	1991	1993	1995	1996
Married/cohabiting couple†	2.0	2.0	1.9	1.9	1.9	1.8	1.8	1.9	1.9	1.9	1.9
Married couple	..	..	..	..	..	..	..	..	..	..	1.9
Cohabiting couple	..	..	..	..	..	..	..	..	..	..	1.7
Lone parent	1.8	1.7	1.7	1.6	1.7	1.6	1.6	1.7	1.7	1.7	1.7
Total: all families with dependent children	2.0	1.9	1.9	1.8	1.8	1.8	1.8	1.8	1.8	1.8	1.8
Bases											
Married/cohabiting couple	*4482*	*4299*	*3701*	*3887*	*3047*	*2890*	*2680*	*2541*	*2453*	*2358*	*2329*
Married couple	*..*	*..*	*..*	*..*	*..*	*..*	*..*	*..*	*..*	*..*	*2086*
Cohabiting couple	*..*	*..*	*..*	*..*	*..*	*..*	*..*	*..*	*..*	*..*	*243*
Lone parent	*382*	*477*	*502*	*558*	*491*	*458*	*543*	*595*	*682*	*658*	*635*
Total	*4864*	*4776*	*4203*	*4445*	*3538*	*3348*	*3223*	*3136*	*3135*	*3016*	*2964*

* Dependent children are persons aged under 16, or aged 16-18 and in full-time education, in the family unit, and living in the household.
† Including married women whose husbands were not defined as resident in the household.

Table 2.6 **Family type and number of dependent children: 1972 to 1996**

Dependent children *   *Great Britain*

| | Percentage of all dependent children in each family type | | | | | | | | | | |
	1972	1975	1979	1981	1983	1985	1989	1991	1993	1995	1996
	%	%	%	%	%	%	%	%	%	%	%
Married/cohabiting couple with											
1 dependent child	16	17	18	18	18	19	18	17	15	16	17
2 or more dependent children	76	74	70	70	69	69	67	66	65	64	63
Lone mother with											
1 dependent child	2	3	3	3	3	4	4	5	6	5	5
2 or more dependent children	5	6	7	7	8	7	9	12	12	14	13
Lone father with											
1 dependent child	0	0	0	1	0	1	1	0	1	1	0
2 or more dependent children	1	1	1	1	1	1	1	1	1	1	1
Base = 100%	*9474*	*9293*	*7803*	*8216*	*6522*	*5966*	*5827*	*5799*	*5794*	*5559*	*5431*

* Dependent children are persons under 16, or aged 16-18 and in full-time education, in the family unit, and living in the household.

Table 2.7 **Age of youngest dependent child by family type**

Families with dependent children *   *Great Britain: 1995 and 1996 combined*

| Family type | | Age of youngest dependent child | | | | *Base =* | Total |
		0-4	5-9	10-15	16 and over	*100%*	
							%
Married/cohabiting couple†	%	42	26	26	7	*4698*	78
Lone mother	%	38	32	24	6	*1192*	20
Lone father	%	11	20	55	14	*107*	2
All lone parents	%	36	31	26	7	*1299*	22
Total	%	41	27	26	7	*5997*	100

* Dependent children are persons aged under 16, or aged 16-18 and in full-time education, in the family unit, and living in the household.
† Including married women whose husbands were not defined as resident in the household.

Table 2.8 **Usual gross weekly household income by family type**

Families with dependent children *   *Great Britain: 1996*

| Family type | | Usual gross weekly household income | | | | | | | | | | |
		£0.01-£100.00	£100.01 -£150.00	£150.01 -£200.00	£200.01 -£250.00	£250.01 -£300.00	£300.01 -£350.00	£350.01 -£400.00	£400.01 -£450.00	£450.01 -£500.00	£500.01 and over	Base = 100%
Married couple	%	3	4	5	5	6	7	8	8	7	48	*1875*
Cohabiting couple	%	6	12	10	8	7	7	6	7	6	31	*221*
Lone mother	%	33	27	12	9	4	4	3	2	1	5	*548*
Single	%	47	22	9	5	2	1	3	3	2	6	*210*
Widowed	%	[4]	[4]	[8]	[21]	[21]	[17]	[4]	[0]	[8]	[12]	*24*
Divorced	%	28	27	15	12	7	1	4	2	1	3	*180*
Separated	%	25	37	13	7	1	9	2	0	0	6	*134*
Lone father	%	27	15	6	12	2	12	2	2	4	19	*52*
All lone parents	%	33	26	11	9	4	4	3	2	2	6	*600*

* Dependent children are persons aged under 16, or aged 16-18 and in full-time education, in the family unit, and living in the household.
† Bases exclude cases where income is not known.

17

Table 2.9 **Stepfamilies by family type**

Stepfamilies with dependent children*
(Family head aged 16-59)   *Great Britain: 1996*

Type of stepfamily	
	%
Couple with child(ren) from the woman's previous marriage†	84
Couple with child(ren) from the man's previous marriage†	12
Couple with child(ren) from both partners' previous marriages†	4
Base = 100%	*170*

* Dependent children are persons under 16, or aged 16-18 and in full-time
   education, in the family unit, and living in the household.

† Includes previous cohabitations.

Table 2.10 **Age by sex: 1971 to 1996**

All persons   *Great Britain*

Age	1971	1975	1979	1981	1983	1985	1989	1991	1993	1995	1996
	%	%	%	%	%	%	%	%	%	%	%
Males											
0- 4	9	8	7	7	7	7	7	8	8	7	7
5-15*	19	18	19	18	18	16	15	15	16	16	16
16-44*	39	40	40	41	41	42	42	41	40	39	39
45-64	24	23	23	22	22	22	23	22	23	24	23
65-74	7	8	8	8	8	9	8	8	9	9	8
75 and over	3	3	4	4	4	4	5	5	5	5	6
Base = 100%	*16908*	*16242*	*14719*	*15735*	*12860*	*12551*	*12157*	*11913*	*11514*	*11376*	*10781*
	%	%	%	%	%	%	%	%	%	%	%
Females											
0- 4	8	6	6	6	7	6	7	7	7	6	7
5-15*	16	17	17	16	15	15	14	14	14	14	15
16-44*	37	38	37	39	39	41	41	39	38	39	39
45-64	24	24	23	22	22	21	21	22	22	24	23
65-74	9	10	10	10	10	10	9	10	10	9	9
75 and over	5	6	7	7	7	8	8	8	8	8	7
Base = 100%	*17871*	*17328*	*15997*	*16675*	*13727*	*13522*	*13112*	*12744*	*12565*	*12009*	*11493*
	%	%	%	%	%	%	%	%	%	%	%
Total											
0- 4	8	7	6	6	7	6	7	7	7	7	7
5-15*	17	17	18	17	16	15	15	15	15	15	15
16-44*	38	39	38	40	40	42	41	40	39	39	39
45-64	24	23	23	22	22	21	22	22	22	24	23
65-74	8	9	9	9	9	9	9	9	10	9	9
75 and over	4	4	5	5	6	6	6	7	7	6	7
Base = 100%	*34779*	*33570*	*30716*	*32410*	*26587*	*26073*	*25269*	*24657*	*24079*	*23385*	*22274*

* 5-14 and 15-44 in 1971 and 1975.

18

Table 2.11 **Sex by age**

All persons   *Great Britain: 1996*

Age		Males	Females	Base = 100%
0- 4	%	50	50	1561
5-15	%	51	49	3449
16-19	%	51	49	1001
20-24	%	48	52	1232
25-29	%	48	52	1645
30-34	%	48	52	1673
35-39	%	48	52	1679
40-44	%	49	51	1492
45-49	%	48	52	1543
50-54	%	51	49	1389
55-59	%	47	53	1083
60-64	%	48	52	1099
65-69	%	47	53	1022
70-74	%	44	56	921
75 and over	%	42	58	1485
Total	%	48	52	22274

Table 2.12 **Percentage living alone, by age: 1973 to 1996**

All persons aged 16 and over   *Great Britain*

	Percentage who lived alone								
	1973	1983	1985	1987	1989	1991	1993	1995	1996
16-24	2	2	4	3	4	3	4	5	4
25-44	2	4	5	6	6	7	8	9	8
45-64	8	9	11	10	11	11	11	12	11
65-74	26	28	29	28	27	29	28	27	31
75 and over	40	47	47	50	48	50	50	51	47
All aged 16 and over	9	11	12	12	13	14	14	15	14
Bases = 100%									
16-24	3811	3498	3367	3558	3137	2819	2574	2318	2233
25-44	8169	7017	7234	7418	7324	7118	6875	6761	6489
45-64	7949	5947	5644	5802	5557	5493	5360	5615	5114
65-74	2847	2494	2210	2389	2231	2196	2303	2129	1943
75 and over	1432	1490	1498	1596	1619	1603	1581	1451	1485
All aged 16 and over	24208	20446	19953	20763	19868	19229	18693	18274	17264

Table 2.13 **Percentage living alone, by age and sex**

All persons aged 16 and over   *Great Britain: 1996*

	Percentage who lived alone		
	Men	Women	Total
16-24	5	3	4
25-44	11	6	8
45-64	10	12	11
65-74	21	39	31
75 and over	31	58	47
All aged 16 and over	12	16	14
All persons*	10	13	11
Bases = 100%			
16-24	*1108*	*1125*	*2233*
25-44	*3136*	*3353*	*6489*
45-64	*2501*	*2613*	*5114*
65-74	*885*	*1058*	*1943*
75 and over	*627*	*858*	*1485*
All aged 16 and over	*8257*	*9007*	*17264*
*All persons**	*10781*	*11493*	*22274*

* Including children.

Table 2.14 **Ethnic group: 1983 to 1996**

All persons   *Great Britain*

Ethnic group	1983	1987	1989	1991	1993	1995	1996
	%	%	%	%	%	%	%
White	95	95	95	94	92	94	94
Indian	2	1	1	2	2	2	2
Pakistani/Bangladeshi	1	1	1	1	1	1	1
Black Caribbean*	1	1	1	1	1	1	1
Remaining groups	1	2	2	2	2	2	2
No answers	1	1	0	0	1	0	0
Base = 100%	*26587*	*26418*	*25269*	*24657*	*24079*	*23385*	*22274*

* West Indian/Guyanese in 1983, 1987 and 1989.

Table 2.15 **Percentage born in the UK by age and ethnic group**

All persons   *Great Britain: 1994-96 combined*

Ethnic group	Percentage born in the United Kingdom			Base = 100%		
	Age			Age		
	Under 25	25 and over	Total	*Under 25*	*25 and over*	*Total*
White	98	95	96	*20392*	*44457*	*64849*
Indian	93	12	47	*503*	*676*	*1179*
Pakistani/Bangladeshi	78	8	48	*512*	*377*	*889*
Black	83	29	49	*365*	*635*	*1000*
Remaining groups	85	29	60	*696*	*576*	*1272*
All ethnic minority groups	85	21	51	*2076*	*2264*	*4340*
Total	97	92	93	*22468*	*46721*	*69189*

Table 2.16 **Average household size by ethnic group of head of household**

Households   *Great Britain: 1994-96 combined*

Ethnic group	Average (mean) household size	Base = numbers of households
White	2.4	27252
Indian	3.7	344
Pakistani/Bangladeshi	4.5	208
Black	2.5	443
Remaining groups	2.6	356
All ethnic minority groups	3.1	1351
Total	2.4	28603

Table 2.17 **Age by ethnic group**

All persons   *Great Britain: 1994-96 combined*

Age	Ethnic group						All
	White	Indian	Pakistani/ Bangladeshi	Black	Remaining groups	All ethnic minority groups	
	%	%	%	%	%	%	%
0- 15	22	31	41	25	41	35	22
16 - 24	10	11	16	12	14	13	10
25 - 44	29	36	27	38	32	33	29
45 - 64	24	17	12	19	11	15	23
65 and over	16	4	3	7	3	4	15
Base = 100%	*64877*	*1183*	*891*	*1000*	*1272*	*4346*	*69223*

Table 2.18 **Sex by ethnic group**

All persons   *Great Britain: 1994-96 combined*

Ethnic group		Male	Female	Base = 100%
White	%	48	52	64877
Indian	%	50	50	1183
Pakistani/Bangladeshi	%	52	48	891
Black	%	49	51	1000
Remaining groups	%	48	52	1272
All ethnic minority groups	%	50	50	4346
Total	%	48	52	69223

Table 2.19 **Region by ethnic group**

All persons   *Great Britain: 1994-96 combined*

Region	Ethnic group						
	White	Indian	Pakistani/ Bangladeshi	Black	Remaining groups	All ethnic minority groups	Total
	%	%	%	%	%	%	%
England							
North	6	0	2	1	1	1	6
Yorkshire and Humberside	9	7	13	3	3	6	9
North West	12	4	16	3	9	8	12
East Midlands	7	12	5	5	5	7	7
West Midlands	9	29	15	14	9	17	10
East Anglia	4	1	0	0	2	1	4
Greater London	9	34	32	62	45	43	11
Outer Metropolitan Area and Outer South East	19	9	13	7	14	11	19
South West	9	1	1	3	7	3	9
Wales	5	1	0	1	2	1	5
Scotland	10	2	2	2	3	2	9
Base = 100%	*64877*	*1183*	*891*	*1000*	*1272*	*4346*	*69223*

3 Housing and consumer durables

Tenure

Trends over time

Changes in tenure during the 1990s show different trends to those of the 1980s. There was an increase in owner occupation during the 1980s which levelled off in the 1990s, but the 1990s has seen a small rise in private renting.

- In the 1980s owner occupation increased from 54% to 66%, but since 1991 it has remained unchanged at 67% of households.
- In 1996 around one in ten households (9%) rented from the private sector compared with 7% in 1991.

The decline in the proportion of households renting social sector housing (council housing, including New Town Corporations, and housing associations) has continued during the 1990s. In 1996:

- nearly a quarter (24%) of households were living in social sector housing;
- less than one fifth (19%) of households rented from councils compared with just over a third (34%) in 1981;
- 5% of households rented from housing associations. In contrast with the rest of the social housing sector this represents a rise; throughout the 1980s 2% of households rented from housing associations.

Table 3.1, Figure 3.A

More detailed information about housing in England from 1993 onwards may be obtained from the Survey of English Housing.[1]

Type of accommodation

The type of accommodation varies considerably with tenure. In 1996:

- almost a quarter of households (24%) who were renting privately lived in converted flats or rooms compared with 3% of households renting from the social sector;
- 92% of owner occupiers lived in a house of some type, compared to 58% households renting from the social sector;
- purpose built flats or maisonettes were most likely to be occupied by households renting from the social sector - 63% of such accommodation was occupied by this group.

Table 3.3

Age of building

The age of the buildings in which households lived was fairly evenly spread across the century but there was substantial variation with tenure. In 1996:

- one in five households (20%) lived in housing built before 1919 and just over one in ten (11%) of households lived in housing built since 1984;
- households renting privately were most likely to live in old housing stock - 43% lived in accommodation built before 1919;
- a small proportion of households (4%) renting from councils lived in accommodation built since 1985 compared with 11% of owner occupiers and 33% of those renting from housing associations.

Table 3.5

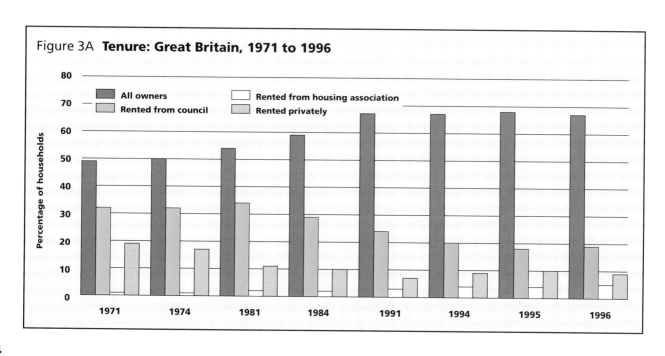

Figure 3A **Tenure: Great Britain, 1971 to 1996**

Household type

Tenure and type of accommodation varied with the number and ages of people in the household. For example:

- around three-quarters (75-77%) of households comprising two adults and no dependent children or large adult households lived in owner occupied accommodation compared with just over a half (52-54%) of single person households, 59% of large families and 68% of small families;   **Table 3.6**
- lone-parent families were the most likely to live in social sector housing (53% compared with 16% of other families);   **Table 3.17**
- 41% of older people living alone occupied social sector housing;   **Table 3.6**
- the households most likely to occupy purpose built flats and maisonettes were those living alone (29% of adults aged 16-59 and 30% of those aged 60 or more);   **Table 3.7**
- lone-parent families were more likely than other families with dependent children to live in purpose built flats and maisonettes (19% compared with 5%).   **Table 3.17**

Income

Gross weekly household income varied with respect to tenure. In 1996:

- households living in social sector housing had the lowest average gross weekly income (£184) while those who were buying with a mortgage had the highest (£543);

- not only did the head of household of those living in social sector housing earn less on average than heads of households in other tenure groups (£134 gross per week compared with £324 among owner occupiers) but so did their partners and other household members. Partners and other household members of owner occupied households contributed on average £136 to the household weekly income compared with an average of £50 among social sector renters.   **Table 3.15**

Cars and Vans

Trends over time

Household access to cars or vans in 1996 remained similar to that in 1995, which continues the trend of a lower rate of increase in car ownership in the 1990s than in the 1980s. In 1996:

- 70% of households had access to a car or van compared with 68% in 1991 and 59% in 1981;
- 24% of households had two or more cars compared with 14% in 1981;
- 4% of households had access to three or more cars. This proportion has remained constant since 1989.   **Table 3.18, Figure 3.B**

Socio-economic group

Access to cars and vans continues to vary according to the socio-economic group of the head of household. In 1996:

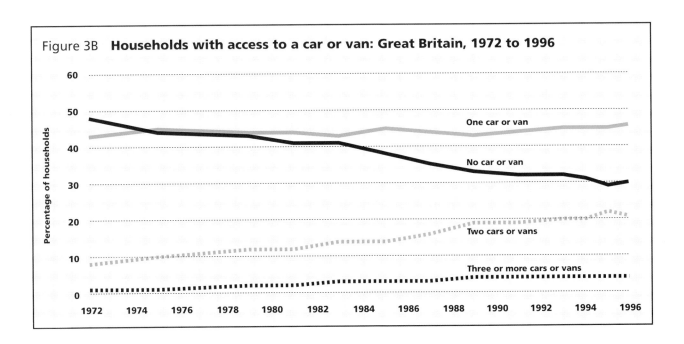

Figure 3B **Households with access to a car or van: Great Britain, 1972 to 1996**

- households headed by unskilled workers were the least likely to have access to a car or van - 45% of these households had no car or van available compared with 23% of junior non-manual workers and 5% of professionals;

- just over half (51%) of households headed by professionals and 58% by employers and managers had access to two or more cars compared with 13% of households headed by an unskilled manual worker. **Table 3.19**

Consumer durables

Trends over time

Various changes have been made to the list of consumer durables used in the survey and in 1996 satellite television was included for the first time.

- 18% of households had a receiver for satellite television.

The availability of the listed consumer durables have all increased since being included in the survey but the rates of increase vary. Particularly noticeable between 1995 and 1996 was the continued growth in ownership of 'entertainment' items:

- CD players (from 52% to 58%);
- video recorders (from 79% to 82%);
- home computers (from 25% to 27%).

Only three types of household appliances showed an increase in availability between 1995 and 1996:

- microwave ovens (from 70% to 74%);
- freezers (from 89% to 91%);
- central heating (from 86% to 88%).
  Table 3.20, Figure 3.C

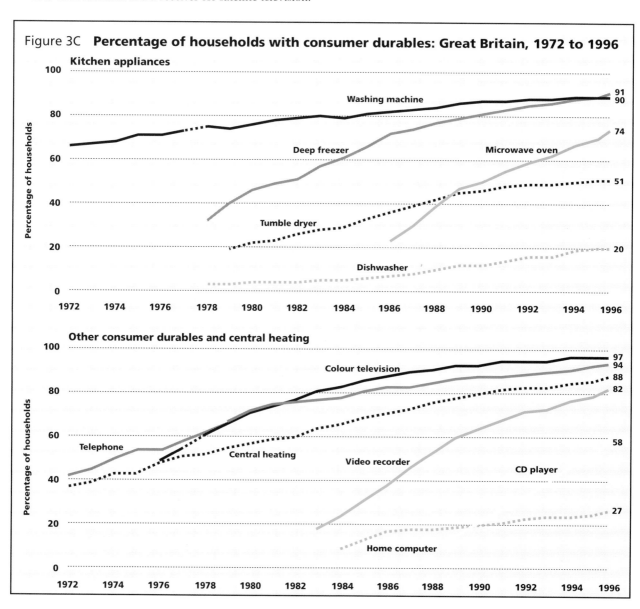

Figure 3C **Percentage of households with consumer durables: Great Britain, 1972 to 1996**

Household type

Households comprising one adult, in particular an older lone adult, were generally the least likely to have each type of consumer durable. The highest proportions of availability were generally among large adult households. For example:

- 42% of households comprising an older lone adult had a video recorder compared with 96% of large adult households and 95% of small family households;
- 70% of older lone adult households and 79% of younger lone adult households had a washing machine compared with almost all households comprising three or more people (98% of small family households and large adult households, and 99% of large family households).

There were some exceptions to the general findings in the availability of CD players, home computers, telephones and central heating.

- CD players and home computers were the only two consumer durables owned by a larger proportion of households comprising one person aged 16-59 than by households comprising two people, one of whom was aged 60 or more (60% compared with 34% and 21% compared with 12% respectively);
- a slightly smaller proportion of households comprising two adults and at least one child had a telephone compared with households with no children or large adult households (94% compared with 97-98%);
- levels of central heating ownership for lone-parent families were similar to single person households (85% compared to 83-84%). **Tables 3.21, 3.17**

Socio-economic group

Households headed by semi or unskilled manual workers were the least likely to have any of the consumer durables listed and those headed by professionals or employers and managers were the most likely. For example, in 1996:

- 64% of professional households had a home computer compared with 15% of unskilled manual households;
- 48% of households headed by employers or managers had a dishwasher compared with 5% of unskilled manual households.

Exceptions to the overall pattern included the proportion of households with:

- televisions (98% of households had a television and there was no difference between the groups);
- satellite televisions. Around a fifth (22%) of both semi and unskilled manual households and 27% of employer and manager households had a satellite television compared with 15-16% of professional, intermediate and junior non-manual households. **Table 3.22**

Gross weekly income

Among households in the lower income ranges, availability of consumer durables increased with income but in the upper ranges there was less variation. For example, in 1996:

- 70% of households in the lowest income group had a telephone compared with 96% of households with a gross weekly income of between £250 to £300 and 99% of households with a gross weekly income of more than £500;
- 66% of households in the lowest income group had a washing machine compared with 93% of households with a gross weekly income of between £250 to £300 and 99% of households with a gross weekly income of more than £500.

But for some consumer durables the increase of availability continued in the upper ranges of income. For example, between an income of £450 to £500 and more than £500 there was an increase in the availability of:

- CD players (from 78% to 85%) and home computers (from 38% to 50%);
- dishwashers (from 26% to 42%) and tumble driers (from 62% to 68%). **Table 3.23**

Reference

1 The latest publication from the Survey of English Housing is: Green, Deacon and Down *Housing in England 1996/7*. TSO (1998)

Table 3.1 **Tenure: 1971 to 1996**

Households   *Great Britain*

Tenure	1971	1975	1979	1981	1983	1985	1989	1991	1993	1994	1995	1996
	%	%	%	%	%	%	%	%	%	%	%	%
Owner occupied, owned outright	22	22	22	23	24	24	24	25	26	25	25	26
Owner occupied, with mortgage	27	28	30	31	33	37	42	42	41	42	42	41
Rented from council*	31	33	34	34	32	28	24	24	22	20	18	19
Rented from housing association	1	1	1	2	2	2	2	3	3	4	4	5
Rented with job or business	5	3	3	2	2	2	2	1	1	1	2	**
Rented privately, unfurnished†	12	10	8	6	5	5	4	4	4	4	5	7
Rented privately, furnished	3	3	2	2	2	2	2	2	3	3	3	3
Base = 100%	*11936*	*11970*	*11432*	*11939*	*9995*	*9933*	*10085*	*9922*	*9823*	*9668*	*9723*	*9155*

*   Council includes local authorities, New Towns and Scottish Homes in 1996.
†   Unfurnished includes the answer 'partly furnished'.
** All tenants whose accommodation goes with the job of someone in the household are allocated to 'rented privately'. Squatters are also included in this category in 1996.

Table 3.2 **Type of accommodation: 1971 to 1996**

Households   *Great Britain*

Type of accommodation*	1971	1975	1979	1981	1983	1985	1989	1991	1993	1994	1995	1996
	%	%	%	%	%	%	%	%	%	%	%	%
Detached house	16	15	17	16	18	19	20	19	19	20	22	21
Semi-detached house	33	34	32	32	32	31	31	32	31	32	31	32
Terraced house	30	28	29	31	31	29	29	29	29	28	28	27
Purpose-built flat or maisonette	13	14	15	15	14	15	14	14	15	14	15	15
Converted flat or maisonette/rooms	6	8	6	5	4	5	4	4	5	4	4	5
With business premises/other	2	1	1	1	1	1	1	1	1	1	1	0
Base = 100%	*11846*	*12041*	*11375*	*11978*	*10003*	*9890*	*10049*	*9917*	*9830*	*9678*	*9730*	*9128*

* Tables for type of accommodation exclude households living in caravans.

Table 3.3 **(a) Type of accommodation by tenure**
(b) Tenure by type of accommodation

Households   *Great Britain: 1996*

Tenure		Type of accommodation*							Base = 100%
		Detached house	Semi-detached house	Terraced house	All houses	Purpose-built flat or maisonette	Converted flat or maisonette/ rooms	All flats/ rooms	
(a)									
Owner occupied, owned outright	%	33	37	22	92	6	2	8	2313
Owner occupied, with mortgage	%	26	36	29	91	6	3	9	3790
All owners	%	29	36	26	92	6	2	8	6103
Rented from council†	%	1	28	31	60	38	2	40	1748
Rented from housing association	%	1	18	31	49	41	10	51	432
Social sector tenants	%	1	26	31	58	39	3	42	2180
Rented privately, unfurnished**	%	16	23	27	66	13	20	34	596
Rented privately, furnished	%	6	10	27	43	23	34	57	243
Private renters††	%	13	19	27	59	16	24	41	842
Total	%	21	32	27	81	15	5	19	9125
(b)									
		%	%	%	%	%	%	%	%
Owner occupied, owned outright		41	29	20	29	10	12	10	25
Owner occupied, with mortgage		53	46	44	47	17	23	18	42
All owners		93	75	64	76	27	35	29	67
Rented from council†		1	17	22	14	50	6	39	19
Rented from housing association		0	3	5	3	13	10	12	5
Social sector tenants		1	19	27	17	63	17	52	24
Rented privately, unfurnished**		5	5	7	5	6	28	11	7
Rented privately, furnished		1	1	3	1	4	19	8	3
Private renters††		6	5	9	7	10	48	19	9
Base = 100%		*1896*	*2947*	*2507*	*7350*	*1346*	*429*	*1775*	*9125*

*   Tables for type of accommodation exclude households living in caravans.
†   Council includes local authorities, New Towns and Scottish Homes in 1996.
** Unfurnished includes the answer 'partly furnished'.
†† All tenants whose accommodation goes with the job of someone in the household are allocated to 'rented privately'. Squatters are also included in this category in 1996.

Table 3.4 **Type of accommodation occupied by households renting from a council compared with other households: 1981 to 1996**

Households   *Great Britain*

Type of accommodation	1981	1987	1989	1991	1993	1994	1995	1996
	%	%	%	%	%	%	%	%
Renting from council								
Detached house	1	1	1	1	1	1	0	1
Semi-detached house	30	28	26	28	26	29	28	28
Terraced house	34	35	34	34	33	33	33	31
Purpose-built flat or maisonette	33	34	36	35	37	37	38	38
Converted flat or maisonette	2	2	3	3	3	1	1	2
Base = 100%	*4007*	*2600*	*2451*	*2339*	*2121*	*1957*	*1770*	*1748*
	%	%	%	%	%	%	%	%
Other households								
Detached house	24	25	26	25	24	25	26	25
Semi-detached house	33	33	33	33	33	33	32	33
Terraced house	29	28	28	28	28	27	27	27
Purpose-built flat or maisonette	6	7	7	8	9	9	10	9
Converted flat or maisonette	7	5	5	5	6	5	4	5
Base = 100%	*7904*	*7511*	*7573*	*7578*	*7699*	*7711*	*7953*	*7379*
	%	%	%	%	%	%	%	%
All households								
Detached house	16	18	20	19	19	20	22	21
Semi-detached house	32	32	31	32	31	32	31	32
Terraced house	31	30	29	29	29	28	28	27
Purpose-built flat or maisonette	15	14	14	14	15	14	15	15
Converted flat or maisonette	5	5	4	4	5	4	4	5
Base = 100%	*11911*	*10111*	*10024*	*9917*	*9820*	*9668*	*9723*	*9127*

Table 3.5 **Age of building by tenure**

Households   *Great Britain: 1996*

Age of building* containing household's accommodation	Owners			Social sector tenants			Private renters			Total
	Owned outright	With mortgage	All owners	Council†	Housing association	Social sector tenants	Unfurnished private**	Furnished private	Private Renters††	
(a)	%	%	%	%	%	%	%	%	%	%
Before 1919	22	21	21	3	17	6	44	40	43	20
1919-1944	23	21	21	18	11	16	19	24	21	20
1945-1964	25	18	20	41	9	35	14	10	13	23
1965-1984	24	27	26	34	30	34	15	18	16	27
1985 or later	7	14	11	4	33	10	8	8	8	11
Base = 100%	*2300*	*3771*	*6071*	*1663*	*423*	*2086*	*583*	*233*	*819*	*8976*

* For an assessment of the reliability of age of building estimates, see Birch F, Age of buildings (OPCS Social Survey Division, GHS Series No.7, 1974).
†
** See the footnotes to Table 3.3.
††

Table 3.6 **(a) Household type by tenure**
         (b) Tenure by household type

Households   *Great Britain: 1996*

Tenure		Household type							Base = 100%
		1 adult aged 16-59	2 adults aged 16-59	Small family	Large family	Large adult household	2 adults, 1 or both aged 60 or over	1 adult aged 60 or over	
(a)									
Owner occupied, owned outright	%	5	9	4	1	12	39	30	*2338*
Owner occupied, with mortgage	%	11	22	32	8	18	6	2	*3792*
All owners	%	9	17	21	6	16	18	12	*6130*
Rented from council*	%	12	8	19	10	9	15	27	*1748*
Rented from housing association	%	14	7	25	8	7	12	27	*432*
Social sector tenants	%	12	8	20	9	9	14	27	*2180*
Rented privately, unfurnished†	%	20	19	23	4	9	9	16	*599*
Rented privately, furnished	%	37	25	12	3	17	0	5	*243*
Private renters**	%	25	21	20	4	11	7	13	*845*
Total	%	11	15	21	6	14	16	16	*9155*
(b)									Total
		%	%	%	%	%	%	%	%
Owner occupied, owned outright		12	15	5	5	22	61	48	26
Owner occupied, with mortgage		42	60	64	54	54	15	5	41
All owners		54	75	68	59	77	76	52	67
Rented from council*		20	10	17	29	13	17	33	19
Rented from housing association		6	2	6	6	2	3	8	5
Social sector tenants		26	13	23	35	15	21	41	24
Rented privately, unfurnished†		12	8	7	4	4	4	6	7
Rented privately, furnished		9	4	2	1	3	0	1	3
Private renters**		20	12	9	6	8	4	7	9
Base = 100%		*1037*	*1412*	*1913*	*580*	*1263*	*1488*	*1462*	*9155*

*
†   See the footnotes to Table 3.I.
**

Table 3.7 **Type of accommodation by household type**

Households   *Great Britain: 1996*

Household type		Type of accommodation*							Base = 100%
		Detached house	Semi-detached house	Terraced house	All houses	Purpose-built flat or maisonette	Converted flat or maisonette/ rooms	All flats/ rooms	
One adult aged 16-59	%	8	20	26	54	29	17	46	*1030*
Two adults aged 16-59	%	20	33	28	81	13	6	19	*1408*
Small family	%	21	34	32	88	9	3	12	*1909*
Large family	%	21	36	34	92	7	1	8	*579*
Large adult household	%	28	38	27	93	5	1	7	*1261*
Two adults, one or both aged 60 or over	%	29	35	23	87	10	2	13	*1485*
One adult aged 60 or over	%	15	27	24	66	30	4	34	*1455*
Total	%	21	32	27	81	15	5	19	*9127*

* See the first footnote to Table 3.3.

Table 3.8 **Persons per room: 1971 to 1996**

Households   *Great Britain*

Persons per room	1971	1975	1979	1982	1985	1989	1991	1993	1994	1995	1996
	%	%	%	%	%	%	%	%	%	%	%
Under 0.5	37	39	41	43	45	48	50	51	51	52	51
0.5 to 0.65	25	25	26	26	26	26	24	24	24	25	24
0.66 to 0.99	24	23	23	22	21	20	19	19	18	18	19
1	9	8	7	7	6	5	5	5	5	5	5
Over 1 to 1.5	4	3	2	2	1	1	1	1	2	1	1
Over 1.5	1	0	0	0	0	0	0	0	0	0	0
Base = 100%	*11990*	*12096*	*11484*	*10238*	*9982*	*10085*	*9646*	*9663*	*9697*	*9754*	*9154*
Mean persons per room	..	0.57	0.57	0.56	0.52	0.50	0.50	0.49	0.49	0.48	0.49

Table 3.9 **Persons per room and mean household size by tenure**

Households   *Great Britain: 1996*

Persons per room*	Tenure									Total
	Owners			Social sector tenants			Private renters			
	Owned outright	With mortgage	All owners	Council†	Housing association	Social sector tenants	Unfur-nished private**	Furnished private	Private renters††	
	%	%	%	%	%	%	%	%	%	%
Under 0.5	75	40	53	48	40	47	49	30	44	51
0.5 to 0.65	18	28	24	23	25	23	28	34	30	24
0.66 to 0.99	5	26	18	19	25	20	18	21	18	19
1	1	5	4	7	9	7	5	13	7	5
Over 1	0	1	1	3	2	3	1	2	1	1
Base =100%	*2337*	*3790*	*6127*	*1748*	*432*	*2180*	*599*	*243*	*845*	*9152*
Mean persons per room	0.37	0.54	0.47	0.51	0.55	0.52	0.47	0.57	0.50	0.49
Mean household size	1.92	2.92	2.54	2.26	2.19	2.25	2.15	2.11	2.14	2.43

* Boxed figures indicate median density of occupation.
†
** | See the footnotes to Table 3.3.
††

Table 3.10   **Closeness of fit relative to the bedroom standard by tenure**

Households   *Great Britain: 1996*

Difference from bedroom standard (bedrooms)	Tenure									Total
	Owners			Social sector tenants			Private renters			
	Owned outright	With mortgage	All owners	Council*	Housing association	Social sector tenants	Unfur-nished private†	Furnished private	Private renters**	
	%	%	%	%	%	%	%	%	%	%
1 or more below standard	1	2	2	4	4	4	3	5	3	2
Equals standard	11	23	19	49	65	52	36	59	43	29
1 above standard	37	42	40	33	25	31	38	21	33	37
2 or more above standard	51	32	39	14	6	12	23	15	20	31
Base =100%	*2338*	*3792*	*6130*	*1748*	*432*	*2180*	*599*	*243*	*845*	*9155*

*   Council includes local authorities, New Towns and Scottish Homes in 1996.
†   Unfurnished includes the answer 'partly furnished'.
** All tenants whose accommodation goes with the job of someone in the household are allocated to 'rented privately'. Squatters are also included in this category in 1996.

Table 3.11 (a) Age of head of household by tenure
(b) Tenure by age of head of household

Heads of household   *Great Britain: 1996*

Tenure		Age of head of household*								Base = 100%
		Under 25	25-29	30-44	45-59	60-64	65-69	70-79	80 and over	
(a)										
Owner occupied, owned outright	%	0	1	5	21	13	17	30	13	2338
Owner occupied, with mortgage	%	2	11	46	34	4	2	2	0	3792
All owners	%	1	7	30	29	8	8	13	5	6130
Rented from council†	%	4	8	24	19	8	9	19	10	1748
Rented from housing association	%	5	11	27	17	6	6	14	13	432
Social sector tenants	%	5	9	24	18	7	8	18	10	2180
Rented privately, unfurnished**	%	11	17	31	16	3	5	10	8	599
Rented privately, furnished	%	29	29	29	7	0	1	3	1	243
Private renters††	%	16	20	30	13	2	4	8	6	845
Total	%	3	9	29	25	7	7	13	6	9155
(b)										Total
		%	%	%	%	%	%	%	%	%
Owner occupied, owned outright		2	2	5	21	48	60	57	51	26
Owner occupied, with mortgage		24	51	66	56	24	9	6	3	41
All owners		26	53	70	77	72	69	63	54	67
Rented from council†		25	19	16	14	21	22	27	29	19
Rented from housing association		7	6	4	3	4	4	5	10	5
Social sector tenants		31	25	20	18	25	26	32	38	24
Rented privately, unfurnished**		20	13	7	4	3	4	5	8	7
Rented privately, furnished		22	9	3	1	0	0	1	1	3
Private renters††		43	22	10	5	3	5	6	8	9
Base = 100%		318	783	2633	2280	646	680	1220	595	9155

* Boxed figures indicate median age-groups.

† ⎤
** ⎬ See the footnotes to Table 3.3.
†† ⎦

Table 3.12 Tenure by sex and marital status of head of household

Heads of household   *Great Britain: 1996*

Tenure	Males						Females						Total
	Married	Cohabiting	Single	Widowed	Divorced/ separated	All males	Married	Cohabiting	Single	Widowed	Divorced/ separated	All females	
	%	%	%	%	%	%	%	%	%	%	%	%	%
Owner occupied, owned outright	27	6	15	56	13	25	††	††	13	49	12	29	26
Owner occupied, with mortgage	54	57	33	7	37	49	††	††	24	7	31	19	41
All owners	80	63	48	63	50	74	††	††	37	55	43	47	67
Rented from council*	12	15	19	27	29	15	††	††	30	32	37	32	19
Rented from housing association	2	7	5	5	7	3	††	††	10	7	9	8	5
Social sector tenants	14	22	24	32	36	18	††	††	40	39	46	41	24
Rented privately, unfurnished†	4	11	13	4	9	6	††	††	13	6	9	9	7
Rented privately, furnished	1	4	15	1	4	2	††	††	10	0	2	3	3
Private renters **	5	15	28	5	14	8	††	††	23	6	11	12	9
Base = 100%	*4942*	*598*	*564*	*335*	*383*	*6822*	*13*	*4*	*603*	*1032*	*681*	*2333*	*9155*

```
 *
 †    See the footnotes to Table 3.1.
**
†† Base too small to enable reliable analysis to be made.
```

Table 3.13   **(a) Socio-economic group and economic activity status of head of household by tenure**
(b) Tenure by socio-economic group and economic activity status of head of household

Heads of households   *Great Britain: 1996*

Socio-economic group and economic activity status of head of household*	Tenure									Total
	Owners			Social sector tenants			Private renters			
	Owned outright	With mortgage	All owners	Council†	Housing association	Social sector tenants	Unfurnished private**	Furnished private	Private Renters††	
(a)	%	%	%	%	%	%	%	%	%	%
Economically active heads:										
Professional	1	8	5	0	0	0	5	7	6	4
Employers and managers	6	26	18	2	5	3	13	12	13	14
Intermediate non-manual	3	12	9	2	4	2	9	14	10	7
Junior non-manual	3	8	6	5	4	5	6	8	7	6
Skilled manual and own account non-professional	11	26	20	13	10	12	16	8	14	18
Semi-skilled manual and personal service	4	9	7	11	11	11	13	13	13	8
Unskilled manual	1	2	1	4	4	4	3	4	4	2
Economically inactive heads	70	10	33	63	62	63	35	34	34	41
Base = 100%	*2330*	*3725*	*6055*	*1714*	*426*	*2140*	*583*	*214*	*799*	*8994*
(b)										*Base = 100%*
Economically active heads:										
Professional	%	8	78	86	1	1	2	8	4	12	*374*
Employers and managers	%	11	76	87	3	2	4	6	2	8	*1252*
Intermediate non-manual	%	12	69	81	4	2	7	8	4	13	*646*
Junior non-manual	%	14	56	70	16	4	19	7	4	10	*507*
Skilled manual and own account non-professional	%	16	61	77	14	3	16	6	1	7	*1608*
Semi-skilled manual and personal service	%	13	43	55	25	6	31	10	4	13	*758*
Unskilled manual	%	9	29	38	39	8	47	10	4	14	*194*
Economically inactive heads	%	45	11	55	30	7	37	6	2	8	*3655*
Total	%	26	41	67	19	5	24	6	2	9	*8994*

*   Excluding members of the Armed Forces, and economically active full-time students and those who were unemployed and had never worked.

†
** See the footnotes to Table 3.3.
††

Table 3.14 (a) Length of residence of head of household by tenure
(b) Tenure by length of residence of head of household

Heads of household   *Great Britain: 1996*

Length of residence* (years)		Tenure									Total
		Owners			Social sector tenants			Private renters			
		Owned outright	With mortgage	All owners	Council†	Housing association	Social sector tenants	Unfurn-ished** private	Furnished private	Private Renters††	
(a)		%	%	%	%	%	%	%	%	%	%
Less than 12 months		2	8	6	10	16	11	30	55	38	10
12 months but less than 2 years		3	8	6	8	13	9	16	19	17	8
2 years but less than 3 years		3	8	6	7	11	8	9	7	8	7
3 years but less than 5 years		4	13	9	12	16	13	10	8	9	10
5 years but less than 10 years		12	25	20	18	18	18	8	7	7	19
10 years or more		77	38	53	45	25	41	28	4	21	47
Base = 100%		2338	3792	6130	1748	432	2180	599	243	845	9155
(b)											*Base = 100%*
Less than 12 months	%	5	34	39	19	8	26	20	14	34	*926*
12 months but less than 2 years	%	9	42	52	20	8	28	13	7	20	*697*
2 years but less than 3 years	%	11	51	61	19	8	27	8	3	12	*607*
3 years but less than 5 years	%	10	51	62	23	7	30	6	2	8	*929*
5 years but less than 10 years	%	16	57	73	19	5	24	3	1	4	*1695*
10 years or more	%	42	33	75	18	3	21	4	0	4	*4301*
Total	%	26	41	67	19	5	24	7	3	9	*9155*

*   Boxed figures indicate median length of residence.

†
** } See the footnotes to Table 3.3.
††

Table 3.15 Usual gross weekly income by tenure

Households   *Great Britain: 1996*

Usual gross weekly income (£)	Tenure									Total
	Owners			Social sector tenants			Private renters			
	Owned outright	With mortgage	All owners	Council*	Housing association	Social sector tenants	Unfurnished private†	Furnished private	Private renters**	
Income of head of household										
Mean	225	380	324	131	145	134	223	222	223	268
Lower quartile	100	208	137	74	77	74	87	69	80	100
Median	162	330	265	103	108	104	154	147	150	200
Upper quartile	276	478	418	157	165	158	294	274	289	355
Base	*2338*	*3792*	*6130*	*1748*	*432*	*2180*	*599*	*243*	*845*	*9155*
Income of head of household and partner										
Mean	265	500	413	153	173	157	266	243	258	335
Lower quartile	107	272	169	75	82	76	95	67	81	113
Median	192	443	344	117	123	118	189	146	175	239
Upper quartile	338	642	553	187	198	190	346	306	337	462
Base	*2338*	*3792*	*6130*	*1748*	*432*	*2180*	*599*	*243*	*845*	*9155*
Total household income										
Mean	312	543	460	181	195	184	303	329	310	377
Lower quartile	132	311	206	84	87	85	108	82	100	134
Median	224	478	391	133	134	134	212	220	213	286
Upper quartile	395	692	610	222	220	222	396	450	404	515
Base	*2338*	*3792*	*6130*	*1748*	*432*	*2180*	*599*	*243*	*845*	*9155*

*
† See the footnotes to Table 3.1.
**

Table 3.16 Housing tenure by ethnic group of head of household

Households   *Great Britain: 1994-96 combined*

Tenure	White	Indian	Pakistani/ Bangladeshi	Black*	Remaining groups	All ethnic minority groups	Total
	%	%	%	%	%	%	%
Owner occupied, owned outright	26	22	13	9	10	13	25
Owner occupied, with mortgage	42	61	42	33	39	43	42
Rented with job or business	2	2	0	2	2	2	2
Rented from council or from housing association	23	8	30	47	28	30	23
Rented privately unfurnished	5	3	8	5	7	5	5
Rented privately furnished	3	4	7	5	14	7	3
Base = 100%	*27154*	*344*	*208*	*443*	*356*	*1351*	*28505*

* Black includes Black Caribbean, Black African and other Black groups.

Table 3.17   **Housing profile by family type: lone-parent families compared with other families**

Families with dependent children*   *Great Britain: 1995 and 1996 combined*

	Lone-parent families	Other families
	%	%
Tenure		
Owner occupied, owned outright	7	6
Owner occupied, with mortgage	28	71
Rented with job or business	1	3
Rented from council or from housing association	53	16
Rented privately unfurnished	9	3
Rented privately furnished	3	1
Central heating	%	%
Yes	85	92
No	15	8
Type of accommodation	%	%
Detached house	7	28
Semi-detached house	31	37
Terraced house	39	29
Purpose-built flat or maisonette	19	5
Converted flat or maisonette/rooms	4	1
With business premises/other	0	0
Bedroom standard	%	%
2 or more below standard	1	0
1 below standard	10	5
Equals standard	57	37
1 above standard	29	44
2 or more above standard	4	14
Persons per room	%	%
Under 0.5	19	6
0.5-0.99	73	75
1.0-1.49	8	18
1.5 or above	0	1
Base = 100%	*1297*	*4692*

* Dependent children are persons aged under 16, or aged 16-18 and in full-time education, in the family unit, and living in the household.

Table 3.18   **Cars or vans: 1972 to 1996**

Households   *Great Britain*

Cars or vans	1972	1975	1979	1981	1983	1985	1989	1991	1993	1994	1995	1996
	%	%	%	%	%	%	%	%	%	%	%	%
Households with:												
no car or van	48	44	43	41	41	38	33	32	32	31	29	30
one car or van	43	45	44	44	43	45	43	44	45	45	45	46
two cars or vans	8	10	12	12	14	14	19	19	20	20	22	21
three or more cars or vans	1	1	2	2	3	3	4	4	4	4	4	4
Base = 100%	*11624*	*11929*	*11459*	*11989*	*10053*	*9963*	*10085*	*9910*	*9851*	*9699*	*9758*	*9158*

Table 3.19 Availability of a car or van by socio-economic group of head of household

Households   *Great Britain: 1996*

Number of cars or vans available to household	Socio-economic group of head of household*								Total
	Economically active heads							Economic-ally inactive heads	
	Professional	Employers and managers	Intermediate non-manual	Junior non-manual	Skilled manual and own account non-professional	Semi-skilled manual and personal service	Unskilled manual		
	%	%	%	%	%	%	%	%	%
None	5	5	12	23	11	32	45	52	30
1	45	38	55	54	55	52	42	41	46
2 or more	51	58	33	23	34	17	13	7	24
Base = 100%	374	1252	647	507	1608	758	194	3656	8996

* Excluding members of the Armed Forces, and economically active full-time students and those who were unemployed and had never worked.

Table 3.20 Consumer durables, central heating and cars: 1972 to 1996

Households   *Great Britain*

	1972	1975	1979	1981	1983	1985	1989	1991	1993	1994	1995	1996
Percentage of households with:												
Television												
colour	93	96	66 ⌉ 97	74 ⌉ 97	81 ⌉ 98	86 ⌉ 98	93 ⌉ 98	95 ⌉ 98	95 ⌉ 98	97 ⌉ 99	97 ⌉ 98	97 ⌉ 99
black and white only			31 ⌋	23 ⌋	17 ⌋	11 ⌋	5 ⌋	4 ⌋	3 ⌋	2 ⌋	2 ⌋	2 ⌋
satellite TV	..	..	..	..	..	..	..	..	..	..	..	18
Video recorder	..	..	..	..	18	31	60	68	73	77	79	82
CD player	..	..	..	..	..	..	15	27	39	47	52	58
Home computer	..	..	..	..	..	13	19	21	24	24	25	27
Microwave oven	..	..	..	..	..	..	47	55	62	67	70	74
Refrigerator*	73	88	92	93	94	95	..	..	..	..	..	..
Deep freezer*	..	..	40	49	57	66	79	83	86	88	89	91
Washing machine	66	71	74	78	80	81	86	87	88	89	90	90
Tumble drier	..	..	19	23	28	33	45	48	49	50	51	51
Dishwasher	..	..	3	1	5	6	12	14	16	19	20	20
Telephone	42	54	67	75	77	81	87	88	90	91	93	94
Central heating	37	43	55	59	64	69	78	82	83	85	86	88
A car or van	43 ⌉ 52	45 ⌉ 56	44 ⌉ 57	44 ⌉ 59	43 ⌉ 59	45 ⌉ 62	43 ⌉ 67	44 ⌉ 67	45 ⌉ 68	45 ⌉ 69	45 ⌉ 71	46 ⌉ 70
- more than 1	9 ⌋	11 ⌋	11 ⌋	14 ⌋	17 ⌋	17 ⌋	23 ⌋	23 ⌋	23 ⌋	24 ⌋	26 ⌋	24 ⌋
Base = 100%	11663	11929	11490	11718	10068	9993	10085	9955	9850	9699	9757	9156

* Fridge freezers are attributed to both 'refrigerator' and 'deep freezer' from 1979 on.

Table 3.21 **Consumer durables, central heating and cars by household type**

Households   *Great Britain: 1996*

Consumer durables	Household type							
	1 adult aged 16-59	2 adults aged 16-59	Small family	Large family	Large adult household	2 adults, 1 or both aged 60 or over	1 adult aged 60 or over	Total
Percentage of households with:								
Television								
colour	92	99	98	98	99	99	93	97
black and white only	3	1	0	1	0	1	4	2
satellite TV	12	20	26	28	27	11	4	18
Video recorder	76	93	95	94	96	80	42	82
CD player	60	73	77	73	84	34	13	58
Home computer	21	30	39	44	44	12	2	27
Microwave oven	65	83	86	82	86	70	47	74
Deep freezer/fridge freezer	80	94	96	98	97	94	77	91
Washing machine	79	95	98	99	98	93	70	90
Tumble drier	33	56	64	71	67	45	25	51
Dishwasher	8	23	28	29	33	16	5	20
Telephone	87	97	94	94	97	98	90	94
Central heating	84	90	91	90	90	89	83	88
Car or van - more than 1	4	36	32	32	55	13	0	24
Base = 100%	*1037*	*1413*	*1913*	*580*	*1262*	*1489*	*1462*	*9156*

Table 3.22 **Consumer durables, central heating and cars by socio-economic group of head of household**

Heads of household   *Great Britain: 1996*

Consumer durables	Socio-economic group of head of household*								Economically inactive heads
	Economically active heads								
	Professional	Employers and managers	Intermediate non-manual	Junior non-manual	Skilled manual and own account non-professional	Semi-skilled manual and personal service	Unskilled manual	Total	
Percentage of households with:									
Television									
colour	97	98	97	98	98	97	98	98	96
black and white	1	1	1	0	1	1	2	1	3
satellite TV	16	27	15	16	28	22	22	23	10
Video recorder	91	95	92	91	94	89	86	93	66
CD player	83	83	79	72	74	65	61	75	31
Home computer	64	50	46	28	29	19	15	37	11
Microwave oven	78	87	81	80	86	77	69	83	61
Deep freezer/fridge freezer	94	95	92	94	95	93	87	94	86
Washing machine	97	98	94	95	97	91	87	95	83
Tumble drier	64	69	57	55	60	52	43	60	38
Dishwasher	43	48	25	20	23	8	5	27	10
Telephone	99	99	98	97	96	91	81	96	92
Central heating	98	94	92	92	88	83	87	90	85
Car or van - more than one	51	58	33	23	34	17	13	36	7
Base = 100%	*374*	*1252*	*647*	*507*	*1607*	*758*	*194*	*5339*	*3656*

* Excluding members of the Armed Forces, and economically active full-time students and those who were unemployed and had never worked.

Table 3.23 **Consumer durables, central heating and cars by usual gross weekly household income**

Households   *Great Britain: 1996*

Consumer durables	Usual gross weekly household income (£)											
	0.01- 50.00	50.01- 100.00	100.01- 150.00	150.01- 200.00	200.01- 250.00	250.01- 300.00	300.01- 350.00	350.01- 400.00	400.01- 450.00	450.01- 500.00	500.01 or more	Total*
Percentage of households with:												
Television												
colour	87	92	96	97	96	99	98	98	99	99	99	97
black and white only	4	5	2	1	2	0	1	1	0	1	0	2
satellite TV	11	7	9	13	15	18	23	21	25	24	25	18
Video recorder	64	52	67	76	85	89	89	92	90	96	96	82
CD player	49	28	32	41	49	59	66	69	73	78	85	58
Home computer	22	6	9	13	18	25	28	28	30	38	50	27
Microwave oven	51	52	63	69	72	75	81	84	81	85	87	74
Deep freezer/fridge freezer	75	78	87	90	91	94	94	96	97	97	97	91
Washing machine	66	74	85	89	88	93	95	96	96	98	99	90
Tumble drier	25	28	37	41	44	53	51	61	58	62	68	51
Dishwasher	9	3	6	8	13	13	15	18	19	26	42	20
Telephone	70	84	91	93	92	96	97	98	99	99	99	94
Central heating	78	82	86	84	84	85	89	90	91	93	95	88
Car or van - more than 1	12	2	4	6	8	13	18	24	26	32	57	24
Base = 100%	*171*	*1098*	*1020*	*740*	*588*	*513*	*500*	*432*	*427*	*386*	*2130*	*9144*

* Total includes no answers to income.

4 Burglaries in private households

Questions on burglary have been asked on the GHS since 1972 and were last included in 1993. The information collected by the GHS supplements other data about burglary, most notably from the British Crime Survey[1]. The data presented in this chapter relates to burglaries in private households in the 12 full calendar months before interview[2] and are limited to those households where the head had been in residence at that address for 12 months or more[3]. Respondents were asked about all burglaries irrespective of whether anything had been stolen or whether they had been reported to the police. The analysis of burglaries includes entry by force, through an unlocked door or window, by false pretences and a few where the burglar had not gained entry.

As the proportion of households who have been burgled is relatively small, analyses where the base is households that have been burgled will be subject to relatively large sampling errors and care should be taken when interpreting these data.

Trends in burglaries and reporting behaviour

The proportion of households who had been burgled at least once during the 12 month reference period was lower than the 1993 figure and similar to the level in 1991. In 1996:

- at 3.3% of households there had been one or more burglaries compared with 4.6% of households in 1993, but this was still higher than the figures for 1986 (2.6%) and earlier;
- the burglary rate, based on the total number of burglaries per 1000 households, showed a similar trend returning to 40 per 1000 in 1996 after rising from 30 per 1000 in 1986 to 40 per 1000 in 1991 and 53 per 1000 in 1993;
- nearly nine out of ten burglaries (89%) were reported

to the police compared with 81% in 1980 and 76% in 1972;   **Table 4.1, Figure 4A**
- the average value of goods stolen in burglaries was £909;
- in one quarter (25%) of burglaries nothing of value was stolen while, at the other end of the scale, goods worth £2000 or more were stolen in 13% of burglaries.
                                                          Table 4.2

Burglaries where higher values of goods were stolen were more likely to have been reported to the police. In 1996,

- nearly all burglaries (98%) involving losses of goods worth £200 or more were reported to the police compared with four out of five (80%) where the goods stolen were worth less than £200.   **Table 4.2**

In 1996, 47% of burglaries involved some insured goods being stolen, 28% of burglaries involved uninsured goods only and, as already noted, 25% involved nothing of value being stolen. The proportion of burglaries involving insured goods was similar to the 1993 figure but there was a significant change in the proportions involving uninsured goods and nothing of value being stolen:

- in 1996, the proportion of burglaries involving uninsured goods only showed an increase rather than a decrease for the first time since 1972, from 22% in 1993 to 28% in 1996;
- the proportion of burglaries where nothing of value was stolen decreased from its highest level (34%) in 1993 to 25% - a level similar to 1991;   **Table 4.3**

In 1996, there was no significant difference between reporting to the police burglaries involving uninsured goods only and those involving insured goods (92% compared with 96%).   **Table 4.4**

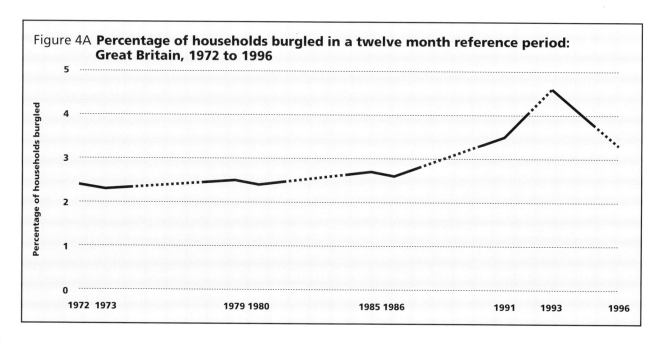

Figure 4A **Percentage of households burgled in a twelve month reference period: Great Britain, 1972 to 1996**

Characteristics of burgled households

The burglary rate showed considerable regional variation with the highest rates in the north of England. In 1996;

- the highest rates were in the North West (69 burglaries per 1000 households) and Yorkshire and Humberside (65 per 1000);
- the lowest rates were in East Anglia (16 per 1000) and the South West (26 per 1000);
- in Scotland the rate was considerably lower than the overall rates for England and for Wales (22 compared with 41 and 55 per 1000 respectively).

Most of the regions followed the overall trend of a decrease in the burglary rate compared with 1993 after a sharp increase between 1991 and 1993. For example:

- burglaries in the North decreased to 40 per 1000 in 1996, having increased from 49 to 74 per 1000 between 1991 and 1993.

There were some exceptions to this. The Scottish rates remained at a similar level in 1996 to 1993 (22 and 26 per 1000) but in Wales the rate increased from 11 to 55 per 1000 households between 1993 and 1996. **Table 4.5**

The burglary rate for metropolitan areas was almost twice that of non-metropolitan areas (60 compared with 31 per 1000), but the average value of goods stolen was higher in non-metropolitan areas - £1017 compared with £793.
Tables 4.5-4.6

The burglary rate varied by tenure, type of accommodation, household type, the age of the head of household and their ethnic group and is partly explained by the association between these characteristics and particular areas.

For example, in 1996:

- private renters and those living in the social rented sector were more likely to be burgled than owner occupiers (61 and 58 per 1000 compared with 32 per 1000); households comprising one adult aged 60 or more had a much lower risk of burglary than other types of household - 23 per 1000 compared with, for example, 59 per 1000 for younger single person households and 55 per 1000 for households comprising adults and children. **Table 4.7**
- households headed by someone aged less than 45 were between two and three times more likely to be burgled than those headed by people aged 45 or more;
- the burglary rate for households where the head of household was from an ethnic minority group was twice as high as for households where the head of household was white (78 per 1000 compared with 38 per 1000). There was also an indication of differences within the

minority groups but small base numbers meant these differences were not significant. **Table 4.8**

The proportion of burglaries reported to the police was higher in non-metropolitan areas - 93% compared with 85% in metropolitan areas. Although there appeared to be some variation with respect to the characteristics of the accommodation and head of household in the percentage of burglaries reported to the police, the small numbers involved meant that none were significant. **Table 4.9**

Comparison of the GHS, British Crime Survey and police statistics

There are a number of differences in the way the GHS and the British Crime Survey collect data on burglary rates, which may explain some of the differences in incidence rates[1], for example: the GHS questions about burglary are asked in the context of a multi-purpose survey as opposed to a survey specifically about crime.

- The 1996 GHS recorded a lower rate of burglaries with a loss than the 1996 BCS. On the 1996 GHS it was 30 per 1000 households in England and Wales compared with 37 per 1000 households on the 1996 BCS. (The 1996 GHS reference period covers 1995/6 and the 1996 BCS refers to burglaries during 1995).
- As would be expected, police statistics for burglaries without a loss are lower than either survey[5] and in 1995 they were 26 per 1000 households. **Table 4.10**

Notes and references

1. Mirrlees-Black C, Mayhew P and Percy A. *1996 British Crime Survey: England and Wales. Home Office Statistical Bulletin, Issue 19/96* Home Office 1996.
2. The reference period of 12 months was adopted by the GHS in 1972 as a balance between the need to minimise problems of recall with the need to retain a long enough period to identify sufficient burglaries for analysis. Use of this time period was examined in detail in 1972 and the results are reported in the 1972 report: OPCS *General Household Survey Report 1972* Section 1.5 HMSO 1975.
3. Data and analysis in this chapter (as in earlier reports) are restricted to households whose head had been in residence for at least 12 months (ie the total reference period for burglaries) - except for the comparison with BCS and police statistics. There is some evidence that recent movers are more likely to be burgled than households who have been resident for longer. Thus it is likely that their exclusion affects the estimates for the incidence of burglary. The 1993 report contains an analysis which indicates that this is the case, but that the effect is the same from year to year. This means that while the estimates presented in the report may be slightly lower than they would be if all households were included, the overall trend data will not be affected. Foster K et al *General Household Survey 1993* Section 4.1 HMSO London 1995.

4. The difficulties in drawing comparisons between these surveys and official statistics are discussed in more detail in the following reports:

    Mayhew P, Elliot D and Dowds L. *The British Crime Survey: Home Office Research Study 111* HMSO 1989.

    Mayhew P, Aye Maung N and Mirrlees-Black C. *The 1992 British Crime Survey: Home Office Research Study 132* HMSO 1993.

    Mayhew P, Mirrlees-Black C and Aye Maung N. *Trends in Crime: findings from the 1994 British Crime Survey. Research Findings No 14* Home Office Research and Statistics Department 1994.

    Mirrlees-Black C, Mayhew P and Percy A. *1996 British Crime Survey: England and Wales. Home Office Statistical Bulletin, Issue 19/96* Home Office 1996.

5. The official statistics[a,b] are based on crimes reported to and recorded by the police but, since not all offences are reported and not all those reported are recorded by the police, changes in the number of offences shown in the official statistics will reflect changes in reporting and recording behaviour as well as any change in the actual number of burglaries committed. Thus the BCS and GHS data can be used to supplement the official statistics to provide information about trends in the proportion of burglaries that go unreported to the police.

    a. Home Office Research and Statistics Department *Notifiable Offences, England and Wales* Home Office (quarterly publication).

    b. Home Office *Criminal Statistics, England and Wales* HMSO (annually).

Table 4.1 **Percentage of households burgled in a 12 month reference period, burglary rate per 1000 households and percentage of burglaries reported to the police: 1972 to 1996**

(a) Households resident at their current address for 12 months or more
(b) Burglaries at households resident at their current address for 12 months or more   Great Britain

Year	(a) Households		(b) Burglaries		
	Percentage of households burgled*	Burglary rate per 1000 households†	Base	Percentage reported to police	Base = 100%**
1972	2.4	29	10725	76	310
1973	2.3	27	10766	76	272
1979	2.5	29	10555	75	304
1980	2.4	27	10878	81	295
1985	2.7	32	9006	87	285
1986	2.6	30	9145	87	263
1991	3.5	40	9100	86	360
1993	4.6	53	8961	86	469
1996	3.3	40	8231	89	317

* Households who were burgled more than once during the reference period are counted only once in the percentage of households burgled.
† Total number of burglaries during the reference period.
** Details collected for a maximum of 3 burglaries at each household.

Table 4.2 **Value of goods stolen and percentage of burglaries reported to police**

Burglaries at households resident at their current address for 12 months or more   Great Britain: 1996

Value of goods stolen	All burglaries*		Percentage of burglaries reported to police		Base = 100%
	%				
Nothing stolen, nil value	25		75%		79
Under £100	14	48	86%	80%	70
£100 but less than £200	8				
£200 but less than £500	16		97%		86
£500 but less than £1000	12				
£1000 but less than £2000	12	52		98%	
£2000 but less than £5000	9		100%		78
£5000 or more	4				
Base = 100%	313		89%		

* Details collected for a maximum of 3 burglaries at each household.

Table 4.3 **Percentage of burglaries in which nothing was stolen and in which insured or uninsured goods were stolen: 1972-1996**

Burglaries at households resident at their current address for 12 months or more   Great Britain

	Some insured goods stolen	Only uninsured goods stolen	Nothing of value stolen	Base =100%
1972/3* %	17	57	26	580
1979/80%	32	43	26	588
1985/6*%	44	38	17	532
1991 %	45	29	27	356
1993 %	44	22	34	463
1996 %	47	28	25	315

* Combined years data.

Table 4.4 **Percentage of burglaries reported to the police by whether the stolen goods were insured**

Burglaries at households resident at their current address for 12 months or more   Great Britain: 1996

Whether the stolen goods were insured	Percentage of burglaries reported to the police	Base = 100%
Some insured goods stolen	96%	147
Only uninsured goods stolen	92%	89
All burglaries in which something of value was stolen	94%	236

Table 4.5 **Burglary rate per 1000 households by region and whether metropolitan or non-metropolitan area: 1985 to 1996**

Households resident at their current address for 12 months or more   *Great Britain*

Region	1985/86	1991	1993	1996	Bases = 100%			
					1985/86	1991	1993	1996
North								
Metropolitan	64 ⎤ 41	39 ⎤ 49	108 ⎤ 74	68 ⎤ 40	438	204	194	206
Non-metropolitan	27 ⎦	56 ⎦	53 ⎦	22 ⎦	672	322	318	315
Yorks and Humberside								
Metropolitan	33 ⎤ 29	42 ⎤ 32	110 ⎤ 87	62 ⎤ 65	1140	552	564	512
Non-metropolitan	20 ⎦	11 ⎦	37 ⎦	70 ⎦	538	272	267	227
North West								
Metropolitan	66 ⎤ 53	63 ⎤ 62	76 ⎤ 72	84 ⎤ 69	1282	654	642	562
Non-metropolitan	34 ⎦	60 ⎦	64 ⎦	46 ⎦	852	402	376	345
East Midlands	16	34	55	30	1260	651	634	637
West Midlands								
Metropolitan	54 ⎤ 45	45 ⎤ 36	55 ⎤ 50	57 ⎤ 47	846	446	415	388
Non-metropolitan	35 ⎦	26 ⎦	44 ⎦	37 ⎦	795	422	407	375
East Anglia	27	22	18	16	699	316	330	310
South East			53	32			2729	2416
Inner London*	65	60	⎤ 67	⎤ 48	797	381	⎤ 1041	⎤ 874
Outer London*	33	53	⎦	⎦	1345	640	⎦	⎦
Outer Metropolitan area	19	37	47 ⎤ 44	24 ⎤ 23	1759	923	886	778
Outer South East†	31	26	40 ⎦	21 ⎦	1578	821	802	764
South West	25	41	47	26	1467	787	780	725
England								
Metropolitan			79 ⎤ 58	62 ⎤ 41			2856	2542
Non-metropolitan			46 ⎦	29 ⎦			4800	4476
Wales	24	32	11	55	904	472	447	454
Scotland								
Metropolitan	49 ⎤ 30	49 ⎤ 34	57 ⎤ 26	20 ⎤ 22	246	103	122	99
Non-metropolitan	27 ⎦	31 ⎦	20 ⎦	23 ⎦	1528	732	736	660
Great Britain								
Metropolitan	50 ⎤ 34	52 ⎤ 40	78 ⎤ 53	60 ⎤ 40	6094	2980	2978	2641
Non-metropolitan	26 ⎦	34 ⎦	40 ⎦	31 ⎦	12052	6120	5983	5590

* Figures for 1993 and 1996 relate to Greater London.
† Figures for 1985/86 relate to South East rest.

Table 4.6 **Average value of goods stolen per burglary and percentage of burglaries where nothing of value was stolen by whether metropolitan or non-metropolitan area**

Burglaries at households resident at their current address for 12 months or more   *Great Britain: 1996*

Area type	Average amount stolen per burglary (£)	Percentage of burglaries where nothing of value stolen	Base =100% All burglaries
Metropolitan	793	29	151
Non-metropolitan	1017	22	162
All households	909	25	313

Table 4.7 **Burglary rate per 1000 households by accommodation and household characteristics**

Households resident at their current address for 12 months or more   *Great Britain: 1996*

Accommodation characteristics	Burglary rate per 1000 households	Base
Tenure		
Owner occupied, owned outright	26	2290
Owner occupied, with mortgage	36	3477
All owners	32	5767
Rented from local authority or New Town	58	1573
Rented from housing association or co-operative	61	362
All social sector tenants	58	1935
Rented privately, unfurnished	53	416
Rented privately, furnished	91	110
All private renters	61	527
Type of accommodation		
Detached house or bungalow	32	1768
Semi-detached house or bungalow	38	2741
Terraced house	49	2263
All houses and bungalows	40	6772
Purpose-built flat or maisonette	38	1131
Converted flat or maisonette/rooms	53	302
All flats or maisonettes	41	1433
Household type		
1 adult 16-59	59 ⎤ 36	814
1 adult aged 60 or over	23 ⎦	1411
2 adults 16-59	39 ⎤ 31	1182
2 adults 1 or both aged 60 or over	25 ⎦	1454
3 or more adults	35	909
Adults and children	55	2416
All households	40	8231

Table 4.8 **Burglary rate per 1000 households by characteristics of head of household**

Households resident at their current address for 12 months or more   *Great Britain: 1996*

Characteristics of head of household	Burglary rate per 1000 households	Base
Age		
16-29	74	698
30-44	63	2331
45-64	24	2769
65 and over	26	2433
Socio-economic group		
Professional	34 ⎤	412
Employers and managers	39 ⎥ 38	1641
Intermediate non-manual	39 ⎥	878
Junior non-manual	39 ⎦	907
Skilled manual and own account non-professional	32 ⎤	2383
Semi-skilled manual and personal service	45 ⎥ 37	1304
Unskilled manual	37 ⎦	437
Ethnic origin		
White	38	7887
Indian	53 ⎤	95
Pakistani/Bangladeshi	56 ⎥ 78	54
Black Caribbean	113 ⎥	71
Remaining groups	89 ⎦	124
All households	40	8231

49

Table 4.9 **Percentage of burglaries reported to police by characteristics of accommodation and head of household**

Burglaries at households resident at their current address for 12 months or more   *Great Britain: 1996*

Characteristics of accommodation and head of household	Percentage of burglaries reported to polce	Base = 100%
Tenure		
Owners	92	181
Social sector tenants	85	104
Private renters	[91]	32
Type of accommodation		
House	88	258
Flat, maisonette or rooms	93	58
Age of head of household		
16-29	90	52
30-64	89	206
65 and over	90	59
Socio-economic group of head of household		
Non-manual	90	142
Manual	88	151
Ethnic group of head of household		
White	90	290
All ethnic minority groups	[78]	27
Type of area		
Metropolitan	85	151
Non-metropolitan	93	166
All households	89	317

Table 4.10 **Burglary rate per 1000 households during 1995 from the GHS, British Crime Survey and official police statistics**

Burglaries with a loss   *England and Wales*

Year of burglary*	Burglaries with a loss		
	GHS†	BCS	Police statistics
1995	30	37	26

* The reference period on the GHS is 1995/6.
† The GHS figures only show England and Wales and to be more comparable with the BCS includes households who were resident at the current address for less than 12 months.

5 Employment

The GHS has collected information about employment issues throughout the life of the survey in order to understand the context in which people live and to help explain various phenomena about them. The GHS has consequently a long time series of information about people's employment (Tables 5.8-5.10(b)), however the principal source for monitoring employment issues is the Labour Force Survey (LFS). Because of the unclustered sample design and larger sample size the LFS results are subject to less sampling error than the GHS and should therefore be used in preference to the GHS as the main source of employment data for monitoring short to mid-term estimates. Data from the LFS are published in the Labour Force Survey Quarterly Bulletin.[1]

In 1996 estimates of men who were economically active were higher on the LFS than the GHS (72% compared with 70%) but there were no significant differences between the surveys for women's economic status (53.6% compared with 53%). Over the last eight years the estimates of the economically active for the two surveys are broadly similar but the GHS has shown more fluctuation than the LFS.   **Table 5.1**

Women with dependent children

Married and cohabiting women with dependent children were more likely than lone mothers to be working and the difference has increased over time. For example:

- in 1977-79, just over a half (52%) of married and cohabiting women with dependent children were working compared with two-thirds (66%) in 1994-96;
- the proportion of lone mothers working fell from 47% in 1977-79 to 42% in 1994-96 with most of the change occurring during the early 1980s.

Both married women with dependent children and lone mothers were more likely to be working part time than full time. In 1994-96:

- 42% of married women and 25% of lone mothers worked part time;
- 24% of married women and 16% of lone mothers worked full time.

Among married women with dependent children there has been an increase in both full and part-time working, whereas among lone mothers there has been a gradual decline in full-time work and the proportion working part time has remained stable.

- The proportion of married women with dependent children working full time has increased steadily from 15% in 1977-79 to 24% in 1994-96. The proportion working part time also increased but at a slower rate from 37% in 1977-79 to 42% in 1994-96.
- The proportion of lone mothers working full time declined from 22% in 1977-79 to 16% in 1994-96. The proportion working part time was at a similar level in 1994-96 as in 1977-79 (25% and 24% respectively).
                            Table 5.2, Figure 5A

Women with dependent children were more likely to be working if their child was aged five or over. In 1994-96:

- 74% of married women whose youngest dependent child was aged five years or over were working compared with 54% if the youngest child was aged under five;
- 51% of lone mothers whose youngest dependent child was aged five or over were working compared with 27% whose youngest dependent child was aged under five.

The age of the youngest child also affected whether women were working full or part time. Both married and lone mothers were more likely to be working full time if their youngest child was aged five or over rather than under five. In 1994-96:

- 28% of married women and 21% of lone mothers whose youngest child was aged five or over were working full time compared with 18% of married women and 9% of lone mothers whose youngest child was under five.   **Table 5.3**

Women with dependent children were less likely to be working if they had three or more children:

- in 1996, 45% of women with three or more dependent children were working compared with 65% of those with one or two children;
- between 1973 and 1996, the proportion of women working with three or more dependent children has remained unchanged but the proportion working with one or two children has increased (from 50% to 65% of those with one dependent child; from 46% to 65% of those with two dependent children).   **Table 5.4**

Whether women with dependent children worked and whether they worked full or part time also varied according to their socio-economic group. In 1994-96:

- 75% of women with dependent children who were professionals, employers or managers were working compared with 57% of unskilled manual women;

- 51% of women with dependent children who were professionals, employers or managers worked full time compared with only 5% of unskilled manual women;

- women who were professionals, employers or managers with a youngest dependent child aged 10 or over were the group of women with dependent children most likely (86%) to be working. About two-thirds (65%) of this group worked full time. **Table 5.5**

Socio-economic group

Since 1975, there has been an increase in the proportion of people working as employers and managers and a decline, particularly among women, in the proportion of semi-skilled manual workers. Most of this increase had occurred by the end of the 1980s but since then there has been little change. For example:

- the proportion working as employers or managers increased between 1975 and 1989 from 15% to 20% of

men and from 4% to 9% of women. In 1996, 22% of men and 9% of women were employers and managers;

- the proportion of women in the semi-skilled manual and personal service socio-economic group fell from 31% in 1975 to 22% in 1991. There was no further significant change in the 1990s. In 1996, 23% of women were in semi-skilled and personal service occupations.

Unemployment rates varied by socio-economic group and sex. For example in 1996:

- 20% of men who were in the unskilled manual group were unemployed compared with 1% of professionals and 4% of employers and managers;

- 6% of women in the unskilled manual group were unemployed compared with 3% of professionals and 2% of employers and managers. **Tables 5.6-5.7**

Reference

1. *Labour Force Survey Quarterly Bulletin*, The Stationery Office, London.

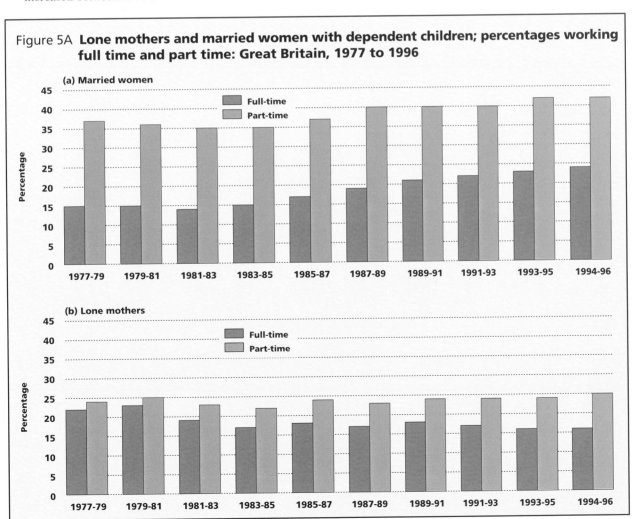

Figure 5A **Lone mothers and married women with dependent children; percentages working full time and part time: Great Britain, 1977 to 1996**

Table 5.1 **Economic status by sex: Labour Force Survey 1989-1996 and General Household Survey 1989-1996***

Persons aged 16 and over   *Great Britain*

	Labour Force Survey						General Household Survey†					
	1989	1991	1993	1994	1995	1996	1989	1991	1993	1994	1995	1996
	%	%	%	%	%	%	%	%	%	%	%	%
Men												
Economically active**	75.6	74.8	72.7	72.6	72.3	72.0	75	75	72	72	72	70
Working	70.1	68.1	63.7	64.4	65.1	65.1	70	67	62	64	65	64
Unemployed	5.4	6.8	8.9	8.2	7.2	6.9	5	8	10	8	7	6
Economically inactive	24.4	25.2	27.3	27.4	27.7	28.0	25	25	28	28	28	30
Base = 100%	*21065*	*21168*	*21319*	*21479*	*21559*	*21654*	*9313*	*8983*	*8643*	*8488*	*8578*	*8117*
	%	%	%	%	%	%	%	%	%	%	%	%
Women												
Economically active**	53.0	53.1	52.9	53.3	53.2	53.6	53	54	53	54	55	53
Working	49.3	49.2	49.0	49.4	49.6	50.2	50	50	48	50	51	50
Unemployed	3.7	3.8	3.9	3.9	3.6	3.4	3	4	5	4	4	3
Economically inactive	47.0	46.9	47.1	46.7	46.8	46.4	47	46	47	46	45	47
Base = 100%	*22680*	*22735*	*22826*	*22798*	*22822*	*22869*	*10317*	*9920*	*9745*	*9504*	*9493*	*8914*
	%	%	%	%	%	%	%	%	%	%	%	%
Total												
Economically active**	63.9	63.6	62.5	62.7	62.5	62.5	64	64	62	62	63	61
Working	59.3	58.3	56.1	56.7	57.1	57.4	60	58	55	57	58	57
Unemployed	4.5	5.2	6.4	6.0	5.4	5.1	4	6	7	6	5	4
Economically inactive	36.1	36.4	37.5	37.3	37.5	37.5	36	36	38	38	37	39
Base = 100%	*43745*	*43903*	*44145*	*44277*	*44381*	*44522*	*19630*	*18903*	*18388*	*17992*	*18071*	*17031*

*   Up to 1991 the LFS data are based on an annual survey carried out in the Spring of each year and show figures grossed to national estimates with the base figures shown in thousands. From 1992 onwards the LFS became a continuous survey. The data shown here come from the Spring quarter. The GHS data are from the annual survey which runs from April to March of the following year and are ungrossed.

†   The GHS unemployment figures for 1989 are those under the old definition. From 1991 onwards unemployment figures are using the new GHS definition based on the ILO definition of unemployment.

** From 1985 full-time students were classified as 'working' 'unemployed' or 'inactive' according to their own reports of what they were doing in the reference week; in previous years they were all classified as 'inactive'. From 1985 people on YT were classified as 'working' if they were with an employer for work experience in the reference week, or as 'inactive' if at college. Since 1989 all those on schemes YT, ET and (1989 only) JTS have been classified as 'working'.
Since 1991 an 'unemployed' person is someone who has been looking for work in the four weeks prior to interview and would be available to start work in the next two weeks, or is waiting to start a job. This has had the effect of reclassifying some informants from 'economically inactive' to 'economically active' and vice versa. See Chapter 5 GHS 1991 Report for further information.

The Labour Force Survey is the main source for economic activity data.

Table 5.2 **Lone mothers and married women with dependent children: percentages working full time and part time by marital status: 1977 to 1996**

Women with dependent children*   *Great Britain*

Marital status and whether working full time or part time	1977-79	1979-81	1981-83	1983-85	1985-87	1987-89	1989-91	1991-93	1993-95	1994-96
	Percentages working full time and part time									
Lone mothers										
Single										
Working full time	25	27	18	9	14	12	11	11	13	14
Working part time	11	11	12	11	13	14	16	18	17	18
All working†	36	38	30	20	27	27	29	30	30	32
Base = 100%	*230*	*271*	*289*	*287*	*319*	*432*	*550*	*655*	*718*	*699*
Widowed										
Working full time	16	17	14	15	13	20	24	20	14	16
Working part time	34	32	29	37	35	38	31	26	26	36
All working†	50	49	44	52	48	58	55	46	41	52
Base = 100%	*253*	*218*	*194*	*151*	*112*	*102*	*104*	*96*	*91*	*88*
Divorced										
Working full time	26	27	21	23	22	20	24	20	20	20
Working part time	26	29	27	24	29	26	30	29	30	31
All working†	52	56	48	47	50	46	55	50	51	52
Base = 100%	*495*	*532*	*569*	*559*	*565*	*539*	*577*	*617*	*651*	*614*
Separated										
Working full time	19	18	18	15	16	15	18	20	18	15
Working part time	24	26	23	22	23	24	25	25	25	25
All working†	44	45	41	37	39	40	44	46	43	41
Base = 100%	*301*	*320*	*280*	*252*	*258*	*278*	*331*	*376*	*414*	*431*
All lone mothers										
Working full time	22	23	19	17	18	17	18	17	16	16
Working part time	24	25	23	22	24	23	24	24	24	25
All working†	47	49	42	39	42	40	43	41	40	42
Base = 100%	*1279*	*1341*	*1332*	*1249*	*1254*	*1351*	*1562*	*1744*	*1874*	*1832*
Married** women with dependent children										
Working full time	15	15	14	15	17	19	21	22	23	24
Working part time	37	36	35	35	37	40	40	40	42	42
All working†	52	52	49	50	54	59	62	63	65	66
Base = 100%	*11693*	*11392*	*10004*	*8823*	*8654*	*8237*	*7627*	*7433*	*7195*	*7064*

*   Persons aged under 16, or aged 16-18 and in full-time education, in the family unit and living in the household.

†   Including a few women whose hours of work were not known, and from 1989 those on YT, ET and (in 1989 only) JTS.

** Including married women whose husbands were not defined as resident in the household: see Appendix A, 'Lone parent'.

The Labour Force Survey is the main source for economic activity data.

Table 5.3 **Married women and lone mothers with dependent children: percentages working full time and part time by age of youngest dependent child: 1977 to 1996**

*Women with dependent children**   *Great Britain*

Age of youngest dependent child and whether woman working full time or part time	1977-79	1979-81	1981-83	1983-85	1985-87	1987-89	1989-91	1991-93	1993-95	1994-96
				Percentages working full time and part time						
Married† women with dependent children										
Under 5 years										
Working full time	5	6	6	6	9	12	14	14	17	18
Working part time	22	22	19	22	25	28	32	34	36	36
All working**	27	28	25	28	34	40	46	49	53	54
Base = 100%	*4374*	*4244*	*3838*	*3626*	*3560*	*3448*	*3263*	*3268*	*3111*	*2975*
5 years or over										
Working full time	21	21	20	21	22	24	27	27	27	28
Working part time	45	45	44	44	46	48	47	45	46	46
All working**	66	66	64	65	68	73	74	73	74	74
Base = 100%	*7319*	*7148*	*6166*	*5197*	*5094*	*4789*	*4364*	*4165*	*4084*	*4089*
All ages										
Working full time	15	15	14	15	17	19	21	22	23	24
Working part time	37	36	35	35	37	40	40	40	42	42
All working**	52	52	49	50	54	59	62	63	65	66
Base = 100%	*11693*	*11392*	*10004*	*8823*	*8654*	*8237*	*7627*	*7433*	*7195*	*7064*
Lone mothers										
Under 5 years										
Working full time	13	12	7	7	9	8	8	7	9	9
Working part time	13	12	11	9	11	13	14	15	16	17
All working**	26	24	18	16	20	21	23	23	25	27
Base = 100%	*382*	*397*	*434*	*441*	*472*	*566*	*703*	*802*	*778*	*728*
5 years or over										
Working full time	26	28	25	23	23	23	27	24	22	21
Working part time	29	31	29	29	32	29	32	31	29	30
All working**	56	59	54	52	55	53	60	56	51	51
Base = 100%	*897*	*944*	*898*	*808*	*782*	*785*	*859*	*958*	*1096*	*1104*
All ages										
Working full time	22	23	19	17	18	17	18	17	16	16
Working part time	24	25	23	22	24	23	24	24	24	25
All working**	47	49	42	39	42	40	43	41	40	42
Base = 100%	*1279*	*1341*	*1332*	*1249*	*1254*	*1351*	*1562*	*1760*	*1874*	*1832*

* Persons aged under 16, or aged 16-18 and in full time education, in the family unit and living in the household.
† Including married women whose husbands were not defined as resident in the household: see Appendix A, 'Lone parent'.
** Including a few women whose hours of work were not known, and from 1989 those on YT, ET and (in 1989 only) JTS.

The Labour Force Survey is the main source for economic activity data.

Table 5.4 **Economic activity of women of working age with dependent children, 1973 to 1996: percentages working full time, working part time, and unemployed by number of dependent children**

Women aged 16-59 with dependent children   *Great Britain*

Number of dependent children* and economic activity†	1973	1975	1979	1981	1983	1985	1989	1991	1993	1994	1995	1996
					Percentages							
1 dependent child												
Working full time	21	21	20	20	19	21	24	28	28	29	29	27
Working part time	29	33	33	33	33	33	35	33	35	33	37	37
All working**	50	54	53	53	52	54	59	63	64	63	66	65
Unemployed	..	..	2	5	5	5	4	7	6	6	6	4
(Economically active)			55	58	57	59	64	69	70	69	72	69
Base = 100%	*1638*	*1749*	*1638*	*1680*	*1361*	*1348*	*1272*	*1203*	*1205*	*1244*	*1154*	*1173*
2 dependent children												
Working full time	14	13	13	12	13	15	19	20	18	20	20	21
Working part time	31	37	40	38	33	37	44	40	43	43	42	43
All working**	46	50	54	50	46	52	63	61	62	64	62	65
Unemployed	..	..	2	4	5	4	3	6	7	4	5	4
(Economically active)			56	54	51	56	66	67	68	68	68	68
Base = 100%	*1726*	*1849*	*1692*	*1855*	*1437*	*1401*	*1336*	*1272*	*1296*	*1269*	*1244*	*1189*
3 or more dependent children												
Working full time	14	11	13	13	8	10	14	13	10	12	12	11
Working part time	30	36	36	26	28	32	34	34	31	34	32	33
All working**	44	48	49	39	36	43	49	47	42	47	44	45
Unemployed	..	..	2	4	4	4	2	5	7	3	6	4
(Economically active)			51	44	40	46	51	53	49	51	50	49
Base = 100%	*1091*	*1061*	*777*	*793*	*656*	*518*	*529*	*570*	*550*	*571*	*546*	*524*
All with dependent children												
Working full time	17	16	16	15	14	17	20	22	21	23	22	22
Working part time	30	35	36	34	32	35	39	36	38	37	38	39
All working**	47	51	52	49	46	51	59	59	59	60	60	61
Unemployed	..	..	2	4	5	4	4	6	7	5	6	4
(Economically active)			55	54	51	56	63	65	65	65	66	65
Base = 100%	*4455*	*4659*	*4107*	*4328*	*3454*	*3267*	*3137*	*3045*	*3051*	*3084*	*2944*	*2886*

* Persons aged under 16, or aged 16-18 and in full-time education, in the family unit and living in the household.

† From 1985 full-time students were classified as 'working' 'unemployed' or 'inactive' according to their own reports of what they were doing in the reference week; in previous years they were all classified as 'inactive'. From 1985 people on YT were classified as 'working' if they were with an employer for work experience in the reference week, or as 'inactive' if at college. Since 1989 all those on schemes YT, ET and (1989 only) JTS have been classified as 'working'.
Since 1991 an 'unemployed' person is someone who has been looking for work in the four weeks prior to interview and would be available to start work in the next two weeks, or is waiting to start a job. This has had the effect of reclassifying some informants from 'economically inactive' to 'economically active' and vice versa. See Chapter 5 GHS 1991 Report for further information.

** Including a few women whose hours of work were not known. From 1989 persons on Government schemes such as YT have been excluded from the full-time and part-time categories but they were included in the 'all working' subtotal. Prior to 1989 those on Government schemes who were treated as economically active were classified according to hours worked.

The Labour Force Survey is the main source for economic activity data.

Table 5.5 Economic activity of women of working age: percentages working full time, working part time, and unemployed by own socio-economic group and age of youngest dependent child

Women aged 16-59   *Great Britain: 1994-96 combined*

Age of youngest dependent child and economic activity*	Socio-economic group					
	Professional or employer/ manager	Intermediate and junior non-manual	Skilled manual and own account non-professional	Semi-skilled manual and personal service	Unskilled manual	Total
	Percentages					
Youngest child aged 0-4						
Working full time	39	17	20	9	2	17
Working part time	25	37	41	25	47	34
All working†	64 ⎤ 67	54 ⎤ 60	61 ⎤ 63	34 ⎤ 40	50 ⎤ 53	51 ⎤ 56
Unemployed	3 ⎦	6 ⎦	3 ⎦	6 ⎦	4 ⎦	5 ⎦
Base = 100%	*380*	*1814*	*270*	*780*	*220*	*3464*
Youngest child aged 5-9						
Working full time	54	21	31	14	4	22
Working part time	25	47	40	43	54	44
All working†	79 ⎤ 83	69 ⎤ 75	71 ⎤ 75	58 ⎤ 63	57 ⎤ 66	66 ⎤ 72
Unemployed	3 ⎦	6 ⎦	4 ⎦	6 ⎦	9 ⎦	6 ⎦
Base = 100%	*231*	*1057*	*181*	*560*	*157*	*2186*
Youngest child aged 10 or over						
Working full time	65	32	41	21	8	32
Working part time	21	48	37	50	58	45
All working†	86 ⎤ 90	80 ⎤ 83	78 ⎤ 82	71 ⎤ 75	66 ⎤ 72	77 ⎤ 81
Unemployed	3 ⎦	3 ⎦	4 ⎦	3 ⎦	7 ⎦	3 ⎦
Base = 100%	*307*	*1355*	*233*	*620*	*209*	*2724*
All with dependent children						
Working full time	51	23	30	14	5	23
Working part time	24	43	39	38	53	40
All working†	75 ⎤ 79	66 ⎤ 71	69 ⎤ 73	52 ⎤ 58	57 ⎤ 63	64 ⎤ 68
Unemployed	3 ⎦	5 ⎦	4 ⎦	5 ⎦	6 ⎦	5 ⎦
Base = 100%	*918*	*4226*	*684*	*1960*	*586*	*8374*
No dependent children						
Working full time	78	56	48	41	9	53
Working part time	8	22	25	25	50	23
All working†	87 ⎤ 89	79 ⎤ 83	74 ⎤ 78	67 ⎤ 74	60 ⎤ 65	76 ⎤ 81
Unemployed	2 ⎦	4 ⎦	5 ⎦	7 ⎦	5 ⎦	5 ⎦
Base = 100%	*1413*	*4892*	*719*	*1958*	*611*	*9593*
Total**						
Working full time	68	41	39	27	7	39
Working part time	14	32	32	31	51	31
All working†	82 ⎤ 85	73 ⎤ 78	72 ⎤ 76	60 ⎤ 66	59 ⎤ 64	70 ⎤ 75
Unemployed	3 ⎦	5 ⎦	4 ⎦	6 ⎦	5 ⎦	5 ⎦
Base = 100%	*2342*	*9146*	*1409*	*3941*	*1202*	*18040*

* See the first two footnotes to Table 5.4 for definitions of dependent child and economic activity.

† Including a few women whose hours of work were not known and those on YT and ET.

** Total is not equal to the sum of totals with and without dependent children because the dependency of some children could not be established.

The Labour Force Survey is the main source for economic activity data.

Table 5.6 **Socio-economic group by sex: 1975 to 1996**

All persons aged 16 and over   *Great Britain*

Socio-economic group*	1975	1979	1981	1983	1985	1989	1991	1993	1994	1995	1996
	%	%	%	%	%	%	%	%	%	%	%
Men											
Professional	5	6	4	5	6	7	7	7	7	7	6
Employers and managers	15	15	15	17	19	20	19	20	21	21	22
Intermediate and junior non-manual	17	17	17	15	17	16	17	17	17	17	17
Skilled manual and own account non-professional	41	40	41	39	37	38	38	37	35	35	35
Semi-skilled manual and personal service	17	17	18	18	16	15	14	14	14	15	15
Unskilled manual	5	5	5	5	5	5	5	4	5	4	5
Base = 100%	*10902*	*10280*	*10880*	*8886*	*8787*	*8815*	*8596*	*8089*	*7948*	*8004*	*7573*
	%	%	%	%	%	%	%	%	%	%	%
Women											
Professional	1	1	1	1	1	1	1	2	2	2	2
Employers and managers	4	5	5	6	7	9	9	10	11	10	9
Intermediate and junior non-manual	46	45	46	46	48	47	48	49	48	49	50
Skilled manual and own account non-professional	9	9	9	9	9	9	9	8	8	8	9
Semi-skilled manual and personal service	31	30	29	30	27	25	22	22	22	22	23
Unskilled manual	9	10	10	9	7	8	11	10	9	8	8
Base = 100%	*11799*	*11102*	*11743*	*9754*	*9439*	*9600*	*9254*	*9009*	*8698*	*8720*	*8137*
	%	%	%	%	%	%	%	%	%	%	%
Total											
Professional	3	3	2	3	3	4	4	4	4	4	4
Employers and managers	9	10	9	11	13	14	14	15	16	15	15
Intermediate and junior non-manual	32	32	32	31	33	32	33	34	33	34	34
Skilled manual and own account non-professional	24	24	24	24	23	23	23	22	21	21	21
Semi-skilled manual and personal service	24	24	24	24	22	20	18	18	18	19	19
Unskilled manual	7	8	8	7	6	7	8	7	7	6	6
Base = 100%	*22701*	*21382*	*22623*	*18640*	*18226*	*18415*	*17850*	*17098*	*16646*	*16724*	*15710*

* The socio-economic group shown is based on the informant's own job (or last job if not in employment). Excluding those in the Armed Forces and any who have never worked.

The Labour Force Survey is the main source for economic activity data.

Table 5.7 **Economically active persons: unemployment rate by socio-economic group and sex: 1975 to 1996**

Economically active persons aged 16 and over   *Great Britain*

Socio-economic group*	1975	1979	1981	1983	1985	1989	1991	1993	1994	1995	1996	Base (1996)† = 100%
						Percentages unemployed						
Men												
Professional	1	0	3	3	1	2	3	5	4	1	1	364
Employers and managers	2	2	4	3	3	2	6	5	4	4	4	1197
Intermediate and junior non-manual	2	3	5	6	6	4	8	9	9	6	5	1016
Skilled manual and own account non-professional	4	4	10	12	11	7	10	15	12	10	7	1810
Semi-skilled manual and personal service	6	8	18	20	19	11	16	18	16	16	14	805
Unskilled manual	15	17	26	32	30	27	28	31	26	24	20	211
Total	4	4	10	11	10	7	10	11	10	9	7	5403
Women												
Professional	4	3	2	7	0	1	2	4	3	3	3	119
Employers and managers	2	3	2	4	5	2	5	5	3	3	2	498
Intermediate and junior non-manual	3	3	6	7	7	4	7	6	6	6	5	2360
Skilled manual and own account non-professional	3	4	8	7	8	4	8	8	4	6	5	370
Semi-skilled manual and personal service	4	5	11	13	12	8	11	12	10	10	6	855
Unskilled manual	1	4	6	5	3	7	8	11	9	7	6	254
Total	3	4	7	8	8	5	8	8	6	6	5	4456
Total												
Professional	1	1	2	3	1	2	3	4	4	2	1	483
Employers and managers	2	2	4	3	4	2	5	6	4	4	4	1695
Intermediate and junior non-manual	3	3	6	7	7	4	7	7	7	6	5	3376
Skilled manual and own account non-professional	3	4	10	12	11	7	10	12	11	10	7	2180
Semi-skilled manual and personal service	5	7	14	17	15	9	13	15	12	13	10	1660
Unskilled manual	7	9	14	17	17	16	16	18	17	14	12	465
Total	4	4	9	10	9	6	9	10	8	8	6	9859

* See the footnote to Table 5.6.
† Bases for earlier years are of a similar size.

The Labour Force Survey is the main source for economic activity data.

Table 5.8 **Economic activity of men, 1975 to 1996: percentage economically active by age**

Men aged 16 and over   *Great Britain*

Age	1975	1979	1981	1983	1985	1989	1991	1993	1994	1995	1996	Base (1996)* = 100%
					Percentage economically active†							
16-17	55	56	47	40	65	72	68	63	61	65	66	303
18-24	89	91	89	89	91	91	89	83	84	87	84	754
25-34	98	98	97	97	97	97	97	94	94	95	94	1556
35-44	98	98	98	97	98	96	95	93	94	94	93	1512
45-54	98	96	95	94	93	92	92	92	90	89	87	1439
55-59	94	88	90	85	82	82	79	76	72	73	75	513
60-64	84	75	73	63	53	54	52	51	49	50	43	531
65 and over	16	15	11	9	8	8	8	7	9	9	6	1509
16-64	93	92	90	88	89	89	88	86	86	86	84	6608
Total	81	79	77	75	76	75	75	72	72	72	70	8117

* Bases for earlier years are of a similar order of magnitude and can be found in GHS Reports for each year.
† From 1985 full-time students were classified as 'working', 'unemployed' or 'inactive' according to their own reports of what they were doing in the reference week; in previous years they were all classified as 'inactive'. From 1985 people on YTS were classified as 'working' if they were with an employer for work experience in the reference week, or as 'inactive' if at college. Since 1989 all those on schemes YTS, ET and (1989 only) JTS have been classified as 'working'.
Since 1991 an 'unemployed' person is someone who has been looking for work in the four weeks prior to interview and would be available to start work in the next two weeks, or is waiting to start a job. This has had the effect of reclassifying some informants from 'economically inactive' to 'economically active' and vice versa. See Chapter 5 GHS 1991 Report for further information.

The Labour Force Survey is the main source for economic activity data.

Table 5.9 **Economic activity of non-married and married women, 1975 to 1996: percentage economically active by age**

Women aged 16 and over   *Great Britain*

Marital status and age	1975	1979	1981	1983	1985	1989	1991	1993	1994	1995	1996	Base (1996)* = 100%
					Percentage economically active†							
Non-married women												
16-17	52	53	40	41	66	70	74	58	63	61	60	244
18-24	82	79	83	81	81	79	79	75	72	74	75	571
25-34	76	76	76	69	74	76	70	69	70	71	70	526
35-44	75	70	75	70	78	77	78	70	68	74	60	352
45-54	77	72	74	67	73	72	76	70	75	73	70	285
55-59	62	61	61	53	51	51	55	53	58	55	45	124
60-64	34	23	23	17	16	21	23	19	26	27	22	135
65 and over	6	5	4	4	2	3	2	2	3	3	2	1107
16-59	72	70	70	67	74	74	74	69	69	70	67	2102
Total	42	42	44	41	45	46	46	43	45	46	44	3344
Married women												
16-17	††	††	††	††	††	††	††	††	††	††	††	5
18-24	54	52	57	52	62	67	71	74	73	77	68	257
25-34	52	55	51	52	57	68	71	72	73	74	74	1175
35-44	66	70	69	69	69	75	77	79	77	79	76	1270
45-54	67	68	69	68	67	75	75	74	77	76	73	1188
55-59	49	55	54	52	50	54	55	56	53	53	53	443
60-64	26	25	21	20	20	21	25	22	25	26	22	430
65 and over	6	6	5	4	4	4	5	4	5	5	5	802
16-59	59	62	61	60	62	70	72	73	73	74	72	4338
Total	51	52	51	49	51	57	59	59	60	60	58	5570
All 16-59	62	64	64	62	66	72	73	72	72	73	70	6440

* Bases for earlier years are of a similar size and can be found in GHS Reports for each year.
† See the second footnote to Table 5.8.
** Single, widowed, divorced and separated women.
†† Base too small to enable reliable analysis to be made.

The Labour Force Survey is the main source for economic activity data.

Table 5.10(a) Economic activity of men by age: 1975-1996

Men aged 16 and over   *Great Britain*

Age and economic activity*	1990 rules						ILO guidelines						
	1975	1979	1981	1983	1985	1989	1991	1991	1992	1993	1994	1995	1996
	%	%	%	%	%	%	%	%	%	%	%	%	%
16-17													
Working	62	60	57	53	56	64	52	52	56	50	46	54	52
Unemployed	7	9	13	15	13	8	13	16	15	13	15	11	14
Inactive	31	30	30	32	31	28	36	32	29	37	39	35	34
Base = 100%	*489*	*483*	*558*	*413*	*389*	*356*	*295*	*293*	*279*	*263*	*278*	*273*	*303*
18-24													
Working	85	86	75	71	73	80	73	73	73	65	69	70	71
Unemployed	6	7	16	22	18	11	16	16	16	18	16	17	13
Inactive	9	8	9	8	9	9	11	11	12	17	16	13	16
Base = 100%	*1402*	*1351*	*1532*	*1281*	*1240*	*1161*	*1099*	*1095*	*1012*	*979*	*888*	*877*	*754*
25-34													
Working	95	94	86	86	88	91	87	87	83	83	84	87	86
Unemployed	3	4	10	11	10	6	10	10	12	12	9	8	8
Inactive	1	2	3	3	3	3	3	3	4	6	6	5	6
Base = 100%	*2250*	*2105*	*2192*	*1652*	*1743*	*1715*	*1796*	*1793*	*1715*	*1731*	*1610*	*1596*	*1556*
35-49													
Working	94	94	90	89	89	90	88	89	87	84	85	87	86
Unemployed	4	4	7	7	8	5	7	6	8	9	8	7	6
Inactive	2	2	2	4	3	5	5	5	5	7	6	6	8
Base = 100%	*2871*	*2552*	*2806*	*2384*	*2419*	*2556*	*2391*	*2384*	*2433*	*2359*	*2458*	*2404*	*2250*
50-59													
Working	93	88	85	80	77	79	76	76	74	72	73	72	76
Unemployed	3	4	7	9	9	8	9	9	9	11	7	7	5
Inactive	4	8	8	10	14	13	15	15	17	17	20	21	19
Base = 100%	*1832*	*1814*	*1804*	*1408*	*1331*	*1332*	*1314*	*1310*	*1310*	*1200*	*1251*	*1326*	*1214*
60-64													
Working	81	70	64	52	49	51	45	46	45	44	43	45	39
Unemployed	3	4	9	11	4	4	5	6	7	7	5	5	4
Inactive	16	25	27	37	47	46	50	48	48	49	51	50	57
Base = 100%	*880*	*676*	*772*	*708*	*709*	*617*	*574*	*566*	*610*	*552*	*505*	*577*	*531*
65 and over													
Working	15	15	11	9	8	8	8	8	7	7	9	9	6
Unemployed	0	0	0	0	0	0	0	0	0	0	0	0	0
Inactive	84	85	89	91	92	92	92	92	93	93	91	91	94
Base = 100%	*1731*	*1768*	*1840*	*1593*	*1498*	*1576*	*1580*	*1542*	*1617*	*1559*	*1498*	*1525*	*1509*
Total													
Working	79	76	71	67	68	70	66	67	64	62	64	65	64
Unemployed	3	4	8	10	8	5	8	8	9	9	8	7	6
Inactive	18	20	21	24	24	25	26	25	27	28	28	28	30
Base = 100%	*11455*	*10749*	*11504*	*9439*	*9329*	*9313*	*9049*	*8983*	*8976*	*8643*	*8488*	*8578*	*8117*

* From 1985 full-time students were classified as 'working' 'unemployed' or 'inactive' according to their own reports of what they were doing in the reference week; in previous years they were all classified as 'inactive'. From 1985 people on YT were classified as 'working' if they were with an employer for work experience in the reference week, or as 'inactive' if at college. Since 1989 all those on schemes YT, ET and (1989 only) JTS have been classified as 'working'.

Since 1991 an 'unemployed' person is someone who has been looking for work in the four weeks prior to interview and would be available to start work in the next two weeks, or is waiting to start a job . This has had the effect of reclassifying some informants from 'economically inactive' to 'economically active' and vice versa. See Chapter 5 GHS 1991 Report for further information.

The Labour Force Survey is the main source for economic activity data.

Table 5.10(b) Economic activity of women by age: 1975-1996

Women aged 16 and over   *Great Britain*

Age and economic activity*	1990 rules							ILO guidelines					
	1975	1979	1981	1983	1985	1989	1991	1991	1992	1993	1994	1995	1996
	%	%	%	%	%	%	%	%	%	%	%	%	%
16-17													
Working	60	63	53	52	53	62	60	60	55	45	50	49	48
Unemployed	6	7	13	14	12	7	11	13	14	14	13	12	12
Inactive	35	30	35	34	35	30	29	26	32	42	37	39	40
Base = 100%	*460*	*473*	*532*	*411*	*373*	*336*	*288*	*286*	*291*	*257*	*235*	*264*	*249*
18-24													
Working	67	65	65	61	62	69	66	67	65	64	61	67	66
Unemployed	4	5	11	12	13	6	9	10	10	11	11	8	7
Inactive	29	30	24	27	25	25	25	24	24	25	28	25	27
Base = 100%	*1367*	*1421*	*1601*	*1271*	*1278*	*1206*	*1090*	*1081*	*1076*	*1002*	*957*	*828*	*828*
25-34													
Working	53	56	51	50	56	67	64	64	64	65	67	66	68
Unemployed	2	3	5	6	5	4	5	6	6	6	5	7	4
Inactive	45	41	44	44	39	30	31	30	30	29	28	27	27
Base = 100%	*2336*	*2170*	*2232*	*1834*	*1837*	*1859*	*1957*	*1945*	*1888*	*1859*	*1885*	*1886*	*1701*
35-49													
Working	66	69	66	66	68	74	73	73	73	73	73	74	71
Unemployed	2	2	4	4	4	3	4	5	5	5	4	4	3
Inactive	32	29	30	30	29	24	23	22	22	22	23	22	26
Base = 100%	*3020*	*2609*	*2889*	*2416*	*2455*	*2587*	*2479*	*2466*	*2564*	*2492*	*2515*	*2493*	*2416*
50-59													
Working	59	60	59	55	53	59	59	59	60	58	62	60	58
Unemployed	1	1	3	3	3	2	3	4	4	4	2	3	3
Inactive	40	38	38	42	44	39	38	36	37	39	36	37	39
Base = 100%	*1963*	*1973*	*1930*	*1502*	*1395*	*1356*	*1333*	*1323*	*1368*	*1242*	*1200*	*1358*	*1246*
60-64													
Working	29	24	21	18	18	20	22	23	22	20	25	25	22
Unemployed	0	0	0	1	0	1	0	1	1	1	1	1	0
Inactive	71	76	79	81	82	79	77	76	77	79	75	74	78
Base = 100%	*1050*	*815*	*859*	*812*	*785*	*710*	*638*	*614*	*590*	*610*	*592*	*621*	*565*
65 and over													
Working	6	5	4	4	3	3	3	3	3	3	4	4	3
Unemployed	0	0	0	0	0	0	0	0	0	0	0	0	0
Inactive	94	95	95	96	97	97	97	97	96	97	96	96	97
Base = 100%	*2683*	*2641*	*2754*	*2371*	*2193*	*2263*	*2205*	*2205*	*2223*	*2283*	*2120*	*2043*	*1909*
Total													
Working	47	47	45	43	45	50	49	50	50	48	50	51	50
Unemployed	2	2	4	5	4	3	4	4	5	5	4	4	3
Inactive	51	50	50	53	51	47	47	46	46	48	46	45	47
Base = 100%	*12879*	*12102*	*12797*	*10617*	*10316*	*10317*	*9990*	*9920*	*10000*	*9745*	*9504*	*9493*	*8914*

* See the footnote to Table 5.10(a).

The Labour Force Survey is the main source for economic activity data.

Table 5.11   **Economic activity of women of working age, 1973 to 1996: percentages working full time, working part time, and unemployed by marital status**

Women aged 16-59   *Great Britain*

Marital status and economic activity*	1973	1975	1979	1981	1983	1985	1989	1991	1993	1994	1995	1996
						Percentages						
Single												
Working full time	72	66	63	57	53	53	54	46	41	41	41	42
Working part time	3	4	4	5	5	13	14	18	18	16	20	21
All working†	76	71	67	62	58	66	72	67	61	60	62	64
Unemployed	3	5	6	11	13	12	6	10	11	12	9	8
(economically active)	78	75	73	73	71	78	78	77	72	72	72	72
Base = 100%	*1550*	*1551*	*1712*	*1985*	*1585*	*1635*	*1629*	*1501*	*1474*	*1492*	*1435*	*1379*
Widowed, divorced, or separated												
Working full time	41	39	36	31	28	32	36	36	34	32	35	27
Working part time	21	21	22	25	21	24	22	24	21	24	24	25
All working†	63	61	59	56	49	56	58	61	55	56	60	52
Unemployed	3	4	5	8	8	8	7	7	8	7	8	6
(economically active)	66	64	64	64	57	64	65	68	63	63	68	58
Base = 100%	*688*	*706*	*748*	*815*	*704*	*691*	*699*	*750*	*802*	*791*	*787*	*717*
All non-married												
Working full time	62	58	54	50	45	47	48	43	38	38	39	37
Working part time	9	9	9	10	10	16	17	20	19	19	21	22
All working†	72	67	64	60	55	63	68	65	59	58	61	60
Unemployed	3	4	6	10	12	11	6	9	10	10	9	7
(economically active)	74	72	70	70	67	74	74	74	69	69	70	67
Base = 100%	*2238*	*2257*	*2460*	*2800*	*2289*	*2326*	*2328*	*2251*	*2276*	*2283*	*2222*	*2096*
Married												
Working full time	25	25	26	25	25	27	32	34	33	36	34	34
Working part time	28	32	33	32	31	32	35	33	35	34	35	34
All working†	54	58	60	57	57	59	68	67	69	70	69	67
Unemployed	1	2	2	4	4	4	2	5	5	3	4	3
(economically active)	55	59	62	61	60	62	70	72	73	73	74	72
Base = 100%	*6746*	*6889*	*6186*	*6385*	*5145*	*5012*	*5016*	*4850*	*4572*	*4505*	*4599*	*4338*
Total												
Working full time	34	33	34	33	31	33	37	37	35	36	36	35
Working part time	23	26	26	25	25	27	29	29	30	29	30	30
All working†	58	60	61	58	56	60	68	67	65	66	67	66
Unemployed	2	2	3	6	6	6	4	6	6	5	5	4
(economically active)	60	62	64	64	62	66	72	73	72	72	73	70
Base = 100%	*8984*	*9146*	*8646*	*9185*	*7434*	*7338*	*7344*	*7101*	*6848*	*6788*	*6821*	*6434*

* See the footnote to Table 5.10(a).

† Including a few women whose hours of work were not known. From 1989 persons on Government schemes such as YT have been excluded from the full-time and part-time categories but they were included in the 'all working' subtotal. Prior to 1989 those on Government schemes who were treated as economically active were classified according to hours worked.

The Labour Force Survey is the main source for economic activity data.

Table 5.12 **Economic activity of women of working age, 1973 to 1996: percentages working full time, working part time, and unemployed by age of youngest dependent child**

Women aged 16-59   *Great Britain*

Age of youngest dependent child* and economic activity†	1973	1979	1981	1983	1985	1989	1991	1993	1994	1995	1996
						Percentages					
Youngest child aged 0-4											
Working full time	7	6	6	5	8	12	13	14	16	16	16
Working part time	18	22	18	18	22	29	29	32	30	32	33
All working**	25 27	28 31	25 30	24 29	30 36	41 46	43 50	46 54	47 52	49 55	49 53
Unemployed	2	3	5	5	6	5	6	7	5	6	4
Base = 100%	*1936*	*1527*	*1604*	*1386*	*1339*	*1325*	*1352*	*1372*	*1320*	*1210*	*1188*
Youngest child aged 5-9											
Working full time	18	16	13	13	14	19	22	17	22	20	21
Working part time	42	44	43	40	46	49	44	44	41	41	41
All working**	61 63	61 64	57 61	54 59	60 63	69 72	67 74	61 69	64 69	61 68	63 68
Unemployed	2	3	5	6	3	3	7	8	5	7	4
Base = 100%	*1258*	*1157*	*1155*	*813*	*769*	*809*	*741*	*740*	*786*	*809*	*760*
Youngest child aged 10 or over											
Working full time	30	26	26	25	28	31	35	33	32	31	30
Working part time	37	45	43	42	42	43	40	42	44	43	44
All working**	67 68	72 73	69 73	66 70	70 73	75 77	76 81	75 79	76 79	75 79	75 78
Unemployed	1	1	4	4	3	3	5	4	3	4	3
Base = 100%	*1247*	*1423*	*1569*	*1255*	*1166*	*1003*	*952*	*939*	*978*	*925*	*938*
All with dependent children											
Working full time	17	16	15	14	17	20	22	21	23	22	22
Working part time	30	36	34	32	35	39	36	38	37	38	39
All working**	47 49	52 55	49 54	46 51	51 56	59 63	59 65	59 65	60 65	60 66	61 65
Unemployed	2	2	4	5	4	4	6	7	5	6	4
Base = 100%	*4441*	*4107*	*4328*	*3454*	*3274*	*3137*	*3045*	*3051*	*3084*	*2944*	*2886*
No dependent children											
Working full time	52	51	48	46	47	51	48	46	48	46	45
Working part time	17	18	18	18	21	22	23	23	22	25	24
All working**	69 71	69 73	66 72	65 72	67 75	75 78	72 78	71 77	71 78	72 77	70 75
Unemployed	2	3	7	8	7	4	6	6	6	5	5
Base = 100%	*4515*	*4504*	*4836*	*3943*	*4043*	*4192*	*4045*	*3773*	*3671*	*3862*	*3530*
Total											
Working full time	34	34	33	31	33	37	37	35	36	36	35
Working part time	23	26	25	25	27	29	29	30	29	31	30
All working**	58 60	61 64	58 64	56 62	60 66	68 72	67 73	65 72	66 72	67 72	66 70
Unemployed	2	3	6	6	6	4	6	6	5	5	4
Base = 100%	*8956*	*8611*	*9164*	*7397*	*7317*	*7329*	*7090*	*6824*	*6755*	*6806*	*6416*

*   Persons aged under 16, or aged 16-18 and in full-time education, in the family unit and living in the household.

†   See the footnote to Table 5.10(a).

** Including a few women whose hours of work were not known. From 1989 persons on Government schemes such as YT have been excluded from the full-time and part-time categories but included in the 'all working' subtotal. Prior to 1989 those on Government schemes who were treated as economically active were classified according to hours worked.

The Labour Force Survey is the main source for economic activity data.

Table 5.13 **Economic activity of married couples of working age with dependent children by number of dependent children and by age of youngest dependent child**

Married couples with husband aged 16-64 and wife
aged 16-59 and with dependent children*

Great Britain: 1996

Economic activity† of husband and wife	Number of dependent children			Age of youngest dependent child			All couples with dependent children
	1	2	3 or more	0-4	5-9	10 or over	
	%	%	%	%	%	%	%
Husband working							
Wife:							
working** - full time	28 ⎫65	20 ⎫64	12 ⎫49	17 ⎫52	21 ⎫64	29 ⎫72	22 ⎫62
- part time	37 ⎭	44 ⎭	37 ⎭	35 ⎭	44 ⎭	43 ⎭	40 ⎭
unemployed	3	2	2	3	3	2	3
economically inactive	19	22	32	33	20	13	23
Total	87	89	84	89	87	86	87
Husband unemployed							
Wife:							
working	1	2	0	1	2	2	1
unemployed	1	1	1	1	1	1	1
economically inactive	3	3	7	5	3	2	3
Total	5	5	8	6	6	5	6
Husband economically inactive							
Wife:							
working	3	3	1	1	2	4	3
unemployed	0	0	0	0	0	0	0
economically inactive	5	3	6	4	4	5	4
Total	8	6	8	5	7	9	7
	%	%	%	%	%	%	%
All couples							
Wife:							
working** - full time	30 ⎫69	23 ⎫68	13 ⎫51	18 ⎫54	23 ⎫69	31 ⎫78	24 ⎫66
- part time	40 ⎭	45 ⎭	38 ⎭	36 ⎭	46 ⎭	46 ⎭	42 ⎭
unemployed	4	3	4	4	4	3	4
economically inactive	27	28	45	42	27	20	31
Base = 100%	*872*	*993*	*413*	*946*	*584*	*748*	*2278*

* Persons aged under 16, or aged 16-18 and in full-time education, in the family unit and living in the household.

† See the footnote to Table 5.10(a).

** Including a few women whose hours of work were not known and those on YT and ET.

The Labour Force Survey is the main source for economic activity data.

Table 5.14 **Economic activity of women: percentages working and unemployed by marital status and age: 1986 and 1996**

Women aged 16 and over   *Great Britain*

Marital status and age	1986				1996			
	Economically active*			Base =100%	Economically active*			Base =100%
	Working	Unem- ployed	Total		Working	Unem- ployed	Total	
				Percentages				
Married								
16-17	58	7	65	*424*	62	6	68	*262*
18-24								
25-34	57	6	63	*1464*	70	3	74	*1175*
35-44	67	3	71	*1596*	73	3	76	*1270*
45-54	67	3	70	*1133*	71	2	73	*1188*
55-59	51	1	52	*534*	50	2	53	*443*
60-64	19	0	19	*513*	22	0	22	*430*
65 and over	3	0	3	*892*	5	0	5	*802*
16-59	62	4	66	*5151*	69	3	72	*4338*
Total	50	3	54	*6556*	56	2	58	*5570*
Single								
16-17	56	13	69	*375*	48	11	60	*244*
18-24	74	11	85	*825*	69	7	76	*556*
25-34	79	5	84	*273*	70	7	76	*384*
35-44	71	12	83	*77*	65	7	72	*112*
45-54	69	6	75	*107*	54	6	60	*83*
55-59								
60-64	6	0	6	*278*	5	0	5	*134*
65 and over								
16-59	70	10	80	*1657*	64	8	72	*1379*
Total	61	9	70	*1935*	59	7	66	*1513*
Widowed/divorced/separated								
16-17	[27]	[3]	[30]	*30*	†	†	†	*14*
18-24								
25-34	50	10	59	*157*	48	6	54	*142*
35-44	61	9	70	*198*	49	5	54	*236*
45-54	62	5	67	*169*	66	6	72	*222*
55-59	42	8	50	*116*	40	4	44	*103*
60-64	20	1	21	*209*	21	0	21	*121*
65 and over	2	0	2	*1272*	2	0	2	*987*
16-59	54	8	61	*670*	52	6	58	*717*
Total	20	3	22	*2151*	23	2	25	*1825*
Total								
16-17	56	13	69	*378*	48	12	60	*249*
18-24	68	9	77	*1276*	66	7	73	*828*
25-34	59	6	66	*1894*	68	4	73	*1701*
35-44	67	4	71	*1871*	69	3	73	*1618*
45-54	67	3	70	*1372*	70	3	73	*1472*
55-59	50	3	52	*687*	48	3	51	*567*
60-64	19	0	20	*766*	22	0	22	*565*
65 and over	2	0	2	*2398*	3	0	3	*1909*
16-59	63	6	69	*7478*	66	4	70	*6434*
Total	46	4	50	*10642*	50	3	53	*8908*

* See the footnote to Table 5.10(a).
† Base too small for reliable analysis.

The Labour Force Survey is the main source for economic activity data.

Table 5.15 **Economic activity of men: percentages working and unemployed by marital status and age: 1986 and 1996**

Men aged 16 and over   *Great Britain*

Marital status and age	1986				1996			
	Economically active*			Base =100%	Economically active*			Base =100%
	Working	Unem-ployed	Total		Working	Unem-ployed	Total	
				Percentages				
Married								
16-17	83	15	98	231	81	10	91	122
18-24								
25-34	90	8	98	1293	90	6	96	1045
35-44	92	6	98	1545	91	3	95	1223
45-54	87	6	94	1171	84	5	89	1224
55-59	76	8	85	578	73	5	78	444
60-64	49	8	57	550	41	4	45	439
65 and over	8	0	8	1167	8	0	8	1059
16-64	84	7	91	5368	82	5	87	4497
Total	71	6	77	6535	68	4	72	5556
Single								
16-17	54	14	68	407	52	14	67	301
18-24	71	20	91	1016	69	14	83	631
25-34	81	12	93	411	78	11	89	442
35-44	74	18	92	156	76	13	88	165
45-54	65	17	83	103	63	15	78	92
55-59	46	17	63	81	[30]	[4]	[34]	47
60-64								
65 and over	10	0	10	111	5	0	5	80
16-64	69	16	86	2174	68	13	81	1678
Total	66	16	82	2285	65	12	77	1758
Widowed/divorced/separated								
16-17	†	†	†	6	†	†	†	2
18-24								
25-34	79	13	92	164	63	20	83	60
35-44					72	12	84	117
45-54	72	16	88	99	71	7	77	123
55-59	48	15	63	127	36	9	45	113
60-64								
65 and over	6	0	6	334	3	0	3	370
16-64	67	15	82	396	61	11	71	415
Total	39	8	47	730	33	6	39	785
Total								
16-17	54	14	68	407	52	14	66	303
18-24	74	19	92	1253	71	13	84	753
25-34	88	9	97	1773	86	8	94	1547
35-44	89	7	97	1796	88	5	93	1505
45-54	85	8	92	1373	82	6	87	1439
55-59	74	10	84	669	69	6	75	512
60-64	49	7	56	667	39	4	43	531
65 and over	8	0	8	1612	6	0	6	1509
16-64	79	10	89	7938	77	7	84	6590
Total	67	8	76	9550	64	6	70	8099

* See the footnote to Table 5.10(a).
† Base too small to enable reliable analysis to be made.

The Labour Force Survey is the main source for economic activity data.

Table 5.16 **Composition of the labour force, 1975 to 1996: economic activity and employment status for men and non-married and married women**

Economically active persons aged 16 and over   *Great Britain*

Economic activity* and employment status	1975	1979	1981	1983	1985	1989	1991	1993	1994	1995	1996
	%	%	%	%	%	%	%	%	%	%	%
Men											
Employees	86	85	79	75	77	77	74	72	74	75	77
Self-employed	10	10	11	12	12	16	16	16	17	17	15
Unemployed	4	5	10	13	11	7	10	12	10	8	8
Base = 100%	*9302*	*8486*	*8914*	*7052*	*7071*	*7027*	*6661*	*6142*	*6012*	*6063*	*5641*
	%	%	%	%	%	%	%	%	%	%	%
Non-married women											
Employees	91	90	84	80	82	87	86	85	84	86	87
Self-employed	3	2	2	3	3	5	4	4	5	2	6
Unemployed	5	8	13	16	14	8	10	11	11	9	8
Base = 100%	*1843*	*1871*	*2107*	*1628*	*1792*	*1813*	*1705*	*1596*	*1593*	*1599*	*1427*
	%	%	%	%	%	%	%	%	%	%	%
Married women											
Employees	93	91	88	86	87	88	87	87	89	88	89
Self-employed	5	6	6	7	7	9	9	9	9	9	8
Unemployed	3	3	6	6	6	3	5	5	3	4	3
Base = 100%	*4318*	*3999*	*4052*	*3254*	*3271*	*3661*	*3570*	*3415*	*3385*	*3470*	*3199*

* See the footnote to Table 5.10(a).

The Labour Force Survey is the main source for economic activity data.

Table 5.17 **Number of people employed by the self-employed by sex**

Self-employed men and women aged 16 and over   *Great Britain: 1996*

Number of employees	Men	Women	Total
	%	%	%
Self-employed without employees	75	80	76
Self-employed with employees			
1-5 employees	16	13	15
6-24 employees	7	5	6
25 or more employees	2	2	2
Total with employees	25	20	24
No answer to whether employees	0	0	0
Base = 100%	*832*	*325*	*1157*

The Labour Force Survey is the main source for economic activity data.

Table 5.18 Composition of the labour force, 1979 to 1996: economic activity and whether man, or non-married or married woman

Economically active persons aged 16 and over   *Great Britain*

Economic activity,* sex, and marital status	1979	1981	1983	1985	1989	1991	1993	1994	1995	1996
	%	%	%	%	%	%	%	%	%	%
Working full time										
Men	54	51	49	49	47	46	43	43	44	45
Non-married women	10 ⌐75	9 ⌐71	9 ⌐69	9 ⌐69	9 ⌐70	8 ⌐68	8 ⌐65	8 ⌐66	8 ⌐66	8 ⌐67
Married women	12	11	11	11	13	14	14	15	14	14
Working part time										
Men	2	2	2	3	3	3	4	4	4	4
Non-married women	2 ⌐20	3 ⌐19	2 ⌐19	3 ⌐20	4 ⌐22	4 ⌐21	4 ⌐23	4 ⌐23	5 ⌐24	5 ⌐25
Married women	15	14	14	14	15	14	15	15	15	15
All working†										
Men	56	53	52	52	52	50	48	48	49	50
Non-married women	12 ⌐95	12 ⌐90	11 ⌐89	13 ⌐90	13 ⌐94	13 ⌐91	13 ⌐89	13 ⌐90	13 ⌐91	13 ⌐93
Married women	27	25	26	25	28	28	29	29	29	30
Unemployed										
Men	3	6	8	6	4	6	7	6	5	5
Non-married women	1 ⌐5	2 ⌐10	2 ⌐11	2 ⌐10	1 ⌐6	2 ⌐9	2 ⌐11	2 ⌐9	2 ⌐9	1 ⌐7
Married women	1	2	2	2	1	2	2	1	2	1
	%	%	%	%	%	%	%	%	%	%
All economically active										
Men	59	59	59	58	56	55	55	54	54	55
Non-married women	13	14	14	15	15	14	14	15	15	14
Married women	28	27	27	27	29	30	31	31	31	31
Base = 100%	*14356*	*15073*	*11934*	*12134*	*12501*	*12084*	*11311*	*11236*	*11380*	*10389*

* See the footnote to Table 5.10(a).

† Including a few persons whose hours of work were not known. From 1989 persons on Government schemes such as YT have been excluded from the full-time and part-time categories but they were included in the 'all working' subtotal. Prior to 1989 those on Government schemes who were treated as economically active were classified according to hours worked.

The Labour Force Survey is the main source for economic activity data.

Table 5.19 **Composition of the labour force, 1975 to 1996: economic activity and employment status for men and non-married and married women**

Economically active persons aged 16 and over　　　　　　　　　　　　*Great Britain*

Economic activity* and employment status	1975	1979	1981	1983	1985	1989†	1991	1993	1994	1995	1996
	%	%	%	%	%	%	%	%	%	%	%
Men											
Employees**											
working full time	..⌐86	82⌐85	76⌐79	72⌐75	73⌐77	70⌐74	68⌐72	65⌐70	66⌐72	66⌐73	70⌐77
working part time	..⌐	3⌐	2⌐	3⌐	3⌐	4⌐	4⌐	5⌐	6⌐	6⌐	6⌐
Self-employed	10	10	11	12	12	17	16	16	16	17	15
Government schemes	..	..	..	..	..	2	1	1	1	1	1
Unemployed	4	5	10	13	11	7	10	13	11	10	8
Base = 100%	*9302*	*8486*	*8914*	*7052*	*7071*	*7027*	*6699*	*5698*	*6047*	*6124*	*5660*
	%	%	%	%	%	%	%	%	%	%	%
Non-married women											
Employees**											
working full time	..⌐91	72⌐90	66⌐84	63⌐80	60⌐82	61⌐83	54⌐81	52⌐80	51⌐78	51⌐81	51⌐83
working part time	..⌐	17⌐	18⌐	17⌐	22⌐	22⌐	27⌐	28⌐	27⌐	30⌐	32⌐
Self-employed	3	2	2	3	3	5	4	4	5	5	5
Government schemes	..	..	..	..	..	4	3	3	2	2	2
Unemployed	5	8	13	16	14	8	12	14	14	12	10
Base = 100%	*1843*	*1871*	*2107*	*1628*	*1792*	*1813*	*1740*	*1548*	*1643*	*1644*	*1465*
	%	%	%	%	%	%	%	%	%	%	%
Married women											
Employees**											
working full time	..⌐93	39⌐91	38⌐88	38⌐86	39⌐87	41⌐87	42⌐85	40⌐85	44⌐87	42⌐86	43⌐88
working part time	..⌐	52⌐	50⌐	48⌐	48⌐	47⌐	42⌐	45⌐	43⌐	44⌐	45⌐
Self-employed	5	6	6	7	7	9	9	8	9	9	8
Government schemes	..	..	..	..	..	0	0	0	0	0	0
Unemployed	3	3	6	6	6	3	7	6	4	5	4
Base = 100%	*4318*	*3999*	*4052*	*3254*	*3271*	*3661*	*3645*	*3396*	*3396*	*3489*	*3226*

* See the footnote to Table 5.10(a).
† Base numbers for 1989 include people on college-based Government schemes.
** Totals include a few persons whose hours of work were not known.

The Labour Force Survey is the main source for economic activity data.

Table 5.20 **Composition of the male labour force of working age: socio-economic group by whether working or unemployed**

Men aged 16-64　　　　　　　　　　　　*Great Britain: 1996*

Socio-economic group*	Economically active men†			All men aged 16-64
	Working	Unemployed	Total	
	%	%	%	%
Professional	7	1	7	6
Employers and managers	23	13	22	22
Intermediate non-manual	11	6	11	10
Junior non-manual	8	8	8	8
Skilled manual and own account non-professional	33	33	34	35
Semi-skilled manual and personal service	14	29	15	15
Unskilled manual	3	11	4	4
Base = 100%	*4908*	*397*	*5305*	*6079*

* Excluding those in the Armed Forces and any who have never worked.
† See the footnote to Table 5.10(a).

The Labour Force Survey is the main source for economic activity data.

Table 5.21 Unemployed married men of working age and all married men of working age by number of dependent children: 1973 to 1996

Married men aged 16-64*

Great Britain

Number of dependent children†	1973	1975	1979	1981	1983	1985	1989	1991	1993	1994	1995	1996
	%	%	%	%	%	%	%	%	%	%	%	%
Unemployed married men with:												
1 dependent child	14	24	23	18	19	25	17	17	19	23	19	19
2 dependent children	19	19	25	22	21	24	18	26	20	21	21	25
3 dependent children	11	11	11	15	13	13	18	16	17	20	18	17
4 or more dependent children	15	17	8	9	7	8						
(total)	59	70	68	63	61	70	53	59	56	64	58	60
No dependent children	41	30	32	37	39	30	47	41	44	36	42	40
Base = 100%	176	204	202	506	442	391	223	340	393	312	252	210
	%	%	%	%	%	%	%	%	%	%	%	%
All married men with:												
1 dependent child	21	21	22	21	21	21	19	19	18	19	18	20
2 dependent children	23	24	25	25	24	24	22	22	23	22	22	22
3 dependent children	9	9	8	8	8	7	9	9	9	10	9	9
4 or more dependent children	5	4	3	3	2	2						
(total)	58	59	58	58	56	54	51	50	51	51	49	51
No dependent children	42	41	42	42	44	46	49	50	49	49	51	49
Base = 100%	6882	7109	6231	6548	5274	5203	5211	5006	4750	4680	4759	4484

* Data for 1973 to 1979 exclude a small number of married men with no wife in the household.

† Persons aged under 16, or 16-18 and in full-time education, in the family unit and living in the household.

The Labour Force Survey is the main source for economic activity data.

Table 5.22 Duration of unemployment at time of interview, for unemployed men: 1975 to 1996

All unemployed men aged 16 and over

Great Britain

Length of time unemployed*	1975	1979	1981	1983	1985	1989	1991	1993	1994	1995	1996
	%	%	%	%	%	%	%	%	%	%	%
Less than 1 month	22	16	8	7	7	13	9	7	10	11	10
1 month but less than 3 months	22	19	14	11	10	17	14	12	15	14	18
3 months but less than 6 months	18	18	18	12	13	13	20	14	12	13	10
6 months but less than 1 year	17	17	23	16	16	13	22	19	18	17	17
1 year but less than 2 years	21	30	22	21	15	13	18	21	15	11	13
2 years or more			15	33	39	31	17	26	31	34	32
Base = 100%	370	386	861	806	702	491	656	739	607	542	446

* See Appendix A, 'Unemployed persons'.

The Labour Force Survey is the main source for economic activity data.

Table 5.23   Economic status of women with dependent children by family type

Women with dependent children*   *Great Britain: 1996*

Family type		Working full time	Working part time	Total working†	Unemployed	Inactive	Base = 100%
Married mother	%	24	44	68	3	29	2073
Cohabiting mother	%	22	25	48	8	44	241
Lone mother	%	16	27	43	5	52	578
Single	%	14	21	36	6	58	218
Widowed	%	20	47	67	3	30	30
Divorced	%	20	31	52	5	42	186
Separated	%	11	26	37	4	59	144

* Dependent children are persons aged under 16, or aged 16-18 and in full-time education, in the family unit, and living in the household.

† Total includes those on Government Schemes and those whose hours of work were not known.

The Labour Force Survey is the main source for economic activity data.

Table 5.24   Lone mothers and married women with dependent children: percentage working full time and part time by age of youngest dependent child and marital status

Women with dependent children*   *Great Britain: 1994-96 combined*

Age of youngest dependent child and whether woman working full time or part time	Lone mothers					Married† women with dependent children
	Single	Widowed	Divorced	Separated	All lone mothers	
	Percentage working full time and part time					
Under 5 years:						
Working full time	10	**	10	8	9	18
Working part time	14	**	25	18	17	36
All working††	25	**	35	26	27	54
Base = 100%	*441*	*7*	*119*	*162*	*729*	*2979*
5 years and over:						
Working full time	20	17	23	19	21	28
Working part time	24	35	32	30	30	46
All working††	44	52	56	49	51	74
Base = 100%	*260*	*83*	*500*	*270*	*1113*	*4107*
All ages:						
Working full time	14	16	20	15	16	24
Working part time	18	36	31	25	25	42
All working††	32	51	52	41	42	66
Base = 100%	*701*	*90*	*619*	*432*	*1842*	*7086*

*   Dependent children are persons aged under 16, or aged 16-18 and in full-time education, in the family unit, and living in the household.

†   Including married women whose husbands were not defined as resident in the household: See Appendix A.

** Base too small to enable reliable analysis to be made.

†† 'All working' includes those on Government Schemes and those whose hours of work were not known.

The Labour Force Survey is the main source for economic activity data.

Table 5.25 Socio-economic group by sex: 1971 to 1996

All persons   *Great Britain*

Socio-economic group*	1971†	1975	1979	1983	1985	1989	1991	1993	1994	1995	1996
	%	%	%	%	%	%	%	%	%	%	%
Males											
Professional	5	5	6	5	6	7	8	7	7	7	6
Employers and managers	15	15	15	17	19	20	19	20	21	21	21
Intermediate and junior non-manual	18	17	17	16	17	17	18	19	18	19	19
Skilled manual and own account non-professional	40	41	40	39	37	36	36	35	33	33	33
Semi-skilled manual and personal service	17	18	17	18	16	15	14	15	15	15	16
Unskilled manual	5	4	5	6	5	5	5	5	5	5	5
Base = 100%	*14320*	*15664*	*14068*	*12081*	*11728*	*11689*	*11535*	*11076*	*10943*	*10877*	*10296*
	%	%	%	%	%	%	%	%	%	%	%
Females											
Professional	4	4	5	4	5	6	6	6	6	6	5
Employers and managers	14	13	14	15	17	19	18	18	20	20	20
Intermediate and junior non-manual	24	23	23	23	25	24	25	27	25	26	25
Skilled manual and own account non-professional	33	34	32	31	29	28	28	27	26	26	27
Semi-skilled manual and personal service	20	21	20	21	19	18	17	16	17	17	17
Unskilled manual	6	5	6	6	5	5	6	6	6	5	5
Base = 100%	*14932*	*16452*	*15075*	*12841*	*12221*	*12572*	*12279*	*12049*	*11734*	*11510*	*10961*

* Married women whose husbands were in the household are classified according to their husband's occupation; children under 16 are classified according to their father's occupation. No answers, members of the Armed Forces, full-time students and those who have never worked are excluded.

† England and Wales in 1971.

The Labour Force Survey is the main source for economic activity data.

Table 5.26 (a) Socio-economic group by sex and age
(b) Age and sex by socio-economic group

All persons   *Great Britain: 1996*

		Socio-economic group*					
		Professional	Employers and managers	Intermediate and junior non-manual	Skilled manual and own account non-professional	Semi-skilled manual and personal service	Unskilled manual	Total
(a)		%	%	%	%	%	%	%
Males								
0 - 4		6	7	9	6	9	8	7
5 - 15		19	17	18	15	16	16	16
16 - 44		37	33	45	35	41	41	38
45 - 64		25	28	18	28	20	18	24
65 - 74		8	8	6	10	8	11	8
75 and over		5	8	5	6	6	5	6
Base = 100%		*638*	*2193*	*1918*	*3393*	*1649*	*505*	*10296*
		%	%	%	%	%	%	%
Females								
0 - 4		7	8	6	8	6	5	7
5 - 15		17	18	11	17	14	12	15
16 - 44		41	35	45	33	40	29	38
45 - 64		26	26	18	28	20	24	24
65 - 74		7	7	10	9	10	15	9
75 and over		1	5	9	5	10	15	7
Base = 100%		*573*	*2175*	*2788*	*2991*	*1870*	*564*	*10961*
(b)								*Base = 100%*
Males								
0 - 4	%	5	20	22	27	20	6	*738*
5 - 15	%	7	22	20	30	16	5	*1694*
16 - 44	%	6	18	22	31	17	5	*3898*
45 - 64	%	6	24	14	38	13	4	*2472*
65 - 74	%	5	20	13	40	15	7	*875*
75 and over	%	5	27	14	33	17	4	*619*
Total	%	6	21	19	33	16	5	*10296*
Females								
0 - 4	%	6	23	22	30	15	4	*757*
5 - 15	%	6	24	19	31	16	4	*1640*
16 - 44	%	6	18	30	24	18	4	*4156*
45 - 64	%	6	22	20	33	15	5	*2578*
65 - 74	%	4	16	28	26	18	8	*1030*
75 and over	%	1	15	33	18	22	11	*800*
Total	%	5	20	25	27	17	5	*10961*

* See the first footnote to Table 5.25.

The Labour Force Survey is the main source for economic activity data.

6 Occupational and personal pension schemes

Pension scheme membership[1]

At the time of the 1996 interview:

* 75% of men in full-time work were currently members either of an occupational or a personal pension scheme compared with 65% of women working full time and 33% of women working part time. Some respondents were members of both types of scheme;
* employees below the age of 25 and over the age of 55 were less likely to belong to a pension scheme than those in other age groups.   **Table 6.1, Figure 6A**

Membership of current employer's pension scheme

Membership of an employer's pension scheme varied according to the sex of the respondent and whether or not they worked full or part time.

* Among those working full time, men were more likely than women to belong to an employer's pension scheme (58% compared with 53%), although the proportion of full-time employees who were offered a scheme by their employer was similar for both groups (74% and 73% respectively);
* membership of an employer's pension scheme was nearly five times as likely among men working full time as those working part time (58% compared with 12%) and just over twice as likely among women working full time as those working part time (53% compared with 26%). To some extent this reflects the higher proportion of full than part-time employees who were offered a pension scheme by their employer;

* among those working part time, women were more likely than men to work for an employer who offered a pension scheme (53% compared with 46%) and were more likely to belong to a scheme if one was provided (26% compared with 12%).   **Table 6.2**

Trends in membership of an occupational pension scheme

Since July 1988, employees have been given the choice of starting their own personal pension in place of SERPS (State Earnings Related Pension Scheme). Previously those not in an occupational scheme could arrange to pay for a personal pension plan but they could not leave SERPS. As a result of this change in the rules, the time series shown in Table 6.3 is not strictly comparable from 1988 with previous years. Since 1988:

* the proportion of men working full time who were in an employer's pension scheme decreased from 64% in 1988 to 58% in 1996. This partly reflects the decline in the proportion of employees who were offered a pension scheme by their employer (from 78% in 1988 to 74% in 1996);
* the proportion of full-time female employees who were offered a pension scheme by their employer has not changed significantly since 1988 (74% in 1988, 73% in 1996) and neither has the proportion of women who were members of a scheme (54% in 1988, 53% in 1996);
* the proportion of women in part-time work who were offered a pension scheme increased from 48% in 1988 to 53% in 1996. Among women in part-time work, membership of an employers pension scheme more

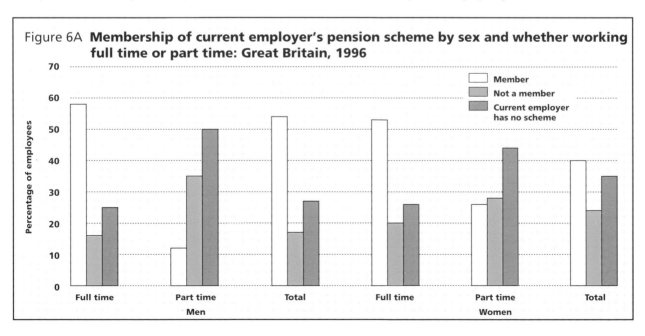

Figure 6A **Membership of current employer's pension scheme by sex and whether working full time or part time: Great Britain, 1996**

than doubled from 12% in 1988 to 26% in 1996;
- the proportion of women in part-time work who did not know whether their employer had a scheme decreased from 10% in 1987 to 2% in 1996.

Tables 6.2-6.4

Membership of a personal pension scheme

Membership of a personal pension scheme also varied according to the sex and age of the respondent. In 1996:

- 26% of men in full-time work were members of a personal pension scheme compared with 18% of women working full time and 9% of women working part time;
- among men working full time, those aged 25-34 were most likely (35%) to belong to a personal pension scheme;
- among women working full time, those aged 25-44 were most likely to belong to a personal pension scheme (24% of those aged 25-34; 22% of those aged 35-44);
- employees below the age of 25 whether working full or part time were the least likely to belong to a personal pension scheme. **Table 6.1**

Characteristics of employees in pension schemes

Socio-economic group
There was considerable variation in membership of employer's and personal pension schemes between socio-

economic groups. For example in the years 1994-96 combined:

- among full-time employees, three-quarters (75%) of professional men and two-thirds (66%) of professional women belonged to an employer's pension scheme compared with 39% of men and 28% of women in unskilled manual occupations;
- professional women in full-time employment were twice as likely as those in unskilled manual occupations (24% compared with 12%) to belong to a personal pension scheme. Among men working full time, there was more variation in membership of a personal pension scheme. The highest proportion of men with a personal pension scheme were employers and managers (33%) and skilled manual workers (32%).
- of women in part-time work, about a half (51%) of all professional women were members of their employer's scheme compared with only 11% of unskilled manual workers. Furthermore, professional women were nearly five times as likely as unskilled manual workers to belong to a personal pension scheme (24% compared with 5%). **Tables 6.5, Figure 6B**

Income
The higher their gross weekly income, the more likely men and women working full time were to belong to their employer's pension scheme. For example in 1996:

- among those working full time, 75% of men and 82% of women with gross weekly earnings between £500 and £600 had an occupational pension compared with 26% of men and 30% of women earning between £100 and £200. **Table 6.6**

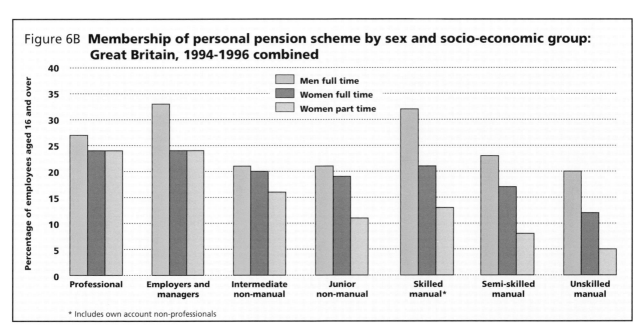

Figure 6B **Membership of personal pension scheme by sex and socio-economic group: Great Britain, 1994-1996 combined**

Length of time with current employer

The likelihood of belonging to an employer's pension scheme increased with the length of time respondents had worked for their current employer. For example:

- 27% of men who had been working full time for their current employer for less than two years belonged to their employer's pension scheme compared with 76% of those who had been with their employer for at least five years;
- for women, comparable figures were 27% and 71% respectively for those working full time; 13% and 39% for those working part time.

Among women but not among men, the likelihood of belonging to a personal pension scheme also increased with the length of time they had worked for their current employer. For example:

- 15% of women working full time for their employer for less than two years belonged to a personal pension scheme compared with 20% who had worked for their employer for at least five years;
- for women working part time, the comparable figures were 7% and 11%. **Table 6.7**

Size of establishment

Among all types of employee, the likelihood of belonging to an employer's pension scheme increased with the size of the establishment in which they worked, mainly because larger employers are more likely to offer their employees a pension scheme. For example:

- 34% of men working full time in an establishment with 3-24 employees belonged to their employer's pension scheme compared with 86% working in an establishment with 1000 or more employees;
- the comparable figures for women working full time were 36% and 75% and for women working part time, 15% and 61%.

Both men and women working full time in smaller establishments were the most likely to belong to a personal pension scheme. For example:

- 34% of men working full time in an establishment with 3-24 employees belonged to a personal pension scheme compared with 15% working in an establishment with 1000 or more employees;
- the comparable figures for women working full time were 23% and 10%. **Table 6.8**

Industry

There was a wide difference in pension scheme membership (for both employer's and personal pension schemes) between industry groups, reflecting differences in the proportion of employers in each industry group who provided a scheme.

For the years 1994-1996 combined:

- men working full time in public and other personal services were the most likely to belong to an employer's pension scheme (81%) and the least likely to belong to a personal pension scheme (15%);
- conversely, men working full time in agriculture, forestry and fishing were the least likely group of all men working full time to belong to an employer's pension (26%) but the most likely to have a personal pension (45%);
- among women working full time, those employed in the coal mining, energy and water supply industries, or public and other personal services, were most likely to belong to an employer's pension scheme (71% and 68% respectively) and those working in distribution, hotels, catering and repairs were least likely (30%) **Tables 6.9**

The self-employed and personal pension scheme membership

Among the self-employed who worked full time, men were more likely than women to belong to a personal pension scheme and the difference was greater than among full-time employees. Of those working full time:

- 64% of self-employed men compared with 41% of self-employed women were currently in a personal pension scheme;
- of the self-employed who worked part time, 30% of men and 24% of women were currently members of a personal pension scheme (this difference is not statistically significant due to the small sample size);
- women in this group were less likely than men to have ever been a member of a personal pension scheme (31% and 50% respectively).

The longer self-employed people had been in their current employment, the more likely they were to belong to a personal pension scheme. For example:

- 72% of men working full time who had been self-employed for at least five years belonged to a personal

79

pension scheme compared with 39% of those who had
been self-employed less than two years;

• the same pattern can be seen for full-time self-
employed women although the number in the sample
who had been self-employed for less than five years is
too small to make a reliable comparison.

Table 6.10-6.11

Notes

1   The figures shown in Table 6.1 for current pension
scheme membership in 1996 are lower than in
previous years because prior to 1996, the proportion
of individuals who were members of an occupational
pension and the proportion with a personal pension
were added together, not taking into account individuals who may be contributing to both.

Table 6.1 **Current pension scheme membership by age and sex**

Employees aged 16 and over excluding YT and ET　　　　　　　　　　　　　　*Great Britain: 1996*

Pension scheme members	Age						
	16-17	18-24	25-34	35-44	45-54	55 and over	Total
				Percentages			
Men full time							
Occupational pension*	[5]	23	53	69	71	59	58
Personal pension	[0]	16	35	28	23	17	26
Any pension	[5]	36	77	84	84	70	75
Women full time							
Occupational pension*	†	27	56	64	61	58	53
Personal pension	†	9	24	22	15	12	18
Any pension	†	34	72	76	70	65	65
Women part time							
Occupational pension*	0	6	25	34	31	19	26
Personal pension	0	1	15	9	12	4	9
Any pension	0	7	37	40	41	23	33
Bases=100%							
Men full time	43	426	1108	1078	906	376	3937
Women full time	15	370	677	487	458	136	2143
Women part time	87	156	405	523	470	267	1908

* Including a few people who were not sure if they were in a scheme but thought it possible.
† Base too small to enable reliable analysis to be made.

Table 6.2 **Membership of current employer's pension scheme by sex and whether working full time or part time**

Employees aged 16 and over excluding YT and ET　　　　　　　　　　　　　　*Great Britain: 1996*

Pension scheme coverage	Men			Women		
	Working full time	Working part time	Total*	Working full time	Working part time	Total*
	%	%	%	%	%	%
Present employer has a pension scheme						
Member†	58	12	54	53	26	40
Not a member	16 ⎤74	35 ⎤46	17 ⎤72	20 ⎤73	28 ⎤53	24 ⎤64
Does not know if a member	0 ⎦	0 ⎦	0 ⎦	0 ⎦	0 ⎦	0 ⎦
Present employer does not have a pension scheme	25	50	27	26	44	35
Does not know if present employer has a pension scheme - not a member	1	4	1	1	2	1
Base = 100%	3937	334	4287	2143	1908	4057

* Including a few people whose hours of work were not known.
† Including a few people who were not sure if they were in a scheme but thought it possible.

Table 6.3 **Membership of current employer's pension scheme by sex: 1975 to 1996**

Employees aged 16 and over excluding YT and ET*   *Great Britain*

Pension scheme members†	1975	1979	1983	1987	1988	1989	1991	1992	1993	1994	1995	1996
						Percentages						
Full-time												
Men	63	68	66	63	64	64	61	62	60	60	58	58
Women	47	55	55	52	54	55	55	54	54	53	55	53
Total	59	65	61	59	61	61	59	59	58	58	57	56
Women part-time employees	..	..	13	11	12	15	17	19	19	19	24	26
Bases = 100%												
Full-time												
Men	*7321*	*6887*	*5087*	*5129*	*4941*	*4906*	*4563*	*4313*	*3976*	*4006*	*4062*	*3937*
Women	*2772*	*2324*	*2256*	*2562*	*2595*	*2602*	*2484*	*2396*	*2239*	*2345*	*2331*	*2143*
Total	*10093*	*9211*	*7343*	*7691*	*7536*	*7508*	*7047*	*6709*	*6215*	*6351*	*6393*	*6080*
Women part-time employees	*..*	*..*	*1638*	*2126*	*2015*	*2102*	*1977*	*2067*	*1938*	*1930*	*2038*	*1908*

* Prior to 1985 full-time students are excluded. Figures for 1987-1993 include full-time students who were working but exclude those on Government schemes. This represents a re-classification from that used in the GHS 1987 and 1988 reports. Figures for 1987 and 1988 have been re-calculated accordingly and may therefore differ from previously published data.

† Including a few people who were not sure if they were in a scheme but thought it possible.

Table 6.4 Membership of current employer's pension scheme by sex: 1983 to 1996

*Employees aged 16 and over excluding YT and ET**   *Great Britain*

Pension scheme coverage	1983		1987		1988		1989		1991		1992		1993		1994		1995		1996	
	%		%		%		%		%		%		%		%		%		%	
Men full time																				
Present employer has a pension scheme																				
Member†	66		63		64		64		61		62		60		60		58		58	
Not a member	10	77	12	74	13	78	14	79	16	77	15	77	16	76	15	75	16	74	16	74
Does not know if a member	1		0		0		0		1		0		0		0		0		0	
Present employer does not have a pension scheme	22		22		19		19		21		21		22		24		25		25	
Does not know if present employer has a pension scheme - not a member	2		3		3		2		2		2		2		1		1		1	
Base = 100%	*5087*		*5129*		*4941*		*4906*		*4563*		*4313*		*3976*		*4006*		*4062*		*3937*	
	%		%		%		%		%		%		%		%		%		%	
Women full time																				
Present employer has a pension scheme																				
Member†	55		52		54		55		55		54		54		53		55		53	
Not a member	17	72	16	68	19	74	21	76	21	77	22	77	22	77	19	73	20	76	20	73
Does not know if a member	0		1		0		0		0		0		0		0		0		0	
Present employer does not have a pension scheme	24		28		23		21		20		21		22		27		24		26	
Does not know if present employer has a pension scheme - not a member	4		4		3		3		3		2		2		1		1		1	
Base = 100%	*2256*		*2562*		*2595*		*2602*		*2484*		*2396*		*2239*		*2345*		*2331*		*2143*	
	%		%		%		%		%		%		%		%		%		%	
Women part time																				
Present employer has a pension scheme																				
Member†	13		11		12		15		17		19		19		19		24		26	
Not a member	39	53	34	46	35	48	37	52	34	52	34	54	35	55	33	52	32	55	28	53
Does not know if a member	0		0		0		0		1		0		0		0		0		0	
Present employer does not have a pension scheme	40		44		42		40		39		39		38		45		42		44	
Does not know if present employer has a pension scheme - not a member	7		10		9		7		8		7		7		3		3		2	
Base = 100%	*1638*		*2126*		*2015*		*2102*		*1977*		*2067*		*1938*		*1930*		*2038*		*1908*	

* See the footnotes to Table 6.3.
†

Table 6.5 Current pension scheme membership by sex and socio-economic group

Employees aged 16 and over excluding YT and ET *Great Britain: 1994-1996 combined*

Pension scheme members	Socio-economic group†							
	Professional	Employers and managers	Intermediate non-manual	Junior non-manual	Skilled manual and own account non-professional	Semi-skilled manual and personal service	Unskilled manual	Total
				Percentages				
Men full time								
Occupational pension*	75	68	72	62	48	46	39	59
Personal pension	27	33	21	21	32	23	20	27
Any pension	89	88	85	75	72	64	54	77
Women full time								
Occupational pension*	66	63	68	51	41	30	28	54
Personal pension	24	24	20	19	21	17	12	20
Any pension	79	78	80	65	56	46	39	67
Women part time								
Occupational pension*	51	43	41	25	17	16	11	23
Personal pension	24	24	16	11	13	8	5	10
Any pension	67	59	53	34	30	23	16	33
Bases=100%								
Men full time	973	2831	1356	1065	3448	1725	399	12005
Women full time	225	1220	1635	2098	335	1092	88	6819
Women part time	51	211	861	2100	166	1313	715	5876

* Including a few people who were not sure if they were in a scheme but thought it possible.

† Members of the Armed Forces, full-time students and those who have never worked are not shown as separate categories but are included in the figures for all persons.

Table 6.6 Current pension scheme membership by sex and usual gross weekly earnings: all employees

Employees aged 16 and over excluding YT and ET *Great Britain: 1996*

Pension scheme members	Usual gross weekly earnings (£)							
	0.01-100.00	100.01-200.00	200.01-300.00	300.01-400.00	400.01-500.00	500.01-600.00	600.01 or more	Total†
				Percentages				
Men full time								
Occupational pension*	45	26	50	68	78	75	82	58
Personal pension	17	19	29	27	26	29	33	26
Any pension	57	42	71	85	91	90	93	75
Women full time								
Occupational pension*	37	30	61	73	83	82	[83]	53
Personal pension	13	17	18	25	21	16	[24]	18
Any pension	47	43	74	85	90	91	[88]	65
Women part time								
Occupational pension*	13	45	67	**	**	**	**	26
Personal pension	7	11	25	**	**	**	**	9
Any pension	19	53	80	**	**	**	**	33
Bases=100%								
Men full time	111	497	858	684	434	234	330	3937
Women full time	115	615	617	277	142	57	42	2143
Women part time	1130	475	102	14	6	4	2	1908

* Including a few people who were not sure if they were in a scheme but thought it possible.

† Totals include no answers to income.

** Base too small to enable reliable analysis to be made.

Table 6.7 **Current pension scheme membership by sex and length of time with current employer**

Employees aged 16 and over excluding YT and ET   *Great Britain: 1996*

Pension scheme members	Length of time with current employer			
	Less than 2 years	2 years, but less than 5 years	5 years or more	Total†
	Percentages			
Men full time				
Occupational pension*	27	47	76	58
Personal pension	26	32	24	26
Any pension	48	67	89	75
Women full time				
Occupational pension*	27	46	71	53
Personal pension	15	19	20	18
Any pension	38	60	82	65
Women part time				
Occupational pension*	13	20	39	26
Personal pension	7	9	11	9
Any pension	18	28	47	33
Bases=100%				
Men full time	*999*	*738*	*2200*	*3937*
Women full time	*627*	*427*	*1087*	*2143*
Women part time	*696*	*400*	*811*	*1908*

* Including a few people who were not sure if they were in a scheme but thought it possible.
† Including a few where length of time in job was not known.

Table 6.8 **Current pension scheme membership by sex and number of employees in the establishment**

Employees aged 16 and over excluding YT and ET   *Great Britain: 1996*

Pension scheme members	Number of employees at establishment					
	1-2	3-24	25-99	100-999	1000 or more	Total†
	Percentages					
Men full time						
Occupational pension*	35	34	55	70	86	58
Personal pension	37	34	28	22	15	26
Any pension	63	61	73	81	90	75
Women full time						
Occupational pension*	[22]	36	54	61	75	53
Personal pension	[22]	23	20	16	10	18
Any pension	[41]	52	65	71	80	65
Women part time						
Occupational pension*	9	15	26	41	61	26
Personal pension	7	9	9	12	11	9
Any pension	15	22	33	48	69	33
Bases=100%						
Men full time	*86*	*940*	*1043*	*1403*	*401*	*3937*
Women full time	*41*	*576*	*559*	*690*	*262*	*2143*
Women part time	*115*	*785*	*486*	*389*	*113*	*1908*

* Including a few people who were not sure if they were in a scheme but thought it possible.
† Includes a few people for whom the number of employees at establishment was not known.

Table 6.9 Current pension scheme membership by sex and industry group

Employees aged 16 and over excluding YT and ET   *Great Britain: 1994-96 combined*

Pension scheme members	Industry group†										
	Agriculture, forestry, fishing	Coal mining, energy and water supply	Mining (excl coal), manufact-ure of metals, minerals and chemicals	Metal goods, engineer-ing and vehicle	Other manufact-uring	Construc-tion	Distribu-tion, hotels, catering repairs	Transport and commun-ications	Banking, finance, insurance business services	Public and other personal services	Total
					Percentages						
Men full time											
Occupational pension*	26	72	64	58	52	46	35	65	61	81	59
Personal pension	45	23	32	30	30	33	33	24	32	15	27
Any pension	62	85	83	79	74	71	61	80	80	88	77
Women full time											
Occupational pension*	[29]	71	50	47	43	48	30	57	51	68	54
Personal pension	[22]	22	19	21	21	20	25	17	23	17	20
Any pension	[49]	86	63	63	58	62	51	69	66	77	67
Women part time											
Occupational pension*	[9]	**	[36]	22	22	19	12	38	31	28	23
Personal pension	11	**	[16]	13	11	16	9	6	13	11	10
Any pension	20	**	[48]	32	32	33	19	43	42	37	31
Bases = 100%											
Men full time	*204*	*309*	*275*	*1951*	*1710*	*896*	*1662*	*1134*	*1435*	*2403*	*11979*
Women full time	*41*	*72*	*70*	*439*	*845*	*103*	*995*	*255*	*1137*	*2855*	*6812*
Women part time	*54*	*14*	*25*	*140*	*402*	*67*	*1884*	*139*	*514*	*2629*	*5868*

*   Including a few people who were not sure if they were in a scheme but thought it possible.
†   Standard Industrial Classification, 1992.
** Base too small for reliable analysis to be made.

Table 6.10 Membership of personal pension scheme by sex and whether working full time or part time: self-employed persons

Self-employed persons aged 16 and over   *Great Britain: 1996*

Pension scheme coverage	Men			Women		
	Working full time	Working part time	Total*	Working full time	Working part time	Total
	%	%	%	%	%	%
Informant belongs to a personal pension scheme	64	30	59	41	24	31
Informant no longer has a personal pension scheme	11	20	12	3	7	5
Informant has never had a personal pension scheme	25	50	29	56	69	63
Base = 100%	*696*	*122*	*824*	*140*	*182*	*322*

* Including a few people whose hours of work were not known.

Table 6.11 **Membership of personal pension scheme by sex and length of time in self-employment**

Self-employed persons aged 16 and over   *Great Britain: 1996*

	Length of time in self-employment			
	Less than 2 years	2 years, but less than 5 years	5 years or more	Total
	Percentage of self-employed who belong to a personal pension scheme			
Men full time	39	49	72	64
Women full time	[27]	[33]	49	41
Women part time	[14]	[17]	32	24
Bases = 100%				
Men full time	93	116	487	696
Women full time	30	24	86	140
Women part time	44	46	92	182

7 Education

The GHS primarily collects information about education to help explain inter-relationships between different characteristics about people as well as describing the educational levels obtained by them. Education data are also available from the Labour Force Survey (LFS) and with its unclustered sample design and larger sample size the estimates are likely to be more accurate.

Trends over time

There has been a steady increase in the proportion of adults aged 16-69 (not in full-time education) with educational qualifications, rising from 41% in 1975 to 69% in 1995 and 1996.

The increase between 1975 and 1996 was mainly accounted for by the increased proportions with:

- a degree (from 4% to 11%);
- a higher educational qualification below degree level (from 6% to 11%);
- GCE 'A' level standard (from 4% to 12%);
- GCSE grades A-C or equivalent (from 13% to 23%).

Table 7.1

Sex and age

Since the early 1970s, men have continued to be more likely than women to have some form of qualification, although the gap between the sexes has decreased.

- In 1975, 49% of men compared with 35% of women had obtained a qualification but by 1991, the gap had narrowed by a half to 7 percentage points (67% and 60% respectively) and has remained the same throughout the 1990s;

- In 1996, 73% of men compared with 66% of women had obtained a qualification.

The gap in the proportion of men and women with a qualification narrowed between 1975 and 1996 mainly because the proportion who reached GCSE, GCE 'A' level or degree level qualifications has increased at a faster rate among women than among men. **Table 7.1**

In 1996, young people were more likely than older people to have educational qualifications. Those aged 20-29 were about twice as likely as those aged 60-69 to have a qualification (87% compared with 43%). Other differences were:

- 14% of both men and women aged 20-29 had a degree level qualification compared with 5% (10% of men, 1% of women) of those aged 60-69;
- 21% of 20-29 year olds (23% of men, 19% of women) had reached GCE 'A' level standard compared with 4% (5% of men, 3% of women) of those aged 60-69;
- 31% of 20-29 year olds (29% of men, 33% of women) had GCSE grades A-C or equivalent compared with 12% (13% of men, 12% of women) of those aged 60-69.

Table 7.2, Figure 7A

Socio-economic group

There is a strong association between socio-economic group and the qualification level achieved. For the years 1995-1996 combined:

- 58% with a degree level qualification were in the professional, employer and managerial groups compared with 27% of those with GCE 'A' level or equivalent, 17% with GCSE grades A-C and 9% with no qualifications;

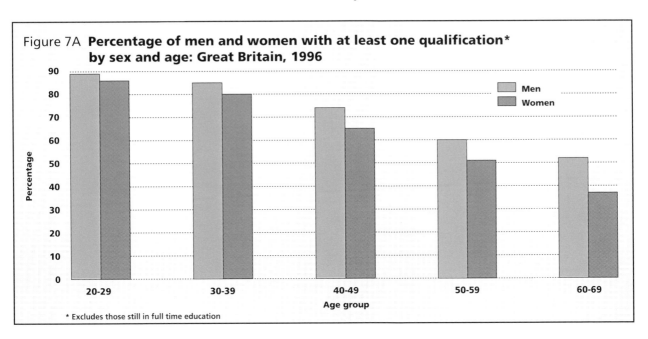

Figure 7A **Percentage of men and women with at least one qualification* by sex and age: Great Britain, 1996**

* Excludes those still in full time education

- 71% with no qualifications were in manual socio-economic groups compared with 41% with GCSE grades A-C, 37% with GCSE 'A' levels and 4% with a degree level qualification.

There was however, a difference in the socio-economic groups of men and women with the same level of qualification. In 1996:

- whereas men with a degree were more likely than women to be in the professional, employer and managerial groups (70% compared with 41%), women were more likely to be in the intermediate non-manual group (44% compared with 21%);
- among those with no qualifications, men were more likely than women to be in manual socio-economic groups (80% compared with 62%) and women were more likely to be in the junior non-manual group (25% compared with 4%).   **Table 7.4(b)**

Economic activity status
The less well qualified people were, the more likely they were to be unemployed. In 1996:

- men aged 16-64 with no qualifications were nearly twice as likely to be unemployed as those with a qualification (11% compared with 6%) and nearly four times as likely to be unemployed as those with higher education qualifications (11% compared with 3%);
- the group most likely (25%) to be unemployed were men in their twenties without qualifications.
                        Table 7.6(a), Figure 7B

The relationship between qualifications and unemployment was less striking among women who were more likely than men to be classified as economically inactive than unemployed. In 1996:

- among women in their twenties and thirties, those without qualifications were the most likely to be classified as economically inactive (58% of those aged 20-29, 47% of those aged 30-39).

Women with qualifications, particularly those with higher educational qualifications were the most likely to be working. For example:

- among women aged 20-29, 90% of those with higher educational qualifications were working compared with 68% of those with a qualification below GCE 'A' level and 35% with no qualification;
- 80% of women aged 30-39 with higher educational qualifications were working compared with 70% of those with a qualification below GCE 'A' level and 48% with no qualifications.   **Table 7.6 (b)**

Earnings
Adults aged 20-69 with higher qualifications had on average, higher earnings than the less well qualified. Compared with the average (median) earnings of all men and women in full-time employment:

- men and women with degrees or equivalent earned 53-54% more than the average;
- men and women with GCSE grades A-C earned less than average (9% and 5% respectively);
- men and women with no qualifications earned less than average (21% and 23% respectively).

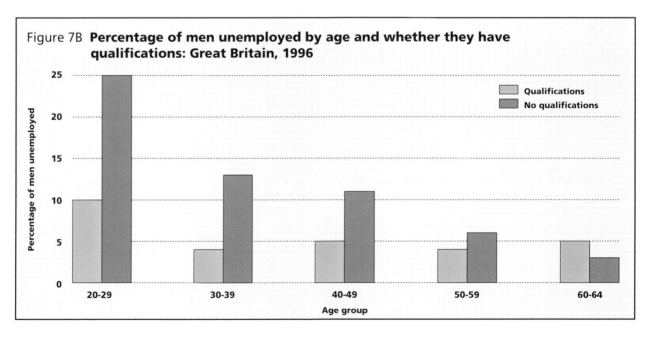

Figure 7B **Percentage of men unemployed by age and whether they have qualifications: Great Britain, 1996**

On average, men earned more than equally qualified women also in full-time employment. The differential in earnings was greatest among those with GCE 'A' levels. In this group, women earned on average 64% of men's earnings.   **Table 7.7**

Lone-parent families

Lone parents were less well qualified than other heads of families. In 1996:

- just over a third (35%) of lone parents had no qualifications compared with 20% of heads of other families. Some difference would be expected as most lone parents are women who are less likely than men to have some form of qualification;
- heads of other families were about three times as likely as lone parents to have a degree or equivalent qualification (16% compared with 5%) and twice as likely to have a higher qualification below degree standard (14% compared with 7%).   **Table 7.8**

Ethnic group

Overall, the educational attainment of ethnic minority groups was similar to the White population but there were differences between groups. In 1996:

- Indian people were more likely than Pakistani, Bangladeshi and Black people, and as likely as the White population, to have obtained a degree level qualification (10%);
- Black people were more likely than any other group to have a higher educational qualification below degree level (14%);
- Pakistani and Bangladeshi people were most likely (40%) to be without qualifications, compared with 31% of Indian, 30% of White and 26% of Black people.   **Table 7.9, Figure 7C**

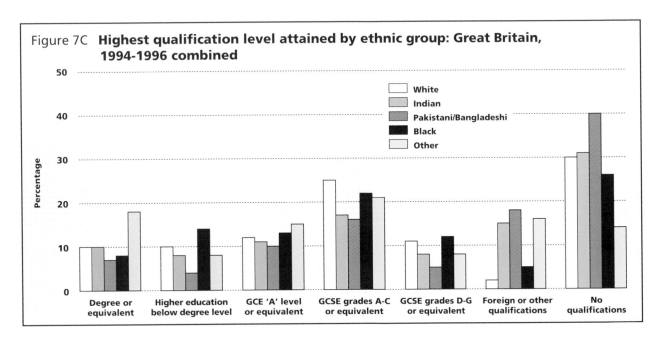

Figure 7C **Highest qualification level attained by ethnic group: Great Britain, 1994-1996 combined**

Table 7.1 **Highest qualification level attained by sex, 1975 to 1996**

Persons aged 16-69, not in full-time education   *Great Britain*

Highest qualification level attained*	1975	1979	1981	1985	1987	1989	1991	1993	1994	1995	1996
	%	%	%	%	%	%	%	%	%	%	%
Degree or equivalent											
Men	6	7	7	9	10	11	11	12	12	14	13
Women	2	3	2	4	5	5	6	7	7	8	8
Total	4	5	5	7	7	8	8	9	10	11	11
Higher education below degree level											
Men	6	6	7	9	10	11	11	11	11	12	12
Women	6	6	6	8	8	8	9	10	9	9	10
Total	6	6	6	8	9	10	10	10	10	11	11
GCE 'A' level or equivalent											
Men	6	8	8	10	11	11	12	15	14	14	14
Women	2	3	3	5	6	5	7	9	9	9	10
Total	4	5	6	7	8	8	9	12	11	11	12
GCSE grades A-C or equivalent											
Men	13	14	15	17	16	18	19	20	22	21	21
Women	12	15	17	19	20	22	24	24	27	25	24
Total	13	14	16	18	18	21	22	22	25	23	23
GCSE grades D-G/commercial qualifications/apprenticeship											
Men	13	12	14	12	13	11	11	10	10	9	10
Women	9	11	12	13	13	13	11	11	12	12	12
Total	11	12	13	13	13	12	11	11	11	11	11
Foreign or other qualifications											
Men	4	4	3	3	3	4	3	3	3	3	2
Women	3	3	3	3	2	3	3	3	2	2	2
Total	4	3	3	3	3	3	3	3	3	2	2
No qualifications											
Men	51	49	46	39	37	34	33	29	28	27	27
Women	65	60	56	47	46	43	40	37	35	34	34
Total	59	55	51	44	42	39	37	33	32	31	31
Base = 100%†											
Men	*9651*	*8767*	*9307*	*7392*	*7764*	*7420*	*7107*	*6580*	*6302*	*6335*	*5811*
Women	*10554*	*9619*	*10135*	*8096*	*8501*	*8170*	*7854*	*7436*	*7208*	*7266*	*6754*
Total	*20205*	*18386*	*19442*	*15488*	*16265*	*15590*	*14961*	*14016*	*13510*	*13601*	*12565*

* For details of qualification level see Appendix A.
† Excludes those who never went to school.

These data are also available from the Labour Force Survey.

Table 7.2 **Highest qualification level attained by sex and age**

Persons aged 16-69 not in full-time education   *Great Britain: 1996*

Highest qualification level attained*	Age						
	16-19	20-29	30-39	40-49	50-59	60-69	Total
	%	%	%	%	%	%	%
Degree or equivalent							
Men	0	14	16	18	10	10	13
Women	0	14	12	9	5	1	8
Total	0	14	14	13	7	5	11
Higher education below degree level							
Men	2	12	14	14	12	8	12
Women	1	7	11	12	10	8	10
Total	2	9	12	13	11	8	11
GCE 'A' level or equivalent							
Men	19	23	16	15	10	5	14
Women	18	19	11	8	6	3	10
Total	19	21	13	11	7	4	12
GCSE grades A-C or equivalent†							
Men	43	29	25	18	15	13	21
Women	45	33	31	23	17	12	24
Total	44	31	28	21	16	12	23
GCSE grades D-G or equivalent/commercial qualifications/apprenticeship							
Men	13	10	11	7	10	14	10
Women	15	11	13	10	12	11	12
Total	14	10	12	9	11	12	11
Foreign or other qualifications							
Men	0	2	2	3	3	3	2
Women	3	2	2	3	2	2	2
Total	1	2	2	3	3	2	2
No qualifications							
Men	23	11	15	26	40	48	27
Women	19	14	20	35	49	63	34
Total	21	13	18	31	45	57	31
*Bases = 100%***							
Men	*197*	*1022*	*1330*	*1243*	*1078*	*941*	*5811*
Women	*186*	*1234*	*1618*	*1457*	*1190*	*1069*	*6754*
Total	*383*	*2256*	*2948*	*2700*	*2268*	*2010*	*12565*

*   For details of qualification level see Appendix A.
†   Corresponds to GCE 'O' level or equivalent/CSE grade 1 in previous years.
** Excludes those who never went to school.

These data are also available from the Labour Force Survey.

Table 7.3 **Educational establishment last attended by sex, 1975 to 1996**

Persons aged 16-69, not in full-time education   *Great Britain*

Latest educational establishment attended*	1975	1979	1981	1983	1985	1987	1989	1991	1993	1994	1995	1996
	%	%	%	%	%	%	%	%	%	%	%	%
School												
Men	87	86	86	84	82	81	79	79	73	71	71	71
Women	87	83	82	81	79	78	77	76	70	69	69	69
Total	87	84	84	83	81	79	78	77	72	70	70	70
College of further education/other college												
Men	9	10	10	9	9	10	11	11	14	15	14	13
Women	12	15	16	15	17	17	17	18	21	20	20	19
Total	11	13	13	12	13	13	14	14	18	18	17	16
Polytechnic												
Men	..	..	..	2	3	3	4	4	4	5	4	5
Women	..	..	..	1	2	2	2	3	3	4	4	4
Total	..	..	..	2	2	3	3	3	4	4	4	5
University												
Men	3	5	5	5	6	6	6	7	9	10	11	11
Women	1	2	2	3	3	3	4	4	5	6	7	8
Total	2	3	3	4	4	5	5	5	7	8	9	9
Base = 100%†												
Men	*9976*	*9201*	*9789*	*7921*	*7933*	*8156*	*7873*	*7586*	*7088*	*7056*	*7153*	*6660*
Women	*10686*	*9771*	*10230*	*8471*	*8211*	*8540*	*8294*	*7987*	*7619*	*7491*	*7606*	*7082*
Total	*20662*	*18972*	*20019*	*16392*	*16144*	*16696*	*16167*	*15573*	*14707*	*14547*	*14759*	*13742*

* Colleges of further education include colleges of education in Scotland, Northern Ireland and ouside the U.K., as well as former colleges of education in England and Wales.
† Excludes those who never went to school.

These data are also available from the Labour Force Survey.

Table 7.4   (a) Highest qualification level attained by sex and socio-economic group

Economically active persons aged 25-69 not in full-time education   *Great Britain: 1995 and 1996 combined*

Highest qualification level attained*	Socio-economic group†							
	Professional	Employers and managers	Intermediate non-manual	Junior non-manual	Skilled manual and own account non-professional	Semi-skilled manual and personal service	Unskilled manual	Total
	%	%	%	%	%	%	%	%
Degree or equivalent								
Men	65	24	30	12	2	1	1	16
Women	68	22	24	4	4	1	0	11
Total	66	24	26	5	2	1	0	14
Higher education below degree level								
Men	17	19	20	13	10	7	2	14
Women	11	19	28	5	4	4	1	11
Total	16	19	25	6	9	5	1	12
GCE 'A' level or equivalent**								
Men	7	17	16	24	15	10	7	15
Women	7	13	9	12	10	8	4	10
Total	7	16	12	14	14	9	5	12
GCSE grades A-C or equivalent**								
Men	5	19	20	29	24	22	20	21
Women	4	23	21	39	28	23	14	27
Total	5	20	20	37	25	23	16	24
GCSE grades D-G or equivalent/ commercial qualifications/ apprenticeship								
Men	0	5	4	7	14	12	12	9
Women	3	8	7	18	14	12	10	12
Total	1	6	6	16	14	12	11	10
Foreign or other qualifications								
Men	3	3	3	2	2	3	4	3
Women	7	2	3	2	2	4	2	2
Total	4	2	3	2	2	3	2	2
No qualifications								
Men	2	12	7	14	33	45	55	23
Women	0	13	9	21	38	47	69	26
Total	2	12	8	20	34	46	64	25
Bases = 100%								
Men	*693*	*2089*	*994*	*570*	*2939*	*1117*	*255*	*8657*
Women	*210*	*999*	*1686*	*2465*	*647*	*1427*	*507*	*7941*
Total	*903*	*3088*	*2680*	*3035*	*3586*	*2544*	*762*	*16598*

*   For details of qualification level see Appendix A. Those who never went to school are excluded.
†   Excludes no answers, members of the Armed Forces, full time students and those who had never worked.
** Including FE qualifications.

These data are also available from the Labour Force Survey.

Table 7.4   (b) **Socio-economic group by sex and highest qualification level attained**

Economically active persons aged 25-69 not in full-time education   *Great Britain: 1995 and 1996 combined*

Highest qualification level attained*		Socio-economic group†							Base = 100%
		Professional	Employers and managers	Intermediate non-manual	Junior non-manual	Skilled manual and own account non-professional	Semi-skilled manual and personal service	Unskilled manual	
Degree or equivalent									
Men	%	33	37	21	5	4	1	0	1393
Women	%	16	25	44	11	3	2	0	911
Total	%	26	32	30	7	3	1	0	2304
Higher education below degree level									
Men	%	10	34	17	6	26	6	0	1171
Women	%	3	22	52	13	3	6	1	898
Total	%	7	29	32	9	16	6	0	2069
GCE 'A' level or equivalent**									
Men	%	4	29	13	11	34	9	1	1276
Women	%	2	17	20	36	8	14	3	785
Total	%	3	24	15	20	24	11	2	2061
GCSE grades A-C or equivalent**									
Men	%	2	22	11	9	40	14	3	1806
Women	%	0	11	17	45	8	16	3	2129
Total	%	1	16	14	28	23	15	3	3935
GCSE grades D-G or equivalent/ commercial qualifications/ apprenticeship									
Men	%	0	15	6	5	53	17	4	772
Women	%	1	8	12	46	10	19	5	962
Total	%	1	11	9	28	29	18	5	1734
Foreign or other qualifications									
Men	%	9	26	15	6	25	15	4	222
Women	%	7	10	24	21	7	27	4	187
Total	%	8	19	19	13	17	20	4	409
No qualifications									
Men	%	1	12	3	4	48	25	7	2017
Women	%	0	6	7	25	12	33	17	2069
Total	%	0	9	5	15	30	29	12	4086
Total									
Men	%	8	24	11	7	34	13	3	8657
Women	%	3	13	21	31	8	18	6	7941
Total	%	5	19	16	18	22	15	5	16598

*
†   See the footnotes to Table 7.4 (a).
**

These data are also available from the Labour Force Survey.

Table 7.5   **(a) Men's highest qualification level attained by their partner's highest qualification level attained**
(b) Women's highest qualification level attained by their partner's highest qualification level attained

Married persons aged 25-69, not in full-time education*   *Great Britain: 1996*

Women's highest qualification level attained†	Men's highest qualification level attained†							
	Degree or equivalent	Higher education below degree level	GCE 'A' level or equivalent	GCSE grades A-C or equivalent	GCSE grades D-G/ commercial qualifications/ apprenticeship	Foreign or other qualifications	No qualifications	Total
(a)	%	%	%	%	%	%	%	%
Degree or equivalent	35	7	7	5	2	13	1	9
Higher education below degree level	21	17	11	9	8	11	4	11
GCE 'A' level or equivalent	10	12	16	11	7	8	4	9
GCSE grades A-C or equivalent	17	32	34	36	22	15	15	25
GCSE grades D-G/commercial qualifications/apprenticeship	8	12	12	14	19	8	11	12
Foreign or other qualifications	2	2	1	2	1	25	2	3
No qualifications	6	17	19	24	42	21	63	32
*Base = 100%***	*543*	*491*	*488*	*754*	*411*	*92*	*1056*	*3835*
(b)								*Base = 100%***
Degree or equivalent	%	58	11	11	11	2	3	3	*318*
Higher education below degree level	%	29	21	13	17	7	2	10	*397*
GCE 'A' level or equivalent	%	17	18	23	24	7	2	10	*317*
GCSE grades A-C or equivalent	%	10	16	18	28	9	1	17	*893*
GCSE grades D-G/commercial qualifications/apprenticeship	%	10	13	13	22	16	1	25	*456*
Foreign or other qualifications	%	14	12	6	14	4	24	26	*96*
No qualifications	%	3	7	8	14	14	2	53	*1238*
Total	%	14	13	13	19	10	2	28	*3715*

* Includes cohabiting persons.
† For details of qualification level see Appendix A.
** Excludes those who never went to school.

These data are also available from the Labour Force Survey.

97

Table 7.6 **Economic activity status by age and highest qualification level attained**
              (a) Men

Men aged 16-64 not in full-time education   *Great Britain: 1996*

Age and economic activity status	Highest qualification level attained*					
	Higher education	GCE 'A' level or equivalent†	Other qualifications	With qualifications	No qualifications	Total
	%	%	%	%	%	%
16-19						
Working	**	[92]	77	81	[53]	74
Unemployed	**	[0]	21	15	[36]	20
Inactive	**	[8]	2	4	[11]	6
Base = 100%	*4*	*38*	*109*	*151*	*45*	*196*
	%	%	%	%	%	
20-29						
Working	93	88	83	87	61	84
Unemployed	6	9	12	10	25	11
Inactive	1	3	5	3	14	5
Base = 100%	*258*	*238*	*409*	*905*	*115*	*1020*
	%	%	%	%	%	%
30-39						
Working	96	92	88	92	69	88
Unemployed	3	4	6	4	13	6
Inactive	1	5	6	4	18	6
Base = 100%	*403*	*219*	*502*	*1124*	*205*	*1329*
	%	%	%	%	%	%
40-49						
Working	92	87	83	88	73	84
Unemployed	3	6	6	5	11	6
Inactive	5	7	11	8	16	10
Base = 100%	*401*	*181*	*342*	*924*	*318*	*1242*
	%	%	%	%	%	%
50-59						
Working	81	83	78	80	68	75
Unemployed	2	6	5	4	6	5
Inactive	16	10	17	16	26	20
Base = 100%	*241*	*108*	*298*	*647*	*431*	*1078*
	%	%	%	%	%	%
60-64						
Working	47	[41]	42	43	30	37
Unemployed	3	[3]	6	5	3	4
Inactive	50	[55]	53	52	67	59
Base = 100%	*86*	*29*	*159*	*274*	*211*	*485*
	%	%	%	%	%	%
16-64						
Working	89	87	80	84	62	79
Unemployed	3	6	8	6	11	7
Inactive	8	7	12	10	27	14
Base = 100%	*1393*	*813*	*1819*	*4025*	*1325*	*5350*

* 'Higher education' = qualifications above GCE 'A' level standard; 'other qualifications' = qualifications below GCE 'A' level standard.
  For details of qualification levels see Appendix A. Those who never went to school are excluded.
† Including FE qualifications.
** Base too small to enable reliable analysis to be made.

These data are also available from the Labour Force Survey.

Table 7.6 **Economic activity status by age and highest qualification level attained
(b) Women**

Women aged 16-59 not in full-time education   *Great Britain: 1996*

Age and economic activity status	Highest qualification level attained*					
	Higher education	GCE 'A' level or equivalent†	Other qualifications	With qualifications	No qualifications	Total
	%	%	%	%	%	%
16-19						
Working	**	[82]	68	71	[46]	66
Unemployed	**	[6]	16	14	[25]	15
Inactive	**	[12]	16	15	[29]	19
Base = 100%	*2*	*33*	*116*	*151*	*35*	*186*
	%	%	%	%	%	%
20-29						
Working	90	80	68	76	35	70
Unemployed	2	3	5	4	8	4
Inactive	7	17	27	20	58	25
Base = 100%	*256*	*240*	*568*	*1064*	*165*	*1229*
	%	%	%	%	%	%
30-39						
Working	80	72	70	73	48	68
Unemployed	3	3	4	4	5	4
Inactive	16	24	26	23	47	28
Base = 100%	*374*	*173*	*749*	*1296*	*321*	*1617*
	%	%	%	%	%	%
40-49						
Working	83	79	75	78	60	72
Unemployed	2	3	4	3	5	4
Inactive	16	18	21	19	35	25
Base = 100%	*306*	*117*	*522*	*945*	*510*	*1455*
	%	%	%	%	%	%
50-59						
Working	64	71	69	67	48	58
Unemployed	3	4	2	2	3	3
Inactive	33	25	30	30	48	39
Base = 100%	*175*	*55*	*375*	*605*	*585*	*1190*
	%	%	%	%	%	%
16-59						
Working	81	77	70	74	51	67
Unemployed	3	4	4	4	5	4
Inactive	17	20	25	22	45	29
Base = 100%	*1113*	*618*	*2330*	*4061*	*1616*	*5677*

* 'Higher education' = qualifications above GCE 'A' level standard; 'other qualifications' = qualifications below GCE 'A' level standard.
  For details of qualification levels see Appendix A. Those who never went to school are excluded.
† Including FE qualifications.
** Base too small to enable reliable analysis to be made.

These data are also available from the Labour Force Survey.

Table 7.7 Usual gross weekly earnings by highest qualification level attained and sex

Persons aged 20-69 in full-time employment*   *Great Britain: 1996*

		Highest qualification level attained†						
		Degree or equivalent	Higher education below degree level	GCE 'A' level or equivalent	GCSE grades A-C or equivalent	GCSE grades D-G or equivalent/ commercial qualifications/ apprenticeship	No qualifications	Total**
Earnings								
Median weekly earnings (£)								
Men	(£)	485	375	337	288	255	251	316
Women	(£)	353	309	216	217	208	177	229
Earnings of women relative								
to those of men	%	73	82	64	75	82	71	72
Lower quartile								
Men	(£)	335	277	246	214	200	191	223
Women	(£)	249	230	163	160	162	140	167
Upper quartile								
Men	(£)	656	493	433	385	350	324	441
Women	(£)	462	400	284	277	259	219	323

* Full-time employment = 31 hours or more per week (26 hours or more for teachers or lecturers) including paid overtime. (The exclusion of overtime would only marginally reduce the numbers in full-time employment.) Full-time students who worked in the reference week are excluded.

† For details of qualification levels see Appendix A. Those who never went to school are excluded.

** Including foreign and 'other'qualifications.

These data are also available from the Labour Force Survey.

Table 7.8 Highest qualification of family head by family type: lone-parent families compared with other families

Families with dependent children* (Family head aged 16-69)   *Great Britain: 1995 and 1996 combined*

Highest qualification level attained	Lone-parent families	Other families
	%	%
Degree or equivalent	5	16
Higher education below degree level	7	14
GCE 'A' level or equivalent	11	16
GCSE grades A-C or equivalent	28	22
GCSE grades D-G or equivalent/commercial qualifications/ apprenticeship	13	8
Foreign or other qualifications	1	3
No qualifications	35	20
Base = 100%	*1268*	*3985*

* Dependent children are persons aged under 16, or aged 16-18 and in full-time education, in the family unit, and living in the household.

These data are also available from the Labour Force Survey.

Table 7.9 Highest qualification level by ethnic group

Persons aged 16-69   *Great Britain: 1994-96 combined*

Highest qualification level attained*	Ethnic group						Total
	White	Indian	Pakistani/ Bangladeshi	Black**	Remaining groups	All ethnic minority groups	
	%	%	%	%	%	%	%
Degree or equivalent	10	10	7	8	18	11	10
Higher education below degree level	10	8	4	14	8	9	10
GCE 'A' level or equivalent	12	11	10	13	15	13	12
GCSE grades A-C or equivalent	25	17	16	22	21	19	24
GCSE grades D-G or equivalent/commercial/ apprenticeship	11	8	5	12	8	9	10
Foreign or other qualifications	2	15	18	5	16	13	3
No qualifications	30	31	40	26	14	27	30
Base = 100%†	39618	650	384	607	617	2258	41876

* For details of qualification level see Appendix A.

† Excludes those who never went to school.

** Black includes Black Caribbean, Black African and other Black groups.

These data are also available from the Labour Force Survey.

101

8 General health and use of health services

The GHS has collected information since 1972 on the self-reported health of the population living in private households and their use of the health service. Questions were addressed to all adults in the household and information concerning any children in the household was collected from the person responsible for them, usually the mother.

In 1996, a standard set of questions known as EuroQol (European Quality of Life) which have been asked in other European countries and on several other surveys in this country were included on the GHS. This series of questions asked adult respondents to make a judgement about their competence to carry out physical and mental functions of daily life. Because these questions were asked prior to the usual GHS questions about respondents' self assessment of their health, it is possible that they may have affected some respondent's answers to these subsequent questions.

Self-reported sickness

The GHS contains two measures of self-reported sickness:

* chronic sickness – defined as longstanding illness, disability or infirmity. Respondents who reported a longstanding illness were also asked whether this limited their activities in any way.
* acute illness – defined as the restriction of normal activities as a result of illness or injury during the two weeks prior to the interview.

The overall trend in the proportion who reported chronic and acute sickness has increased steadily since 1972 but

from the early 1980s the increase in the proportions of the population reporting chronic and acute illness have fluctuated. There was, however, an increase in the prevalence of both chronic and acute illness between 1995 and 1996 but this may be partly explained by the positioning of the EuroQol questions. In 1996:

* 35% reported a longstanding illness compared with 31% in 1995, 30% in 1985 and 21% in 1972;
* 22% had a longstanding illness which limited their activities;
* 16% had an acute illness which restricted activity compared with 14% in 1995, 12% in 1985 and 8% in 1972.

As these measures are based on people's subjective assessment of their health, changes over time may reflect not only changes in the actual prevalence of sickness but in the expectations people have about their health.

Table 8.1, Figure 8A

Age
The prevalence of chronic illness not surprisingly increased markedly with age. In 1996:

* the proportion who reported having a longstanding illness, disability or infirmity increased from only 13% of children aged 0-4 years to 66% of those aged 75 and over;
* the proportion with a longstanding illness which limited their activities increased from 4% of those aged 0-4 years to 52% of those aged 75 and over.

The relationship between acute illness and age was not as marked.

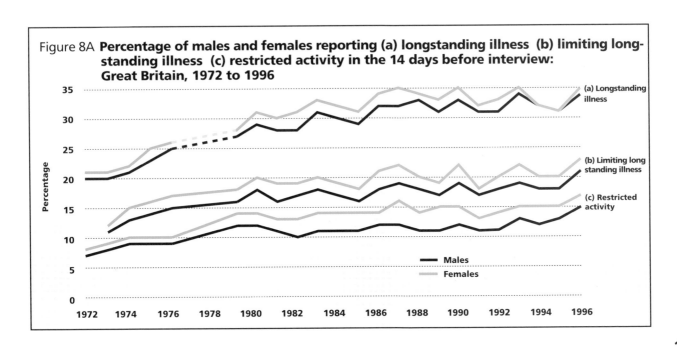

Figure 8A **Percentage of males and females reporting (a) longstanding illness (b) limiting longstanding illness (c) restricted activity in the 14 days before interview: Great Britain, 1972 to 1996**

- The proportion who reported an acute illness which restricted activity in the last two weeks was 10% for children under 16, 14% of those aged 16-44, 20% of those aged 45-74 and 24% of those aged 75 and over.

Table 8.1

Socio-economic group and economic activity status

The relationship between self-reported sickness and socio-economic group differed between chronic and acute illness.

The prevalence of chronic illness was related to the socio-economic group of the head of household and this relationship was particularly strong amongst adults. In 1996:

- among manual households, 24% of men reported a longstanding illness which limited their activities compared with 17% of men in non-manual households. The corresponding figures for women were 25% and 20%.   **Tables 8.2-8.3**

Although adults in manual households were only slightly more likely to report an acute illness than those in non-manual households, the number of days on which they had to cut down on any of the things they usually did because of illness or injury was much higher.

- Men in manual households had on average 35 days of restricted activity per year due to an illness or injury compared with 25 days for men in non-manual households. The corresponding figures for women were 39 and 31 days;
- the average rate of restricted activity was highest in unskilled manual households (51 days per year for men, 50 days per year for women).   **Table 8.4**

The prevalence of self-reported illness amongst adults was also related to their economic activity status and again there was a contrast between the pattern for chronic and acute illness.

- Amongst both men and women, the highest prevalence of chronic longstanding illness which limited activities was reported by those who were economically inactive (51% of men, 41% of women). This is not unexpected as this group includes the elderly, retired and those permanently unable to work because of disability;
- the unemployed reported a higher prevalence of longstanding illness which limited their activities than those who were working (18% compared with 13% of men, 19% compared with 14% of women);
- the economically inactive were the most likely to report

an acute illness (27% of men, 24% of women) and had the highest rates of restricted activity (on average 68 days per year for men and 61 days per year for women);
- the prevalence of acute illness which restricted activities was not significantly different between those who were working and the unemployed.

Tables 8.6-8.7

Longstanding conditions and complaints

Respondents who reported a longstanding illness were asked what was the matter with them. Their responses were recorded and coded into broad categories (details of the coding and an explanation of the limitations of the data are given in the 1989 report). Prevalence is expressed in terms of rates per 1000 persons.

As in previous years, the most common group of conditions causing longstanding illness were:

- disorders of the musculoskeletal system (198 per 1000);
- problems of heart and circulatory system (97 per 1000);
- respiratory problems (74 per 1000).

The prevalence of different conditions and the types of problems reported varied with both age and sex.

- In all age groups, musculoskeletal problems were the most common and amongst those aged 45 and over were more often reported by women than men. The greatest difference was amongst those aged 65 and over (the rates were 342 per 1000 women and 265 per 1000 men aged 65-74; 470 per 1000 women and 310 per 1000 men aged 75 and over);
- women of all ages were more likely to suffer from arthritis than men, but particularly if they were aged 65 or over (the rates were 223 per 1000 women and 148 per 1000 men aged 65-74; 313 per 1000 women, 188 per 1000 men aged 75 and over). Of those aged 65 and over, women were also more likely than men to report other bone and joint problems;
- the musculoskeletal problems reported by people under 45, particularly men, differed from those experienced by older people. Back problems and other bone and joint problems were more prevalent among the under 45s than arthritis;
- amongst those aged 45 and over, heart and circulatory problems were the next most commonly reported complaint, with prevalence increasing with age (the rates were 15 per 1000 of those aged under 45 compared with 252 per 1000 of those aged 75 and over);
- men between the ages of 45 and 74 were more likely to

report a heart or circulatory system complaint than women in the same age groups (the rates were 141 per 1000 men, 124 per 1000 women aged 45-64; 268 per 1000 men, 224 per 1000 women aged 65-74). Among the very elderly aged 75 and over, the reverse was the case;

- of the specific heart conditions reported, women of all ages were more likely than men to report suffering from hypertension (the rates were 36 per 1000 women, 25 per 1000 men).;

- asthma, which was the most frequently reported respiratory illness, was most common amongst those aged under 45 (54 per 1000 men, 55 per 1000 women). Bronchitis and emphysema were most often reported by those aged 65 and over, with the highest rate amongst men aged 75 and over (37 per 1000 men);

Tables 8.8-8.11

Health service utilisation

GP consultations

- During the 1980s, there was a gradual increase in the proportion of people, particularly women, who consulted a NHS GP in the 14 days prior to interview. It rose from 14% of women and 10% of men in 1981 to 17% of women and 12% of men in 1989. Since then, the proportion has fluctuated. In 1996:

- 16% of respondents (19% of women , 13% of men) had consulted a NHS GP in the previous 14 days;

- amongst adults under 65, a higher proportion of women than men had consulted a NHS GP in the last 14 days. The difference was most marked in the 16-44 age group (20% of women, 10% of men);

- in the 16-44 age group, women consulted their GP twice as often as men – on average seven compared with three consultations per year;

Tables 8.19-8.20, Figure 8B

- in 1996, 84% of GP consultations took place in the surgery, a proportion which has remained almost unchanged since the early 1990s;

- between 1971 and 1991, the proportion of GP consultations that took place at home halved from 22% in 1971 to 11% in 1991, whereas the proportion of consultations in the surgery increased from 73% to 81% and the proportion of telephone consultations increased from 4% to 8%;

- those aged 75 and over were the most likely to be visited at home by their GP. In 1996, 27% of consultations by this age group took place at home compared with 4%-11% of those in other age groups;

Tables 8.21-8.22

- women in manual households were more likely than those in non-manual households to have consulted their GP in the last 14 days (20% compared with 17%). Among men there was no significant difference;

- among both men and women, the economically inactive were the most likely to have consulted their GP in the last 14 days (22% and 23% respectively). There was no significant difference in consultation rates between those who were working and the unemployed;

- of those who consulted their GP, about seven out of ten obtained a prescription. **Tables 8.24-8.26**

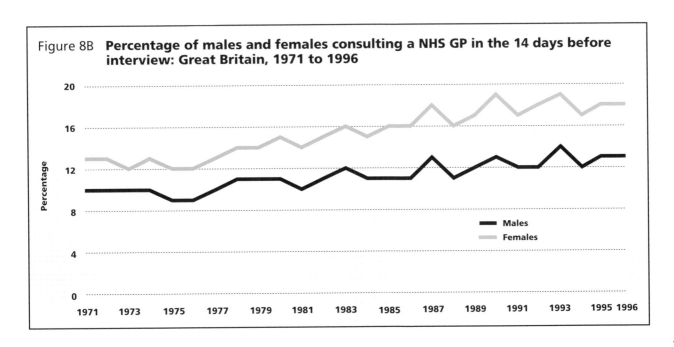

Figure 8B **Percentage of males and females consulting a NHS GP in the 14 days before interview: Great Britain, 1971 to 1996**

Hospital visits

Outpatient visits

The proportion of people who attended an outpatient or casualty department during the three months before interview increased from 10% in 1972 to 14% in 1989. Since then the only significant change has been among the elderly. In 1996:

- 15% of people of all ages attended an outpatient or casualty department in the previous three months;
- attendance rose from 11% of children aged 0-15 to 24% of those aged 75 and over;
- among children under 5, attendance at an outpatient or casualty department was higher among boys than girls (13% of boys, 9% of girls). **Table 8.28**

Day patients

- During the 12 months before interview, 5% of men and 6% of women had been in hospital for treatment as a day patient;
- those admitted to hospital as a day patient spent on average two separate days in hospital during the previous 12 months. **Tables 8.29-8.31**

Inpatients

- The proportion of people admitted to hospital as an inpatient overnight or longer during the twelve months before interview has changed little since the question was first asked in 1982. In 1996, 10% of women and 7% of men had been inpatients in the last year;
- women aged 16-44 were more than twice as likely as men to have been in hospital as an inpatient (12% of women, 5% of men). This is probably due to the inclusion of maternity stays;

- those admitted as an inpatient spent on average seven nights in hospital in the previous 12 months. Those aged 75 and over were in hospital for an average of 13 nights. **Tables 8.32-8.34, Figure 8C**

Health related quality of life

A standard set of questions known as EuroQol which ask respondents to make a judgement about their current state of health, have been asked in several European countries. They were developed to be used on self-completion questionnaires but were included on the GHS in a face-to-face interview.

Adults (aged 16 and over) living in private households were asked to make a judgement about – their mobility; ability to care for themselves; perform usual activities such as work, study, housework, family or leisure activities; and whether they experience pain, depression or anxiety.

On each of these dimensions, respondents rated themselves as having no problems, some problems or severe problems, (see the questionnaire, Appendix D, for detailed wording of questions).

- Most frequently mentioned were pain or discomfort. A third of adults reported these problems and 5% said that their pain or discomfort was severe;
- nearly a fifth (19%) of all adults said that mobility was a problem. Less than 1% said that the problem was so severe that they were confined to bed;
- anxiety or depression were also mentioned by 19% of all adults. Two per cent said they were extremely anxious or depressed. In all age groups, women were

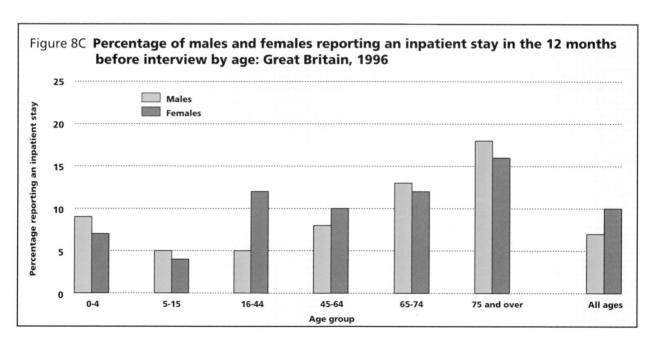

Figure 8C **Percentage of males and females reporting an inpatient stay in the 12 months before interview by age: Great Britain, 1996**

more likely than men to report these problems. Overall, 22% of women compared with 16% of men said they were anxious or depressed;

- 14% of all adults said they had problems performing their usual activities such as work, study, housework, family or leisure activities. Two per cent reported problems which were so severe that they were unable to perform these activities;

- 5% of all adults said they had problems caring for themselves such as washing or dressing. Less than 1% said that these problems were so severe that they were unable to wash or dress themselves.

Table 8.35-8.36

Age

On each of the five dimensions, the proportion reporting a problem increased with age. Between the ages of 16-44 and 75 and over, the proportion reporting problems increased for:

- pain or discomfort from 19% to 61%;
- mobility from 6% to 55%;
- anxiety or depression from 15% to 25%;
- performing usual activities from 6% to 34%
- caring for themselves from 2% to 18%.

On each of these dimensions, women aged 75 and over were more likely than men in the same age group to say they had a problem. Among those aged 75 and over, problems were mentioned relating to:

- pain and discomfort by 65% of women compared with 56% of men;
- mobility by 59% of women compared with 50% of men;
- anxiety or depression by 30% of women compared with 19% of men;
- performing usual activities by 40% of women compared with 27% of men;
- self care by 21% of women compared with 14% of men.

Tables 8.35-8.36

Degree of problems

On the basis of their responses to the questions about each of the five dimensions, respondents were classified into four groups according to the degree of their problems:

- Full health – no problems on any dimension;
- Mild problems – moderate problems on any one dimension, no problems on the remaining dimensions;
- Moderate problems – moderate problems on two dimensions but no problems on the remaining dimensions;

- Substantial problems – either moderate problems on at least three dimensions or severe problems on one dimension.

This classification showed that:

- 58% of all adults but a higher proportion of men than women (60% compared with 55%) had no problems on any dimension. Eighteen per cent of adults had mild problems, 9% had moderate problems and 15% had substantial problems;

- the proportion with problems increased with age. This was most marked amongst those with substantial problems. Seven per cent of those aged 16-44 had a substantial problem increasing to 38% of those aged 75 and over;

- among those aged 75 and over, women were more likely than men to have a substantial problem (44% compared with 30%). **Tables 8.37-8.38**

Visual Analogue Scale

In addition to rating aspects of their health in response to the standard EuroQol questions, respondents were also asked to rate their health using a Visual Analogue Scale (VAS) which is a diagram of a thermometer showing scores ranging from 0 'worst imaginable state of health' to 100 'best imaginable state of health'. Respondents were asked to indicate on the scale, how good their health was on the day of interview.

- The average (mean) score on the VAS was 77, ranging from 80 in the 16-44 age group down to 66 in the 75 and over age group;

- among those aged 75 and over, men had a higher score, that is a better self-assessed state of health, than women (mean score of 68 for men, 65 for women). There was no significant difference in the average scores between men and women in the other age groups. **Table 8.39**

The relationship between a respondent's score on the VAS and their classification based on response to questions about the five dimensions of health showed that:

- those who were classified as having no problems on any of the five dimensions of health had a higher VAS score (84) than those with mild problems (77), moderate problems (70) or substantial problems (53).

Table 8.40

The elderly: activities of daily living

Those aged 65 and over were asked questions about their ability to get out of doors and walk down the road, get up and down stairs and steps, get around the house on the level, get to the toilet and get in and out of bed. These questions have been asked several times since 1980.

Since 1980, there has been a change in the profile of the elderly population living in private households. For example, in 1996:

* one in five (21%) of people aged 65 and over were in the 80 and over age group compared with 16% in 1980;
* the proportion of elderly people living alone had increased from 34% in 1980 to 39% in 1996 and the proportion living just with their spouse increased from 45% to 48%. There was a decrease in the proportion living with others such as a son, daughter or siblings (from 21% in 1980 to 13% in 1996);
* elderly women were more likely than men to live alone (49% compared with 26% in 1996).   **Tables 8.42-8.43**

Mobility

In 1996, among those aged 65 and over:

* 13% said they were unable to manage going out and walking down the road on their own;
* 10% were unable to get up and down stairs unaided;
* only a small proportion (1%) said they could not get around the house even on the level, without help. A similar proportion could not get to the toilet on their own and 2% were unable to get in and out of bed without help.   **Table 8.44**

Problems with getting about increased with age.

* 7% of those aged 65-69 reported that they were unable to manage getting out and walking down the road on their own, and this increased to 37% of those aged 85 and over;
* 20% of those aged 85 and over could not manage to get out of doors at all even with help. This applied to only 3% of those aged 65-69;
* 5% of those aged 65-69 were unable to get up and down stairs and steps unaided, compared with 30% of those aged 85 and over. Fifteen per cent of people aged 85 and over could not manage steps and stairs at all even with help.

Elderly women were more likely to report problems getting about than elderly men, particularly in the older age groups. This is consistent with the findings noted earlier in the chapter, that women were more likely than men to have a musculoskeletal problem. For example:

* 48% of women compared with 16% of men aged 85 and over said they could not go out and walk down the road on their own;
* 40% of women compared with 11% of men aged 85 and over said they could not manage stairs on their own.   **Figure 8D, Tables 8.44-8.45**

The effect of lack of mobility on people's lives varies according to their living arrangements. In 1996:

* 14% of elderly people living alone were unable to go out for a walk on their own and 12% could not manage steps or stairs. Only 1% or less of those living alone were unable to get about the house, get to the toilet or get in and out of bed;

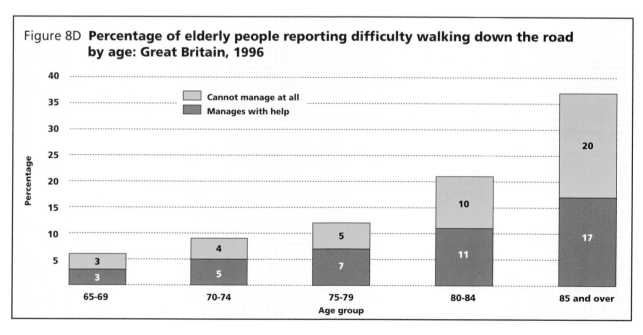

Figure 8D **Percentage of elderly people reporting difficulty walking down the road by age: Great Britain, 1996**

women living in a private household but with people other than their spouse (i.e. in the miscellaneous category) were more likely than those living in other types of household to be unable to get out on their own (23% compared with 17% of women who lived alone and 14% who lived with their spouse). This suggests that they may be living with others because of their need for assistance;

- of all elderly people, those living with their spouse were the most mobile, although 10% of this group were unable to get out on their own and 8% could not manage steps and stairs. **Table 8.46**

Despite the ageing of the general population there has been little change in the prevalence of mobility problems among those aged 65 and over living in private households. This is mainly due to the improved mobility of those aged 80 and over living in private households in 1996 compared with 1980. For example, in 1996:

- 20% of those aged 80-84 were unable to get out of doors compared with 26% in 1980. For those aged 85 and over, the figures were 37% compared with 48%;
- 4% of those aged 85 and over could not get around the house compared with 10% in 1980. **Table 8.48**

Self-care

Respondents were asked whether they could manage four aspects of looking after themselves: bathing, showering or washing all over, dressing and undressing, washing face and hands and feeding themselves. In 1996:

- 9% of all elderly people said they could not bath, shower or wash all over without help;
- 4% were unable to dress and undress themselves unaided;
- very few (1% or less) were unable to wash their face and hands or feed themselves;
- the older people were, the less likely they were to be

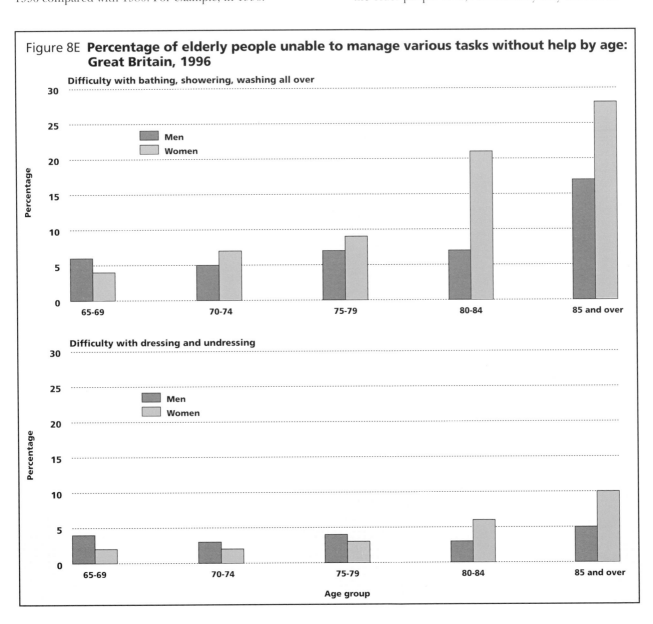

Figure 8E **Percentage of elderly people unable to manage various tasks without help by age: Great Britain, 1996**

able to manage. For example: 24% of those aged 85 and over and 15% of those aged 80-84 were unable to wash all over compared with only 5% of those aged 65-69;

- among those over 80, women were more likely than men to say they needed help with bathing (21% of women compared with 7% of men aged 80-84; 28% of women compared with 17% of men aged 85 and over;

- those living with people other than their spouse (i.e. in the miscellaneous category) were less likely than those in other types of household to be able to cope with self-care. Fourteen per cent were unable to manage at least one of the four aspects of self-care compared with 10% of those living alone and 8% living with their spouse;

- 10% of all elderly people living alone could not manage to bath, shower or wash all over on their own and two per cent were unable to dress and undress without help. **Figure 8E, Tables 8.49-8.50**

Table 8.1 **Trends in self-reported sickness by sex and age, 1972 to 1996: percentage of persons who reported**
(a) longstanding illness
(b) limiting longstanding illness
(c) restricted activity in the 14 days before interview

All persons   *Great Britain*

	1972	1975	1979	1981	1983	1985	1989	1991	1993	1994	1995	1996	*Base (1996)* = 100%*
						(a) Longstanding illness							
Percentage who reported:													
Males													
0- 4	5	8	8	12	11	11	14	13	15	15	14	14	*771*
5-15†	9	11	14	17	17	18	20	17	21	21	20	19	*1736*
16-44†	14	17	21	22	23	21	24	23	26	25	23	27	*4124*
45-64	29	35	39	40	44	42	42	42	45	43	43	46	*2480*
65-74	48	50	50	51	58	55	58	61	62	56	55	61	*884*
75 and over	54	63	56	60	67	58	61	63	64	62	56	64	*626*
Total	20	23	27	28	31	29	31	31	34	32	31	34	*10621*
Females													
0- 4	3	6	6	7	9	9	10	10	12	11	11	13	*786*
5-15†	6	9	10	13	13	13	16	15	16	18	17	16	*1685*
16-44†	13	16	20	21	23	22	24	23	26	24	22	27	*4406*
45-64	31	33	38	41	45	43	43	41	45	41	39	47	*2603*
65-74	48	54	52	58	63	56	57	55	59	57	54	58	*1052*
75 and over	65	61	64	70	70	65	70	65	69	64	66	68	*855*
Total	21	25	28	30	33	31	33	32	35	32	31	35	*11387*
All persons													
0- 4	4	7	7	10	10	10	12	12	13	13	13	13	*1557*
5-15†	8	10	12	15	15	16	18	16	19	20	19	18	*3421*
16-44†	13	16	20	21	23	22	24	23	26	24	23	27	*8530*
45-64	30	34	38	41	44	43	43	41	45	42	41	47	*5083*
65-74	48	52	51	55	61	56	58	58	60	56	55	59	*1936*
75 and over	62	62	61	67	69	63	66	65	67	63	63	66	*1481*
Total	21	24	27	29	32	30	32	31	34	32	31	35	*22008*
						(b) Limiting longstanding illness							
Percentage who reported:													
Males													
0- 4	..	3	2	3	3	4	6	4	5	5	5	4	*771*
5-15†	..	6	7	8	8	8	8	7	9	10	8	8	*1736*
16-44†	..	9	10	10	11	10	10	10	13	13	12	14	*4123*
45-64	..	24	26	26	27	27	26	25	28	27	28	31	*2478*
65-74	..	36	37	35	40	38	37	40	41	38	37	42	*884*
75 and over	..	46	45	44	53	43	44	46	45	45	41	50	*626*
Total	..	14	16	16	18	16	17	17	19	18	18	21	*10618*
Females													
0- 4	..	2	2	3	2	3	2	3	3	4	3	4	*786*
5-15†	..	4	5	6	6	6	7	5	8	8	8	8	*1685*
16-44†	..	9	10	11	12	11	12	11	15	13	13	16	*4405*
45-64	..	22	24	26	28	26	25	25	29	27	26	32	*2601*
65-74	..	39	38	41	45	38	36	34	39	39	37	40	*1052*
75 and over	..	49	54	56	54	51	53	51	52	49	52	53	*854*
Total	..	16	18	19	20	18	19	18	22	20	20	23	*11383*
All persons													
0- 4	..	2	2	3	3	3	4	4	4	4	4	4	*1557*
5-15†	..	5	6	7	7	7	7	6	9	9	8	8	*3421*
16-44†	..	9	10	11	12	10	11	10	14	13	12	15	*8528*
45-64	..	23	25	26	27	26	25	25	29	27	27	32	*5079*
65-74	..	38	37	38	43	38	37	37	40	39	37	41	*1936*
75 and over	..	48	51	52	54	48	50	49	50	48	48	52	*1480*
Total	..	15	17	17	19	17	18	18	20	19	19	22	*22001*

* Bases for earlier years are of a similar size and can be found in GHS reports for each year.
† These age-groups were 5-14 and 15-44 in 1972 to 1978.

111

Table 8.1 - *continued*

All persons   *Great Britain*

	1972	1975	1979	1981	1983	1985	1989	1991	1993	1994	1995	1996	*Base (1996)* = 100%*
						(c) Restricted activity							
Percentage who reported:													
Males													
0- 4	5	10	12	13	15	13	12	11	13	11	11	12	*771*
5-15†	6	9	11	12	12	11	12	11	11	10	10	10	*1733*
16-44†	7	7	10	8	8	9	9	9	11	10	10	13	*4127*
45-64	9	10	14	12	11	11	12	12	15	15	15	18	*2476*
65-74	10	8	12	11	12	13	13	14	16	17	17	19	*884*
75 and over	10	12	17	15	17	17	19	18	17	18	20	23	*626*
Total	7	9	12	11	11	11	11	11	13	12	13	15	*10617*
Females													
0- 4	6	8	10	12	14	13	12	10	10	12	11	9	*786*
5-15†	5	7	11	11	11	12	13	9	11	12	10	9	*1684*
16-44†	8	10	13	11	13	13	13	12	13	13	13	15	*4404*
45-64	9	10	14	13	15	14	15	13	17	17	17	22	*2603*
65-74	10	12	16	17	19	18	19	16	19	21	20	21	*1054*
75 and over	14	13	22	21	20	23	26	21	23	25	26	25	*853*
Total	8	10	14	13	14	14	15	13	15	15	15	17	*11384*
All persons													
0- 4	6	9	11	13	15	13	12	11	11	11	11	10	*1557*
5-15†	6	8	11	12	12	11	12	10	11	11	10	10	*3417*
16-44†	8	9	11	10	11	11	11	10	12	12	12	14	*8531*
45-64	9	10	14	12	13	12	14	13	16	16	16	20	*5079*
65-74	10	11	14	14	16	16	17	15	18	20	19	20	*1938*
75 and over	13	13	20	19	19	21	23	20	21	22	24	24	*1479*
Total	8	9	13	12	13	12	13	12	14	14	14	16	*22001*

* Bases for earlier years are of a similar size and can be found in GHS Reports for each year.
† These age-groups were 5-14 and 15-44 in 1972 to 1978.

Table 8.2 Chronic sickness: prevalence of reported longstanding illness by sex, age and socio-economic group of head of household

All persons   *Great Britain: 1996*

Socio-economic group of head of household*	Males					Females				
	Age					Age				
	0-15	16-44	45-64	65 and over	Total	0-15	16-44	45-64	65 and over	Total
	Percentage who reported longstanding illness									
Professional	19	24	34	51	29	15	23	40	[78]	30
Employers and managers	15	22	35	62	30	16	23	39	60	30
Intermediate non-manual	15	29	46	62	33	8	28	48	60	34
Junior non-manual	22	24	46	69	32	17	32	49	61	40
(group)	17	24	38	61	31	15	26	43	61	33
Skilled manual and own account non-professional	15	27	52	62	37	15	26	49	63	35
Semi-skilled manual and personal service	22	31	49	63	37	19	30	51	66	40
Unskilled manual	22	31	63	72	42	13	36	61	60	45
(group)	18	29	52	63	38	16	28	51	62	37
All persons	17	27	46	62	34	15	27	47	62	35
Bases = 100%										
Professional	152	255	157	83	647	137	256	151	49	593
Employers and managers	530	934	595	341	2400	567	917	582	290	2326
Intermediate non-manual	249	434	224	118	1025	228	495	261	201	1185
Junior non-manual	238	310	129	89	766	236	455	252	343	1286
Skilled manual and own account non-professional	696	1273	932	549	3450	727	1210	843	425	3205
Semi-skilled manual and personal service	403	557	323	230	1513	368	652	374	357	1751
Unskilled manual	121	172	92	81	466	100	157	133	167	557
All persons	2507	4124	2480	1510	10621	2471	4406	2603	1907	11387

* Members of the Armed Forces, persons in inadequately described occupations and all persons who have never worked are not shown as separate categories, but are included in the figure for all persons (see Appendix A for details).

Table 8.3 **Chronic sickness: prevalence of reported limiting longstanding illness by sex, age and socio-economic group of head of household**

All persons   *Great Britain: 1996*

Socio-economic group of head of household*	Males					Females				
	Age					Age				
	0-15	16-44	45-64	65 and over	Total	0-15	16-44	45-64	65 and over	Total
	Percentage who reported limiting longstanding illness									
Professional	8	11	17	35	15	9	12	25	[45]	17
Employers and managers	6	10	21	43	16	6	12	24	43	17
Intermediate non-manual	7	16	27	42	19	4	16	29	39	20
Junior non-manual	8	13	33	51	19	6	20	35	45	27
(group)	7	12	23	43	17	6	15	28	43	20
Skilled manual and own account non-professional	5	15	36	47	24	7	15	34	48	23
Semi-skilled manual and personal service	7	17	35	47	23	8	18	37	48	26
Unskilled manual	9	20	48	53	29	7	24	45	50	34
(group)	6	16	37	48	24	8	17	36	48	25
All persons	7	14	31	45	21	7	16	32	46	23
Bases = 100%										
Professional	152	255	157	83	649	137	256	151	49	593
Employers and managers	530	934	595	341	2400	567	917	552	290	2326
Intermediate non-manual	249	433	224	118	1024	228	495	261	201	1185
Junior non-manual	238	310	129	89	766	236	455	251	343	1285
Skilled manual and own account non-professional	696	1273	931	549	3449	727	1210	842	425	3204
Semi-skilled manual and personal service	403	557	323	230	1513	368	652	374	356	1750
Unskilled manual	121	172	91	81	465	100	157	133	167	557
All persons	2507	4123	2478	1510	10618	2471	4405	2601	1906	11383

* See the footnote to Table 8.2.

Table 8.4 Acute sickness
(a) Prevalence of reported restricted activity in the 14 days before interview, by sex, age, and socio-economic group of head of household
(b) Average number of restricted activity days per person per year, by sex, age, and socio-economic group of head of household

All persons   *Great Britain: 1996*

Socio-economic group of head of household*	Males					Females				
	Age					Age				
	0-15	16-44	45-64	65 and over	Total	0-15	16-44	45-64	65 and over	Total

(a) Percentage who reported restricted activity in the 14 days before interview

Socio-economic group	M 0-15	M 16-44	M 45-64	M 65+	M Total	F 0-15	F 16-44	F 45-64	F 65+	F Total
Professional	12	11	14	19	13	8	13	18	[24]	14
Employers and managers	10	12	14	19	13	10	14	17	18	14
Intermediate non-manual	12	16	15	14	15	8	16	21	18	16
Junior non-manual	13	15	19	28	17	10	20	21	22	19
(non-manual subtotal)	*11*	*13*	*15*	*20*	*14*	*9*	*16*	*19*	*20*	*16*
Skilled manual and own account non-professional	9	13	21	22	16	9	13	23	25	16
Semi-skilled manual and personal service	13	12	19	23	15	10	16	25	25	18
Unskilled manual	12	17	37	20	20	11	15	29	30	22
(manual subtotal)	*10*	*13*	*22*	*22*	*16*	*9*	*14*	*24*	*26*	*18*
All persons	11	13	18	21	15	9	15	22	23	17

(b) Average number of restricted activity days per person per year

Socio-economic group	M 0-15	M 16-44	M 45-64	M 65+	M Total	F 0-15	F 16-44	F 45-64	F 65+	F Total
Professional	14	16	22	47	21	8	21	32	73	25
Employers and managers	14	19	30	50	25	9	25	37	48	27
Intermediate non-manual	11	20	29	37	22	9	28	43	46	31
Junior non-manual	17	20	48	82	31	16	39	50	57	42
(non-manual subtotal)	*14*	*19*	*31*	*52*	*25*	*10*	*28*	*40*	*53*	*31*
Skilled manual and own account non-professional	12	24	51	55	34	13	27	53	72	36
Semi-skilled manual and personal service	15	24	50	60	33	15	32	61	67	42
Unskilled manual	22	41	105	56	51	17	33	75	67	50
(manual subtotal)	*14*	*25*	*54*	*56*	*35*	*14*	*29*	*57*	*69*	*39*
All persons	14	22	44	54	30	12	29	49	61	35

Bases = 100%	M 0-15	M 16-44	M 45-64	M 65+	M Total	F 0-15	F 16-44	F 45-64	F 65+	F Total
Professional	152	255	155	83	645	137	256	151	49	593
Employers and managers	530	936	594	341	2401	567	917	552	290	2326
Intermediate non-manual	248	433	223	118	1022	228	495	261	201	1185
Junior non-manual	238	310	129	89	766	235	455	252	344	1286
Skilled manual and own account non-professional	696	1274	932	549	3451	727	1210	844	425	3206
Semi-skilled manual and personal service	401	558	323	230	1512	368	652	374	356	1750
Unskilled manual	121	172	92	81	466	100	156	132	167	555
All persons	2504	4127	2476	1510	10617	2470	4404	2603	1907	11384

* See the footnote to Table 8.2.

Table 8.5 **Chronic sickness: prevalence of reported longstanding illness by sex, age, and economic activity status**

Persons aged 16 and over   *Great Britain: 1996*

Economic activity status	Men				Women			
	Age				Age			
	16-44	45-64	65 and over	Total	16-44	45-64	65 and over	Total
	Percentage who reported longstanding illness							
Working	24	35	44	28	23	35	33	27
Unemployed	29	42	0	33	28	42	0	31
Economically inactive	46	80	64	65	35	63	63	55
All aged 16 and over	27	46	62	39	27	47	62	41
Bases = 100%								
Working	*3360*	*1736*	*98*	*5194*	*2954*	*1423*	*64*	*4441*
Unemployed	*341*	*131*	*0*	*472*	*212*	*60*	*0*	*272*
Economically inactive	*419*	*613*	*1411*	*2443*	*1233*	*1120*	*1843*	*4196*
All aged 16 and over	*4120*	*2480*	*1509*	*8109*	*4399*	*2603*	*1907*	*8909*

Table 8.6 **Chronic sickness: prevalence of reported limiting longstanding illness by sex, age, and economic activity status**

Persons aged 16 and over   *Great Britain: 1996*

Economic activity status	Men				Women			
	Age				Age			
	16-44	45-64	65 and over	Total	16-44	45-64	65 and over	Total
	Percentage who reported limiting longstanding illness							
Working	11	17	21	13	12	19	12	14
Unemployed	16	24	0	18	17	28	0	19
Economically inactive	37	71	47	51	25	49	47	41
All aged 16 and over	14	31	45	25	16	32	46	27
Bases = 100%								
Working	*3360*	*1734*	*98*	*5192*	*2954*	*1421*	*64*	*4439*
Unemployed	*340*	*131*	*0*	*471*	*212*	*60*	*0*	*272*
Economically inactive	*419*	*613*	*1411*	*2443*	*1232*	*1120*	*1842*	*4194*
All aged 16 and over	*4119*	*2478*	*1509*	*8106*	*4398*	*2601*	*1906*	*8905*

Table 8.7 **Acute sickness**
(a) Prevalence of reported restricted activity in the 14 days before interview, by sex, age and economic activity status
(b) Average number of restricted activity days per person per year, by sex, age, and economic activity status

Persons aged 16 and over   *Great Britain: 1996*

Economic activity status	Men				Women			
	Age				Age			
	16-44	45-64	65 and over	Total	16-44	45-64	65 and over	Total
(a) Percentage who reported restricted activity in the 14 days before interview								
Working	12	12	13	12	13	15	8	13
Unemployed	12	15	0	13	17	18	0	17
Economically inactive	26	39	21	27	20	30	23	24
All aged 16 and over	13	18	21	16	15	22	23	19
(b) Average number of restricted activity days per person per year								
Working	18	24	26	20	22	29	15	24
Unemployed	21	27	0	22	26	38	0	29
Economically inactive	60	103	56	68	44	77	62	61
All aged 16 and over	22	44	54	35	29	50	60	41
Bases = 100%								
Working	*3362*	*1732*	*98*	*5192*	*2955*	*1423*	*65*	*4443*
Unemployed	*341*	*131*	*0*	*472*	*212*	*60*	*0*	*272*
Economically inactive	*420*	*613*	*1411*	*2444*	*1230*	*1120*	*1842*	*4192*
All aged 16 and over	*4123*	*2476*	*1509*	*8108*	*4397*	*2603*	*1907*	*8907*

Table 8.8   **Chronic sickness: rate per 1000 reporting longstanding condition groups, by sex**

Persons aged 16 and over   *Great Britain: 1996*

Condition group	Men	Women	Total
XIII Musculoskeletal system	184	211	198
VII Heart and circulatory system	99	95	97
VIII Respiratory system	76	72	74
III Endocrine and metabolic	34	41	38
IX Digestive system	34	40	37
VI Nervous system	30	35	33
V Mental disorders	22	26	24
VI Eye complaints	19	16	17
VI Ear complaints	19	15	17
X Genito-urinary system	13	14	13
II Neoplasms and benign growths	9	12	11
XII Skin complaints	11	11	11
IV Blood and related organs	2	5	4
Other complaints*	3	5	4
I Infectious diseases	2	2	2
Average number of conditions reported by those with a longstanding illness	1.4	1.5	1.5
Bases = 100% (all persons 16 and over)	*8122*	*8922*	*17044*

* Including general complaints such as insomnia, fainting, generally run down, old age and general infirmity and non-specific conditions such as war wounds or road accident injuries where no further details were given.

Table 8.9 Chronic sickness: rate per 1000 reporting longstanding condition groups, by age

Persons aged 16 and over   *Great Britain: 1996*

Condition group	16-44	45-64	65-74	75 and over
XIII Musculoskeletal system	105	254	307	402
VII Heart and circulatory system	15	132	244	252
VIII Respiratory system	72	63	95	90
III Endocrine and metabolic	17	52	73	60
IX Digestive system	18	46	68	79
VI Nervous system	30	38	35	31
V Mental disorders	25	27	19	18
VI Eye complaints	7	14	25	78
VI Ear complaints	8	17	33	49
X Genito-urinary system	8	14	24	30
II Neoplasms and benign growths	4	13	21	26
XII Skin complaints	12	8	10	18
IV Blood and related organs	2	4	6	8
Other complaints*	3	5	3	9
I Infectious diseases	2	2	2	1
Average number of conditions reported by those with a longstanding illness	1.2	1.5	1.6	1.7
Bases = 100% (all persons 16 and over)	*8537*	*5088*	*1938*	*1481*

* Including general complaints such as insomnia, fainting, generally run down, old age and general infirmity and non-specific conditions such as war wounds or road accident injuries where no further details were given.

Table 8.10 Chronic sickness: rate per 1000 reporting selected longstanding condition groups, by age and sex

Persons aged 16 and over   *Great Britain: 1996*

Condition group			16-44	45-64	65-74	75 and over	All ages
XIII	Musculoskeletal system	Men	110	246	265	310	184
		Women	100	262	342	470	211
VII	Heart and circulatory system	Men	14	141	268	249	99
		Women	15	124	224	254	95
VIII	Respiratory system	Men	73	62	106	107	76
		Women	71	64	86	78	72
III	Endocrine and metabolic	Men	14	48	72	64	34
		Women	20	56	74	57	41
IX	Digestive system	Men	14	46	62	81	34
		Women	22	46	72	77	40
VI	Nervous system	Men	25	32	37	40	30
		Women	34	43	32	25	35
Bases = 100%		*Men*	*4129*	*2483*	*884*	*626*	*8122*
		Women	*4408*	*2605*	*1054*	*855*	*8922*

Table 8.11   **Chronic sickness: rate per 1000 reporting selected longstanding conditions, by age and sex**

Persons aged 16 and over   *Great Britain: 1996*

Condition	Men					Women				
	16-44	45-64	65-74	75 and over	All ages	16-44	45-64	65-74	75 and over	All ages
Musculoskeletal (XIII)										
Arthritis and rheumatism	16	97	148	188	68	22	134	223	313	106
Back problems	50	89	60	30	62	49	83	51	47	59
Other bone and joint problems	44	60	57	91	54	29	45	67	110	46
Heart and circulatory (VII)										
Hypertension	4	43	63	37	25	6	61	76	61	36
Heart attack	1	30	66	75	23	1	28	65	83	24
Stroke	1	9	27	43	10	0	5	17	22	6
Other heart complaints	4	41	80	64	28	4	21	45	58	19
Other blood vessel/embolic disorders	1	12	28	26	9	4	7	16	26	8
Respiratory (VIII)										
Asthma	54	33	51	42	46	55	41	53	39	49
Bronchitis and emphysema	2	11	24	37	10	2	7	13	15	6
Hay fever	12	2	1	0	7	7	2	1	2	4
Other respiratory complaints	6	16	31	29	13	7	13	19	22	12
Bases = 100% (all persons 16 and over)	*4129*	*2483*	*884*	*626*	*8122*	*4408*	*2605*	*1054*	*855*	*8922*

Table 8.12   **Chronic sickness: rate per 1000 reporting selected longstanding condition groups, by socio-economic group of head of household**

Persons aged 16 and over   *Great Britain: 1996*

Condition group	Professional	Employers and managers	Inter-mediate and junior non-manual	Skilled manual and own account non-pro-professional	Semi-skilled manual and personal service	Unskilled manual	Total*
XIII Musculoskeletal system	130	160	205	215	222	264	198
VII Heart and circulatory system	62	75	93	107	119	148	97
VIII Respiratory system	69	66	71	72	85	107	74
III Endocrine and metabolic	26	30	37	40	46	56	38
IX Digestive system	29	26	37	41	44	64	37
VI Nervous system	28	32	32	34	32	34	33
Average number of condition groups reported by those with a longstanding illness	1.32	1.37	1.42	1.48	1.52	1.64	1.45
Bases = 100% (all persons aged 16 and over)	*951*	*3631*	*3315*	*5236*	*2497*	*802*	*17044*

* Persons whose head of household was in the Armed Forces or a full-time student are not shown as separate categories but are included in the totals.

Table 8.13 **Chronic sickness: rate per 1000 reporting selected longstanding condition groups, by age and sex and whether non-manual or manual socio-economic group of head of household**

Persons aged 16 and over   *Great Britain: 1996*

Condition group		Men				Women				All aged 16 and over			
		16-44	45-64	65 and over	Total	16-44	45-64	65 and over	Total	16-44	45-64	65 and over	Total
XIII Musculoskeletal system	Non-manual	93	172	279	149	95	235	318	199	94	205	349	175
	Manual	130	301	285	216	104	285	406	227	117	293	349	222
VII Heart and circulatory system	Non-manual	9	114	233	79	17	91	231	83	13	102	232	81
	Manual	19	165	283	120	15	152	246	109	17	159	264	114
VIII Respiratory system	Non-manual	75	52	82	69	67	59	79	67	71	56	81	68
	Manual	72	73	127	84	77	66	86	75	75	69	106	79
III Endocrine and metabolic	Non-manual	13	42	67	31	18	46	57	34	16	44	61	33
	Manual	14	54	72	39	23	67	77	48	19	60	75	44
IX Digestive system	Non-manual	9	37	59	26	22	33	69	35	16	35	65	31
	Manual	18	54	78	42	21	57	82	46	20	56	80	44
VI Nervous system	Non-manual	18	27	43	25	34	44	38	38	26	36	40	32
	Manual	30	35	36	38	33	42	22	34	32	39	29	33
Base = 100%	*Non-manual*	*1936*	*1106*	*631*	*3673*	*2123*	*1219*	*884*	*4224*	*4059*	*2323*	*1515*	*7897*
	Manual	*2004*	*1349*	*860*	*4213*	*2021*	*1351*	*950*	*4322*	*4025*	*2700*	*1810*	*8535*

Table 8.14 **Acute sickness: average number of restricted activity days per person per year, by sex and age**

All persons   *Great Britain: 1996*

	Number of days			Bases = 100%		
	Males	Females	Total	*Males*	*Females*	*Total*
Age						
0- 4	16	11	14	*771*	*786*	*1557*
5-15	13	12	12	*1733*	*1684*	*3417*
16-44	22	29	26	*4124*	*4403*	*8527*
45-64	44	50	47	*2475*	*2603*	*5078*
65-74	47	55	51	*884*	*1053*	*1937*
75 and over	64	67	66	*626*	*852*	*1478*
Total	30	35	33	*10613*	*11381*	*21994*

Table 8.15 **Self-reported sickness by sex and standard region: percentage of persons who reported**
(a) longstanding illness
(b) limiting longstanding illness
(c) restricted activity in the 14 days before interview

All persons   *Great Britain: 1996*

Standard region*	(a) Longstanding illness	(b) Limiting longstanding illness	(c) Restricted activity	Base = 100%
Males				
England				
North	35	23	17	691
Yorkshire and Humberside	37	23	14	913
North West	34	23	16	1191
East Midlands	37	24	15	791
West Midlands	33	20	14	1024
East Anglia	34	20	14	432
Greater London	31	20	14	1101
Outer Metropolitan area	34	18	14	998
Outer South East	32	18	15	1022
South West	34	19	13	918
All England	34	20	15	9081
Wales	39	26	19	576
Scotland	32	19	17	961
Great Britain	34	21	15	10618
Females				
England				
North	40	26	19	697
Yorkshire and Humberside	35	25	16	994
North West	33	22	16	1295
East Midlands	34	19	13	861
West Midlands	35	22	16	1060
East Anglia	39	22	16	439
Greater London	33	22	16	1225
Outer Metropolitan area	33	19	15	1058
Outer South East	35	23	17	1046
South West	39	26	19	1030
All England	35	23	16	9705
Wales	37	26	19	655
Scotland	34	22	18	1023
Great Britain	35	23	17	11383
All persons				
England				
North	37	25	18	1388
Yorkshire and Humberside	36	24	15	1907
North West	33	22	16	2486
East Midlands	36	22	14	1652
West Midlands	34	21	15	2084
East Anglia	37	21	15	871
Greater London	32	21	15	2326
Outer Metropolitan area	34	18	15	2056
Outer South East	33	20	16	2068
South West	37	23	16	1948
All England	35	22	15	18786
Wales	38	26	19	1231
Scotland	33	21	17	1984
Great Britain	35	22	16	22001

* The data have not been standardised to take account of age or socio-economic group.

Table 8.16   **Prevalence of longstanding illness by sex and health region**

All persons   *Great Britain: 1996*

Health region	Males	Females	All persons
Northern and Yorkshire	36	39	37
Trent	37	34	35
Anglia and Oxford	33	35	34
North Thames	33	34	34
South Thames	32	33	33
South and West	34	38	36
West Midlands	33	34	34
North West	34	33	33
England	34	35	35
Wales	39	37	38
Scotland	32	34	33
Great Britain	34	35	35
Bases = 100%			
Northern and Yorkshire	*1137*	*1192*	*2329*
Trent	*1159*	*1264*	*2423*
Anglia and Oxford	*1198*	*1240*	*2438*
North Thames	*982*	*1088*	*2070*
South Thames	*1152*	*1220*	*2372*
South and West	*1214*	*1328*	*2542*
West Midlands	*1026*	*1063*	*2089*
North West	*1216*	*1314*	*2530*
England	*9084*	*9709*	*18793*
Wales	*576*	*655*	*1231*
Scotland	*961*	*1023*	*1984*
Great Britain	*10621*	*11387*	*22008*

Table 8.17   **Prevalence of limiting longstanding illness by sex and health region**

All persons   *Great Britain: 1996*

Health region	Males	Females	All persons
Northern and Yorkshire	23	27	25
Trent	23	21	22
Anglia and Oxford	18	21	19
North Thames	21	21	21
South Thames	18	22	20
South and West	19	25	22
West Midlands	20	22	21
North West	22	22	22
England	20	23	22
Wales	26	26	26
Scotland	19	22	21
Great Britain	21	23	22
Bases = 100%			
Northern and Yorkshire	*1137*	*1192*	*2329*
Trent	*1159*	*1263*	*2422*
Anglia and Oxford	*1198*	*1240*	*2438*
North Thames	*982*	*1087*	*2069*
South Thames	*1152*	*1219*	*2371*
South and West	*1214*	*1328*	*2542*
West Midlands	*1025*	*1063*	*2088*
North West	*1214*	*1313*	*2527*
England	*9081*	*9705*	*18786*
Wales	*576*	*655*	*1231*
Scotland	*961*	*1023*	*1984*
Great Britain	*10618*	*11383*	*22001*

Table 8.18 **Prevalence of reported restricted activity in the 14 days before interview, by sex and health region**

All persons   *Great Britain: 1996*

Health region	Males	Females	All persons
Northern and Yorkshire	16	17	16
Trent	14	14	14
Anglia and Oxford	13	18	15
North Thames	14	14	14
South Thames	15	17	16
South and West	14	18	16
West Midlands	14	15	15
North West	16	16	16
England	15	16	15
Wales	19	19	19
Scotland	17	18	17
Great Britain	15	17	16
Bases = 100%			
Northern and Yorkshire	*1137*	*1192*	*2329*
Trent	*1158*	*1263*	*2421*
Anglia and Oxford	*1198*	*1241*	*2439*
North Thames	*981*	*1086*	*2067*
South Thames	*1152*	*1220*	*2372*
South and West	*1213*	*1329*	*2542*
West Midlands	*1026*	*1061*	*2087*
North West	*1216*	*1314*	*2530*
England	*9081*	*9705*	*18787*
Wales	*575*	*655*	*1230*
Scotland	*961*	*1023*	*1984*
Great Britain	*10617*	*11384*	*22001*

Table 8.19 Trends in consultations with an NHS GP in the 14 days before interview: 1972 to 1996

All persons   *Great Britain*

	1972	1979	1981	1983	1985	1989	1991	1993	1994	1995	1996	Base (1996)* = 100%
					Percentage consulting GP							
Males												
0- 4	13	19	21	21	22	24	23	23	23	22	23	771
5-15†	7	8	8	10	9	10	10	11	10	9	9	1733
16-44†	8	9	7	8	7	8	9	11	9	10	10	4125
45-64	11	14	12	12	12	12	11	15	13	14	15	2479
65-74	12	15	13	18	15	16	17	21	16	17	19	884
75 and over	19	16	17	20	19	19	21	22	18	22	21	626
Total	10	11	10	12	11	12	12	14	12	13	13	10618
Females												
0- 4	15	15	17	20	21	21	21	22	20	21	20	786
5-15†	6	8	9	9	11	11	11	10	11	13	9	1685
16-44†	15	15	15	17	17	18	17	20	17	18	20	4405
45-64	12	13	13	15	15	17	17	19	19	17	19	2605
65-74	15	17	16	18	17	19	19	20	21	23	21	1053
75 and over	20	23	20	21	20	22	19	23	19	23	23	854
Total	13	14	14	16	16	17	17	19	17	18	19	11388
All persons												
0- 4	14	17	19	20	21	23	22	22	22	21	22	1557
5-15†	7	8	9	10	10	10	10	11	10	11	9	3418
16-44†	12	12	11	12	12	13	13	16	13	14	15	8530
45-64	12	14	12	14	14	15	14	17	16	16	17	5084
65-74	14	16	15	18	16	18	18	21	19	20	20	1937
75 and over	20	21	19	21	20	21	19	22	19	23	22	1480
Total	12	13	12	14	14	15	14	17	15	16	16	22006

* ⎤
† ⎦ See the footnotes to Table 8.1.

Table 8.20   **Average number of NHS GP consultations per person per year: 1972 to 1996**

*All persons**   *Great Britain*

	1972†	1979	1981	1983	1985	1989	1991	1993	1994	1995	1996
Males											
0- 4	4	6	7	7	7	9	7	8	8	7	8
5-15**	2	2	2	3	3	3	3	3	3	3	3
16-44**	3	3	2	2	2	2	3	4	3	3	3
45-64	4	4	4	4	4	4	4	5	4	4	5
65-74	4	5	4	5	5	5	5	6	5	5	6
75 and over	7	5	6	7	6	6	7	7	5	8	7
Total	3	3	3	4	3	4	4	5	4	4	4
Females											
0- 4	5	5	5	6	7	7	7	7	7	7	6
5-15**	2	3	3	3	3	3	3	3	4	4	3
16-44**	5	5	5	5	5	6	5	6	5	6	7
45-64	4	4	4	5	5	5	5	6	6	5	6
65-74	5	5	5	6	5	6	6	6	6	7	7
75 and over	7	8	6	7	7	7	6	7	6	7	7
Total	4	5	4	5	5	6	5	6	6	6	6
All persons											
0- 4	4	5	6	7	7	8	7	8	8	7	7
5-15**	2	2	3	3	3	3	3	3	3	3	3
16-44**	4	4	4	4	4	4	4	5	4	4	5
45-64	4	4	4	4	4	5	4	5	5	5	5
65-74	4	5	4	6	5	6	6	6	6	6	6
75 and over	7	7	6	7	6	7	6	7	6	7	7
Total	4	4	4	4	4	5	5	5	5	5	5

*   Bases for 1996 are shown in Table 8.1. Bases for earlier years are of a similar size and can be found in GHS reports for each year.
†   1972 figures relate to England and Wales.
** These age-groups were 5-14 and 15-44 in 1972 to 1978.

Table 8.21   **(NHS) GP consultations: trends in site of consultation: 1971 to 1996**

Consultations in the 14 days before interview   *Great Britain*

Site of consultation	1971	1979	1981	1983	1985	1989	1991	1993	1994	1995	1996
	%	%	%	%	%	%	%	%	%	%	%
Surgery*	73	76	79	79	79	78	81	84	83	84	84
Home	22	16	14	15	14	14	11	9	10	9	8
Telephone	4	7	7	6	7	8	8	7	8	7	8
Base = 100%	5031	4678	4704	4287	4123	4520	4228	4873	4221	4385	4341

* Includes consultations with a GP at a health centre and those who had answered 'elsewhere'.

Table 8.22   **(NHS) GP consultations: consultations with doctors in the 14 days before interview, by sex and age of person consulting, and by site of consultation**

Consultations in the 14 days before interview

Site of consultation	Males						Females						All persons					
	Age						Age						Age					
	0-4	5-15	16-44	45-64	65-74	75 and over	0-4	5-15	16-44	45-64	65-74	75 and over	0-4	5-15	16-44	45-64	65-74	75 and over
	%	%	%	%	%	%	%	%	%	%	%	%	%	%	%	%	%	%
Surgery*	83	88	89	89	82	74	78	86	86	87	84	59	81	87	87	88	83	65
Home	7	6	4	7	11	22	10	2	4	5	10	30	8	4	4	6	11	27
Telephone	10	6	7	5	7	3	11	12	9	8	6	11	10	9	9	7	6	8
Base = 100%	229	174	498	458	208	160	186	175	1119	616	274	244	415	349	1617	1074	482	404

* Includes consultations with a GP at a health centre and those who had answered 'elsewhere'.

Table 8.23   **(NHS) GP consultations: percentage of persons consulting a doctor in the 14 days before interview, by sex and by site of consultation, and by age and by site of consultation**

Persons who consulted in the 14 days before interview

Site of consultation	Total	Males	Females	Age					
				0-4	5-15	16-44	45-64	65-74	75 and over
	%	%	%	%	%	%	%	%	%
Surgery	87	89	86	86	89	91	90	86	68
At home	8	8	8	9	4	4	5	10	27
Telephone	9	6	10	11	9	10	7	6	9
Base (all persons consulting) = 100% *	3523	1414	2109	336	306	1270	888	394	329

* Percentages add to more than 100 because some people consulted at more than one site during the reference period.

Table 8.24 **(NHS) GP consultations**
(a) Percentage of persons who consulted a doctor in the 14 days before interview, by sex, age, and socio-economic group of head of household
(b) Average number of consultations per person per year, by sex, age, and socio-economic group of head of household

All persons   *Great Britain: 1996*

Socio-economic group of head of household*	Males						Females					
	Age						Age					
	0-4	5-15	16-44	45-64	65 and over	Total	0-4	5-15	16-44	45-64	65 and over	Total
(a) Percentage who consulted a doctor in the 14 days before interview												
Professional	[19]	11	6	10	16	10	[21]	12	17	19	[31]	18
Employers and managers	21	6	9	13	23	12	19	7	18	14	21	16
Intermediate non-manual	30	8	9	16	15	12	16	12	18	17	18	17
Junior non-manual	25	14	12	19	21	16	14	7	24	20	20	20
(grouped above four)	24	9	9	13	21	13	17	9	19	17	21	17
Skilled manual and own account non-professional	23	8	10	16	20	13	27	9	19	21	27	20
Semi-skilled manual and personal service	22	9	12	19	20	15	19	9	22	24	21	20
Unskilled manual	[25]	13	14	23	19	17	[7]	11	16	23	23	19
(grouped above three)	23	9	11	17	20	14	23	9	20	22	24	20
All persons	23	9	10	15	20	13	20	9	20	19	22	19
(b) Average number of consultations per person per year												
Professional	6	4	2	3	4	3	6	3	5	6	11	6
Employers and managers	8	2	3	4	7	4	5	2	6	4	7	5
Intermediate non-manual	11	2	3	5	5	4	5	3	5	5	6	5
Junior non-manual	9	4	4	5	8	5	5	2	9	6	7	7
(grouped above four)	9	3	3	4	7	4	5	2	6	5	7	5
Skilled manual and own account non-professional	7	2	3	5	6	4	9	3	6	7	8	6
Semi-skilled manual and personal service	7	2	4	6	6	5	6	3	8	7	7	7
Unskilled manual	8	4	4	8	7	6	2	3	6	7	8	6
(grouped above three)	7	3	3	5	6	5	7	3	7	7	8	6
All persons	8	3	3	5	6	4	6	3	7	6	7	6
Bases = 100%												
Professional	36	116	255	156	83	646	42	95	256	151	49	593
Employers and managers	150	380	936	595	341	2402	175	392	917	552	290	2326
Intermediate non-manual	77	171	434	225	118	1025	76	152	495	261	201	1185
Junior non-manual	83	155	311	129	89	767	80	155	455	253	344	1287
Skilled manual and own account non-professional	197	499	1271	932	549	3448	231	496	1209	844	424	3204
Semi-skilled manual and personal service	138	263	557	323	230	1511	117	252	653	374	357	1753
Unskilled manual	44	77	172	91	81	465	28	72	156	133	167	556
All persons	771	1733	4125	2479	1510	10618	786	1685	4405	2605	1907	11388

* See the footnote to Table 8.2.

Table 8.25   **(NHS) GP consultations**
  (a) **Percentage of persons who consulted a doctor in the 14 days before interview, by sex, age, and economic activity status**
  (b) **Average number of consultations per person per year, by sex, age, and economic activity status**

All persons aged 16 and over   *Great Britain: 1996*

Economic activity status	Men				Women			
	Age				Age			
	16-44	45-64	65 and over	Total	16-44	45-64	65 and over	Total
(a) Percentage who consulted a doctor in the 14 days before interview								
Working	9	11	15	10	18	17	9	17
Unemployed	8	10	0	9	21	15	0	20
Economically inactive	19	30	20	22	24	23	23	23
All aged 16 and over	10	15	20	13	20	19	22	20
(b) Average number of consultations per person per year								
Working	3	3	5	3	6	5	3	5
Unemployed	2	3	0	3	7	5	0	7
Economically inactive	7	10	6	7	8	8	7	8
All aged 16 and over	3	5	6	4	7	6	7	7
Bases = 100%								
Working	3361	1736	98	5195	2954	1424	65	4443
Unemployed	341	131	0	472	211	60	0	271
Economically inactive	419	612	1411	2442	1233	1121	1842	4196
All aged 16 and over	4121	2479	1509	8109	4398	2605	1907	8910

Table 8.26   **(NHS) GP consultations: percentage of persons consulting a doctor in the 14 days before interview who obtained a prescription from the doctor, by sex, age and non-manual/manual socio-economic group of head of household**

Persons who consulted in the 14 days before interview   *Great Britain: 1996*

Socio-economic group of head of household*	Males					Females				
	Age					Age				
	0-15	16-44	45-64	65 and over	Total	0-15	16-44	45-64	65 and over	Total
Percentage consulting who obtained a prescription										
Non-manual	67	63	66	72	67	69	63	70	80	69
Manual	74	61	75	76	71	70	69	75	74	72
All persons consulting	70	62	71	75	69	69	66	73	76	70
Bases = 100%										
Non-manual	154	175	149	130	608	134	409	201	183	927
Manual	163	213	226	171	773	161	398	298	228	1085
All persons consulting	331	400	381	302	1414	311	869	507	421	2108

* See the footnote to Table 8.2.

Table 8.27 **GP consultations: consultations with doctors in the 14 days before interview by whether consultation was NHS or private**

Consultations in the 14 days before interview   *Great Britain: 1996*

Type of consultation	Males	Females	All persons
	%	%	%
NHS	97	98	97
Private	3	2	3
Base (all consultations) =100%	*1925*	*2857*	*4782*

Table 8.28 **Trends in percentages of persons who reported attending an outpatient or casualty department in a 3 month reference period: 1972 to 1996**

All persons*   *Great Britain*

	1972†	1975	1979	1981	1983	1985	1989	1991	1993	1994	1995	1996
						Percentages						
Males												
0- 4	8	9	13	12	10	13	11	14	14	11	12	13
5-15**	9	8	10	11	10	12	12	11	12	11	11	12
16-44**	11	9	11	11	12	12	12	11	12	12	12	13
45-64	11	10	13	12	13	16	15	15	15	16	16	16
65-74	10	11	15	14	15	16	18	18	20	22	21	20
75 and over	10	12	13	14	19	15	16	22	24	22	26	25
Total	10	10	12	11	12	13	13	13	14	14	14	15
Females												
0- 4	6	8	10	9	9	11	10	11	10	11	12	9
5-15**	6	6	8	8	9	9	9	8	10	9	9	10
16-44**	9	9	12	11	11	12	13	12	12	13	12	13
45-64	11	10	13	13	15	15	17	16	17	17	17	18
65-74	12	12	16	16	18	17	19	18	18	22	21	22
75 and over	13	10	16	16	16	17	20	20	22	22	22	24
Total	10	9	12	12	12	13	14	14	14	15	14	15
All persons												
0- 4	7	9	11	10	10	12	10	13	12	11	12	11
5-15**	8	7	9	10	10	10	11	10	11	10	10	11
16-44**	10	9	11	11	11	12	13	12	12	12	12	13
45-64	11	10	13	13	14	15	16	16	16	16	16	17
65-74	11	11	15	15	17	17	18	18	19	22	21	21
75 and over	12	10	15	15	17	16	18	21	22	22	24	24
Total	10	9	12	12	12	13	14	13	14	14	14	15

*   Bases for 1996 are shown in Table 8.1. Bases for earlier years are of a similar size and can be found in GHS Reports for each year.
†   1972 figures relate to England and Wales.
** These age-groups were 5-14 and 15-44 from 1972 to 1978.

Table 8.29   **Trends in day-patient treatment in the 12 months before interview, 1992 to 1996**

All persons   *Great Britain*

	1992	1993	1994	1995	1996	Base (1996)* = 100%
			Percentage receiving day-patient treatment			
Males						
0- 4	4	4	4	4	5	771
5-15	2	3	3	3	3	1733
16-44	4	5	5	6	5	4124
45-64	4	4	5	7	6	2482
65-74	5	5	6	6	7	884
75 and over	4	3	5	5	6	626
Total	4	4	5	5	5	10620
Females						
0- 4	2	3	3	3	3	786
5-15	2	3	3	2	4	1683
16-44	5	6	7	6	7	4406
45-64	5	5	5	7	8	2605
65-74	4	5	5	5	6	1053
75 and over	3	5	5	5	7	855
Total	4	5	5	5	6	11388
All persons						
0- 4	3	3	3	3	4	1557
5-15	2	3	3	3	3	3416
16-44	4	6	6	6	6	8530
45-64	5	5	5	7	7	5087
65-74	4	5	5	6	7	1937
75 and over	3	4	5	5	6	1481
Total	4	5	5	5	6	22008

* See the first footnote to Table 8.1.

Table 8.30   **Treatment in hospital as a day-patient in the last 12 months**

All persons   *Great Britain: 1996*

Age	Male	Female	Total	Male	Female	Total
		% as day-patient			Bases = 100%	
0-4	5	3	4	771	786	1557
5-15	3	4	3	1733	1683	3416
16-44	5	7	6	4124	4406	8530
45-64	6	8	7	2482	2605	5087
65-74	7	6	7	884	1053	1937
75 and over	6	7	6	626	855	1481
All persons	5	6	6	10620	11388	22008

131

Table 8.31 **Average number of separate days spent in hospital as a day-patient during the last 12 months**

All day-patients   *Great Britain: 1996*

Age	Male	Female	Total	Male	Female	Total
	Average number of days			Base (all day-patients)		
0-4	2	2	2	37	20	57
5-15	2	2	2	48	62	110
16-44	2	2	2	209	327	536
45-64	2	2	2	152	201	353
65-74	1	1	1	62	67	129
75 and over	3	2	2	37	56	93
All persons	2	2	2	545	733	1278

Table 8.32 **Trends in inpatient stays in the 12 months before interview, 1982 to 1996**

All persons   *Great Britain*

	1982	1985	1987	1989	1991	1992	1993	1994	1995	1996	Base (1996)* = 100%
	Percentage with inpatient stay										
Males											
0- 4	14	12	10	12	10	11	10	9	9	9	771
5-15	6	8	6	7	6	6	6	6	5	5	1733
16-44	5	6	6	6	6	6	6	5	5	5	4124
45-64	8	8	9	8	8	9	9	8	9	8	2482
65-74	12	13	12	12	13	16	14	13	15	13	884
75 and over	14	17	20	17	20	18	21	18	21	18	626
Total	7	8	8	8	8	8	8	7	8	7	10620
Females											
0- 4	12	8	8	9	8	10	7	7	8	7	786
5-15	4	5	5	5	4	4	5	5	4	4	1683
16-44	15	16	16	15	15	13	13	12	12	12	4406
45-64	8	8	9	9	9	9	9	8	8	10	2605
65-74	8	18	11	11	11	11	10	11	11	12	1053
75 and over	12	13	14	17	16	17	16	18	20	16	855
Total	11	11	12	12	11	11	11	10	10	10	11388
All persons											
0- 4	13	10	9	10	9	10	9	8	9	8	1557
5-15	5	6	6	6	5	5	5	5	4	4	3416
16-44	10	11	11	11	10	9	9	9	8	9	8530
45-64	8	8	9	9	8	9	9	8	8	9	5087
65-74	10	10	12	11	12	13	12	12	13	12	1937
75 and over	13	15	16	17	18	17	18	18	20	17	1481
Total	9	10	10	10	10	10	9	9	9	9	22008

* See the first footnote to Table 8.1.

Table 8.33 **Inpatient stays and outpatient attendances**
(a) Average number of inpatient stays per 100 persons in a 12 month reference period, by sex and age
(b) Average number of outpatient attendances per 100 persons per year, by sex and age

All persons   *Great Britain: 1996*

Age	(a) Average number of inpatient stays per 100 persons in a 12 month reference period			(b) Average number of outpatient attendances per 100 persons per year			Bases = 100%		
	Males	Females	Total	Males	Females	Total	*Males*	*Females*	*Total*
0- 4	9	9	9	81	52	67	*771*	*786*	*1557*
5-15	12	5	8	82	68	75	*1733*	*1683*	*3416*
16-44	6	17	12	106	110	108	*4124*	*4406*	*8530*
45-64	10	14	12	149	160	155	*2482*	*2605*	*5087*
65-74	16	15	15	180	207	195	*884*	*1053*	*1937*
75 and over	27	23	25	254	185	214	*626*	*855*	*1481*
Total	10	14	12	125	126	126	*10620*	*11388*	*22008*

Table 8.34 **Average number of nights spent in hospital as an inpatient during the last 12 months**

All inpatients   *Great Britain: 1996*

Age	Male	Female	Total	*Male*	*Female*	*Total*
	Average number of nights			*Base (all inpatients)*		
0-4	4	7	5	*65*	*54*	*119*
5-15	3	4	3	*84*	*61*	*145*
16-44	6	6	6	*191*	*525*	*716*
45-64	9	8	8	*171*	*249*	*420*
65-74	8	10	9	*111*	*120*	*231*
75 and over	12	13	13	*102*	*123*	*225*
All persons	7	8	7	*724*	*1132*	*1856*

Table 8.35   **EuroQol dimensions: whether problems with general health by age**

Persons aged 16 and over   *Great Britain: 1996*

	Age group				
	16-44	45-64	65-74	75 and over	Total
	%	%	%	%	%
Pain or discomfort					
No problems	81	61	48	39	67
Some problems	17	33	44	51	28
Severe problems	2	6	8	10	5
Mobility					
No problems	94	79	64	45	81
Some problems	6	21	36	55	19
Severe problems	0	0	0	0	0
Anxiety or depression					
No problems	85	79	78	75	81
Some problems	14	19	20	23	17
Severe problems	2	2	2	2	2
Usual activities					
No problems	94	84	78	66	86
Some problems	6	14	20	29	12
Severe problems	1	2	2	5	2
Self care					
No problems	98	94	92	82	95
Some problems	2	5	8	16	5
Severe problems	0	0	1	2	0
Base = 100%	*7680*	*4724*	*1878*	*1404*	*15687*

Table 8.36   **EuroQol dimensions: whether problems with general health by age and sex**

Persons aged 16 and over   *Great Britain: 1996*

	Men					Women				
	16-44	45-64	65-74	75 and over	Total	16-44	45-64	65-74	75 and over	Total
	%	%	%	%	%	%	%	%	%	%
Pain or discomfort										
No problems	82	61	48	44	68	80	60	49	35	66
Some problems	17	32	46	50	28	18	34	42	52	29
Severe problems	1	7	6	6	4	2	6	9	13	5
Mobility										
No problems	94	78	64	50	82	94	79	63	41	81
Some problems	6	22	36	50	18	6	21	36	59	19
Severe problems	0	0	0	0	0	0	0	0	0	0
Anxiety or depression										
No problems	88	82	80	81	84	82	76	76	70	78
Some problems	11	16	17	18	14	16	21	22	28	19
Severe problems	1	2	2	1	2	2	3	2	2	2
Usual activities										
No problems	95	84	79	73	88	93	83	77	60	85
Some problems	5	13	18	24	11	6	15	21	33	13
Severe problems	1	3	2	3	2	1	2	2	7	2
Self care										
No problems	99	94	92	86	95	98	95	91	79	94
Some problems	1	6	7	13	4	2	5	8	18	5
Severe problems	0	0	1	1	0	0	0	1	2	1
Base = 100%	*3520*	*2217*	*850*	*596*	*7183*	*4160*	*2507*	*1029*	*808*	*8504*

Table 8.37 **EuroQol category by age**

Persons aged 16 and over   *Great Britain: 1996*

EuroQol category	Age group				
	16-44	45-64	65-74	75 and over	Total
	%	%	%	%	%
No problems	72	52	38	25	58
Mild problems	16	19	21	19	18
Moderate problems	6	10	16	18	9
Substantial problems	7	18	25	38	15
Base = 100%	*7679*	*4724*	*1878*	*1404*	*15685*

Table 8.38 **EuroQol category by sex and age**

Persons aged 16 and over   *Great Britain: 1996*

EuroQol category	Men					Women				
	16-44	45-64	65-74	75 and over	Total	16-44	45-64	65-74	75 and over	Total
	%	%	%	%	%	%	%	%	%	%
No problems	74	54	38	30	60	70	50	38	21	55
Mild problems	15	18	23	19	17	16	20	19	19	18
Moderate problems	5	9	16	21	9	6	11	16	16	10
Substantial problems	6	18	23	30	14	8	18	27	44	17
Base = 100%	*3520*	*2217*	*850*	*596*	*7183*	*4159*	*2507*	*1028*	*808*	*8502*

Table 8.39 **Mean score on Visual Analogue Scale (VAS) by sex and age**

Persons aged 16 and over   *Great Britain: 1996*

	Age group				
	16-44	45-64	65-74	75 and over	Total
	Mean VAS score				
Men	81	76	73	68	77
Women	80	76	72	65	76
Total	80	76	72	66	77
Base = 100%					
Men	*3513*	*2204*	*839*	*589*	*7145*
Women	*4151*	*2500*	*1011*	*778*	*8440*
Total	*7664*	*4704*	*1850*	*1367*	*15585*

Table 8.40   **Mean score on Visual Analogue Scale (VAS) by EuroQol category**

Persons aged 16 and over   *Great Britain: 1996*

EuroQol category	Age group				
	16-44	45-64	65-74	75 and over	Total
	Mean VAS score				
No problems	84	85	83	81	84
Mild problems	77	79	76	73	77
Moderate problems	72	70	69	67	70
Substantial problems	58	50	53	53	53
All persons	80	76	72	66	77
Base = 100%					
No problems	*5499*	*2447*	*709*	*342*	*8997*
Mild problems	*1192*	*915*	*384*	*260*	*2751*
Moderate problems	*443*	*473*	*298*	*250*	*1464*
Substantial problems	*528*	*866*	*458*	*513*	*2365*
All persons	*7664*	*4704*	*1850*	*1367*	*15585*

Table 8.41   **EuroQol category: percentage with no problems by region and age**

Persons aged 16 and over   *Great Britain: 1996*

Standard region	Age group				
	16-44	45-64	65-74	75 and over	Total
	Percentage with no problems				
North	72	44	24	23	54
Yorkshire and Humberside	73	45	34	22	54
North West	68	49	39	23	55
East Midlands	74	52	40	24	59
West Midlands	74	51	39	19	58
East Anglia	76	59	42	31	62
Greater London	71	56	42	22	60
Outer Metropolitan area	71	62	40	26	60
Outer South East	69	53	45	28	57
South West	72	58	40	24	59
Wales	73	42	38	29	55
Scotland	75	51	30	29	58
Great Britain	72	52	38	25	58
Base = 100%					
North	*485*	*303*	*117*	*60*	*965*
Yorkshire and Humberside	*620*	*465*	*149*	*128*	*1362*
North West	*858*	*570*	*187*	*124*	*1739*
East Midlands	*556*	*364*	*166*	*94*	*1180*
West Midlands	*726*	*411*	*191*	*128*	*1456*
East Anglia	*306*	*176*	*85*	*68*	*635*
Greater London	*902*	*440*	*160*	*156*	*1658*
Outer Metropolitan area	*734*	*461*	*179*	*141*	*1515*
Outer South East	*688*	*427*	*168*	*166*	*1449*
South West	*673*	*435*	*183*	*142*	*1433*
Wales	*412*	*235*	*113*	*82*	*842*
Scotland	*719*	*437*	*180*	*115*	*1451*
Great Britain	*7679*	*4724*	*1878*	*1404*	*15685*

Table 8.42 **Age of elderly men and women: 1980-1996**

Persons aged 65 and over   *Great Britain*

Age	1980	1985	1991	1994	1996
	%	%	%	%	%
Men					
65-69	41	36	35	33	32
70-74	30	30	26	32	27
75-79	17	22	21	16	23
80-84	9	9	12	12	12
85 and over	3	4	6	6	6
Women					
65-69	34	27	31	27	28
70-74	27	28	24	30	27
75-79	21	23	22	18	21
80-84	11	12	14	14	14
85 and over	8	9	9	11	9
All elderly people					
65-69	37	31	33	30	30
70-74	28	29	25	31	27
75-79	20	22	22	18	22
80-84	10	11	13	13	13
85 and over	6	7	8	9	8
Base = 100%					
Men	*1842*	*1498*	*1580*	*1458*	*1447*
Women	*2674*	*2193*	*2205*	*2043*	*1840*
All elderly people	*4516*	*3691*	*3785*	*3501*	*3287*

Table 8.43 **Household type of elderly men and women: 1980-1996**

Persons aged 65 and over   *Great Britain*

Household type	1980	1985	1991	1994	1996
	%	%	%	%	%
Men					
Lives with spouse only	62	63	62	61	62
Lives alone	17	20	24	24	26
Miscellaneous	21	17	15	15	12
Women					
Lives with spouse only	33	33	36	35	38
Lives alone	45	48	48	49	49
Miscellaneous	22	19	17	16	13
All elderly people					
Lives with spouse only	45	45	46	46	48
Lives alone	34	36	38	39	39
Miscellaneous	21	18	16	15	13
Base = 100%					
Men	*1842*	*1498*	*1580*	*1458*	*1447*
Women	*2674*	*2193*	*2205*	*2043*	*1840*
All elderly people	*4516*	*3691*	*3785*	*3501*	*3287*

137

Table 8.44   **Mobility: percentage unable to manage on their own by sex and age**

Persons aged 65 and over   *Great Britain: 1996*

Activity	Age					
	65-69	70-74	75-79	80-84	85 and over	All aged 65 and over
	Percentage unable to manage on their own					
Going out of doors and walking down the road						
Men	6	7	8	9	16	8
Women	7	11	15	28	48	17
All elderly people	7	9	12	20	37	13
Getting up and down stairs and steps						
Men	4	6	10	8	11	7
Women	6	7	11	20	40	12
All elderly people	5	7	11	15	30	10
Getting around the house (on the level)						
Men	1	1	0	0	1	1
Women	2	1	1	2	6	2
All elderly people	1	1	0	1	4	1
Getting to the toilet						
Men	1	1	1	0	2	1
Women	1	1	1	2	4	1
All elderly people	1	1	1	1	3	1
Getting in and out of bed						
Men	2	2	2	1	3	2
Women	2	2	1	5	5	3
All elderly people	2	2	1	3	4	2
At least one of the above						
Men	6	9	14	13	23	11
Women	8	14	18	32	57	20
All elderly people	7	11	16	25	45	16
Bases = 100%						
Men	*458*	*391*	*335*	*174*	*87*	*1445*
Women	*523*	*505*	*382*	*264*	*162*	*1836*
All elderly people	*981*	*896*	*717*	*438*	*249*	*3281*

Table 8.45   **Mobility: percentage who usually manage with help and percentage who cannot usually manage at all, by sex and age**

Persons aged 65 and over   *Great Britain: 1996*

Activity	Age					
	65-69	70-74	75-79	80-84	85 and over	All aged 65 and over
				Percentages		
Going out of doors and walking down the road						
Usually manages with help						
Men	3	3	5	5	6	4
Women	3	7	9	14	23	9
All elderly people	3	5	7	11	17	6
Cannot usually manage at all						
Men	3	4	4	3	10	4
Women	4	5	7	14	25	8
All elderly people	3	4	5	10	20	6
Bases = 100%						
Men	*458*	*392*	*335*	*174*	*88*	*1447*
Women	*524*	*505*	*383*	*265*	*163*	*1840*
All elderly people	*982*	*897*	*718*	*439*	*251*	*3287*
Getting up and down stairs and steps						
Usually manages with help						
Men	2	4	5	5	8	4
Women	3	4	8	12	19	7
All elderly people	3	4	7	9	15	6
Cannot usually manage at all						
Men	2	2	5	3	3	3
Women	3	3	3	8	21	5
All elderly people	2	3	4	6	15	4
Bases = 100%						
Men	*458*	*392*	*335*	*174*	*88*	*1447*
Women	*524*	*505*	*383*	*265*	*162*	*1839*
All elderly people	*982*	*897*	*718*	*439*	*250*	*3286*

139

Table 8.46 **Mobility: percentage unable to manage on their own by sex, age and household type**

Persons aged 65 and over   *Great Britain: 1996*

Activity	Household type											
	Lives with spouse only			Lives alone			Miscellaneous			All aged 65 and over		
	65-74	75 and over	Total	65-74	75 and over	Total	65-74	75 and over	Total	65-74	75 and over	Total
	Percentage unable to manage on their own											
Going out of doors and walking down the road												
Men	7	8	8	3	11	7	6	14	8	6	10	8
Women	11	22	14	7	25	17	11	36	23	9	26	17
All elderly people	9	13	10	6	21	14	8	29	17	8	19	13
Getting up and down stairs and steps												
Men	6	10	7	2	10	6	4	11	6	5	10	7
Women	8	15	10	6	21	14	6	23	14	7	20	12
All elderly people	7	12	8	5	18	12	5	19	10	6	15	10
Getting around the house (on the level)												
Men	1	0	1	0	0	0	1	2	1	1	0	1
Women	2	2	2	0	1	1	1	4	2	1	2	2
All elderly people	2	1	1	0	1	1	1	4	2	1	1	1
Getting to the toilet												
Men	1	1	1	0	1	0	2	4	2	1	1	1
Women	2	3	2	0	1	0	1	4	2	1	2	1
All elderly people	2	1	2	0	1	0	1	4	2	1	1	1
Getting in and out of bed												
Men	2	2	2	1	0	0	0	7	2	2	2	2
Women	4	5	4	0	2	1	1	3	2	2	3	3
All elderly people	3	3	3	1	2	1	0	4	2	2	2	2
At least one of the above												
Men	9	14	11	4	17	11	6	18	9	7	15	11
Women	12	24	16	9	31	21	11	39	24	11	31	20
All elderly people	10	18	13	8	27	18	8	32	18	9	24	16
Bases = 100%												
Men	*545*	*343*	*888*	*181*	*197*	*378*	*123*	*56*	*179*	*849*	*596*	*1445*
Women	*490*	*203*	*693*	*411*	*492*	*903*	*127*	*113*	*240*	*1028*	*808*	*1836*
All elderly people	*1035*	*546*	*1581*	*592*	*689*	*1281*	*250*	*169*	*419*	*1877*	*1404*	*3281*

Table 8.47 **Mobility: percentage who usually manage with help and percentage who cannot usually manage at all, by sex, age, and household type**

Persons aged 65 and over   *Great Britain: 1996*

Activity	Household type											
	Lives with spouse only			Lives alone			Miscellaneous			All aged 65 and over		
	65-74	75 and over	Total	65-74	75 and over	Total	65-74	75 and over	Total	65-74	75 and over	Total
						Percentages						
Going out of doors and walking down the road												
Usually manages with help												
Men	3	4	4	1	6	4	2	7	3	3	5	4
Women	6	12	8	4	12	8	6	19	12	5	13	9
All elderly people	5	7	5	3	11	7	4	15	8	4	10	6
Cannot usually manage at all												
Men	4	4	4	2	5	3	4	7	5	4	5	4
Women	5	10	6	3	13	8	6	17	11	4	13	8
All elderly people	4	6	5	3	10	7	5	14	8	4	9	6
Bases = 100%												
Men	*546*	*344*	*890*	*181*	*197*	*378*	*123*	*56*	*179*	*850*	*597*	*1447*
Women	*491*	*203*	*694*	*411*	*494*	*905*	*127*	*114*	*241*	*1029*	*811*	*1840*
All elderly people	*1037*	*547*	*1584*	*592*	*691*	*1283*	*250*	*170*	*420*	*1879*	*1408*	*3287*
Getting up and down stairs and steps												
Usually manages with help												
Men	4	5	4	1	6	3	1	7	3	3	5	4
Women	4	8	5	3	12	8	4	15	9	4	11	7
All elderly people	4	6	5	2	10	6	2	12	6	3	9	6
Cannot usually manage at all												
Men	2	5	3	1	4	3	3	4	3	2	5	3
Women	3	7	4	3	9	6	2	8	5	3	8	5
All elderly people	3	6	4	3	8	5	2	6	4	3	7	4
Bases = 100%												
Men	*546*	*344*	*890*	*181*	*197*	*378*	*123*	*56*	*179*	*850*	*597*	*1447*
Women	*491*	*203*	*694*	*411*	*493*	*904*	*127*	*114*	*241*	*1029*	*810*	*1839*
All elderly people	*1037*	*547*	*1584*	*592*	*690*	*1282*	*250*	*170*	*420*	*1879*	*1407*	*3286*

Table 8.48 **Mobility: percentage unable to manage on their own by sex and age: 1980 to 1996**

Persons aged 65 and over   *Great Britain*

	Age														
	65-69					70-74					75-79				
	1980	1985	1991	1994	1996	1980	1985	1991	1994	1996	1980	1985	1991	1994	1996
Percentage unable to:															
walk out of doors	5	5	5	7	7	8	7	6	8	9	13	14	11	13	12
get up and down stairs and steps	3	4	5	6	5	6	5	5	7	7	9	10	9	8	11
get around the house	1	1	1	1	1	1	1	1	1	1	1	2	1	0	0
get to the toilet	1	1	1	2	1	1	1	1	1	1	2	2	1	0	1
get in and out of bed	1	1	1	2	2	2	1	1	2	2	2	3	2	1	1
Bases = 100%	*1634*	*1120*	*1235*	*1032*	*981*	*1237*	*1059*	*936*	*1065*	*896*	*876*	*819*	*809*	*609*	*717*

	80-84					85 and over					All 65 and over				
	1980	1985	1991	1994	1996	1980	1985	1991	1994	1996	1980	1985	1991	1994	1996
Percentage unable to:															
walk out of doors	26	24	16	21	20	48	47	44	37	37	12	13	11	13	13
get up and down stairs and steps	16	17	15	13	15	31	31	27	23	30	8	9	9	9	10
get around the house	3	3	2	2	1	10	6	6	3	4	2	2	2	1	1
get to the toilet	3	2	0	2	1	9	7	5	3	3	2	2	1	1	1
get in and out of bed	3	2	2	2	3	10	7	7	4	4	2	2	2	2	2
Bases = 100%	*442*	*408*	*482*	*457*	*438*	*249*	*256*	*288*	*306*	*249*	*4438*	*3662*	*3750*	*3469*	*3281*

Table 8.49 **Self-care: percentage usually unable to manage on their own by sex and age**

Persons aged 65 and over   *Great Britain: 1996*

Activity	Age					
	65-69	70-74	75-79	80-84	85 and over	All aged 65 and over
	Percentage unable to manage on their own					
Bathing, showering, washing all over						
Men	6	5	7	7	17	7
Women	4	7	9	21	28	10
All elderly people	5	6	8	15	24	9
Dressing and undressing						
Men	4	3	4	3	5	4
Women	2	2	3	6	10	4
All elderly people	3	2	4	5	8	4
Washing face and hands						
Men	0	1	1	1	0	1
Women	1	0	0	2	2	1
All elderly people	1	0	1	1	1	1
Feeding						
Men	0	0	1	0	0	0
Women	1	0	1	1	1	1
All elderly people	0	0	1	1	1	0
At least one of the above						
Men	7	5	9	7	18	8
Women	4	7	10	22	30	11
All elderly people	5	6	9	16	26	10
Bases = 100%						
Men	*458*	*391*	*335*	*174*	*87*	*1445*
Women	*523*	*505*	*382*	*264*	*162*	*1836*
All elderly people	*981*	*896*	*717*	*438*	*249*	*3281*

Table 8.50   **Self-care: percentage usually unable to manage on their own by sex, age and household type**

Persons aged 65 and over   *Great Britain: 1996*

Activity	Household type											
	Lives with spouse only			Lives alone			Miscellaneous			All aged 65 and over		
	65-74	75 and over	Total	65-74	75 and over	Total	65-74	75 and over	Total	65-74	75 and over	Total
	Percentage unable to manage on their own											
Bathing, showering, washing all over												
Men	6	8	7	3	9	6	7	12	9	5	9	7
Women	6	11	7	4	17	11	8	25	16	5	17	10
All elderly people	6	9	7	4	15	10	8	21	13	5	13	9
Dressing and undressing												
Men	4	5	5	0	1	1	4	11	6	3	4	4
Women	3	9	5	1	3	2	1	7	4	2	5	4
All elderly people	4	6	5	1	3	2	2	8	5	3	5	4
Washing face and hands												
Men	1	1	1	0	1	0	1	2	1	1	1	1
Women	1	1	1	0	1	1	0	1	0	0	1	1
All elderly people	1	1	1	0	1	0	0	1	1	0	1	1
Feeding												
Men	0	1	0	0	0	0	0	0	0	0	1	0
Women	0	1	1	0	1	1	0	0	0	0	1	1
All elderly people	0	1	1	0	1	1	0	0	0	0	1	0
At least one of the above												
Men	7	9	8	3	9	6	8	16	11	6	10	8
Women	6	15	9	4	17	12	8	25	16	6	18	11
All elderly people	6	11	8	4	15	10	8	22	14	6	14	10
Bases = 100%												
Men	*545*	*343*	*888*	*181*	*197*	*378*	*123*	*56*	*179*	*849*	*596*	*1445*
Women	*490*	*203*	*693*	*411*	*492*	*903*	*127*	*113*	*240*	*1028*	*808*	*1836*
All elderly people	*1035*	*546*	*1581*	*592*	*689*	*1281*	*250*	*169*	*419*	*1877*	*1404*	*3281*

9 Mobility and mobility aids

Mobility difficulties

Questions about difficulties with mobility and the possession of mobility aids were first asked on the GHS in 1993 and were repeated in 1996. The aim was to provide estimates of the number of people who need aids to get about, and also of the number of aids that people have but do not use. All respondents aged 16 and over were asked these questions. In 1996:

- 8% of all respondents reported having difficulties getting around their home and/or going out of doors and walking down the road without assistance of any kind. This was the same proportion as in 1993;
- 7% said that they had a permanent difficulty with mobility and 1% had a temporary difficulty due to an accident or illness;
- as would be expected, the likelihood of having difficulties with mobility increased with age (among men - from 4% of those aged 16-64 to 42% of those aged 85 and over; among women - from 4% of those aged 16-64 to 67% of those aged 85 and over);
- women were more likely than men to report having a difficulty with mobility (9% compared with 7%). The greatest difference was amongst the very elderly. This is consistent with the finding noted in Chapter 8 (health) that women particularly in the older age groups were more likely than men to have a musculoskeletal problem;
- of those with mobility difficulties, nearly a half (48%) had difficulty getting about both indoors and outdoors. A similar proportion (47%) had problems getting about outdoors only and 5% had problems getting about indoors only. **Tables 9.1-9.2**

Possession of mobility aids

All respondents were asked whether they possessed any aids to mobility such as a walking stick, crutches, walking frame, trolley, wheelchair, buggy or scooter. In 1996:

- nearly three-quarters (74%) of all those with mobility difficulties had at least one of these aids;
- the proportion with mobility difficulties who possessed an aid increased from 63% of those aged 16-64 to 85% in the 75 and over age group;
- 4% of all respondents who did not report a problem with mobility, possessed at least one mobility aid;
- just over two-thirds (68%) of those with mobility aids had just one aid, 23% had two aids and 9% had three or more aids. **Figure 9A, Tables 9.3-9.4**

The possession of an aid varied according to where the problem with mobility was experienced.

- People who experienced problems getting about both indoors and outdoors were the most likely (84%) to have a mobility aid. In comparison, 67% who only had problems getting about outdoors and 54% who only had difficulties getting about their home had an aid. **Table 9.5**

Respondents were asked about the type of assistance required and whether they had the equipment needed.

- 93% who thought they needed a walking aid to help them get about indoors had such an aid compared with fewer (83%) of those who reported needing a wheelchair. The comparable figures for those requiring walking aids or wheelchairs for getting about outdoors were 94% and 79% respectively.

This indicates a level of unmet need but the results should be used with caution as they are based on perception of need rather than a professional assessment. **Table 9.6**

The health service or the social services provided a half of all mobility aids. Twenty nine per cent were bought by the informant or their spouse, 18% were provided by a relative or friend and 2% by a voluntary organisation. **Table 9.7**

Types of mobility aid

Of all the mobility aids which respondents possessed:

- walking sticks accounted for nearly two-thirds (64%);
- the next most common were – manual wheelchairs (12%), walking frames, tripods and zimmer frames (9%), crutches (7%). Electric wheelchairs, buggies or scooters were each possessed by 2% of those with mobility aids.

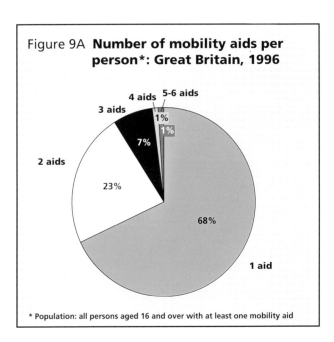

Figure 9A **Number of mobility aids per person*: Great Britain, 1996**

4 aids 1%
5-6 aids 1%
3 aids 7%
2 aids 23%
1 aid 68%

* Population: all persons aged 16 and over with at least one mobility aid

Overall, 84% of all the mobility aids which people possessed were in use.

- Mechanical aids were more likely to be in use than the less expensive walking aids (90% compared with 82%). Crutches were the least likely (73%) of all mobility aids to be in use.
- Of the mobility aids that were in use, mechanical aids were more likely to be in constant or regular use than other types of walking aids (73% compared with 66%).

Tables 9.8-9.9

As would be expected, whether an aid was used indoors or outdoors varied by the type of aid. For example:

- 47% of buggies/scooters were restricted to outdoor use compared with 24% of walking frames;
- 44% of trolleys compared with 12% of walking sticks were used only for getting about inside the home.

Table 9.10

Table 9.1 Percentage of persons reporting mobility difficulties, by sex and by age

Persons aged 16 and over   Great Britain: 1996

	Men						Women						Total
	16-64	65-74	75-79	80-84	85 and over	All men	16-64	65-74	75-79	80-84	85 and over	All women	
	Percentage reporting mobility difficulties												
Permanent difficulties	4	12	19	27	40	6	4	15	21	39	66	8	7
Temporary difficulties	0	1	2	0	1	0	0	1	1	3	1	1	1
All with difficulties	4	12	21	27	42	7	4	15	23	42	67	9	8
Base = 100%*	6395	874	347	182	89	7887	6889	1049	388	272	169	8767	16654

* Excludes persons who did not specify whether difficulties were permanent or temporary.

Table 9.2 Where mobility difficulties were experienced by age

Persons aged 16 and over with mobility difficulties   Great Britain: 1996

Age		Indoors only	Outdoors only	Indoors and outdoors	Bases = 100%
16-64	%	7	44	49	597
65-74	%	3	55	41	269
75 and over	%	3	46	51	477
Total	%	5	47	48	1343

Table 9.4 Percentage of people with mobility aid(s) by type of mobility difficulties

Persons aged 16 and over   Great Britain: 1996

Whether has mobility aid	No difficulties	Temporary difficulties	Permanent difficulties
	%	%	%
Has mobility aid	4	71	74
No mobility aid	96	29	26
Base = 100%	15326	86	1241

Table 9.3 Percentage of people with mobility aid(s) by age and whether has mobility difficulties

Persons aged 16 and over   Great Britain: 1996

Whether has mobility difficulties	16-64	65-74	75 and over	Total
	Percentage with mobility aid(s)			
Has difficulties	63	80	85	74
No difficulties	2	11	21	4
Bases = 100%				
Has difficulties	597	269	477	1343
No difficulties	12700	1655	974	15329

Table 9.5 Percentage of people with mobility aid(s) by where mobility difficulties were experienced

Persons aged 16 and over with mobility difficulties   Great Britain: 1996

Whether or not has at least one mobility aid	Indoors only	Outdoors only	Indoors and outdoors
	%	%	%
Has mobility aid	54	67	84
No mobility aid	46	33	16
Base = 100%	65	633	644

Table 9.6 Percentage of people with the type of equipment they required ('met need')

Population: all aged 16 and over who need a walking aid or wheelchair   *Great Britain: 1996*

Type of assistance required	Percentage with equipment that they required	Base = 100%
Need walking aid indoors	93	495
Need wheelchair indoors	83	71
Need walking aid outdoors	94	740
Need wheelchair outdoors	79	175

Table 9.7 Origin of mobility aids as a percentage of all mobility aids and percentage in use according to origin of aid

All mobility aids   *Great Britain: 1996*

Origin	Percentage of all aids	Percentage in use	Base = 100%
	%	Percentage	
Health/Social Services	50	88	1727
Self/spouse	29	87	990
Relative/friend	18	65	607
Voluntary organisation	2	85	59
Other	1	74	50
Total in use		84	3433
Base = 100%	3433		

Table 9.8 Type of mobility aid as a percentage of all mobility aids and percentage in use according to type of aid

All mobility aids   *Great Britain: 1996*

Type of aid	Percentage of all aids	Percentage in use		Base = 100%
Walking stick	64	81		2233
Crutches	7	73	82	244
Walking frame/tripod/zimmer	9	89		318
Trolley	2	97		69
Manual wheelchair	12	91		433
Electric wheelchair	2	88	90	74
Buggy/scooter	2	91		55
Other	2	93		86
Total in use		84		3512
Base = 100%	3512			

Table 9.9 Regularity of use outdoors of mobility aids by type

All aids in use   *Great Britain: 1996*

Type of aid		When aid used		Base = 100%
		All the time/ regularly	Occasionally	
Walking stick	%	66	34	1664
Crutches	%	58	42	152
Walking frame/ zimmer/tripod	%	71 (66)	29 (34)	174
Trolley	%	[87]	[13]	39
Manual wheelchair	%	73	27	335
Electric wheelchair	%	[80] (73)	[20] (27)	45
Buggy/scooter	%	[67]	[33]	45
Other	%	74	26	53

Table 9.10 Where mobility aids were used by type

All aids in use   *Great Britain: 1996*

Type of aid		Where aid used			Base = 100%
		Indoors only	Outdoors only	Indoors and outdoors	
Walking stick	%	12	55	33	1888
Crutches	%	16	41	42	182
Walking frame/ zimmer/tripod	%	41 (17)	24 (49)	34 (34)	296
Trolley	%	44	29	27	70
Manual wheelchair	%	21	46	32	426
Electric wheelchair	%	36 (23)	40 (46)	24 (32)	70
Buggy/scooter	%	15	47	38	53
Other	%	35	26	39	82

10 Smoking

Trends in cigarette smoking: 1974 - 1996

During the 1970s and 1980s there was a steady fall in the proportion of men and women who smoked cigarettes but this decline has levelled out during the 1990s. A higher proportion of men than women smoked during this period, but the gap has been closing and in 1996 it was negligible. In 1996:

- 29% of men and 28% of women smoked compared with 51% and 41% in 1974 (the first time questions about smoking were asked on the GHS in their current form).

Between 1994 and 1996, there was an increase in the proportion of women who smoked cigarettes bringing the prevalence rate for women back up to the same level as in 1992. This increase was only significant among the 25-34 year old age-group. It is too soon to tell whether this is the start of an upward trend or part of the levelling out of the proportion of women smoking. In 1996:

- 28% of women smoked cigarettes compared with 26% in 1994;
- 34% of women aged 25-34 smoked cigarettes (the same as in 1992) compared with 30% in 1994;
- 29% of men smoked cigarettes compared with 28% in 1994 but this change was not statistically significant.

Cigarette smoking varies according to people's age. In 1996:

- men and women aged 20-24 (43% and 36% respectively) were more likely than any other age-group to smoke cigarettes;

- people aged 60 and over (18% for men and 19% for women) were the least likely to smoke cigarettes.
Figures 10A-10B, Table 10.1

The proportion of ex-regular cigarette smokers, and those who never (or only occasionally smoked) has increased over the life of the survey. For example, in 1996:

- 32% of men and 20% of women were ex-regular smokers compared with 23% of men and 11% of women in 1974;
- men and women aged 60 and over were more likely than any other age-group to be ex-regular smokers (55% and 28% respectively);
- 40% of men had never smoked compared with 25% in 1974. A higher proportion of women had never smoked (53%) but there has been little change since 1974 when it was 49%;
- those aged 16-19 were the most likely group never to have smoked cigarettes (69% of men and 63% of women).
Tables 10.2-10.3

In the 1990s there has been little or no change in the proportions of men and women who were light smokers (under 20 per day), although there has been a slight fall in the proportion of men who were heavy smokers (20 or more per day). In 1996:

- 17% of men and 19% of women smoked fewer than 20 cigarettes per day;
- 11% of men were heavy smokers compared with 15% in 1986 and 26% in 1974;
- 8% of women were heavy smokers compared with 10% in 1986 and 13% in 1974;

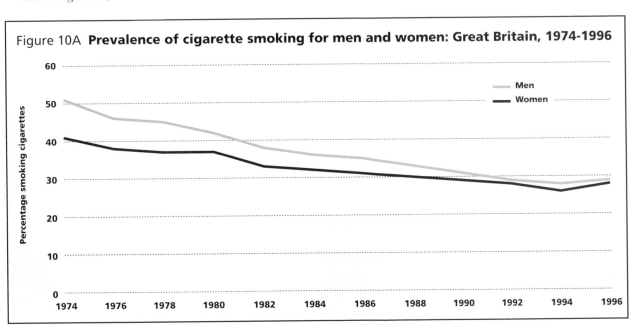

Figure 10A **Prevalence of cigarette smoking for men and women: Great Britain, 1974-1996**

- men (15%) and women (12%) aged 35-49 were the most likely group to be heavy smokers.

Tables 10.4-10.5

Age first started smoking regularly

Over a third (37%) of people who had ever smoked regularly began before they were aged 16 and people in manual social classes were more likely to start smoking early than those in non-manual classes. In 1996, among people who had ever smoked regularly:

- nearly a quarter (24%) from professional households had started smoking before the age of 16 compared with 42% where the head of household's socio-economic group was defined as semi-skilled;
- men were more likely to have started to smoke before the age of 16 than women (41% compared with 32%);
- nearly one in ten women (9%) started smoking when they were aged 25 or more.

Tables 10.6-10.7

Regional variation

In 1976 a higher proportion of people in Scotland smoked cigarettes than in England and Wales and this continues to be the case 20 years later. In 1996:

- 32% of adults in Scotland smoked cigarettes compared with 46% in 1976;
- 27% of adults in Wales were smokers compared with 41% in 1976;
- 28% of adults in England smoked compared with 41% in 1976;
- in England, the prevalence of cigarette smoking was highest in the North (31%) and lowest in East Anglia (25%).

Table 10.8

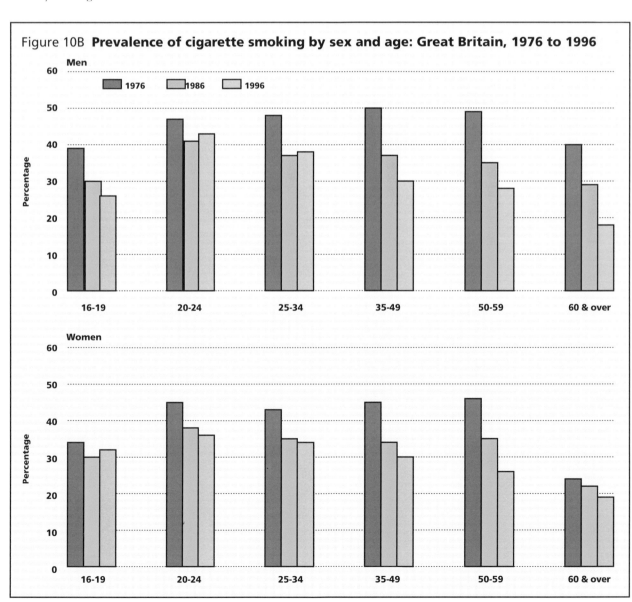

Figure 10B **Prevalence of cigarette smoking by sex and age: Great Britain, 1976 to 1996**

Cigarette smoking and socio-economic group

Smoking behaviour varies according to economic status and socio-economic group and prevalence continues to be higher among those households where the head of household's socio-economic group was classified as manual. In 1996:

- 35% of men in manual households and 21% in non-manual households smoked cigarettes compared with 56% and 45% respectively in 1974;
- men in the unskilled manual group were more than four times as likely to smoke as those in households where the socio-economic group of the head of household was classified as professional (45% compared with 11% respectively);

- women living in semi-skilled and unskilled manual households were more likely to smoke than women in professional households (36% compared with 12%). The pattern was similar when socio-economic group was based on women's own or last job;

  Tables 10.10-10.11

- economically active men were more likely to smoke cigarettes than economically inactive men (31% compared with 24%) and this was found in all socio-economic groups. The lower proportion of male smokers who were economically inactive can be largely explained by the lower prevalence of smoking among older men, who form the majority of the economically inactive group;
- smoking was more prevalent among economically inactive women aged less than 60 than among women who were economically active (35% compared with

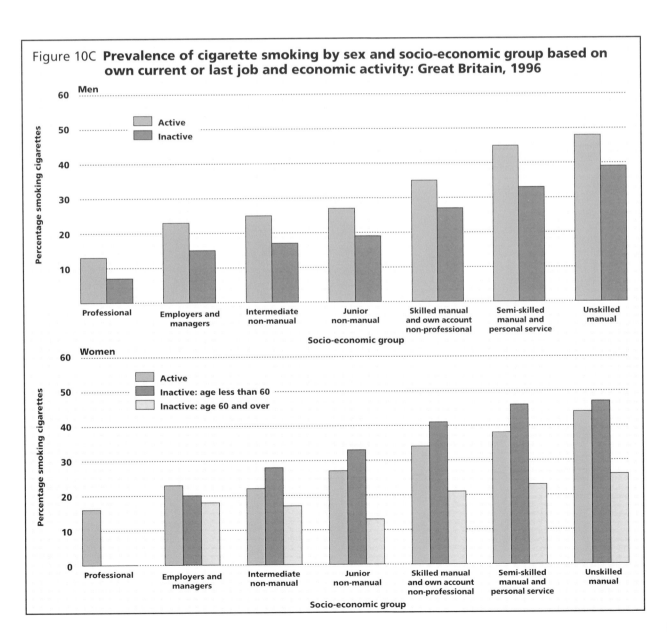

Figure 10C **Prevalence of cigarette smoking by sex and socio-economic group based on own current or last job and economic activity: Great Britain, 1996**

29%). Prevalence was lowest amongst women who were economically inactive and aged 60 or over (19%);

- nearly half of all economically active men and economically inactive women aged 16-59 in the unskilled manual group smoked cigarettes (48% and 47%) - the highest prevalence level of any socio-economic group.

Table 10.12, Figure 10C

Cigarette consumption

Over the period of the survey women smokers have always smoked, on average, fewer cigarettes per week than men. There has, however, been a fall in the number of cigarettes smoked by male smokers between 1974 and 1996 but for women there has been little change. Consumption rates have fallen among younger age-groups but have increased among older age women smokers. In 1996:

- women smokers smoked, on average, 96 cigarettes per week while men smoked, on average, 111 cigarettes per week. In 1974, the average for women smokers was 94 cigarettes per week and for men it was 125;
- male smokers aged 16-19, smoked an average of 82 cigarettes per week compared with 110 in 1974. For women it was 68 per week in 1996 compared with 86 in 1974;
- women aged 60 and over, who smoked, smoked an average of 89 cigarettes per week compared with 68 in 1974. Among men there was no significant difference (107 cigarettes per week in 1996 compared with 100 in 1974). **Table 10.14**

Cigarette type and tar level

The majority of smokers continue to smoke filter cigarettes but in recent years there has been an increase in the proportion smoking hand-rolled cigarettes. In 1996, of those who smoked:

- 75% of men and 93% of women smoked filter cigarettes;
- 23% of men smoked hand-rolled cigarettes compared with 13% in 1974. Throughout much of the 1980s and early 1990s there was little change in the proportion smoking hand-rolled cigarettes but more recently there has been an increase from 18% in 1992 to 21% in 1994 and 23% in 1996;
- 6% of women smoked hand-rolled cigarettes compared with 4% in 1994 and 2% in 1992. The prevalence rate was 1% in 1974. **Tables 10.18-10.19**

Cigarette tar levels have reduced in recent years and therefore for the analysis of the 1996 data a new tar level category has been introduced for manufactured cigarettes.[2] In 1996:

- men were more likely than women smokers to smoke high tar cigarettes (62% compared with 52% respectively);
- younger smokers were the most likely to smoke high tar cigarettes (79% of men and 66% of women aged 16-19);
- men and women smokers in households headed by manual workers (66% and 57% respectively) were more likely than those households headed by non-manual workers (56% and 47%) to smoke high tar cigarettes. **Tables 10.20-10.21**

Prevalence of cigar and pipe smoking

The prevalence of cigar and pipe smoking among men has fallen dramatically over the period of the survey. In 1996:

- 6% of men smoked cigars compared with 34% in 1974;
- 2% of men smoked pipes compared with 12% in 1974;
- nearly one in ten (9%) of men aged 50-59 smoked a cigar;
- fewer than 1% of women smoked cigars. **Tables 10.22-10.23**

Dependence on cigarette smoking

Current cigarette smokers were asked how easy or difficult they would find it to go without smoking for a whole day and whether they would like to give up smoking altogether.

- Almost three-fifths (58%) of current smokers said that they would find it very or fairly difficult to go without smoking for one day.
- Women were more likely than male cigarette smokers to say they would find it difficult to go without smoking for a whole day (61% compared with 56% respectively).
- People smoking 20 or more cigarettes a day were more likely to say it would be difficult to go without smoking for a day than those smoking less than 10 a day (83% compared with 23%).
- Younger smokers were less likely than older smokers to say that they would find it difficult to go a day without smoking (44% of those aged 16-24 compared with 63% of those aged 60 and over).

- Two-thirds of men and women smokers (66% and 67%) said that they would like to give up smoking altogether.
- Smokers aged 60 and over (57% of men and 60% of women) were least likely to want to stop smoking altogether.
- Smokers who said they would find it most difficult to stop smoking for one day were also those who were most likely to want to give up altogether - 70% of this group wanted to stop smoking completely compared with only 50% of those who thought it would be very easy to stop smoking for a day.

One measure of smoking addiction is how long after waking a person smokes their first cigarette of the day. In 1996:

- 15% of smokers had their first cigarette within 5 minutes of waking. A third of both men and women smokers (34% and 33%) had their first cigarette within 15 minutes of waking;

- heavy smokers (those smoking 20 or more cigarettes per day) were most likely to smoke their first cigarette within 5 minutes of waking - 30% did so, compared with only 2% of those who smoked less than 10 cigarettes per day;
- smokers who had their first cigarette within 5 minutes of waking were the most likely to say they would have difficulty in stopping smoking for one day while smokers who had their first cigarette 2 hours or more after waking were the least likely (88% compared with 18%). **Tables 10.24-10.31, Figure 10D**

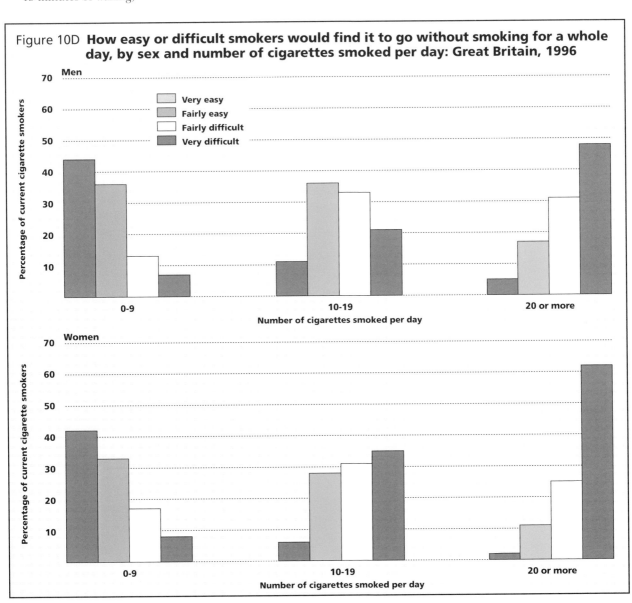

Figure 10D **How easy or difficult smokers would find it to go without smoking for a whole day, by sex and number of cigarettes smoked per day: Great Britain, 1996**

Notes and references

1. Similar targets apply in Wales and Scotland as part of their own health strategies.

2. Tar levels correspond to the most recent available tar yield figures determined by the Laboratory of the Government Chemist and published by the Department of Health.

Very low tar	less than 4mg per cigarette
Low tar	4 but less than 10mg per cigarette
Low to middle tar	10 but less than 12mg per cigarette
Middle tar	12 but less than 15mg per cigarette
High tar	15mg or more per cigarette

3. See *Chapter 4, General Household Survey 1992*, HMSO (1994).

Table 10.1 **Prevalence of cigarette smoking by sex and age: 1974 to 1996**

Persons aged 16 and over   *Great Britain*

Age	1974	1976	1978	1980	1982	1984	1986	1988	1990	1992	1994	1996	Base (1996)* =100%
						Percentage smoking cigarettes							
Men													
16-19	42	39	35	32	31	29	30	28	28	29	28	26	406
20-24	52	47	45	44	41	40	41	37	38	39	40	43	471
25-34	56	48	48	47	40	40	37	37	36	34	34	38	1322
35-49	55	50	48	45	40	39	37	37	34	32	31	30	1947
50-59	53	49	48	47	42	39	35	33	28	28	27	28	1090
60 and over	44	40	38	36	33	30	29	26	24	21	18	18	1936
All aged 16 and over	51	46	45	42	38	36	35	33	31	29	28	29	7172
Women													
16-19	38	34	33	32	30	32	30	28	32	25	27	32	403
20-24	44	45	43	40	40	36	38	37	39	37	38	36	567
25-34	46	43	42	44	37	36	35	35	34	34	30	34	1615
35-49	49	45	43	43	38	36	34	35	33	30	28	30	2321
50-59	48	46	42	44	40	39	35	34	29	29	26	26	1202
60 and over	26	24	24	24	23	23	22	21	20	19	17	19	2393
All aged 16 and over	41	38	37	37	33	32	31	30	29	28	26	28	8501
Total													
16-19	40	36	34	32	30	31	30	28	30	27	27	29	809
20-24	48	46	44	42	40	38	39	37	38	38	39	39	1038
25-34	51	45	45	46	38	38	36	36	35	34	32	36	2937
35-49	52	48	45	44	39	37	36	36	34	31	30	30	4268
50-59	51	47	45	45	41	39	35	33	29	29	27	27	2292
60 and over	34	31	30	29	27	26	25	23	21	20	17	18	4329
All aged 16 and over	45	42	40	39	35	34	33	32	30	28	27	28	15673

* Bases for earlier years are of a similar size and can be found in GHS Reports for each year.

Table 10.2 **Ex-regular cigarette smokers by sex and age: 1974 to 1996**

Persons aged 16 and over   *Great Britain*

Age	1974	1976	1978	1980	1982	1984	1986	1988	1990	1992	1994	1996	Base (1996)* = 100%
						Percentage of ex-regular cigarette smokers							
Men													
16-19	3	5	4	5	4	5	5	4	4	5	5	5	406
20-24	9	11	9	8	9	8	11	10	8	8	7	10	471
25-34	18	20	18	18	20	20	20	17	16	16	16	13	1322
35-49	21	27	26	27	32	31	33	31	32	29	27	27	1947
50-59	30	33	35	35	38	37	38	41	42	41	40	41	1090
60 and over	37	43	43	45	47	48	52	53	52	55	55	55	1936
All 16 and over	23	27	27	28	30	30	32	32	32	32	31	32	7172
Women													
16-19	4	5	5	4	6	6	7	5	6	5	6	5	403
20-24	9	10	8	9	9	9	9	8	8	9	10	11	567
25-34	12	13	14	13	15	16	16	16	14	15	14	13	1615
35-49	10	12	13	13	15	17	20	21	20	22	21	18	2321
50-59	13	15	18	17	19	18	18	19	20	22	22	25	1202
60 and over	11	14	16	19	20	22	23	25	27	29	29	28	2393
All 16 and over	11	12	14	14	16	17	18	19	19	21	21	20	8501

* See the footnote to Table 10.1.

Table 10.3 **Percentage who have never smoked cigarettes regularly by sex and age: 1974 to 1996**

Persons aged 16 and over   *Great Britain*

Age	1974	1976	1978	1980	1982	1984	1986	1988	1990	1992	1994	1996	*Base (1996)* = 100%*
					Percentage who have never smoked regularly								
Men													
16-19	56	56	61	62	65	66	65	69	68	67	67	69	*406*
20-24	38	42	46	48	50	52	47	53	54	52	53	47	*471*
25-34	26	32	33	34	39	39	43	46	48	50	50	49	*1322*
35-49	24	23	26	27	28	30	30	32	34	39	42	43	*1947*
50-59	16	18	17	18	20	24	26	26	31	31	33	31	*1090*
60 and over	18	18	18	19	20	22	19	22	24	24	27	28	*1936*
All 16 and over	25	27	29	30	32	34	34	35	37	38	40	40	*7172*
Women													
16-19	58	61	62	63	64	62	62	67	62	70	67	63	*403*
20-24	47	45	49	51	51	55	54	55	53	54	52	54	*567*
25-34	42	45	44	43	48	48	48	50	52	51	55	53	*1615*
35-49	41	43	44	44	47	47	46	44	48	49	51	52	*2321*
50-59	38	39	39	39	41	43	47	48	51	49	52	49	*1202*
60 and over	63	62	60	57	57	55	55	54	54	52	54	53	*2393*
All 16 and over	49	50	49	49	51	51	51	51	52	52	54	53	*8501*

* See the footnote to Table 10.1.

Table 10.4 Cigarette-smoking status by sex: 1974 to 1996

Persons aged 16 and over   *Great Britain*

	1974	1976	1978	1980	1982	1984	1986	1988	1990	1992	1994	1996
						Percentages						
Men												
Current cigarette smokers												
Light (under 20 per day)	25	22	22	21	20	20	20	18	17	17	17	17
Heavy (20 or more per day)	26	24	23	21	18	16	15	15	14	12	12	11
Total current cigarette smokers	51	46	45	42	38	36	35	33	31	29	28	29
Ex-regular cigarette smokers	23	27	27	28	30	30	32	32	32	32	31	32
Never or only occasionally smoked cigarettes	25	27	29	30	32	34	34	35	37	38	40	40
Base = 100%	9852	10888	10480	10454	9199	8417	8874	8673	8106	8417	7642	7172
Women												
Current cigarette smokers												
Light (under 20 per day)	28	24	23	23	22	22	21	20	20	19	18	19
Heavy (20 or more per day)	13	14	13	13	11	10	10	10	9	9	8	8
Total current cigarette smokers	41	38	37	37	33	32	31	30	29	28	26	28
Ex-regular cigarette smokers	11	12	14	14	16	17	18	19	19	21	21	20
Never or only occasionally smoked cigarettes	49	50	49	49	51	51	51	51	52	52	54	53
Base = 100%	11480	12554	12156	12100	10641	9788	10304	10122	9445	9764	9108	8501

Table 10.5 Cigarette-smoking status by sex and age

Persons aged 16 and over   *Great Britain: 1996*

Age		Current cigarette smokers			Current non-smokers of cigarettes		Base =100%
		Light (under 20 per day)	Heavy (20 or more per day)	All current smokers	Ex-regular cigarette smokers	Never or only occasionally smoked cigarettes	
Men							
16-19	%	21	5	26	5	69	406
20-24	%	30	13	43	10	47	471
25-34	%	25	13	38	13	49	1322
35-49	%	15	15	30	27	43	1947
50-59	%	15	13	28	41	31	1090
60 and over	%	12	6	18	55	28	1936
All aged 16 and over	%	17	11	29	32	40	7172
Women							
16-19	%	29	3	32	5	63	403
20-24	%	29	7	36	11	54	567
25-34	%	25	9	34	13	53	1615
35-49	%	18	12	30	18	52	2321
50-59	%	16	10	26	25	49	1202
60 and over	%	14	5	19	28	53	2393
All aged 16 and over	%	19	8	28	20	53	8501

Table 10.6 **Age started smoking regularly by socio-economic group of head of household**

Persons aged 16 and over who had ever smoked regularly   *Great Britain: 1996*

Age started smoking regularly	Socio-economic group of head of household							
	Professional	Employers and managers	Intermediate non-manual	Junior non-manual	Skilled manual and own account non-professional	Semi-skilled manual and personal service	Unskilled manual	All persons
	%	%	%	%	%	%	%	%
Under 16	24	32	30	33	41	42	38	37
16-17	28	29	28	26	28	27	25	28
18-19	25	20	22	16	15	14	14	17
20-24	17	14	15	15	10	11	11	12
25 and over	6	5	6	10	6	6	11	6
Base = 100%	*305*	*1538*	*823*	*748*	*2749*	*1408*	*449*	*8020*

Table 10.7 **Age started smoking regularly by sex**

Persons aged 16 and over who had ever smoked regularly   *Great Britain: 1996*

Age started smoking regularly	Men	Women	All
	%	%	%
Under 16	41	32	37
16-17	27	28	28
18-19	17	17	17
20-24	11	13	12
25 and over	4	9	6
Base = 100%	*4295*	*3991*	*8286*

Table 10.8 **Prevalence of cigarette smoking by sex and standard region: 1976 to 1996**

Persons aged 16 and over   *Great Britain*

Standard region*	1976	1978	1980	1982	1984	1986	1988	1990	1992	1994	1996	Base† (1996) =100%
						Percentage smoking cigarettes						
Men												
England												
North	49	43	44	43	36	38	37	33	28	29	28	430
Yorkshire and Humberside	45	43	44	39	41	35	32	29	28	29	30	606
North West	50	46	45	37	36	34	32	34	29	26	30	805
East Midlands	46	43	44	35	33	33	34	29	27	28	25	547
West Midlands	47	44	40	39	35	38	29	31	28	25	28	663
East Anglia	45	44	40	35	27	36	30	28	30	27	24	305
Greater London	46	48	44	38	42	36	38	32	32	32	32	773
Outer Metropolitan Area	41	40	38	35	33	32	30	31	26	26	24	705
Outer South East	45	44	43	37	32	32	32	29	30	28	29	668
South West	43	43	36	35	30	31	29	29	28	27	28	646
All England	45	44	42	37	35	34	32	31	29	28	28	6148
Wales	46	44	45	36	42	33	35	30	32	28	28	367
Scotland	50	48	46	45	43	37	36	33	34	31	33	657
Great Britain	46	45	42	38	36	35	33	31	29	28	29	7172
Women												
England												
North	42	39	39	38	35	33	35	31	32	27	32	532
Yorkshire and Humberside	35	36	38	32	38	32	31	29	28	28	25	756
North West	42	41	41	35	35	35	34	33	30	28	30	934
East Midlands	37	36	35	31	30	29	31	28	23	24	27	631
West Midlands	39	34	35	32	31	31	29	28	25	23	28	791
East Anglia	33	33	32	25	20	28	28	24	25	21	25	329
Greater London	38	37	36	34	33	31	31	29	26	26	27	885
Outer Metropolitan Area	35	34	33	29	28	29	28	27	27	24	25	811
Outer South East	32	31	35	30	30	29	25	27	26	25	26	779
South West	37	37	32	33	29	27	26	25	23	22	26	785
All England	37	36	36	32	32	31	30	28	27	25	27	7233
Wales	37	37	39	34	32	30	28	31	33	27	27	475
Scotland	43	42	42	39	35	35	37	35	34	29	31	793
Great Britain	38	37	37	33	32	31	30	29	28	26	28	8501
All persons												
England												
North	45	41	41	41	36	35	36	32	31	28	31	962
Yorkshire and Humberside	40	39	40	35	39	34	32	29	28	28	28	1362
North West	46	43	43	36	35	35	33	33	30	27	30	1739
East Midlands	41	39	39	33	31	31	32	28	25	26	26	1178
West Midlands	43	39	37	35	33	34	29	29	26	24	28	1454
East Anglia	39	38	36	30	24	31	29	26	27	24	25	634
Greater London			40	36	37	33	34	31	29	29	29	1658
Outer Metropolitan Area	39	39	35	32	30	31	29	29	26	25	25	1516
Outer South East			39	33	31	30	28	28	28	27	28	1447
South West	40	39	34	34	30	29	28	27	25	24	27	1431
All England	41	40	39	35	33	32	31	29	28	26	28	13381
Wales	41	40	42	35	37	31	31	31	32	27	27	842
Scotland	46	45	44	42	39	36	37	34	34	30	32	1450
Great Britain	42	40	39	35	34	33	32	30	28	27	28	15673

* The data have not been standardised to take account of age or socio-economic group.

† Bases for earlier years are of a similar size and can be found in GHS Reports for each year.

161

Table 10.9 Prevalence of cigarette smoking by sex and health region in England

Persons aged 16 and over   *England: 1996*

Health region	Men	Women	Total
		Percentage smoking cigarettes	
Northern and Yorkshire	29	29	29
Trent	27	27	27
Anglia and Oxford	26	25	26
North Thames	31	27	29
South Thames	31	27	29
South and West	25	25	25
West Midlands	28	28	28
North West	29	30	30
All England	28	27	28
Bases = 100%			
Northern and Yorkshire	*714*	*900*	*1614*
Trent	*798*	*940*	*1738*
Anglia and Oxford	*814*	*925*	*1739*
North Thames	*682*	*789*	*1471*
South Thames	*801*	*922*	*1723*
South and West	*857*	*1014*	*1871*
West Midlands	*664*	*793*	*1457*
North West	*818*	*950*	*1768*
All England*	*6148*	*7233*	*13381*

* Addresses are classified to health regions according to their full postcode, but to standard regions according to postcode sector only.

Table 10.10 Cigarette-smoking status by sex and socio-economic group of head of household

Persons aged 16 and over   *Great Britain: 1996*

Socio-economic group of head of household		Current cigarette smokers			Current non-smokers of cigarettes		Base = 100%
		Light (under 20 per day)	Heavy (20 or more per day)	All current smokers	Ex-regular cigarette smokers	Never or only occasionally smoked cigarettes	
Men							
Professional	%	8	3	11	30	59	447
Employers and managers	%	12	8	21	33	47	1652
Intermediate and junior non-manual	%	17	9	25	32	43	1177
Skilled manual and own account							
non-professional	%	19	13	31	34	35	2413
Semi-skilled manual & personal service	%	24	16	40	30	30	983
Unskilled manual	%	26	19	45	24	32	298
Total non-manual	%	13	8	21	32	47	3276
Total manual	%	21	14	35	32	33	3694
All aged 16 and over*	%	17	11	29	32	40	7172
Women							
Professional	%	9	2	12	17	71	432
Employers and managers	%	12	6	18	21	61	1672
Intermediate and junior non-manual	%	21	7	27	20	53	1929
Skilled manual and own account							
non-professional	%	20	10	30	20	50	2346
Semi-skilled manual & personal service	%	24	13	36	19	45	1328
Unskilled manual	%	25	11	36	20	43	435
Total non-manual	%	16	6	22	20	58	4033
Total manual	%	22	11	33	20	47	4109
All aged 16 and over*	%	19	8	28	20	53	8501

* Persons whose head of household was in the Armed Forces or a full-time student are not shown as separate categories but are included in the total.

Table 10.11   Prevalence of cigarette smoking by sex and socio-economic group: 1974 to 1996

Persons aged 16 and over   *Great Britain*

Socio-economic group*	1974	1976	1978	1980	1982	1984	1986	1988	1990	1992	1994	1996	Base (1996)† =100%
							Percentage smoking cigarettes						
Men													
Professional	29	25	25	21	20	17	18	16	16	14	16	12	*431*
Employers and managers	46	38	37	35	29	29	28	26	24	23	20	20	*1483*
Intermediate and junior non-manual	45	40	38	35	30	30	28	25	25	25	24	24	*1288*
Skilled manual and own account non-professional	56	51	49	48	42	40	40	39	36	34	33	32	*2365*
Semi-skilled manual and personal service	56	53	53	49	47	45	43	40	39	39	38	41	*1105*
Unskilled manual	61	58	60	57	49	49	43	43	48	42	40	41	*314*
Total non-manual	45	37	36	33	28	28	26	24	23	22	21	21	*3202*
Total manual	56	52	51	49	44	43	40	40	38	36	35	35	*3784*
All aged 16 and over*	51	46	45	42	38	36	35	33	31	29	28	29	*7172*
Women													
Professional	25	28	23	21	21	15	19	17	16	13	12	11	*410*
Employers and managers	38	35	33	33	29	29	27	26	23	21	20	18	*1553*
Intermediate and junior non-manual	38	36	33	34	30	28	27	27	27	27	23	28	*2187*
Skilled manual and own account non-professional	46	42	42	43	39	37	36	35	32	31	29	30	*2162*
Semi-skilled manual and personal service	43	41	41	39	36	37	35	37	36	35	32	36	*1417*
Unskilled manual	43	38	41	41	41	36	33	39	36	35	34	36	*444*
Total non-manual	38	35	32	32	29	27	26	25	25	23	21	22	*4150*
Total manual	45	41	41	41	38	37	36	36	34	33	31	33	*4023*
All aged 16 and over*	41	38	37	37	33	32	31	30	29	28	26	28	*8501*

* Socio-economic group corresponds to the present job of those currently working and to the last job of those not currently working. Married women whose husbands were in the household are classified according to their husband's occupation. Members of the Armed Forces, persons in inadequately described occupations and all persons who have never worked have not been shown as separate categories but are included in the figures shown as totals.

† See the footnote to Table 10.1.

Table 10.12 **Prevalence of cigarette smoking by sex and socio-economic group based on own current or last job, whether economically active or inactive, and, for economically inactive women, age**

Persons aged 16 and over   *Great Britain: 1996*

Socio-economic group*	Men			Women				
	Active	Inactive	Total	Active	Inactive 16-59	Inactive 60 and over	Total inactive	Total
				Percentage smoking cigarettes				
Professional	13	7	12	16	†	†	†	17
Employers and managers	23	15	20	23	20	18	18	21
Intermediate non-manual	25	17	23	22	28	17	22	22
Junior non-manual	27	19	25	27	33	13	22	25
Skilled manual and own account non-professional	35	27	32	34	41	21	28	31
Semi-skilled manual and personal service	45	33	41	38	46	23	33	35
Unskilled manual	48	39	45	44	47	26	33	38
All aged 16 and over	31	24	29	29	35	19	26	28
Bases=100%								
Professional	*321*	*96*	*417*	*106*	*13*	*6*	*19*	*125*
Employers and managers	*1028*	*444*	*1472*	*470*	*87*	*158*	*245*	*715*
Intermediate non-manual	*515*	*161*	*676*	*854*	*244*	*298*	*542*	*1396*
Junior non-manual	*395*	*118*	*513*	*1399*	*459*	*641*	*1100*	*2499*
Skilled manual and own account non-professional	*1528*	*810*	*2338*	*349*	*110*	*217*	*327*	*676*
Semi-skilled manual and personal service	*710*	*320*	*1030*	*799*	*424*	*521*	*945*	*1744*
Unskilled manual	*161*	*118*	*279*	*243*	*140*	*261*	*401*	*644*
All aged 16 and over	*4879*	*2288*	*7167*	*4460*	*1822*	*2212*	*4034*	*8494*

* Full-time students, members of the Armed Forces, and those who have never worked are not shown as separate categories but are included in the totals.

† Base too small to enable reliable analysis to be made.

Table 10.13 **Cigarette-smoking status by sex and marital status**

Persons aged 16 and over   *Great Britain: 1996*

Marital status		Current cigarette smokers			Current non-smokers of cigarettes		Base = 100%
		Light (under 20 per day)	Heavy (20 or more per day)	Total	Ex-regular cigarette smokers	Never or only occasionally smoked cigarettes	
Men							
Single	%	24	12	35	12	53	*1484*
Married/cohabiting	%	15	10	26	36	38	*4931*
Married couple	%	14	10	24	38	37	*4393*
Cohabiting couple	%	27	15	42	19	39	*538*
Widowed/divorced/separated	%	18	14	32	39	29	*757*
All aged 16 and over	%	17	11	29	32	40	*7172*
Women							
Single	%	27	6	33	10	57	*1365*
Married/cohabiting	%	16	9	25	21	54	*5355*
Married couple	%	15	8	23	22	55	*4770*
Cohabiting couple	%	28	14	42	18	40	*585*
Widowed/divorced/separated	%	21	9	31	23	46	*1781*
All aged 16 and over	%	19	8	28	20	53	*8501*

Table 10.14 **Average weekly cigarette consumption per smoker by sex and age: 1974 to 1996**

Current cigarette smokers aged 16 and over   *Great Britain*

Age	1974	1976	1978	1980	1982	1984	1986	1988	1990	1992	1994	1996	Standard deviation (1996)	Base (1996)* = 100%
						Mean number of cigarettes per week								
Men														
16-19	110	106	98	99	87	87	86	84	89	81	71	82	47.7	104
20-24	132	135	122	113	114	107	108	109	110	92	94	101	65.4	203
25-34	136	138	134	135	121	114	110	120	115	100	107	102	61.2	505
35-49	138	141	138	140	137	130	133	136	135	130	126	126	68.1	588
50-59	127	130	137	130	129	126	120	132	121	129	142	119	64.2	303
60 and over	100	108	104	102	109	103	103	102	106	102	99	107	61.1	341
All aged 16 and over	125	129	127	124	121	115	115	120	118	112	114	111	64.6	2044
Women														
16-19	86	89	90	84	76	80	77	79	80	70	70	68	45.2	129
20-24	99	110	101	102	100	91	85	95	92	88	90	79	47.1	202
25-34	108	109	113	111	109	105	101	103	103	97	97	92	52.5	552
35-49	104	112	109	115	108	107	112	113	106	111	104	109	57.7	694
50-59	91	103	101	105	101	98	99	102	107	105	106	109	53.7	313
60 and over	68	75	79	73	77	80	84	81	81	81	89	89	51.4	448
All aged 16 and over	94	101	101	102	98	96	97	99	97	97	97	96	54.6	2338

* See the footnote to Table 10.1.

Table 10.15 **Average weekly cigarette consumption per smoker by sex and socio-economic group: 1974 to 1996**

*Current cigarette smokers aged 16 and over**   *Great Britain*

Socio-economic group*	1974	1976	1978	1980	1982	1984	1986	1988	1990	1992	1994	1996	Standard deviation (1996)	Base (1996)† = 100%
						Mean number of cigarettes per week								
Men														
Professional	107	103	100	98	108	108	85	109	101	99	103	90	60.2	52
Employers and managers	134	132	128	125	139	121	130	132	126	123	122	121	70.1	298
Intermediate and junior non-manual	118	124	120	120	109	108	103	113	104	100	103	99	63.6	306
Skilled manual and own account non-professional	130	133	131	130	126	121	118	122	122	114	119	115	62.0	755
Semi-skilled manual and personal service	120	128	126	122	118	108	114	117	117	111	107	110	64.6	451
Unskilled manual	117	118	120	118	120	114	110	111	120	109	118	117	65.7	129
All aged 16 and over*	125	129	127	124	121	115	115	120	118	112	114	111	64.6	2044
Women														
Professional	82	81	72	86	73	78	82	90	94	74	93	82	61.2	45
Employers and managers	97	101	94	96	97	93	101	101	96	95	94	99	56.9	274
Intermediate and junior non-manual	89	98	97	95	92	93	91	88	90	86	83	87	52.7	606
Skilled manual and own account non-professional	100	107	107	110	106	101	99	104	100	106	106	102	54.2	657
Semi-skilled manual and personal service	92	102	103	103	98	99	101	102	102	98	100	101	53.2	512
Unskilled manual	91	96	102	97	93	96	92	104	99	103	106	99	57.5	159
All aged 16 and over*	94	101	101	102	98	96	97	99	97	97	97	96	54.6	2338

* See the first footnote to Table 10.11
† See the footnote to Table 10.1.

Table 10.16 **Number of cigarettes smoked per day by sex: 1974 to 1996**

Current cigarette smokers aged 16 and over   *Great Britain*

No. of cigarettes smoked per day	1974	1976	1978	1980	1982	1984	1986	1988	1990	1992	1994	1996
	%	%	%	%	%	%	%	%	%	%	%	%
Men												
Under 10	18	18	18	19	15	20	21	19	19	24	23	22
10-19	31	30	31	31	35	36	36	35	36	35	36	39
20-29	36	36	36	36	37	35	32	34	34	31	31	29
30 or more	15	16	15	14	13	10	11	12	11	10	10	10
Base = 100%	*4968*	*4986*	*4618*	*4394*	*3323*	*3045*	*3057*	*2849*	*2487*	*2469*	*2142*	*2044*
Women												
Under 10	31	28	29	27	23	28	28	27	26	27	27	28
10-19	36	35	35	37	41	40	40	40	42	42	43	41
20-29	27	29	28	29	30	27	27	28	27	27	26	26
30 or more	6	8	8	7	6	5	5	5	4	4	4	4
Base = 100%	*4627*	*4728*	*4426*	*4416*	*3274*	*3127*	*3171*	*3076*	*2734*	*2693*	*2332*	*2338*

Table 10.17 **Number of cigarettes smoked per day by sex and age**

Current cigarette smokers aged 16 and over   *Great Britain: 1996*

Age		Men				Base = 100%	Women				Base = 100%
		No. of cigarettes smoked per day					No. of cigarettes smoked per day				
		Under 10	10-19	20-29	30 or more		Under 10	10-19	20-29	30 or more	
16-19	%	32	50	16	2	*104*	50	40	9	1	*129*
20-24	%	29	42	23	7	*203*	39	42	18	1	*202*
25-29	%	30	38	26	7	*265*	35	41	21	3	*292*
30-34	%	23	42	27	8	*240*	27	45	25	3	*260*
35-49	%	16	35	35	14	*588*	20	39	33	7	*694*
50-59	%	20	34	33	13	*303*	20	41	34	5	*313*
60 and over	%	20	47	25	9	*341*	31	43	22	4	*448*
All aged 16 and over	%	22	39	29	10	*2044*	28	41	26	4	*2338*

Table 10.18 **Type of cigarette smoked by sex: 1974 to 1996**

Current cigarette smokers aged 16 and over   *Great Britain*

Type of cigarette smoked	1974	1976	1978	1980	1982	1984	1986	1988	1990	1992	1994	1996
	%	%	%	%	%	%	%	%	%	%	%	%
Men												
Mainly filter	69	71	75	77	72	77	78	79	80	80	78	75
Mainly plain	18	15	11	8	7	6	4	3	2	2	2	1
Mainly hand-rolled	13	14	14	15	21	17	18	18	18	18	21	23
Base = 100%	*4993*	*4989*	*4646*	*4422*	*3469*	*3062*	*3072*	*2849*	*2510*	*2473*	*2150*	*2052*
Women												
Mainly filter	91	93	95	95	94	95	96	96	97	97	96	93
Mainly plain	8	6	4	3	3	2	1	1	1	1	1	1
Mainly hand-rolled	1	1	1	1	3	3	2	2	2	2	4	6
Base = 100%	*4600*	*4697*	*4421*	*4441*	*3522*	*3144*	*3192*	*3076*	*2748*	*2698*	*2336*	*2341*

Table 10.19   **Type of cigarette smoked by age and sex**

Current cigarette smokers aged 16 and over   Great Britain: 1996

Type of cigarette smoked	Age					
	16-24	25-34	35-49	50-59	60 and over	All aged 16 and over
	%	%	%	%	%	%
Men						
Mainly filter	86	78	72	70	73	75
Mainly plain	1	0	1	1	3	1
Mainly hand-rolled	13	22	27	29	24	23
Base=100%	*307*	*507*	*589*	*305*	*344*	*2052*
Women						
Mainly filter	92	93	93	96	94	93
Mainly plain	2	0	0	1	2	1
Mainly hand-rolled	7	7	7	4	4	6
Base=100%	*331*	*552*	*695*	*313*	*450*	*2341*

Table 10.20   **Tar levels* by sex and age**

Current smokers of manufactured† cigarettes aged 16 and over   Great Britain: 1996

		Tar level								Base = 100%
		Very low	Low	Low to middle	Middle to high	High	Very high	No regular brand	New brand/ don't know	
Men										
16-19	%	0	4	9	6	79	0	0	2	*90*
20-24	%	3	15	5	6	69	0	0	2	*177*
25-34	%	10	16	9	7	55	0	0	2	*394*
35-49	%	6	7	11	9	64	0	0	3	*430*
50-59	%	6	6	12	9	62	0	0	6	*216*
60 and over	%	6	7	15	10	60	0	0	3	*258*
Total	%	7	10	10	8	62	0	0	3	*1565*
Women										
16-19	%	3	14	6	6	66	2	0	3	*119*
20-24	%	10	18	12	5	52	0	0	3	*186*
25-34	%	10	16	12	6	53	0	0	2	*515*
35-49	%	10	9	18	8	52	0	0	3	*641*
50-59	%	11	8	20	6	51	0	0	3	*301*
60 and over	%	8	7	25	7	49	0	0	3	*433*
Total	%	9	11	17	7	52	0	0	3	*2195*
Total										
16-19	%	1	10	7	6	72	1	0	3	*209*
20-24	%	7	16	8	6	60	0	0	3	*363*
25-34	%	10	16	11	6	54	0	0	2	*909*
35-49	%	8	8	15	8	57	0	0	3	*1071*
50-59	%	9	7	16	7	56	0	0	4	*517*
60 and over	%	7	7	21	8	53	0	0	3	*691*
Total	%	8	11	14	7	56	0	0	3	*3760*

* Tar levels have been grouped differently in 1996 to previous years.

Tar levels per cigarette :	Very low	Low	Low to middle	Middle	High
	Less than 4mg	4<10mg	10<12mg	12<15mg	15+mg

† Twenty three per cent of male smokers and 6 per cent of female smokers said they mainly smoked hand-rolled cigarettes and have been excluded from this analysis.

Table 10.21 Tar levels* by socio-economic group of head of household

Current smokers of manufactured† cigarettes aged 16 and over Great Britain: 1996

Socio-economic group of head of household		Tar levels								Base = 100%
		Very low	Low	Low to middle	Middle to high	High	Very high	No regular brand	New brand/ don't know	
Men										
Professional	%	[16]	[25]	[2]	[9]	[45]	[0]	[0]	[2]	44
Employers and managers	%	11	14	12	7	55	0	0	2	286
Intermediate and junior non-manual	%	9	11	9	8	59	0	0	3	236
Skilled manual and own account non-professional	%	4	6	12	8	66	0	0	4	560
Semi-skilled manual and personal service	%	4	7	9	9	67	0	0	3	289
Unskilled manual	%	2	8	9	15	64	0	0	2	89
Total non-manual	%	11	14	10	7	56	0	0	2	566
Total manual	%	4	7	11	9	66	0	0	3	938
All aged 16 and over**	%	7	10	10	8	62	0	0	3	1564
Women										
Professional	%	[10]	[19]	[19]	[8]	[38]	[0]	[2]	[4]	48
Employers and managers	%	14	14	17	7	45	0	0	2	289
Intermediate and junior non-manual	%	13	12	18	4	50	0	0	2	492
Skilled manual and own account non-professional	%	8	10	18	8	55	0	0	2	665
Semi-skilled manual and personal service	%	6	9	15	8	58	0	0	4	453
Unskilled manual	%	7	10	17	5	56	0	0	5	147
Total non-manual	%	13	13	18	6	47	0	0	2	829
Total manual	%	7	9	16	7	57	0	0	3	1265
All aged 16 and over**	%	9	11	17	7	52	0	0	3	2194

*† See the footnotes to Table 10.20.
** See the footnote to Table 10.10.

Table 10.22 Prevalence of smoking by sex and type of product smoked: 1974 to 1996

Persons aged 16 and over Great Britain

	1974	1976	1978	1980	1982	1984	1986	1988	1990	1992	1994	1996
						Percentage smoking						
Men												
Cigarettes*	51	46	45	43	38	37	35	33	31	29	28	29
Pipe	12	11	10	..	..	..	6	4	4	4	3	2
Cigars†	34	31	16	14	12	10	10	9	8	7	6	6
All smokers**	64	60	55	50††	45††	43††	44	40	38	36	33	33
Base = 100%	9862	10894	10439	10433	9171	8377	8884	8673	8119	8427	7662	7186
Women												
Cigarettes*	41	38	37	37	33	32	31	30	29	28	26	28
Cigars†	3	3	1	0	0	0	1	0	0	0	0	0
All smokers**	41	39	37	37	34	33	31	31	29	28	26	28
Base = 100%	11419	12515	12079	12067	10559	9681	10312	10122	9455	9772	9137	8512

* Figures for cigarettes include all smokers of manufactured and hand-rolled cigarettes.
† For 1974 and 1976 the figures include occasional cigar smokers, that is, those who smoked less than one cigar a month.
** The percentages for cigarettes, pipes and cigars add to more than the percentage for all smokers because some people smoked more than one type of product.
†† In 1980, 1982 and 1984 men were not asked about pipe smoking, and therefore the figures for all smokers exclude those who smoked only a pipe.

Table 10.23 **Prevalence of smoking by type of product smoked by sex and age**

Persons aged 16 and over *Great Britain: 1996*

Age	Men					Women			
	Cigarettes*	Pipe†	Cigars†	All smokers**	Base = 100%	Cigarettes*	Cigars†	All smokers	Base = 100%
	Percentage smoking					Percentage smoking			
16-19	25	0	3	25	*418*	31	1	31	*413*
20-24	43	1	4	44	*472*	36	0	36	*567*
25-29	41	0	6	43	*651*	37	0	37	*790*
30-34	36	1	4	38	*671*	32	0	32	*825*
35-49	30	1	7	36	*1948*	30	0	30	*2321*
50-59	28	3	9	35	*1090*	26	0	26	*1203*
60 and over	18	5	5	25	*1936*	19	0	19	*2393*
All aged 16 and over	29	2	6	33	*7186*	28	0	28	*8512*

* Figures for cigarettes include all smokers of both manufactured and hand-rolled cigarettes.

† Young people aged 16-17 were not asked about cigar or pipe-smoking.

** See the third footnote to Table 10.22.

Table 10.24 **How easy or difficult smokers would find it to go without smoking for a whole day, by sex and number of cigarettes smoked per day**

Current cigarette smokers aged 16 and over *Great Britain: 1996*

Ease or difficulty of not smoking for a day	Number of cigarettes per day			
	20 or more	10-19	0-9	Total*
	%	%	%	%
Men				
Very easy	5	11	44	16
Fairly easy	17	36	36	28
Fairly difficult	31	33	13	27
Very difficult	48	21	7	29
Base=100%	*792*	*799*	*445*	*2044*
	%	%	%	%
Women				
Very easy	2	6	42	15
Fairly easy	11	28	33	24
Fairly difficult	25	31	17	25
Very difficult	62	35	8	36
Base=100%	*711*	*963*	*659*	*2336*
	%	%	%	%
All smokers				
Very easy	4	8	43	15
Fairly easy	14	31	34	26
Fairly difficult	28	32	15	26
Very difficult	55	29	8	32
Base=100%	*1503*	*1762*	*1104*	*4380*

* Includes a few smokers who did not say how many cigarettes a day they smoked.

Table 10.25 **Whether would like to give up smoking altogether, by sex and number of cigarettes smoked per day**

Current cigarette smokers aged 16 and over   *Great Britain: 1996*

Whether would like to give up altogether	Number of cigarettes per day			
	20 or more	10-19	0-9	Total*
Men	%	%	%	%
Yes	66	69	62	66
No	34	31	38	34
Base=100%	*785*	*784*	*434*	*2009*
Women	%	%	%	%
Yes	69	70	59	67
No	31	30	41	33
Base=100%	*707*	*945*	*648*	*2303*
All smokers	%	%	%	%
Yes	68	70	60	67
No	32	30	40	33
Base=100%	*1492*	*1729*	*1082*	*4312*

* Includes a few smokers who did not say how many cigarettes a day they smoked.

Table 10.26 **Proportion of smokers who would like to stop smoking altogether, by sex and whether they would find it easy or difficult to go without smoking for a whole day**

Current cigarette smokers aged 16 and over   *Great Britain: 1996*

	Ease or difficulty of not smoking for a day				
	Very easy	Fairly easy	Fairly difficult	Very difficult	Total
	Percentage who would like to stop altogether				
Men	51	66	71	71	66
Women	50	66	73	69	67
All smokers	50	66	72	70	66
Bases=100%					
Men	*311*	*564*	*553*	*576*	*2004*
Women	*349*	*551*	*576*	*823*	*2299*
All smokers	*660*	*1115*	*1129*	*1399*	*4303*

Table 10.27 **Time between waking and the first cigarette, by sex and number of cigarettes smoked per day**

Current cigarette smokers aged 16 and over   *Great Britain: 1996*

Time between waking and the first cigarette	Number of cigarettes per day			
	20 or more	10-19	0-9	Total*
	%	%	%	%
Men				
Less than 5 minutes	29	9	3	16
5 - 14 minutes	26	17	5	18
15 - 29 minutes	17	17	7	15
30 minutes but less than 1 hour	17	24	9	18
1 hour but less than 2 hours	8	18	15	14
2 hours or more	3	15	61	20
Base=100%	*793*	*804*	*444*	*2048*
	%	%	%	%
Women				
Less than 5 minutes	32	11	1	15
5 - 14 minutes	30	18	4	18
15 - 29 minutes	16	19	6	14
30 minutes but less than 1 hour	15	22	10	16
1 hour but less than 2 hours	6	16	15	13
2 hours or more	1	15	63	24
Base=100%	*713*	*962*	*658*	*2336*
	%	%	%	%
All smokers				
Less than 5 minutes	30	10	2	15
5 - 14 minutes	28	17	5	18
15 - 29 minutes	16	18	6	14
30 minutes but less than 1 hour	16	23	10	17
1 hour but less than 2 hours	7	17	15	13
2 hours or more	2	15	62	22
Base=100%	*1506*	*1766*	*1102*	*4384*

* Includes a few smokers who did not say how many cigarettes a day they smoked.

171

Table 10.28 **Proportion of smokers who would find it difficult to go without smoking for a whole day, by sex, age and number of cigarettes smoked per day**

Current cigarette smokers aged 16 and over   *Great Britain: 1996*

Number of cigarettes smoked per day	Age					
	16-24	25-34	35-49	50-59	60 and over	Total
			Percentages			
Men						
20 or more	72	81	78	77	83	78
10 - 19	45	53	55	57	59	54
0 - 9	14	13	20	31	31	20
All smokers*	43	52	61	61	62	56
Women						
20 or more	92	84	87	87	89	87
10 - 19	58	66	65	67	72	66
0 - 9	16	25	20	37	31	24
All smokers*	45	58	65	69	64	61
Total						
20 or more	80	82	82	82	86	83
10 - 19	51	60	61	62	66	60
0 - 9	15	20	20	34	31	23
All smokers*	44	55	63	65	63	58
Bases=100%						
Men						
20 or more	79	170	291	137	115	792
10 - 19	137	199	202	104	157	799
0 - 9	90	134	93	61	67	445
*All smokers**	307	504	587	304	342	2044
Women						
20 or more	52	144	278	122	115	711
10 - 19	136	235	274	127	191	963
0 - 9	143	171	142	63	140	659
*All smokers**	331	550	695	312	448	2336
Total						
20 or more	131	314	569	259	230	1503
10 - 19	273	434	476	231	348	1762
0 - 9	233	305	235	124	207	1104
*All smokers**	638	1054	1282	616	790	4380

* Includes a few smokers who did not say how many cigarettes a day they smoked.

172

Table 10.29 **Proportion of smokers who would like to give up smoking altogether, by sex, age and number of cigarettes smoked per day**

Current cigarette smokers aged 16 and over   *Great Britain: 1996*

Number of cigarettes smoked per day	Age					
	16-24	25-34	35-49	50-59	60 and over	Total
			Percentages			
Men						
20 or more	55	65	72	65	62	66
10 - 19	70	76	71	70	57	69
0 - 9	61	68	64	56	52	62
All smokers*	63	70	71	65	57	66
Women						
20 or more	67	70	74	66	59	69
10 - 19	74	72	69	68	67	70
0 - 9	66	63	59	52	51	59
All smokers*	69	69	69	64	60	67
Total						
20 or more	60	68	73	66	60	68
10 - 19	72	74	70	69	63	70
0 - 9	64	66	61	54	51	60
All smokers*	67	70	70	65	59	67
Bases=100%						
Men						
20 or more	*74*	*170*	*290*	*136*	*115*	*785*
10 - 19	*123*	*198*	*203*	*102*	*158*	*784*
0 - 9	*82*	*133*	*92*	*61*	*66*	*434*
All smokers*	*279*	*502*	*586*	*301*	*341*	*2009*
Women						
20 or more	*51*	*145*	*274*	*122*	*115*	*707*
10 - 19	*129*	*231*	*271*	*127*	*187*	*945*
0 - 9	*133*	*172*	*140*	*63*	*140*	*648*
All smokers*	*313*	*548*	*686*	*312*	*444*	*2303*
Total						
20 or more	*125*	*315*	*564*	*258*	*230*	*1492*
10 - 19	*252*	*429*	*474*	*229*	*345*	*1729*
0 - 9	*215*	*305*	*232*	*124*	*206*	*1082*
All smokers*	*592*	*1050*	*1272*	*613*	*785*	*4312*

* Includes a few smokers who did not say how many cigarettes a day they smoked.

Table 10.30 **Proportion of smokers who have their first cigarette within five minutes of waking, by sex, age and number of cigarettes smoked per day**

Current cigarette smokers aged 16 and over   *Great Britain: 1996*

Number of cigarettes smoked per day	Age					
	16-24	25-34	35-49	50-59	60 and over	Total
			Percentages			
Men						
20 or more	25	36	29	22	30	29
10 - 19	9	11	5	10	12	9
0 - 9	4	0	3	5	4	3
All smokers*	12	17	17	14	17	16
Women						
20 or more	25	37	36	22	30	32
10 - 19	7	14	10	13	11	11
0 - 9	3	1	1	0	1	1
All smokers*	8	16	18	14	12	15
Total						
20 or more	25	37	32	22	30	30
10 - 19	8	13	8	12	11	10
0 - 9	3	1	2	2	2	2
All smokers*	10	16	18	14	15	15
Bases=100%						
Men						
20 or more	*79*	*170*	*291*	*138*	*115*	*793*
10 - 19	*137*	*201*	*203*	*104*	*159*	*804*
0 - 9	*91*	*134*	*91*	*61*	*67*	*444*
*All smokers**	*308*	*505*	*586*	*305*	*344*	*2048*
Women						
20 or more	*52*	*145*	*278*	*123*	*115*	*713*
10 - 19	*136*	*235*	*274*	*127*	*190*	*962*
0 - 9	*141*	*172*	*141*	*63*	*141*	*658*
*All smokers**	*329*	*552*	*694*	*313*	*448*	*2336*
Total						
20 or more	*131*	*315*	*569*	*261*	*230*	*1506*
10 - 19	*273*	*436*	*477*	*231*	*349*	*1766*
0 - 9	*232*	*306*	*232*	*124*	*208*	*1102*
*All smokers**	*637*	*1057*	*1280*	*618*	*792*	*4384*

* Includes a few smokers who did not say how many cigarettes a day they smoked.

Table 10.31 **How easy or difficult smokers would find it to go without smoking for a whole day, by sex and time between waking and the first cigarette**

Current cigarette smokers aged 16 and over   *Great Britain: 1996*

Ease or difficulty of not smoking for a day	Time between waking and the first cigarette						
	Less than 5 minutes	5 - 14 minutes	15 - 29 minutes	30 minutes but less than 1 hour	1 hour but less than 2 hours	2 hours or more	Total
	%	%	%	%	%	%	%
Men							
Very easy	3	3	6	11	14	48	16
Fairly easy	11	23	29	32	38	37	28
Fairly difficult	24	33	36	33	34	10	28
Very difficult	61	42	29	25	13	4	29
Base=100%	*321*	*368*	*296*	*367*	*277*	*412*	*2041*
	%	%	%	%	%	%	%
Women							
Very easy	2	4	5	5	14	45	15
Fairly easy	7	13	21	28	38	34	24
Fairly difficult	18	29	34	32	27	15	25
Very difficult	73	54	41	34	21	6	36
Base=100%	*340*	*409*	*333*	*384*	*297*	*568*	*2331*
	%	%	%	%	%	%	%
All smokers							
Very easy	3	3	5	8	14	46	15
Fairly easy	9	18	24	30	38	35	26
Fairly difficult	21	31	35	32	31	13	26
Very difficult	67	48	36	30	17	5	32
Base=100%	*661*	*777*	*629*	*751*	*574*	*980*	*4372*

Table 10.32 **Cigarette-smoking status by age and sex: 1996 General Household Survey**

Persons aged 16 and over   *England: 1996*

Cigarette-smoking status*	Age							
	16-24	25-34	35-44	45-54	55-64	65-74	75 and over	Total
	%	%	%	%	%	%	%	%
Men								
Current smokers:								
Less than 10	11	11	5	5	4	4	2	6
10, less than 20	16	15	11	9	9	9	5	11
20 or more	8	12	15	13	12	6	2	11
Total current cigarette smokers†	34	38	31	28	26	19	9	28
Ex-regular smokers	8	12	25	34	48	56	61	32
Never or only occasionally smoked cigarettes	58	50	44	38	27	25	30	40
Base = 100%	*732*	*1163*	*1104*	*1100*	*806*	*729*	*514*	*6148*
Women								
Current smokers:								
Less than 10	15	11	6	6	6	7	3	8
10, less than 20	14	14	12	11	11	9	4	11
20 or more	6	8	11	12	8	5	2	8
Total current cigarette smokers†	35	33	29	30	25	21	9	27
Ex-regular smokers	8	13	18	22	24	30	30	20
Never or only occasionally smoked cigarettes	57	54	53	48	51	48	61	53
Base = 100%	*826*	*1395*	*1312*	*1221*	*926*	*856*	*697*	*7233*

* Current smokers of cigars and pipes only are classified according to their cigarette-smoking status ie. 'never regularly smoked' or 'ex-regular smoker'.
† Includes those for whom number of cigarettes was not known.

Table 10.33 **Cigarette-smoking status by age and sex: 1996 Health Survey**

Persons aged 16 and over   *England: 1996*

Cigarette-smoking status*	Age							
	16-24	25-34	35-44	45-54	55-64	65-74	75 and over	Total
	%	%	%	%	%	%	%	%
Men								
Current smokers:								
Less than 10	13	10	8	5	5	6	5	7
10, less than 20	18	15	11	9	8	7	6	11
20 or more	6	13	15	17	11	6	3	11
All current smokers†	38	39	34	30	23	19	14	30
Ex-regular smokers	5	13	22	35	43	53	63	30
Never regularly smoked	57	48	44	35	33	28	24	40
Base = 100%	*938*	*1363*	*1410*	*1324*	*996*	*895*	*554*	*7480*
Women								
Current smokers:								
Less than 10	14	11	8	7	6	6	5	8
10, less than 20	16	13	11	11	10	10	4	11
20 or more	5	10	11	11	8	4	1	8
All current smokers†	35	34	30	29	24	20	10	27
Ex-regular smokers	8	14	18	25	25	33	32	21
Never regularly smoked	57	52	53	47	51	47	58	51
Base = 100%	*1101*	*1675*	*1603*	*1492*	*1087*	*1100*	*881*	*8939*

* Current smokers of cigars and pipes only are classified according to their cigarette-smoking status ie. 'never regularly smoked' or 'ex-regular smoker'.
† Includes those for whom number of cigarettes was not known.

Table 10.34 Cigarette-smoking status and alcohol consumption level by sex

Persons aged 16 and over — *Great Britain: 1996*

	Consumption level (units per week)*				Base = 100%
	Non-drinker/ very low	Low/ moderate	Fairly high/ high	Very high	
	Percentage of men				
Men					
Current cigarette smokers					
Light (under 20 per day)	2	9	5	1	
Heavy (20 or more per day)	2	5	3	2	
Total current cigarette smokers	4	14	7	3	
Ex-regular cigarette smokers	4	19	7	1	
Never or only occasionally smoked cigarettes	7	25	7	1	
					7159
	Percentage of women				
Women					
Current cigarette smokers					
Light (under 20 per day)	5	10	3	1	
Heavy (20 or more per day)	2	4	1	0	
Total current cigarette smokers	8	14	5	1	
Ex-regular cigarette smokers	6	11	2	0	
Never or only occasionally smoked cigarettes	19	29	4	1	
					8482

* Consumption level (units per week)

	Very low	Low	Moderate	Fairly high	High	Very high
Men	Under 1	1-10	11-21	22-35	36-50	51 and over
Women	Under 1	1-7	8-14	15-25	26-35	36 and over

Table 10.35 Current cigarette-smoking behaviour and alcohol consumption level by sex and age

Persons aged 16 and over — *Great Britain: 1996*

	Men				Women			
	16-24	25-44	45-64	65 and over	16-24	25-44	45-64	65 and over
	%	%	%	%	%	%	%	%
Current non-smokers*								
Non-drinker/very low	13	6	10	22	17	17	24	45
Drinker†								
Low/moderate	35	42	46	49	38	44	40	33
Fairly high/high	14 ⎤ 52	15 ⎤ 59	14 ⎤ 63	11 ⎤ 62	9 ⎤ 49	8 ⎤ 52	7 ⎤ 48	4 ⎤ 39
Very high	4 ⎦	3 ⎦	3 ⎦	2 ⎦	2 ⎦	1 ⎦	1 ⎦	1 ⎦
Current smokers								
Non-drinker/very low	2	4	5	4	4	6	10	9
Drinker†								
Low/moderate	16	18	14	8	19	18	13	6
Fairly high/high	11 ⎤ 33	9 ⎤ 31	6 ⎤ 22	3 ⎤ 11	7 ⎤ 30	6 ⎤ 25	4 ⎤ 18	1 ⎤ 8
Very high	6 ⎦	4 ⎦	2 ⎦	1 ⎦	3 ⎦	2 ⎦	1 ⎦	0 ⎦
Base = 100%	872	2628	2214	1445	965	3182	2509	1836

* Those who have never or only occasionally smoked and ex-regular cigarette smokers are included in the current non-smokers category.

† Consumption level (units per week):

	Very low	Low	Moderate	Fairly high	High	Very high
Men	Under 1	1-10	11-21	22-35	36-50	51 and over
Women	Under 1	1-7	8-14	15-25	26-35	36 and over

177

Table 10.36 Alcohol consumption level (AC rating) by sex and cigarette-smoking status

Persons aged 16 and over   *Great Britain: 1996*

Alcohol consumption level*	Current cigarette smokers			Current non-smokers of cigarettes		All aged 16 and over†
	Heavy (20 or more per day)	Light (under 20 per day)	Total**	Ex-regular smokers	Never/only occasionally smoked	
	%	%	%	%	%	%
Men						
Non-drinker/very low	14	14	14	14	17	15
Low/moderate	46	52	50	60	62	58
Fairly high/high	25 ⎤ 40	26 ⎤ 34	26 ⎤ 36	21 ⎤ 26	18 ⎤ 21	21 ⎤ 27
Very high	15 ⎦	8 ⎦	11 ⎦	5 ⎦	3 ⎦	6 ⎦
Base = 100%	*791*	*1248*	*2049*	*2258*	*2852*	*7169*
Women						
Non-drinker/very low	29	28	28	29	36	33
Low/moderate	49	52	51	56	54	54
Fairly high/high	17 ⎤ 21	16 ⎤ 21	16 ⎤ 21	12 ⎤ 15	8 ⎤ 10	11 ⎤ 14
Very high	5 ⎦	4 ⎦	5 ⎦	2 ⎦	1 ⎦	2 ⎦
Base = 100%	*712*	*1622*	*2337*	*1673*	*4482*	*8496*

*   See the footnote to Table 10.34.
†   Total includes no answers to cigarette-smoking status.
** Total includes no answers to number of cigarettes smoked per day.

Table 10.37 Cigarette-smoking status by sex and alcohol consumption level (AC rating)

Persons aged 16 and over   *Great Britain: 1996*

Alcohol consumption level*		Current cigarette smokers			Current non-smokers of cigarettes		Base = 100%
		Heavy (20 or more per day)	Light (under 20 per day)	Total†	Ex-regular smokers	Never/only occasionally smoked	
Men							
Non-drinker/very low	%	10	15	26	29	45	*1093*
Low/moderate	%	9	16	25	33	43	*4132*
Fairly high/high	%	13	22	35	32	33	*1511*
Very high	%	28	24	52	25	23	*423*
All aged 16 and over**	%	11	17	29	32	40	*7172*
Women							
Non-drinker/very low	%	7	16	24	18	59	*2771*
Low/moderate	%	8	18	26	21	53	*4556*
Fairly high/high	%	12	27	40	22	39	*972*
Very high	%	20	36	56	19	25	*193*
All aged 16 and over†**	%	8	19	28	20	53	*8501*

*   See the footnote to Table 10.34.
†   Total includes no answers to number of cigarettes smoked per day.
** Total includes cases where alcohol consumption level could not be calculated.

178

11 Drinking

Questions about drinking alcohol have been included in the GHS every two years since 1978 and since 1984, trends have been measured in terms of alcohol consumption level (AC).

Sensible Drinking[1] , the 1995 report of an inter-departmental review of the scientific and medical evidence on the effects of drinking alcohol, concluded that daily benchmarks were more appropriate than the previously recommended weekly levels since they could help individuals decide how much to drink on single occasions and to avoid episodes of intoxication with their attendant health and social risks. The Department of Health's advice on sensible drinking is now based on these daily benchmarks. Revised targets to reflect this new advice are being considered in the context of the Government's new alcohol strategy. In the absence of new targets, the previous recommended weekly maximum levels of 21 units for men and 14 units for women have been retained to provide ready comparability with previous GHS data.

More details relating to the health effects of drinking alcohol and a full description of the methodology can be found in Appendix A.

Trends in alcohol consumption: 1984 - 1996

Since 1984, alcohol consumption levels (units per week) have remained fairly constant for men, while for women there has been a gradual increase. In 1996:

- 27% of men aged 18 and over were drinking more than 21 units per week, which represented no change since the increase from 25% to 27% between 1984 and 1986;

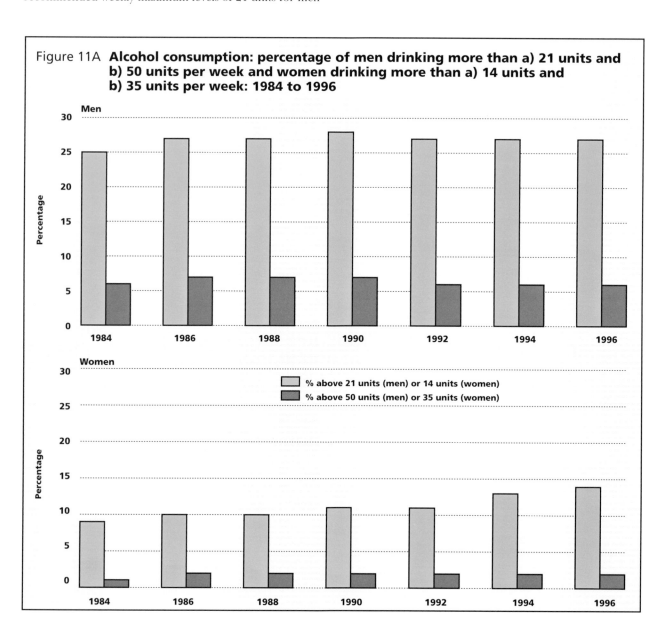

Figure 11A **Alcohol consumption: percentage of men drinking more than a) 21 units and b) 50 units per week and women drinking more than a) 14 units and b) 35 units per week: 1984 to 1996**

% above 21 units (men) or 14 units (women)
% above 50 units (men) or 35 units (women)

- 14% of women aged 18 and over were drinking more than 14 units a week, which continued the gradual increase from 9% in 1984;

- there has been no change in the proportion of men or women with very high levels of alcohol consumption (6% of men drank more than 50 units per week and 2% of women drank more than 35 units per week);

Figure 11A, Table 11.1

- the proportion of non-drinkers has remained unchanged since 1984 at 7% of men and 13% of women ;

Table 11.1

- the number of units consumed averaged over drinkers and non-drinkers showed similar trends, with no change between 1992 and 1996 among men aged 16 and over (15.9 and 16.0 units per week respectively), but an increase among women from 5.4 units per week in 1992 to 6.3 units per week in 1996. **Table 11.2**

The overall trends among men and women varied with age:

- since 1984, the proportion of men aged 18-24 who were exceeding 21 units per week has fluctuated but in 1996 reached its highest level at 41%;

- although there was no change between 1994 and 1996 for any other age groups, there was continuing evidence of an increase in consumption among men aged 65 and over from 12% in 1984 through to 18% in 1996;

- for women in every age group there has been an increase in alcohol consumption since 1984; the largest increase was among the youngest women (18-24) of whom the proportion drinking more than 14 units per week increased from 15% in 1984 to 24% in 1996;

- the proportion of women aged 65 and over who drink more than 14 units a week doubled between 1984 and 1996 - from 3% to 7%;

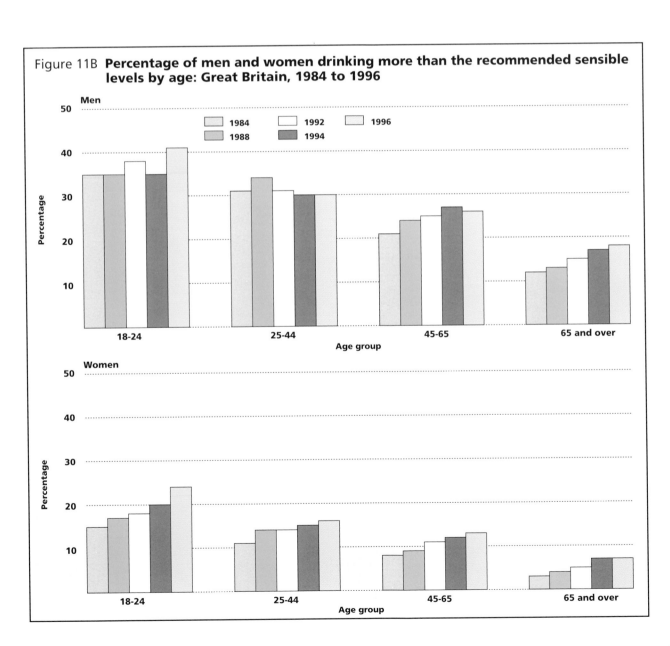

Figure 11B **Percentage of men and women drinking more than the recommended sensible levels by age: Great Britain, 1984 to 1996**

- 18-24 year old women were the only age group to show an increase in the proportion of the heaviest drinkers (more than 35 units per week) from 3% in 1984 to 6% in 1996.   **Figure 11B, Table 11.3**

Drinking and the Health of the Nation

In the 1992 White Paper 'The Health of the Nation', the Department of Health set a range of targets for reducing the risk factors for coronary heart disease and stroke. One of these was to reduce the proportion of men in England drinking more than 21 units a week from 28% in 1990 to 18% in 2005 and the proportion of women drinking more than 14 units a week from 11% to 7% in the same period. The GHS figures show that, to date, there has been little progress towards meeting these targets. The alcohol consumption figures for England were similar to those for Great Britain:

- the proportion of women aged 18 and over in England who exceeded 14 units per week has increased from 11% in 1990 to 14% in 1996;
- at 28% there has been no overall change between 1990 and 1996 in the proportion of men aged 18 and over in England drinking more than 21 units per week.
                            Figure 11C, Table 11.4

It should be noted that the Department of Health's advice on sensible drinking is now based on daily benchmarks (see Appendix A). Revised targets to reflect this new advice are being considered in the context of the Government's new alcohol strategy.

The variation in alcohol consumption with age and sex

Despite the continuing increase in levels of consumption among women, their consumption is still much lower than that of men. In 1996, the proportion of women drinking more than 14 units per week was lower than the proportion of men who drank more than 21 units per week and a higher proportion of women than men were non-drinkers. In 1996, among people aged 16 and over:

- women were almost twice as likely as men to be non-drinkers (13% compared with 7%);
- there was, however, no difference between the proportions of men and women aged 16-24 who were non-drinkers (8% and 9% respectively);
- in every age group, men were more likely to drink more than 21 units per week than women were to drink more than 14 units per week. For example, 18% of men aged 65 and over did so compared with 7% of women in this age group;
- in every age group, there was a higher proportion of women than men who consumed less than one unit per week. For example, 13% of 16-24 year old women were drinking less than one unit per week compared with 6% of men of the same age.   **Table 11.5**

Alcohol consumption was higher among the younger age groups. The 1996 figures showed:

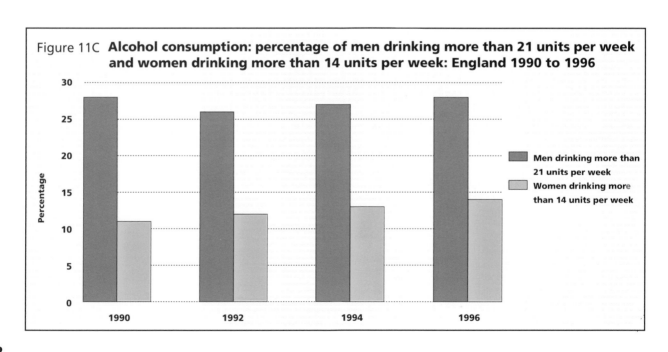

Figure 11C **Alcohol consumption: percentage of men drinking more than 21 units per week and women drinking more than 14 units per week: England 1990 to 1996**

- 35% of men aged 16-24 were drinking more than 21 units per week compared with 18% of those aged 65 and over; the equivalent figures for women drinking more than 14 units per week were 22% and 7%;
- the proportion of non drinkers was lower in the younger age groups in particular among women. The proportions varied from 9% of the youngest women to 24% of the oldest;
- men in the youngest age group drank nearly twice as much on average as those in the oldest age group (20.3 units per week compared with 11.0), while the figures for women, although lower, showed a consumption which was nearly three times higher among the youngest compared with the oldest age groups (9.5 units per week compared with 3.5).   **Figure 11D, Table 11.5**

Regional variation in alcohol consumption

In 1996, levels of alcohol consumption were similar for men in England, Scotland and Wales but women in Scotland were less likely than women elsewhere to drink more than 14 units per week.

- Around one quarter of men in each country were drinking more than 21 units per week (27% in England, and 25% in both Scotland and Wales);
- 11% of women in Scotland were drinking more than 14 units per week compared with 14% of women in England and 16% of women in Wales.   **Table 11.6**

Consumption levels among men varied by region in England and showed a north-south geographical divide. There was little variation among women. In 1996:

- up to a third of men in the North, Yorkshire and Humberside and North West exceeded 21 units per week (33%, 30% and 31% respectively) compared with a quarter or less in Greater London, the Outer Metropolitan area of the South East, the South West (all 25%) and East Anglia (23%);
- the proportion of women exceeding 14 units per week was highest in the North West at 18% and ranged between 12% and 15% across the rest of the country.
          Table 11.6

The variations across the NHS Regional Office areas[2] showed similar trends to those found for the standard regions. For example, in 1996:

- 32% of men in the Northern and Yorkshire NHS Regional Office area were drinking more than 21 units per week compared with 23% of men in North Thames.
          Table 11.7

Social and economic characteristics

Consumption varied with respect to most of the socio-economic variables examined. Men who were single, in a household headed by an employer/manager or intermediate non-manual worker, or who had a household income at the upper end of the range were more likely to drink more than 21 units per week. Women in each of these categories and those in households headed by a professional or who were full-time rather than part-time workers were more likely to drink more than 14 units per week. In 1996:

- over a third of single men (35%) and a fifth of single women (21%) were drinking more than 21 units per

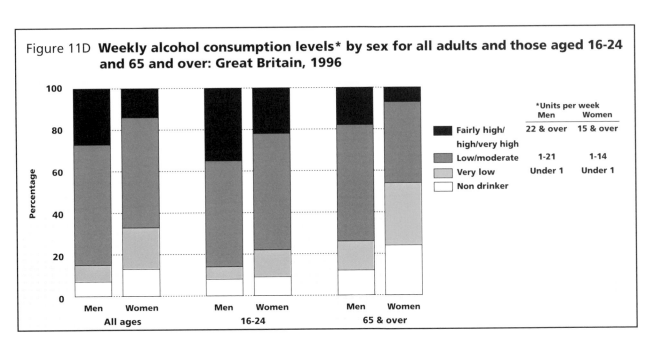

Figure 11D **Weekly alcohol consumption levels* by sex for all adults and those aged 16-24 and 65 and over: Great Britain, 1996**

week and 14 units per week respectively compared with 24% of married men and 13% of married women;

- a higher proportion of widowed, separated and divorced men than of married men were drinking more than 21 units per week (28% compared with 24%), while for women the opposite was true (9% compared with 13% drank more than 14 units per week). **Table 11.8**

- women in households headed by a professional or employer/manager were three times more likely than those in unskilled households to exceed 14 units per week (18% in both the higher groups compared with 6% in unskilled households);

- just under a third of men in households headed by employers/managers (29%) or intermediate non-manual workers (30%) were drinking more than 21 units per week compared with 23% of men in households headed by unskilled manual workers. **Table 11.9**

- men and women in the highest household income group (more than £500 gross per week) were more likely to exceed 21 units per week and 14 units per week respectively than those in other income groups; 34% of men and 20% of women did so compared with 14% to 27% of men in other income groups and 9% to 14% of women;

- among men and women the proportion of non-drinkers was higher among the lower income groups. For example, 13% of men and 20% of women were non-drinkers in households where the usual gross weekly income was between £100 and £150 compared with 3% of men and 7% of women in the highest income group (more than £500 gross per week). **Table 11.10**

- there was no significant difference between people in employment and those who were unemployed in the proportions of men drinking more than 21 units per week and the proportions of women drinking more than 14 units per week (31% and 29% of men and 18% and 19% of women);

- women in full-time employment had higher consumption levels on average than those in part-time employment (8.9 units per week compared with 7.1 units). **Table 11.l2**

Self-assessment of alcohol consumption

When asked to assess their levels of drinking in 1996, 42% of men who drank assessed themselves as 'moderate' drinkers compared with 29% of women. Although there was a consistent correlation between self-assessment and the alcohol consumption rating, among those at the upper end of the consumption range there was a tendency to understate the amount they drank.

- Over half the men (56%) defined as having a very high consumption level assessed themselves as drinking 'quite a lot' or 'heavily' compared with 17% of those defined in the fairly high consumption category;

- 40% of men and 43% of women in the very high consumption category assessed themselves as drinking 'moderately'. **Table 11.13**

Drinking and health

Analyses of the relationship between drinking and health presented in earlier reports have concluded that the higher rates of morbidity found among the non-drinkers were largely accounted for by pre-existing ill health and the age distribution of the group, although they did not provide a complete explanation. In 1996, the data supported these earlier conclusions.

- Among men and women the prevalence of limiting longstanding illness was higher among non-drinkers (39% and 43%) and those who drank less than one unit per week (42% and 34%) than among other drinkers. For example the prevalence among moderate drinkers was 22% for men and 20% for women.

- Differences were less marked for the prevalence of acute illness or restricted activity within the 14 days prior to interview. **Table 11.14**

- A comparison of the prevalence of longstanding illness with that which would be expected given the age distribution of each group shows that prevalence was still significantly higher among men and women who were non-drinkers and among men who drank less than one unit per week. **Table 11.15**

- Among non-drinkers, 52% of men and 58% of women were lifetime abstainers while 48% of men and 42% of women had stopped drinking. **Table 11.16**

- Not surprisingly, lifetime abstainers were far less likely to give health reasons for not drinking than those who had stopped drinking (4% of men and 5% of women compared with 50% of both men and women who had stopped drinking). **Table 11.17**

- Age-standardised figures show that the prevalence of limiting longstanding illness among men who were lifetime abstainers was no different from that which would be expected given the age distribution of the group. Among women lifetime abstainers, however, there was a significantly higher prevalence of limiting longstanding illness compared with that which would be expected given the age distribution of the group.

- Men and women who had stopped drinking, and in particular those who had stopped drinking for health reasons, were the most likely to have a longstanding illness.

- Those who had stopped drinking for any reason were also significantly more likely than would be expected from their age distribution to report an acute illness as were men and women who drank less than one unit per week, women who were lifetime abstainers and men who drank 51 or more units per week.

Figure 11E, Table 11.18

Notes

1 See *Sensible Drinking The Report of an Inter-Departmental Working Group. Department of Health* (1995).

2 As the GHS sample is designed to be representative within Standard Regions rather than the areas covered by regional offices, these data should be treated with caution. See section 3.6.1 in the Health chapter of Thomas, M et al *General Household Survey 1992*, HMSO(1994).

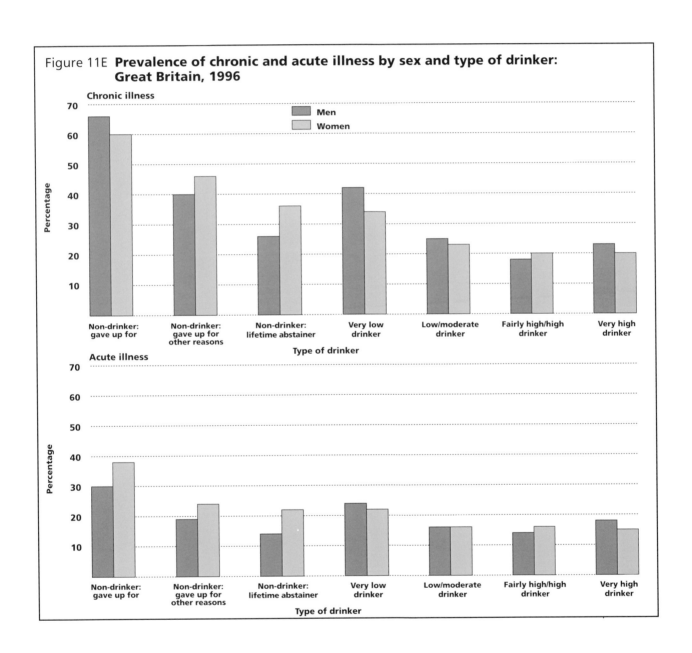

Figure 11E **Prevalence of chronic and acute illness by sex and type of drinker: Great Britain, 1996**

Table 11.1 **Alcohol consumption level (AC rating) by sex: 1984 to 1996**

Persons aged 18 and over   *Great Britain*

Alcohol consumption level (units per week)	1984		1986		1988		1990		1992		1994		1996	
	%		%		%		%		%		%		%	
Men														
Non-drinker	7		6		7		6		6		7		7	
Very low (under 1)	10		9		10		9		10		9		8	
Low (1-10)	37		36		35		36		36		35		35	
Moderate (11-21)	21		22		22		22		22		22		23	
Fairly high (22-35)	12		14		13		13		14		15		15	
High (36-50)	6	25	6	27	7	27	7	28	7	27	6	27	7	27
Very high (51+)	6		7		7		7		6		6		6	
Base = 100%	*8044*		*8415*		*8371*		*7844*		*8150*		*7411*		*6902*	
	%		%		%		%		%		%		%	
Women														
Non-drinker	13		11		12		12		12		14		13	
Very low (under 1)	24		24		23		23		23		21		20	
Low (1-7)	41		41		40		40		39		37		37	
Moderate (8-14)	14		14		14		14		15		15		16	
Fairly high (15-25)	6		7		7		7		8		9		9	
High (26-35)	2	9	2	10	2	10	2	11	2	11	2	13	2	14
Very high (36+)	1		2		2		2		2		2		2	
Base = 100%	*9399*		*9845*		*9814*		*9150*		*9490*		*8906*		*8284*	

Table 11.2 **Mean weekly alcohol consumption in units, by sex and age: 1992 to 1996**

Persons aged 16 and over   *Great Britain*

Age	Men			Women			All persons		
	1992	1994	1996	1992	1994	1996	1992	1994	1996
16-24	19.1	17.4	20.3	7.3	7.7	9.5	12.9	12.3	14.7
25-44	18.2	17.5	17.6	6.3	6.2	7.2	11.8	11.4	11.9
45-64	15.6	15.5	15.6	5.3	5.3	5.9	10.2	10.2	10.5
65 and over	9.7	10.0	11.0	2.7	3.2	3.5	5.6	6.0	6.8
Total	15.9	15.4	16.0	5.4	5.4	6.3	10.2	10.0	10.7
Bases = 100%									
16-24	*1144*	*951*	*881*	*1271*	*1069*	*969*	*2415*	*2020*	*1850*
25-44	*3056*	*2855*	*2628*	*3492*	*3437*	*3182*	*6548*	*6292*	*5810*
45-64	*2598*	*2376*	*2215*	*2828*	*2560*	*2509*	*5426*	*4936*	*4724*
65 and over	*1597*	*1454*	*1445*	*2156*	*2038*	*1836*	*3753*	*3492*	*3281*
Total	*8395*	*7636*	*7169*	*9747*	*9104*	*8496*	*18142*	*16740*	*15665*

Table 11.3 Alcohol consumption: percentages exceeding sensible amounts by sex and age: 1984 to 1996

Persons aged 18 and over   *Great Britain*

Age	Men							Women						
	1984	1986	1988	1990	1992	1994	1996	1984	1986	1988	1990	1992	1994	1996
Percentage who drank more than 21/14 units														
18-24	35	39	35	36	38	35	41	15	19	17	18	18	20	24
25-44	31	32	34	33	31	30	30	11	13	14	13	14	15	16
45-64	21	23	24	25	25	27	26	8	8	9	10	11	12	13
65 and over	12	13	13	14	15	17	18	3	3	4	5	5	7	7
Total	25	27	27	28	27	27	27	9	10	10	11	11	13	14
Percentage who drank more than 50/35 units														
18-24	11	14	11	13	11	11	12	3	4	3	4	4	4	6
25-44	8	8	9	9	7	7	6	2	2	2	2	2	2	2
45-64	5	5	6	6	6	6	5	1	1	1	1	1	2	2
65 and over	2	2	2	3	2	3	3	0	0	0	1	0	1	1
Total	6	7	7	7	6	6	6	1	2	2	2	2	2	2
Bases = 100%														
18-24	*1112*	*1106*	*1054*	*904*	*899*	*726*	*631*	*1176*	*1196*	*1222*	*1069*	*1014*	*871*	*761*
25-44	*3054*	*3273*	*3185*	*3045*	*3056*	*2855*	*2612*	*3422*	*3646*	*3530*	*3369*	*3492*	*3437*	*3179*
45-64	*2431*	*2528*	*2557*	*2386*	*2598*	*2376*	*2214*	*2681*	*2724*	*2749*	*2593*	*2828*	*2560*	*2508*
65 and over	*1447*	*1508*	*1575*	*1509*	*1597*	*1454*	*1445*	*2120*	*2279*	*2313*	*2119*	*2156*	*2038*	*1836*
Total	*8044*	*8415*	*8371*	*7844*	*8150*	*7411*	*6902*	*9399*	*9845*	*9814*	*9150*	*9490*	*8906*	*8284*

Table 11.4 Alcohol consumption: percentages exceeding sensible amounts, by sex: 1990 to 1996

Persons aged 18 and over   *England*

	1990	1992	1994	1996
Men	28	26	27	28
Women	11	12	13	14
Bases = 100%				
Men	*6737*	*7066*	*6411*	*5913*
Women	*7789*	*8153*	*7668*	*7046*

Table 11.5 **Alcohol consumption level (AC rating) and mean weekly number of units by sex and age**

Persons aged 16 and over   *Great Britain: 1996*

Alcohol consumption level (units per week)	Age				
	16-24	25-44	45-64	65 and over	Total
	%	%	%	%	%
Men					
Non-drinker	8	5	6	12	7
Very low (under 1)	6	5	9	14	8
Low (1-10)	32	33	35	39	35
Moderate (11-21)	18	26	24	18	23
Fairly high (22-35)	16	16	15	10	15
High (36-50)	9 ⎱ 35	7 ⎱ 30	6 ⎱ 26	4 ⎱ 18	7 ⎱ 27
Very high (51+)	10	6	5	3	6
Mean weekly units	20.3	17.6	15.6	11.0	16.0
Base = 100%	*880*	*2612*	*2214*	*1445*	*7151*
	%	%	%	%	%
Women					
Non-drinker	9	8	13	24	13
Very low (under 1)	13	14	21	30	20
Low (1-7)	36	42	38	29	37
Moderate (8-14)	20	19	15	10	16
Fairly high (15-25)	12	11	9	5	9
High (26-35)	4 ⎱ 22	3 ⎱ 16	2 ⎱ 13	1 ⎱ 7	2 ⎱ 14
Very high (36+)	5	2	2	1	2
Mean weekly units	9.5	7.2	5.9	3.5	6.3
Base = 100%	*968*	*3179*	*2508*	*1836*	*8491*

Table 11.6 Alcohol consumption level (AC rating) by sex and region

Persons aged 16 and over   *Great Britain: 1996*

Region		Alcohol consumption level*								Mean weekly units	Base = 100%
		Non-drinker	Very low	Low	Moderate	Fairly high	High	Very high	Total high		
Men											
North	%	9	7	27	24	15	10	8	33	19.1	432
Yorkshire and Humberside	%	7	9	32	23	17	7	6	30	16.8	606
North West	%	6	8	33	22	15	8	8	31	18.4	804
East Midlands	%	6	7	36	25	15	6	5	26	15.3	550
West Midlands	%	9	6	33	24	16	7	5	28	16.2	664
East Anglia	%	4	10	40	22	14	6	4	23	13.7	305
South East:	%	8	9	37	21	14	6	6	26	15.2	2138
Greater London	%	11	10	35	19	13	6	6	25	14.5	770
Outer Metropolitan area	%	6	7	38	24	14	6	5	25	15.4	702
Outer South East	%	6	9	37	20	14	8	6	27	15.8	666
South West	%	6	9	36	24	14	5	6	25	15.0	646
England	%	7	8	35	23	15	7	6	27	16.1	6145
Wales	%	6	9	41	19	14	5	6	25	15.0	367
Scotland	%	7	7	33	28	15	5	5	25	16.2	657
Great Britain	%	7	8	35	23	15	7	6	27	16.0	7169
Women											
North	%	17	19	36	15	10	2	2	13	5.9	532
Yorkshire and Humberside	%	12	19	36	18	9	3	3	15	6.6	754
North West	%	11	19	35	17	10	5	4	18	7.9	933
East Midlands	%	10	20	39	19	9	2	1	12	5.8	630
West Midlands	%	16	19	36	16	8	2	2	12	5.9	790
East Anglia	%	12	22	39	14	9	2	2	13	5.5	330
South East:	%	14	20	37	16	8	3	2	13	6.2	2473
Greater London	%	20	22	33	12	8	2	2	13	5.6	884
Outer Metropolitan area	%	11	18	40	18	9	3	2	14	6.4	811
Outer South East	%	11	20	37	18	8	3	3	14	6.7	778
South West	%	9	19	41	17	10	2	2	13	6.1	785
England	%	13	20	37	16	9	3	2	14	6.3	7227
Wales	%	13	18	38	15	10	3	3	16	6.8	476
Scotland	%	13	21	39	16	8	1	2	11	5.5	793
Great Britain	%	13	20	37	16	9	2	2	14	6.3	8496

* Consumption level (units per week):

	Very low	Low	Moderate	Fairly high	High	Very high	Total high
Men	under 1	1-10	11-21	22-35	36-50	51 and over	22 and over
Women	under 1	1-7	8-14	15-25	26-35	36 and over	15 and over

Table 11.7 **Alcohol consumption: percentages exceeding sensible amounts, by sex and health region in England**

Persons aged 16 and over   *England: 1996*

Health region	Percentage drinking more than 21/14 units		Percentage drinking more than 50/35 units		Bases = 100%	
	Men	**Women**	**Men**	**Women**	*Men*	*Women*
Northern and Yorkshire	32	15	7	2	716	899
Trent	27	12	6	1	801	938
Anglia and Oxford	25	15	6	3	814	926
North Thames	23	11	4	2	679	787
South Thames	27	14	7	2	798	922
South and West	26	13	5	2	855	1014
West Midlands	28	12	5	2	665	792
North West	31	18	8	4	817	949
All England	27	14	6	2	6145	7227

Table 11.8 **Alcohol consumption level (AC rating) and mean weekly number of units by sex, marital status and presence of children**

Persons aged 16 and over   *Great Britain: 1996*

Alcohol consumption level (units per week)	Marital status					
	Married			Single	Widowed/ divorced/ separated	Total
	With dependent children	Without dependent children	Total* married			
	%	%	%	%	%	%
Men						
Non-drinker	6	7	6	9	10	7
Very low (under 1)	6	10	8	7	11	8
Low (1-10)	37	37	37	29	32	35
Moderate (11-21)	25	23	24	20	20	23
Fairly high (22-35)	15	14	14	17	13	15
High (36-50)	6 ⎫ 26	5 ⎫ 23	6 ⎫ 24	9 ⎫ 35	8 ⎫ 28	7 ⎫ 27
Very high (51+)	5 ⎭	4 ⎭	5 ⎭	10 ⎭	7 ⎭	6 ⎭
Mean weekly units	15.5	14.1	14.7	20.1	16.3	16.0
Base = 100%	*1950*	*2947*	*4909*	*1487*	*755*	*7151*
	%	%	%	%	%	%
Women						
Non-drinker	9	13	12	11	19	13
Very low (under 1)	15	20	18	17	27	20
Low (1-7)	44	37	40	34	32	37
Moderate (8-14)	18	17	17	17	13	16
Fairly high (15-25)	10	9	9	12	6	9
High (26-35)	2 ⎫ 13	3 ⎫ 13	2 ⎫ 13	4 ⎫ 21	2 ⎫ 9	2 ⎫ 14
Very high (36+)	2 ⎭	2 ⎭	2 ⎭	5 ⎭	2 ⎭	2 ⎭
Mean weekly units	6.2	6.1	6.1	8.9	4.7	6.3
Base = 100%	*2244*	*3091*	*5348*	*1363*	*1780*	*8491*

* Totals married with dependent children and without dependent children do not always sum to the total married as the dependency of some children could not be established.

Table 11.9 Alcohol consumption level (AC rating) and mean weekly number of units by sex and socio-economic group of the head of household

Persons aged 16 and over   *Great Britain: 1996*

Alcohol consumption level (units per week)	Professional	Employers and managers	Intermediate non-manual	Junior non-manual	Skilled manual and own account non-profess-ional	Semi-skilled manual and personal service	Unskilled manual	Total
	%	%	%	%	%	%	%	%
Men								
Non-drinker	6	5	5	6	7	10	11	7
Very low (under 1)	5	5	7	9	10	10	12	8
Low (1-10)	37	35	35	36	35	34	35	35
Moderate (11-21)	26	25	23	24	22	21	19	23
Fairly high (22-35)	16	16	18	12	14	12	12	15
High (36-50)	6 ⎤25	7 ⎤29	7 ⎤30	8 ⎤24	7 ⎤27	6 ⎤25	5 ⎤23	7 ⎤27
Very high (51+)	3 ⎦	6 ⎦	6 ⎦	4 ⎦	6 ⎦	7 ⎦	6 ⎦	6 ⎦
Mean weekly units	14.6	17.1	17.1	14.8	16.0	15.5	13.4	16.0
Base = 100%	*447*	*1650*	*700*	*475*	*2411*	*985*	*299*	*7151*
	%	%	%	%	%	%	%	%
Women								
Non-drinker	7	9	10	12	13	18	22	13
Very low (under 1)	13	13	17	24	21	24	30	20
Low (1-7)	41	40	40	36	38	34	32	37
Moderate (8-14)	22	20	18	16	16	13	10	16
Fairly high (15-25)	12	13	9	8	8	7	4	9
High (26-35)	3 ⎤18	2 ⎤18	3 ⎤15	2 ⎤12	3 ⎤13	2 ⎤11	0 ⎤6	2 ⎤14
Very high (36+)	3 ⎦	3 ⎦	3 ⎦	2 ⎦	2 ⎦	2 ⎦	1 ⎦	2 ⎦
Mean weekly units	7.9	7.5	7.2	5.7	5.9	5.3	3.5	6.3
Base = 100%	*432*	*1672*	*916*	*1014*	*2340*	*1330*	*434*	*8491*

* Members of the Armed Forces, persons in inadequately described occupations and all persons who have never worked are not shown as separate categories but are included in the figures for all persons.

Table 11.10 **Alcohol consumption level (AC rating) by sex and usual gross weekly household income**

Persons aged 16 and over   *Great Britain: 1996*

Alcohol consumption level (units per week)	Usual gross weekly household income (£)								
	0.01 - 100.00	100.01 - 150.00	150.01 - 200.00	200.01 - 250.00	250.01 - 300.00	300.01 - 400.00	400.01 - 500.00	500.01 or more	Total*
	%	%	%	%	%	%	%	%	%
Men									
Non-drinker	11	13	12	10	8	5	4	3	7
Very low (under 1)	14	15	13	11	10	7	7	4	8
Low (1-10)	31	42	34	33	40	38	39	31	35
Moderate (11-21)	18	16	20	19	20	23	25	27	23
Fairly high (22-35)	11	8	11	13	11	15	14	19	15
High (36-50)	7 / 27	2 / 14	5 / 21	7 / 27	5 / 22	6 / 27	6 / 25	9 / 34	7 / 27
Very high (51+)	8	4	5	6	5	5	6	7	6
Mean weekly units	17.1	9.6	13.3	15.8	13.7	15.8	15.7	19.1	16.0
Base = 100%	*463*	*597*	*519*	*447*	*436*	*822*	*755*	*2238*	*7169*
	%	%	%	%	%	%	%	%	%
Women									
Non-drinker	19	20	20	14	10	11	8	7	13
Very low (under 1)	30	28	22	21	22	19	15	13	20
Low (1-7)	32	32	33	37	39	40	42	40	37
Moderate (8-14)	10	11	13	15	16	18	21	20	16
Fairly high (15-25)	5	6	7	8	9	8	8	13	9
High (26-35)	1 / 9	2 / 9	3 / 12	3 / 13	2 / 13	2 / 12	3 / 14	3 / 20	2 / 14
Very high (36+)	2	2	2	2	2	2	3	3	2
Mean weekly units	4.4	4.5	5.3	6.1	5.8	6.1	7.2	8.2	6.3
Base = 100%	*951*	*859*	*665*	*533*	*457*	*864*	*792*	*2254*	*8496*

* Includes people who did not provide income data, and 12 cases of nil income.

Table 11.11 Alcohol consumption level (AC rating) and mean weekly number of units by sex and usual gross weekly earnings

(a) Men aged 16-64 in full-time employment

Great Britain: 1996

Alcohol consumption level (units per week)	Usual gross weekly earnings (£)								Total*
	0.01 - 100.00	100.01 - 150.00	150.01 - 200.00	200.01 - 250.00	250.01 - 300.00	300.01 - 350.00	350.01 - 400.00	400.01 or more	
	%	%	%	%	%	%	%	%	%
Non-drinker	7	8	6	3	4	2	2	2	4
Very low (under 1)	5	7	8	5	5	5	5	2	5
Low (1-10)	40	34	36	33	34	36	31	33	34
Moderate (11-21)	23	21	21	22	24	27	30	31	26
Fairly high (22-35)	12	15	15	22	16	17	18	18	17
High (36-50)	8 ⎤ 25	11 ⎤ 31	8 ⎤ 30	8 ⎤ 37	8 ⎤ 32	5 ⎤ 30	7 ⎤ 33	8 ⎤ 32	8 ⎤ 32
Very high (51+)	4 ⎦	5 ⎦	7 ⎦	7 ⎦	8 ⎦	7 ⎦	8 ⎦	6 ⎦	7 ⎦
Mean weekly units	15.0	17.7	18.7	19.2	18.3	17.4	19.4	18.7	18.4
Base = 100%	179	228	363	480	497	401	354	1129	3935

(b) Women aged 16-64 in full-time employment

Great Britain: 1996

Alcohol consumption level (units per week)	Usual gross weekly earnings (£)							Total*
	0.01 - 100.00	100.01 - 150.00	150.01 - 200.00	200.01 - 250.00	250.01 - 300.00	300.01 - 350.00	350.01 or more	
	%	%	%	%	%	%	%	%
Non-drinker	11	8	6	5	7	4	3	6
Very low (under 1)	11	14	14	11	8	8	7	11
Low (1-7)	42	38	41	40	42	42	43	41
Moderate (8-14)	17	16	18	22	25	22	26	21
Fairly high (15-25)	11	15	13	12	11	18	15	13
High (26-35)	4 ⎤ 19	5 ⎤ 24	4 ⎤ 22	4 ⎤ 22	4 ⎤ 18	1 ⎤ 23	4 ⎤ 21	4 ⎤ 21
Very high (36+)	3 ⎦	4 ⎦	4 ⎦	6 ⎦	3 ⎦	4 ⎦	1 ⎦	4 ⎦
Mean weekly units	7.8	9.3	8.9	10.2	8.4	8.9	8.8	8.9
Base = 100%	159	258	379	381	249	157	388	2114

* Total includes people who did not provide earnings data.

193

Table 11.12 Alcohol consumption level (AC rating) and mean weekly number of units by sex and economic activity status

(a) Men aged 16-64   *Great Britain: 1996*

Alcohol consumption level (units per week)	Economic activity status			
	Working	Unemployed	Economically inactive	Total
	%	%	%	%
Non-drinker	4	9	12	6
Very low (under 1)	5	10	13	7
Low (1-10)	34	32	35	34
Moderate (11-21)	26	20	19	24
Fairly high (22-35)	17	15	10	16
High (36-50)	8 ⎱ 31	6 ⎱ 29	5 ⎱ 20	7 ⎱ 29
Very high (51+)	7	9	5	7
Mean weekly units	18.1	17.3	13.3	17.3
Base = 100%	*4366*	*418*	*936*	*5720*

(b) Women aged 16-64   *Great Britain: 1996*

Alcohol consumption level (units per week)	Economic activity status					
	Working full time	Working part time	All working*	Unemployed	Economically inactive	Total
	%	%	%	%	%	%
Non-drinker	6	6	6	14	17	10
Very low (under 1)	11	16	13	18	23	17
Low (1-7)	41	44	42	34	36	40
Moderate (8-14)	21	19	20	15	14	18
Fairly high (15-25)	13	11	12	11	7	10
High (26-35)	4 ⎱ 21	3 ⎱ 16	3 ⎱ 18	3 ⎱ 19	2 ⎱ 10	3 ⎱ 16
Very high (36+)	4	2	3	5	2	3
Mean weekly units	8.9	7.1	8.0	8.0	5.2	7.1
Base = 100%	*2114*	*1967*	*4138*	*256*	*2259*	*6653*

* Including a few women who did not specify their hours of work.

194

Table 11.13 **Self-image of drinking by sex and alcohol consumption level (AC rating)**

Drinkers aged 16 and over *Great Britain: 1996*

Drinking self-image	Alcohol consumption level*						
	Very low	Low	Moderate	Fairly high	High	Very high	Total
	%	%	%	%	%	%	%
Men							
Hardly drink at all	82	27	4	1	1	2	19
Drink a little	17	50	28	10	5	2	29
Drink a moderate amount	1	23	65	72	60	40	42
Drink quite a lot	0	0	4	17	32	46	9
Drink heavily	0	0	0	0	2	10	1
Base = 100%	*587*	*2496*	*1638*	*1043*	*468*	*422*	*6654*
	%	%	%	%	%	%	%
Women							
Hardly drink at all	83	30	7	3	2	5	33
Drink a little	16	51	37	16	8	7	35
Drink a moderate amount	1	19	55	71	65	43	29
Drink quite a lot	0	0	2	10	25	41	3
Drink heavily	0	0	0	0	0	4	0
Base = 100%	*1668*	*3175*	*1380*	*761*	*211*	*193*	*7388*

* Consumption level (units per week):						
	Very low	Low	Moderate	Fairly high	High	Very high
Men	under 1	1-10	11-21	22-35	36-50	51 and over
Women	under 1	1-7	8-14	15-25	26-35	36 and over

Table 11.14 **Prevalence of limiting longstanding illness and restricted activity by sex and alcohol consumption level**

All persons aged 16 and over *Great Britain: 1996*

Alcohol consumption level*	Men	Women	Base = 100% Men	Women
Percentage with limiting longstanding illness				
Non-drinker	39	43	*507*	*1101*
Very low	42	34	*587*	*1666*
Low	27	24	*2497*	*3174*
Moderate	22	20	*1636*	*1381*
Fairly high	18	19	*1044*	*761*
High	19	21	*470*	*211*
Very high	23	20	*423*	*193*
Total	26	27	*7164*	*8487*
Percentage with restricted activity in the last 14 days				
Non-drinker	19	26	*508*	*1104*
Very low	24	22	*588*	*1667*
Low	17	17	*2496*	*3175*
Moderate	14	15	*1638*	*1382*
Fairly high	15	14	*1044*	*760*
High	14	22	*470*	*211*
Very high	18	15	*423*	*193*
Total	17	19	*7167*	*8492*

* See the footnote to Table 11.13.

Table 11.15 **Prevalence of limiting longstanding illness and restricted activity by sex and alcohol consumption level: age standardised**

All persons aged 16 and over   *Great Britain: 1996*

Alcohol consumption level*	Men			Women		
	Observed	Expected	Observed/ expected	Observed	Expected	Observed/ expected
Percentage with limiting longstanding illness†						
Non-drinker	39	29	136**	43	32	133**
Very low	42	31	137**	34	31	109**
Low	27	27	101	24	26	93**
Moderate	22	25	88**	20	24	81**
Fairly high	18	24	74**	19	24	81**
High	19	23	83**	21	22	96
Very high	23	22	104**	20	22	88
Total	26	26	100	27	27	100
Percentage with restricted activity in the last 14 days†						
Non-drinker	19	17	113	26	20	133**
Very low	24	18	135**	22	20	111**
Low	17	17	104	17	18	93**
Moderate	14	16	84**	15	18	83**
Fairly high	15	16	91	14	18	81**
High	14	16	85	22	18	125
Very high	18	16	112	15	18	83
Total	17	17	100	19	19	100

* Consumption level (units per week):

	Very low	Low	Moderate	Fairly high	High	Very high
Men	under 1	1-10	11-21	22-35	36-50	51 and over
Women	under 1	1-7	8-14	15-25	26-35	36 and over

† For a full explanation of observed and expected percentages, see Appendix A.
** Ratio significantly different from 100.

Table 11.16 **Age distributions of lifetime abstainers and those who had stopped drinking, by sex**

Non-drinkers aged 16 and over   *Great Britain: 1996*

	Lifetime abstainers		Those who had stopped drinking	
	Men	Women	Men	Women
	%	%	%	%
16-24	22	10	7	4
25-44	27	25	27	23
45-64	23	27	27	30
65 and over	27	38	39	43
Base = 100%	*255*	*617*	*233*	*440*

Table 11.17 **Main reason for not drinking, by sex and whether was a lifetime abstainer or had stopped drinking**

Non-drinkers aged 16 and over   *Great Britain: 1996*

Reason for not drinking	Lifetime abstainers			Those who had stopped drinking		
	Men	Women	Total	Men	Women	Total
	%	%	%	%	%	%
Religion	40	22	27	8	3	5
Don't like it	39	57	51	13	28	23
Parents' advice	9	9	9	0	1	1
Health reasons	4	5	5	50	50	50
Can't afford it	2	1	1	12	5	7
Other	6	6	6	17	13	15
Base = 100%	*255*	*614*	*869*	*233*	*437*	*670*

Table 11.18 **Prevalence of limiting longstanding illness and restricted activity by sex, type of drinker, and for those who had given up drinking, reason for stopping: age standardised**

Persons aged 16 and over   *Great Britain: 1996*

Alcohol consumption level*	Men			Women		
	Observed	Expected	Observed/ expected	Observed	Expected	Observed/ expected
Percentage with limiting longstanding illness†						
Non-drinkers						
Stopped: health reason	66	33	201**	60	35	171**
Stopped: other reason	40	29	135**	46	32	143**
Lifetime abstainer	26	26	99	36	31	116**
Drinkers						
Occasional (very low)	42	31	138**	34	31	110**
Low/moderate	25	26	96**	23	25	89**
Fairly high/high	18	24	77**	20	24	84**
Very high	23	22	104	20	22	88
All aged 16 and over	26	26	100	27	27	100
Percentage with restricted activity in the last 14 days†						
Non-drinkers						
Stopped: health reason	30	18	170**	38	20	184**
Stopped: other reason	19	17	110	24	20	122**
Lifetime abstainer	14	16	83	22	20	115
Drinkers						
Occasional (very low)	24	18	135**	22	20	112
Low/moderate	16	16	96**	16	18	90**
Fairly high/high	14	16	89**	16	18	90
Very high	18	16	112	15	18	83
All aged 16 and over	17	17	100	19	19	100

* Consumption level (units per week):

	Very low	Low	Moderate	Fairly high	High	Very high
Men	under 1	1-10	11-21	22-35	36-50	51 and over
Women	under 1	1-7	8-14	15-25	26-35	36 and over

† For a full explanation of observed and expected percentages, see Appendix A.

** Ratio significantly different from 100.

12 Marriage and cohabitation

At the beginning of the GHS interview, the person answering the household questionnaire is asked about the marital status of each household member. Later in the interview, there are specific questions which are addressed to all household members aged 16-59 present at the interview, to check their legal marital status and whether they are cohabiting. The responses to these questions are described in this chapter.

Marital status

In 1996:

- 22% of men and 17% of women were single;
- 61% of men and 55% of women were married;
- women were three times as likely as men to be widowed (12% compared with 4%) – reflecting the tendency of women to marry at an earlier age and to live longer than men;
- 8% of women and 5% of men were divorced or separated - the higher proportion of women among divorced and separated people is largely accounted for by the higher proportion of men than women of the same age who remarry following a divorce.

Table 12.1

Cohabitation

In 1996:

- 22% of non-married men and women aged 16-59 (that is those not currently married and living with their spouse) were cohabiting;
- those most likely to be cohabiting were non-married

men in their late twenties or early thirties and non-married women in their early twenties to early thirties. Around a third of each of these groups were cohabiting;

Table 12.3, Figure 12A

- people who were divorced were more likely to be cohabiting than those who were single, widowed or separated (among men - 36% of divorced, 20% of separated, 19% of single and 10% of widowed were cohabiting; among women - 27% of divorced, 23% of single, 9% of separated and 6% of widowed were cohabiting);
- among the divorced and separated, men were more likely to cohabit than women (36% of divorced men compared with 27% of divorced women; 20% of separated men compared with 9% of separated women).

Table 12.4

Trends in the legal marital status of women

Between 1979 and 1996, the proportion of women aged 18-49[1] who were legally married[2] fell from 74% to 57%. Most of this decrease had occurred by the early 1990s and since then there has been little change.

Over the same period (1979-1996):

- the proportion of women aged 18-49 who were single increased from 18% in 1979 to 29% in 1992. Since then there has been no significant change;
- the proportion of women in the same age group who were divorced increased from 4% in 1979 to 9% in 1993 and since then has remained unchanged;

Table 12.6

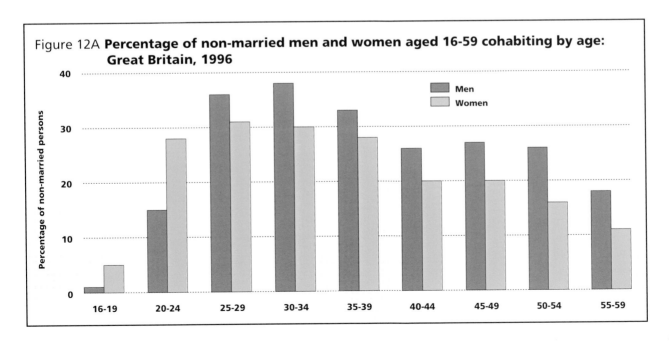

Figure 12A **Percentage of non-married men and women aged 16-59 cohabiting by age: Great Britain, 1996**

- the proportion of non-married women aged 18-49 who were cohabiting more than doubled from 11% in 1979 to 26% in 1996. Most of this increase occurred in the 1980s;
- in the early 1980s, the highest prevalence of cohabitation was among divorced and separated women, with about a fifth of each of these groups cohabiting;
- since the mid 1980s, the prevalence of cohabitation has increased among divorced women; in 1996, 31% of divorced women were cohabiting. The prevalence of cohabitation among separated women has declined from 20% in 1985 to 7% in 1996.

Table 12.7, Figure 12B

Cohabitation among women and the presence of dependent children

In 1996, nearly a third (30%) of non-married women aged 16-59 with dependent children were cohabiting compared with 19% of those with no dependent children.

The relationship between cohabitation and the presence of dependent children varied with legal marital status. For example:

- among single women, 41% with dependent children were cohabiting compared with 19% of those with no dependent children;
- among the divorced, 31% with dependent children were cohabiting compared with 27% without dependent children.

Table 12.8

Trends in marital separation and remarriage

Over the past thirty years, the trend has been for the first marriages of those who married aged under 30 to last for successively shorter periods of time.

Among women married for the first time before aged 30:

- the proportion of first marriages which began between 1965 and 1969 and ended within three years was 3% and the proportion ending within five years was 6%;
- twenty years later (first marriages which began between 1985 and 1989) the proportion ending within 3 and 5 years had increased to 12% and 18% respectively;
- of first marriages which began between 1965 and 1969, 15% had ended in separation within 10 years, compared with nearly a quarter (23%) of first marriages which began between 1980 and 1984.

Among men married for the first time before aged 30:

- the proportion of first marriages which ended within three years increased from 3% of marriages which began between 1965 and 1969 to 7% of those between 1985 and 1989. The proportion ending within 5 years increased from 7% to 11% over the same period. The proportion ending within 10 years increased from 14% of those which began between 1965 and 1969 to 24% of those which began between 1980 and 1984.

Table 12.9

The trend is even more marked among teenage women.

- 6% of first marriages entered into between 1965 and 1969 by women aged under 20 ended within three years and 9% ended within five years;

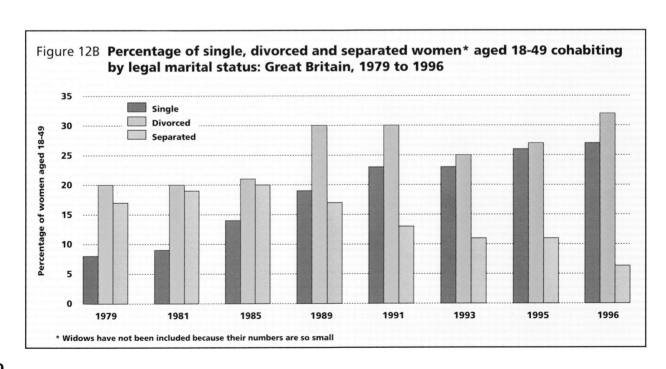

Figure 12B **Percentage of single, divorced and separated women* aged 18-49 cohabiting by legal marital status: Great Britain, 1979 to 1996**

* Widows have not been included because their numbers are so small

- 19% of first marriages among teenage women which began twenty years later (between 1985 and 1989) ended within three years and nearly a third (32%) ended within five years.   **Table 12.10**

Between 23% and 31% of men and similar proportions (22% and 31%) of women who separated since 1981 when they were under 35 remarried within four years.

Tables 12.11-12.12

Notes

1   See Appendix A for an explanation of why some analyses refer to women aged 18-49 while others refer to women aged 16-59.

2   See Appendix A for a definition of 'legal marriage'.

Table 12.1   **Sex by marital status**

All persons aged 16 and over   *Great Britain: 1996*

Marital status*	Men	Women
	%	%
Married	61	55
Cohabiting	7	7
Single	22	17
Widowed	4	12
Divorced	4 ⎤ 5	6 ⎤ 8
Separated	1 ⎦	2 ⎦
Base = 100%	8257	9007

* Marital status as recorded at the beginning of the interview.

Table 12.2 **(a) Age by sex by marital status**
(b) Marital status by sex by age

Persons aged 16 and over   Great Britain: 1996

Age	Marital status*						
	Married	Cohabiting	Single	Widowed	Divorced	Separated	Total
(a)	%	%	%	%	%	%	%
Men							
16-24	1	14	53	0	0	1	13
25-34	15	48	26	0	9	27	19
35-44	22	19	9	1	27	23	19
45-54	23	13	5	5	26	22	18
55-64	17	4	3	10	19	16	13
65-74	13	1	3	32	15	7	11
75 and over	8	1	2	52	4	5	8
Base = 100%	*4984*	*617*	*1846*	*353*	*324*	*115*	*8239*
	%	%	%	%	%	%	%
Women							
16-24	2	28	54	0	0	5	12
25-34	19	39	25	0	15	29	19
35-44	24	17	7	1	28	36	18
45-54	23	10	4	4	27	17	16
55-64	17	4	2	12	15	7	13
65-74	11	1	4	34	10	4	12
75 and over	5	1	4	48	4	2	10
Base = 100%	*4985*	*617*	*1570*	*1107*	*499*	*223*	*9001*
	%	%	%	%	%	%	%
Total							
16-24	1	21	53	0	0	4	13
25-34	17	43	25	0	13	28	19
35-44	23	18	8	1	28	31	18
45-54	23	11	5	5	27	19	17
55-64	17	4	2	12	16	10	13
65-74	12	1	3	33	12	5	11
75 and over	6	1	3	49	4	3	9
Base = 100%	*9969*	*1234*	*3416*	*1460*	*823*	*338*	*17240*

Age		Married	Cohabiting	Single	Widowed	Divorced	Separated	Base = 100%
(b)								
Men								
16-24	%	3	8	89	0	0	0	*1107*
25-34	%	48	19	30	0	2	2	*1588*
35-44	%	73	8	11	0	6	2	*1532*
45-54	%	80	5	6	1	6	2	*1454*
55-64	%	83	2	4	3	6	2	*1046*
65-74	%	74	1	6	13	5	1	*885*
75 and over	%	62	1	5	29	2	1	*627*
Total	%	61	7	22	4	4	1	*8239*
Women								
16-24	%	8	16	75	0	0	1	*1124*
25-34	%	55	14	23	0	4	4	*1721*
35-44	%	72	7	7	1	9	5	*1628*
45-54	%	77	4	4	3	9	3	*1477*
55-64	%	75	2	3	12	7	1	*1135*
65-74	%	53	1	6	35	5	1	*1054*
75 and over	%	28	0	7	62	2	0	*858*
Total	%	55	7	17	12	6	2	*9001*
Total								
16-24	%	6	12	82	0	0	1	*2231*
25-34	%	51	16	26	0	3	3	*3309*
35-44	%	72	7	9	1	7	3	*3160*
45-54	%	78	5	5	2	7	2	*2931*
55-64	%	79	2	4	8	6	2	*2181*
65-74	%	63	1	6	25	5	1	*1943*
75 and over	%	42	1	6	48	2	1	*1485*
Total	%	58	7	20	8	5	2	*17240*

* Marital status as recorded at the beginning of the interview.

Table 12.3 **Percentage cohabiting by sex and age**

Men and women aged 16-59   *Great Britain: 1996*

Age	Percentage cohabiting		Base = 100%	
	All	Non-married*	All	Non-married*
Men				
16-19	1	1	418	417
20-24	15	17	471	441
25-29	24	37	644	412
30-34	14	36	668	264
35-39	9	31	684	204
40-44	6	23	618	155
45-49	5	26	639	129
50-54	4	21	628	135
55-59	3	17	461	76
Total	10	22	5231	2233
Women				
16-19	6	6	411	409
20-24	25	30	566	481
25-29	17	32	790	421
30-34	11	31	824	297
35-39	8	27	840	240
40-44	5	18	723	198
45-49	5	19	752	177
50-54	4	15	655	155
55-59	3	10	546	136
Total	9	22	6107	2514

* Men and women describing themselves as 'separated' were, strictly speaking, legally married. However, because the separated can cohabit, they have been included in the 'non-married' category.

Table 12.4 **Percentage cohabiting by legal marital status and age**

Men and women aged 16-59   *Great Britain: 1995 and 1996 combined*

Legal marital status*	Percentage cohabiting					Bases = 100%				
	16-24	25-34	35-49	50-59	Total	16-24	25-34	35-49	50-59	Total
Men										
Married	-	-	-	-	-	74	1335	3003	1844	6256
Non-married										
Single	9	36	21	7	19	1748	1194	524	160	3626
Widowed	0	†	†	[7]	10	0	1	13	45	59
Divorced	†	50	36	28	36	1	98	393	195	687
Separated	†	20	22	17	20	8	71	129	60	268
	9	36	27	17	22					
Total	8	18	7	3	9	1831	2699	4062	2304	10896
Women										
Married	-	-	-	-	-	187	1932	3428	1890	7437
Non-married										
Single	17	34	22	9	23	1716	1097	385	101	3299
Widowed	0	†	6	5	6	0	5	79	168	252
Divorced	†	35	27	18	27	11	244	602	280	1137
Separated	[9]	9	9	7	9	22	148	222	56	448
	17	31	21	12	22					
Total	16	14	6	3	9	1936	3426	4716	2495	12573

* Men and women describing themselves as 'separated' were, strictly speaking, legally married. However, because the separated can cohabit they have been included in the 'non-married' category.

† Base too small to enable reliable analysis to be made.

203

Table 12.5 **Cohabiters: age by sex**

Cohabiting persons aged 16-59   *Great Britain: 1996*

Age	Men	Women
	%	%
16-19	1	4
20-24	15	26
25-29	30	24
30-34	19	16
35-39	13	11
40-44	7	6
45-49	7	6
50-54	6	4
55-59	3	2
Base = 100%	*501*	*564*

Table 12.6 **Legal marital status of women aged 18-49: 1979 to 1996**

Women aged 18-49   *Great Britain*

Legal marital status*	1979	1981	1983	1985	1989	1991	1992	1993	1994	1995	1996
	%	%	%	%	%	%	%	%	%	%	%
Married	74	72	70	68	63	61	59	59	57	58	57
Non-married											
Single	18	20	21	22	26	26	29	28	29	28	29
Widowed	1	1	1	1	1	1	1	1	1	1	1
Divorced	4	5	6	6	7	8	8	9	9	9	9
Separated	3	3	2	3	3	3	4	4	4	4	4
Base = 100%	*6006*	*6524*	*5285*	*5364*	*5483*	*5359*	*5364*	*5171*	*5123*	*4953*	*4695*

* See the first footnote to Table 12.4.

Table 12.7 **Percentage of women aged 18-49 cohabiting by legal marital status: 1979 to 1996**

Women aged 18-49   *Great Britain*

Legal marital status*	1979		1981		1985		1989		1991		1992		1993		1994		1995		1996	
							Percentage cohabiting													
Married	-		-		-		-		-		-		-		-		-		-	
Non-married																				
Single	8		9		14		19		23		21		23		24		26		28	
Widowed	0	11	6	12	5	16	9	21	2	23	[9]	21	[8]	22	[19]	23	[8]	25	[5]	26
Divorced	20		20		21		30		30		28		25		28		27		31	
Separated	17		19		20		17		13		12		11		10		11		7	
Total	3		3		5		8		9		9		9		10		10		11	
Bases = 100%																				
Married	*4461*		*4674*		*3653*		*3457*		*3265*		*3160*		*3053*		*2913*		*2864*		*2683*	
Non-married																				
Single	*1061*		*1303*		*1175*		*1433*		*1416*		*1532*		*1431*		*1486*		*1405*		*1361*	
Widowed	*61*		*66*		*55*		*55*		*55*		*46*		*49*		*43*		*40*		*44*	
Divorced	*256*		*314*		*338*		*387*		*448*		*432*		*453*		*468*		*437*		*421*	
Separated	*167*		*167*		*143*		*151*		*175*		*194*		*185*		*209*		*206*		*186*	
Total	*6006*		*6524*		*5364*		*5483*		*5359*		*5364*		*5171*		*5119*		*4952*		*4695*	

* See the first footnote to Table 12.4.

204

Table 12.8 **Women aged 16-59: percentage cohabiting by legal marital status and whether has dependent children in the household**

Women aged 16-59   *Great Britain: 1996*

Legal marital status	Percentage cohabiting			Bases = 100%		
	Has dependent children	*No dependent children*	Total	*Has dependent children*	*No dependent children*	*Total**
Married	-	-	-	*2000*	*1581*	*3593*
Non-married						
Single	41	19	24	*368*	*1262*	*1634*
Widowed	0	6	5	*24*	*100*	*124*
Divorced	31	27	29	*266*	*277*	*548*
Separated	5	14	8	*150*	*63*	*213*
(Non-married grouped)	*30*	*19*	*22*			
Total	9	10	9	*2808*	*3283*	*6112*

* Totals with dependent children and without dependent children do not sum to the total because the dependency of some children could not be established.

Table 12.9 **Cumulative percentages of men and women separated within a given period by year of marriage**

Persons born 1938-76 and first married aged under 30   *Great Britain: 1996*

Year of marriage	Percentage of first marriages ending in separation within:				Base = 100%
	3 years	5 years	10 years	20 years	
Men					
1965-69	3	7	14*	26*	*477*
1970-74	5	10	20*	28*	*488*
1975-79	8	11*	18*		*423*
1980-84	9	14	24*		*382*
1985-89	7	11*			*348*
Women					
1965-69	3*	6*	15*	26*	*555*
1970-74	5	10*	18*	30*	*589*
1975-79	7*	11*	21*		*532*
1980-84	8*	12*	23		*477*
1985-89	12*	18*			*449*

* Analysis was done using life table technique so that account could be taken of people who were widowed. The asterisked cells are those affected.

Table 12.10 **Cumulative percentages of women separated within a given period by age at, and year of, marriage**

Women born 1938-76 and first married aged under 30   *Great Britain: 1996*

Age at marriage Year of marriage	Percentage of first marriages ending in separation within:				Base = 100%
	3 years	5 years	10 years	20 years	
Less than 20					
1965-69	6	9	23*	36	180
1970-74	8	14*	27*	39*	212
1975-79	11*	19*	30*		176
1980-84	20	27	38		101
1985-89	19	32			69
20-24					
1965-69	2*	5*	12*	23*	326
1970-74	3	9	15	26*	315
1975-79	5	8	17		274
1980-84	5*	9*	21*		303
1985-89	12	18			257
25-29					
1965-69	2	4	8	10	49
1970-74	2	3	5*	20*	62
1975-79	2	6	12		82
1980-84	1	4*	10*		73
1985-89	8	11			123

* See the footnote to Table 12.9.

Table 12.11 **Cumulative percentages of men remarried within a given period following separation, by year of separation**

*Men aged 16-59 who were under 35 when
their first marriage ended in separation*   *Great Britain: 1995 and 1996 combined*

Year of separation*		Percentages remarried within:							Base = 100%
		1 year	2 years	3 years	4 years	6 years	8 years	10 years	
1967-70	%	0	2	18	34	58	68	73	93
1969-72	%	1	9	25	37	58	66	74	142
1971-74	%	1	9	21	33	54	63	70	159
1973-76	%	1	7	18	30	52	61	67	162
1975-78	%	1	11	24	37	56	65	69	180
1977-80	%	1	11	25	38	57	67	69	216
1979-82	%	1	9	21	31	49	61	64	194
1981-84	%	1	7	20	31	48	60	65	167
1983-86	%	1	8	20	30	45	58		171
1985-88	%	2	7	18	26	37			180
1987-90	%	1	4	16	23				191
1989-92	%	1	5						165

* The groupings overlap in order to extend the trend series.

Table 12.12 Cumulative percentages of women remarried within a given period following separation, by year of separation

Women aged 16-59 who were under 35 when their first marriage ended in separation

Great Britain: 1995 and 1996 combined

Year of separation*		Percentages remarried within:							Base = 100%
		1 year	2 years	3 years	4 years	6 years	8 years	10 years	
1967-70	%	1	10	23	38	50	60	67	124
1969-72	%	1	9	23	40	56	65	70	161
1971-74	%	1	6	19	33	51	62	70	205
1973-76	%	4	9	18	29	47	59	66	255
1975-78	%	4	14	21	31	48	59	62	264
1977-80	%	2	13	21	29	44	52	56	261
1979-82	%	2	10	21	26	41	47	52	271
1981-84	%	3	9	21	28	41	47	51	274
1983-86	%	2	10	21	31	42	48		270
1985-88	%	1	9	18	27	36			264
1987-90	%	1	8	15	22				279
1989-92	%	0	6						303

* See the footnote to Table 12.11.

13 Sports and leisure activities

The current format of questions about participation in sports and leisure activities has been used in the GHS at three year intervals since 1987. Sports and leisure activities include all active leisure pursuits with the exception of gardening and DIY which are considered separately. Walking is included only where the walk was for pleasure and of 2 miles or more, but all cycling is included. In 1996, new questions on the use of leisure facilities and competitive participation were introduced. Appendix A gives full details of the methodology.

Sports participation

In 1996, almost two-thirds of adults (64%) had taken part in some sport or physical activity during the four weeks before interview. Leisure walks of 2 miles or more contributed considerably to this total; the exclusion of respondents whose only activity had been those long walks reduced the overall participation figure to 46%. In 1996:

- 45% of adults said they had been for a walk of two miles or more in the four weeks before interview;
- indoor swimming was the next most popular activity; 13% of adults had been swimming in the four weeks before interview;
- only three other activities were mentioned by more than 10% of adults: keep fit/yoga - including aerobics and exercise classes (12%), cue sports - snooker/billiards/pool (11%) and cycling (11%);
- among the most popular sports, cycling and keep fit/yoga had the highest frequency of participation among participants at around twice a week (8 times in the four week reference period for cycling and 7 for keep/fit yoga);
- some of the less frequently mentioned sports also attracted a comparatively high frequency of participation - participants in weight lifting, horse riding and gymnastics all took part around twice a week on average. **Table 13.1**

Participation rates over a twelve month reference period were also collected. In 1996:

- 81% of people said they had taken part in at least one activity in the year before interview, which reduced to 66% when walking is excluded; **Figure 13A**
- based on annual participation, indoor swimming was still the most popular activity after walking (35%). The annual rates for the other most popular sports were all around 20% (keep fit/yoga and cycling both at 21% and cue sports at 19%);

- cycling had the highest average annual frequency of participation per adult at 11.6 days per adult per year. This compared with 10.8 for keep fit/yoga and 5.9 for indoor swimming. **Table 13.1**

Participation rates were different for men and women. Men were more likely than women to have participated in at least one activity in either the four weeks or twelve months before interview. Men also had higher participation rates than women in each activity with the exception of indoor swimming and keep fit/yoga. In 1996:

- seven out of ten men (71%) compared with six out of ten women (58%) had participated in at least one activity in the four week reference period;
- walking was the most popular activity for both men and women in the four week reference period but for men the next most popular was the cue sports while for women keep fit/yoga took second place together with swimming; **Table 13.3 Figure 13B**
- 54% of men and 38% of women had taken part in at least one activity other than walking;
- the greatest differences in participation between men and women were found for:
     cue sports - 20% of men compared with 4% of women had participated in the four weeks before the interview
     soccer - 10% of men and less than 1% of women
     cycling - 15% and 8% respectively

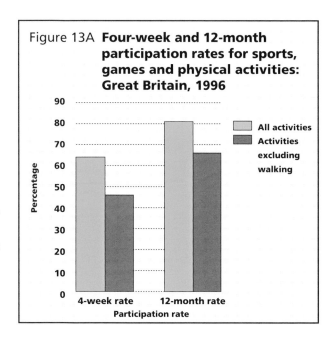

Figure 13A **Four-week and 12-month participation rates for sports, games and physical activities: Great Britain, 1996**

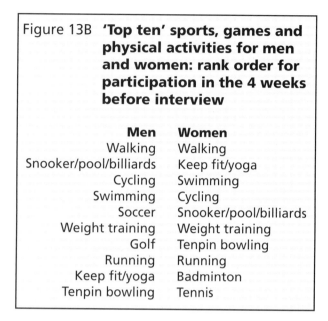

Figure 13B 'Top ten' sports, games and physical activities for men and women: rank order for participation in the 4 weeks before interview

Men	Women
Walking	Walking
Snooker/pool/billiards	Keep fit/yoga
Cycling	Swimming
Swimming	Cycling
Soccer	Snooker/pool/billiards
Weight training	Weight training
Golf	Tenpin bowling
Running	Running
Keep fit/yoga	Badminton
Tenpin bowling	Tennis

- participation rates for women were significantly higher than for men in:

  indoor swimming - 15% of women compared with 11% of men had participated in the four weeks before the interview

  keep fit/yoga - 17% of women and 7% of men.

Table 13.3 Figure 13C

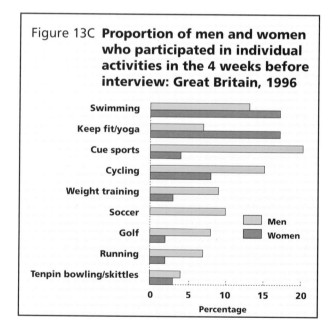

Figure 13C Proportion of men and women who participated in individual activities in the 4 weeks before interview: Great Britain, 1996

Trends in sports participation

There has been no significant change in overall participation in sports since the increase between 1987 and 1990; the overall participation rate which excludes respondents whose only activity had been long walks has shown a slight decline since 1990.

- The proportion of adults who had participated in at least one sport (including long walks) in the four week reference period increased from 61% in 1987 to 65% in 1990 since when it has remained at a similar level. In 1996 it was 64%.

- Participation rates excluding walking have declined slightly from 48% in 1990 to 46% in 1996.
- Four week participation rates in most specific activities showed little change between 1993 and 1996 with the exception of walking which increased from 41% to 45%.
- Since 1987, there has been a small but gradual increase in four week participation rates for cycling from 8% to 11% and a gradual decrease in the rates for cue sports (15% to 11%).
- Four week participation rates for swimming and keep fit/yoga reflected the trend in the overall participation rate with no change since an increase between 1987 and 1990.   **Table 13.4 Figure 13D**

The overall trends varied for men and women. For example:

- among women there has been no significant change in the overall four week participation rate including walking since it increased from 52% in 1987 to 57% in 1990. The rate excluding walking, at 38% in 1996, was not significantly different from the 1990 figure of 39%;
- four week participation rates for men have shown a slight fall since 1990 for both the rate including walking (from 73% in 1990 to 71% in 1996) and excluding walking (from 58% in 1990 to 54% in 1996);

Table 13.5

Participation rates by age

The proportion of adults who had taken part in at least one sport or physical activity in the four weeks before interview was lower with each successive age group. This age difference was more pronounced when walking was excluded from the overall measure. In 1996:

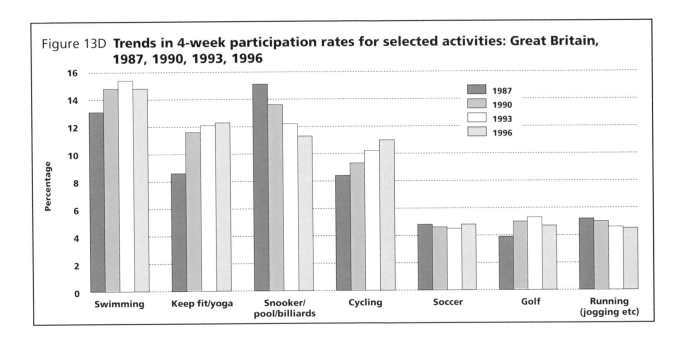

Figure 13D **Trends in 4-week participation rates for selected activities: Great Britain, 1987, 1990, 1993, 1996**

- 86% of 16-19 year olds had taken part in at least one activity in the four week reference period (including walking) compared with 81% of 20-24 year olds and 77% of 25-29 year olds; the equivalent figures at the upper end of the age range were 55% of 60-69 year olds and 31% of people aged 70 or more;
- participation rates which excluded walking ranged from 78% of 16-19 year olds to 13% of people aged 70 or more.

Some activities did not follow this general trend, in particular:

- participation in walking maintained fairly similar levels up to the 60-69 age group (52% of 16-19 year olds compared with 45% of those aged 60-69);
- participation in swimming and keep fit/yoga maintained similar levels between the ages of 16 and 44.

Table 13.7

The decrease in participation with age was similar for both men and women, although in each age group participation levels were lower for women than for men. For example:

- in 1996, 69% of 16-19 year old women took part in at least one activity in the four week reference period (excluding walking) compared with 87% of 16-19 year old men, the equivalent figures for people aged 70 or more were 9% of women and 18% of men. **Table 13.8**

Participation rates by social and economic characteristics

Unskilled manual workers and adults who were economically inactive were the least likely to participate in any sports or physical activities including walking. These findings applied to both men and women and were not attributable to the different age structures of the groups. In 1996:

- four-week participation rates of professional people were almost twice those of unskilled manual workers (80% compared with 45%). The rates excluding walking were almost three times as high (63% compared with 23%); **Tables 13.9-13.11**
- walking was the activity with the highest rate of participation for all socio-economic groups, but there were still large differences between the participation rates of professional and unskilled manual workers (56% compared with 33%);
- nearly a quarter (23%) of those in the professional group had swum in the four weeks before interview compared with 6% of unskilled manual workers. Apart from walking, no activity among unskilled manual workers had a participation rate of more than 7%; **Table 13.10**
- men and women who were economically inactive had lower participation rates than those who were in work or unemployed. For example, 52% of economically

inactive men had participated in at least one sport or physical activity in the four week reference period compared with 79% of men in full-time work (the equivalent figures for women were 45% and 69%). Although the former group comprises older people, age-standardised ratios indicated that these differences were not the effect of age alone;   **Table 13.12**

- age-standardised ratios indicated that men and women in households where the youngest child was aged 5-15 were more likely to participate in sport and physical activity than would be expected on the basis of the age composition of this group.   **Table 13.13**

Participation by region

There was some variation between regions in the participation rates for the four weeks before interview. Adults living in the North, West Midlands and Yorkshire and Humberside regions were the least likely to have taken part in some sport or physical activity during the four weeks before interview (57%, 59% and 61% respectively) and those living in the South West, East Anglia or the two South East regions outside of London were the most likely (66%, 67%, 68% and 67% respectively). Adults living in Scotland also had high participation rates (66%). These overall variations were generally reflected in the three most popular activities. In 1996:

- half of adults in Scotland (50%), the South West (49%) and the South East regions excluding London (48%) had taken a walk of at least two miles in the four weeks before interview compared with 39% of those living in the West Midlands and East Anglia;
- 22% of East Anglians had cycled in the four weeks before interview compared with no more than 15% in any other region;
- participation rates for swimming ranged from 11% in the North to 18% in the South West region.

Table 13.14

Use of facilities

One of the new questions on sports participation introduced in the 1996 GHS concerned the type of facility used for participation in each type of sport (excluding walking) among those who had participated in the four weeks before interview. It should be noted that some variation in the type of facility used will reflect differences in sports participation. In 1996:

- nearly one in four adults (24%) had used an indoor facility which was mainly for sport (eg a sports centre or indoor swimming pool) and about one in ten (11%) had used an outdoor facility which was mainly for sport (eg playing field or outdoor swimming pool);
- other sporting activity took place in indoor facilities not mainly used for sport such as village halls (12%), outdoors in a natural setting (14%) and 7% took place at home (the respondent's or someone else's);
- 15% of people used a facility that belonged to a school, college or university.   **Table 13.15**

Use of facilities varied between men and women:

- men were more than three times as likely as women to use an outdoor sports facility (18% compared with 5%):
- but there was considerably less difference between the proportion of men and women who used indoor sports facilities (26% of men and 23% of women) or took part in sport in their homes (8% and 6% respectively).

Table 13.15

Club membership, competition and tuition

Among people who had participated in at least one activity (excluding walking) in the four weeks before interview, club membership during that period varied considerably from activity to activity, as did participation in organised competition and tuition within the twelve months prior to interview. In general, activities with a high club membership also had a higher than average proportion of participants who took part in organised competition. For example:

- bowls, golf and soccer were all activities with both a comparatively high proportion of club members and of competitive participation. Just over two-thirds (67%) of bowls players, 47% of golfers and 34% of soccer players belonged to clubs in the four weeks before interview while 58%, 42% and 43% respectively had participated in organised competitions in the twelve months before interview;
- club membership and competitive participation was lowest among cyclists (2% and 2%), swimmers (11% and 2%) and tenpin bowlers (4% and 8%);
- participants in horse riding, keep fit/yoga, weight training, weight lifting and golf were the most likely to have received tuition in the twelve months before interview (48%, 40%, 26%, 26% and 20% respectively).

Table 13.17

Club membership, participation in organised competition and tuition varied according to the age, sex and socio-economic group of participants. It is likely that some of this variation reflected the different types of sports in which men and women of different ages participated. In 1996:

- about four out of ten men (41%) and one in four women (25%), who participated in at least one activity (excluding walking) in the four weeks before interview, had belonged to a club during that period so that they could participate in specific activities;
- club membership among male sports participants was highest in the oldest and youngest age groups (48% of men aged 60 or more and 46% of men aged 16-19 compared with 38% of men aged 25-44);
- club membership among women sports participants increased with age from 17% of women aged 16-19 to 37% of those aged 70 or more;
- nearly one in three men (32%) and one in ten women (10%), who had participated in at least one activity excluding walking, had participated in organised competition in the twelve months before interview;
- men aged 16-19 who participated in sport were the most likely to take part in organised competition and men aged 70 or over were the least likely (41% compared with 23%);
- women sports players in the youngest and oldest age groups were twice as likely as those aged 30-44 to have participated competitively (14% and 15% compared with 7%);

- women sports participants were more likely than male sports participants to have received tuition to improve their performance in the twelve months before interview (27% compared with 19%). **Table 13.18**
- a fifth (20%) of men who were sports participants and who were in non-manual occupations had received tuition in the twelve months before interview compared with 14% of male sports participants who were in manual occupations;
- the equivalent figures for women sports participants were 30% of those in non-manual occupations and 21% of those in manual occupations. **Table 13.19**

Participation in leisure activities

Questions about participation in leisure activities have been included in the sports section of GHS since 1977 but with a reduced format since 1990 in which respondents have been asked about participation in selected recreational activities in the four weeks before interview. In addition to the provision of information about specific leisure activities, information from these questions also provides a benchmark against which to measure the popularity of sports and physical activities. Participation in the recreational activities listed in the question was generally much higher than in sports and physical activities. In the four weeks before interview in 1996:

- the vast majority of people had watched television (99%) and a high proportion had listened to the radio (88%) and listened to records or tapes (78%);

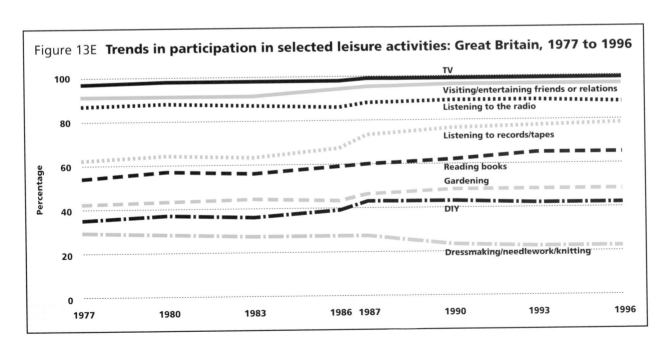

Figure 13E **Trends in participation in selected leisure activities: Great Britain, 1977 to 1996**

- two out of three adults had read books and more women than men had done so (71% compared with 58%) but there was little variation with age;
- DIY was more popular than gardening for men (58% compared with 52%) while the opposite was true for women (30% and 45% respectively);
- more than one third of women (37%) had done some dressmaking, needlework or sewing compared with 3% of men.   **Table 13.20**
- 46% of adults aged 70 or more had listened to records or tapes compared with 98% aged 16-19;
- 61% of adults aged 60-69 had gardened compared with 15% of 16-19 year olds and 35% of adults aged 25-29;
- around two-thirds of men aged between 30 and 59 had done some DIY compared with a third of those aged 16-19.   **Table 13.20**

Between 1993 and 1996 there has been no change in the participation rates of any of the listed leisure activities, but there have been a number of changes since 1977.

- in 1996, nearly two-thirds of adults (65%) had read books in the four weeks before interview compared with just over half (54%) in 1977;
- the participation rates for gardening increased from 42% to 48% in the same period but participation rates for sewing, needlework and knitting decreased from 29% to 22%.   **Table 13.21 Figure 13E**

Attendance at leisure classes

In 1996, 6% of adults had attended a leisure class[1] in the four weeks before interview; in 1993 it was 8%. Attendance at classes varied with age, sex, socio-economic group and economic activity.

- Women were twice as likely as men to be attending a class (8% compared with 4%).   **Table 13.23**
- Adults in non-manual occupations were twice as likely to attend classes as those with manual occupations (9% compared with 4%), a difference which was more evident among women.
- Men in part-time work were more likely to attend leisure classes in the four weeks before interview than those in full-time work or unemployed men (9% compared with 4% and 5%).   **Table 13.26**

Notes and references

1 'Leisure and recreation classes' includes any course or class which does not lead to an examination or qualification, i.e. they are courses which are not designed to further people's career or job prospects. Interviewers were instructed that classes must be regular and have a teacher, instructor or supervisor.

Table 13.1 **Sports, games and physical activities:**
(a) participation rates in the 4 weeks before the interview
(b) participation rates in the 12 months before the interview
(c) average frequency of participation per participant in 4 weeks before the interview
(d) average frequency of participation per adult per year

All persons aged 16 and over   *Great Britain: 1996*

Active sports, games and physical activities*	(a)	(b)	(c)	(d)
Walking†	44.5	68.2	..	..
Any swimming	14.8	39.6	4	8.2
Swimming: indoor	12.8	35.1	4	5.9
Swimming: outdoor	2.9	14.9	6	2.3
Keep fit/yoga	12.3	20.7	7	10.8
Snooker/pool/billiards	11.3	19.2	4	6.6
Cycling	11.0	21.4	8	11.6
Weight training	5.6	9.8	7	5.3
Any soccer	4.8	8.5	5	3.3
Soccer: outdoor	3.8	6.9	5	2.3
Soccer: indoor	2.1	4.8	4	1.0
Golf	4.7	11.0	4	2.5
Running (jogging, etc.)	4.5	8.0	6	3.5
Darts**	..	8.6	..	..
Tenpin bowls/skittles	3.4	15.5	2	0.7
Badminton	2.4	7.0	3	1.0
Tennis	2.0	7.1	4	1.0
Any bowls	1.9	4.6	6	1.4
Carpet bowls	1.1	3.0	5	0.8
Lawn bowls	0.9	2.8	6	0.7
Fishing	1.7	5.3	3	0.7
Table tennis	1.5	5.3	3	0.6
Squash	1.3	4.1	4	0.6
Weight lifting	1.3	2.6	8	1.3
Horse riding	1.0	3.0	8	1.0
Cricket	0.9	3.3	3	0.4
Shooting	0.8	2.8	4	0.4
Self defence	0.7	1.7	6	0.6
Climbing	0.7	2.5	2	0.2
Basketball	0.7	2.0	3	0.3
Rugby	0.6	1.3	4	0.3
Ice skating	0.6	3.2	1	0.1
Netball	0.5	1.4	3	0.2
Sailing	0.4	2.3	4	0.3
Motor sports	0.4	1.6	3	0.2
Canoeing	0.4	1.6	2	0.1
Hockey	0.3	1.1	4	0.2
Skiing	0.3	2.6	4	0.2
Athletics-track & field	0.2	1.2	5	0.2
Gymnastics	0.2	0.7	6	0.2
Windsurfing, boardsailing	0.2	1.1	2	0.1
At least one activity (exc. walking)††	45.6	65.9		
At least one activity††	63.6	81.4		
Base = 100%	*15696*	*15696*		

* Includes only activities in which more than 0.5% of men or of women participated in the 12 months before interview.
† In 1996 respondents were not asked how often they went walking.
** In 1996 respondents were asked about darts only in relation to the last twelve months and not the last four weeks.
†† Total includes those activities not separately listed.

Table 13.2 **Seasonal variation in sports, games and physical activities: participation rates in the 4 weeks before interview by quarter**

Persons aged 16 and over   *Great Britain: 1996*

Active sports, games and physical activities*	Month of interview				All months
	Jan-Mar 1997	Apr-Jun 1996	Jul-Sep 1996	Oct-Dec 1996	
	Percentage participating in the 4 weeks before interview†				
Usually outdoor					
Walking	42	47	48	41	45
Cycling	9	12	14	9	11
Golf	3	5	6	4	5
Running (jogging, etc.)	5	4	5	4	5
Soccer	4	4	4	3	4
Swimming	1	2	6	2	3
Tennis	1	2	4	1	2
Fishing	1	1	3	2	2
Horse riding	1	1	1	1	1
Lawn bowls	0	1	2	0	1
Cricket	0	1	2	0	1
Shooting	1	1	1	1	1
Climbing	1	0	1	1	1
Rugby	1	1	0	1	1
Athletics-track & field	0	0	0	0	0
Netball	0	1	0	1	0
Sailing	0	0	1	0	0
Motor sports	0	1	1	0	0
Canoeing	0	0	1	0	0
Hockey	0	0	0	1	0
Skiing	1	0	0	0	0
At least one outdoor activity (exc. walking)	20	27	33	22	25
At least one outdoor activity (inc. walking)	49	56	60	49	54
Usually indoor					
Swimming	11	13	16	10	13
Keep fit/yoga	13	13	12	11	12
Snooker/pool/billiards	12	12	11	10	11
Weight training	6	6	5	6	6
Tenpin bowls/skittles	4	4	3	3	3
Badminton	3	2	3	2	2
Soccer	2	2	2	2	2
Table tennis	1	2	2	2	2
Squash	1	1	1	1	1
Weight lifting	1	1	1	1	1
Carpet bowls	1	1	1	1	1
Self defence	1	1	1	1	1
Basketball	1	1	1	0	1
Ice skating	1	1	0	1	1
At least one indoor activity	36	37	36	33	35
At least one activity (exc. walking)**	44	47	50	41	46
At least one activity**	62	66	67	59	64
Base = 100%	*4178*	*3665*	*4136*	*3717*	*15696*

*   Includes only activities in which more than 0.5% of men or of women participated in the 4 weeks before interview in the most popular quarter for each activity.

†   For each activity, the figure for the quarter(s) with the highest participation rate is underlined.

** Total includes those activities not separately listed.

Table 13.3 **Sports, games and physical activities, participation rates by sex**
  (a) participation rates in the 4 weeks before interview
  (b) participation rates in the 12 months before interview

Persons aged 16 and over   *Great Britain: 1996*

Active sports, games and physical activities*	(a) Percentage participating in 4 weeks before interview			(b) Percentage participating in 12 months before interview		
	Men	Women	Total	Men	Women	Total
Walking	49	41	45	73	64	68
Any swimming	13	17	15	37	41	40
Swimming: indoor	11	15	13	32	37	35
Swimming: outdoor	3	3	3	17	14	15
Keep fit/yoga	7	17	12	10	29	21
Snooker/pool/billiards	20	4	11	33	8	19
Cycling	15	8	11	27	16	21
Weight training	9	3	6	14	6	10
Any soccer	10	0	5	18	1	8
Soccer: outdoor	8	0	4	14	1	7
Soccer: indoor	4	0	2	10	0	5
Golf	8	2	5	19	4	11
Running (jogging, etc.)	7	2	5	12	5	8
Tenpin bowls/skittles	4	3	3	18	13	15
Badminton	3	2	2	8	6	7
Tennis	2	2	2	9	6	7
Any bowls	2	1	2	6	3	5
Carpet bowls	1	1	1	4	2	3
Lawn bowls	1	1	1	4	2	3
Fishing	3	0	2	10	1	5
Table tennis	2	1	2	7	4	5
Squash	2	0	1	7	2	4
Weight lifting	2	1	1	4	1	3
Horse riding	0	1	1	2	4	3
Cricket	2	0	1	7	0	3
Shooting	2	0	1	5	1	3
Self defence	1	0	1	3	1	2
Climbing	1	0	1	4	1	2
Basketball	1	0	1	3	1	2
Rugby	1	0	1	3	0	1
Ice skating	0	1	1	3	3	3
Netball	0	1	0	0	2	1
Sailing	1	0	0	3	1	2
Motor sports	1	0	0	3	0	2
Canoeing	1	0	0	2	1	2
Hockey	0	0	0	1	1	1
Skiing	1	0	0	3	2	3
Athletics - track & field	0	0	0	2	1	1
Gymnastics	0	0	0	1	1	1
Windsuring, boardsailing	0	0	0	2	1	1
At least one activity (exc. walking)†	54	38	46	72	60	66
At least one activity†	71	58	64	87	77	81
Base = 100%	*7186*	*8510*	*15696*	*7186*	*8510*	*15696*

* Includes only activities in which more than 0.5% of men or of women participated in the 12 months before interview.
† Total includes those activities not separately listed.

Table 13.4   **Trends in participation in sports, games and physical activities: 1987, 1990, 1993 and 1996**

Persons aged 16 and over   *Great Britain*

Active sports, games and physical activities*	Percentage participating in the 4 weeks before interview				Percentage participating in the 12 months before interview				Average number of occasions of participation in 4 weeks			
	1987	1990	1993	1996	1987	1990	1993	1996	1987	1990	1993	1996
Walking	38	41	41	45	60	65	65	68	8	8	8	..
Swimming	13	15	15	15	35	42	43	40	4	4	4	4
Keep fit/yoga	9	12	12	12	14	19	20	21	9	9	8	7
Snooker/pool/billiards	15	14	12	11	23	22	20	19	6	5	5	4
Cycling	8	9	10	11	15	17	19	21	10	10	10	8
Weight training†	5	5	5	6	8	9	10	10	8	7	8	7
Weight lifting				1				2				8
Soccer	5	5	4	5	9	9	8	8	4	5	5	5
Golf	4	5	5	5	9	12	12	11	4	4	4	4
Running (jogging, etc)	5	5	5	5	11	9	8	8	7	6	6	6
Tenpin bowls/skittles	2	4	4	3	6	11	15	15	2	2	2	2
Badminton	3	3	3	2	8	9	7	7	3	3	3	3
Tennis	2	2	2	2	7	7	7	7	4	4	4	4
Lawn/carpet bowls	2	2	2	2	4	5	4	5	6	6	6	5
Fishing	2	2	2	2	6	6	6	5	3	3	3	3
Table tennis	2	2	2	2	6	5	5	5	4	4	3	3
Squash	3	3	2	1	7	6	5	4	4	4	4	4
Horse riding	1	1	1	1	3	3	3	3	7	6	7	8
At least one activity (exc. walking)**	45	48	47	46	62	67	68	66				
At least one activity**	61	65	64	64	78	82	82	81				
Base = 100%	*19529*	*17574*	*17552*	*15696*	*19529*	*17574*	*17552*	*15696*				

*   Activities are listed in descending order of 4 week participation rate for all adults in 1996. Includes only activities in which more than 1.0% of all persons participated in 4 weeks before interview in 1996 and sports for which results are available for all years.

†   In 1987-93 these categories were combined. In 1996 they were asked separately.

** Total includes those activities not separately listed.

Table 13.5 **Trends in participation in sports, games and physical activities in the 4 weeks before interview by sex: 1987, 1990, 1993 and 1996**

Persons aged 16 and over   *Great Britain*

Active sports, games and physical activities*	Men				Women			
	1987	1990	1993	1996	1987	1990	1993	1996
				Percentage participating in the 4 weeks before interview				
Walking	41	44	45	49	35	38	37	41
Any swimming	..	14	15	13	..	15	16	17
Swimming: indoor	10	11	12	11	11	13	14	15
Swimming: outdoor	4	4	4	3	3	4	3	3
Keep fit/yoga	5	6	6	7	12	16	17	17
Snooker/pool/billiards	27	24	21	20	5	5	5	4
Cycling	10	12	14	15	7	7	7	8
Weight training	7	8	9	9	2	2	3	3
Weight lifting				2				1
Any soccer	10	10	9	10	0	0	0	0
Golf	7	9	9	8	1	2	2	2
Running (jogging, etc.)	8	8	7	7	3	2	2	2
Tenpin bowls/skittles	2	5	5	4	1	3	3	3
Badminton	4	4	3	3	3	3	2	2
Tennis	2	2	3	2	1	2	2	2
Any bowls	2	3	3	2	1	1	2	1
Fishing	4	4	4	3	0	0	0	0
Table tennis	4	3	2	2	1	1	1	1
Squash	4	4	3	2	1	1	1	0
Horse riding	0	1	0	0	1	1	1	1
At least one activity (exc. walking)†	57	58	57	54	34	39	39	38
At least one activity†	70	73	72	71	52	57	57	58
Base = 100%	*9086*	*8119*	*8062*	*7186*	*10443*	*9455*	*9490*	*8510*

* Includes only activities in which more than 1.0% of all adults participated in 4 weeks before interview in 1996.

† Total includes those activities not separately listed.

Table 13.6 **Trends in participation in sports, games and physical activities in the 4 weeks before interview by age: 1987, 1990, 1993 and 1996**

Persons aged 16 and over   *Great Britain*

	Year	Age							Total
		16-19	20-24	25-29	30-44	45-59	60-69	70 and over	
		Percentage participating in the 4 weeks before interview							
At least one activity (exc walking)	1987	80	69	63	56	35	23	10	45
	1990	82	72	67	59	42	28	12	48
	1993	81	71	65	58	43	28	16	47
	1996	78	70	63	57	40	30	13	46
At least one activity	1987	86	77	74	71	56	47	26	61
	1990	87	81	78	73	63	54	31	65
	1993	86	80	77	73	64	51	33	64
	1996	86	81	77	73	63	55	31	64
Bases = 100%	*1987*	*1384*	*1821*	*1827*	*5162*	*4140*	*2654*	*2541*	*19529*
	1990	*1096*	*1439*	*1723*	*4695*	*3778*	*2437*	*2406*	*17574*
	1993	*899*	*1379*	*1649*	*4768*	*3959*	*2301*	*2597*	*17552*
	1996	*829*	*1039*	*1441*	*4372*	*3686*	*2024*	*2305*	*15696*

Table 13.7 **Sports, games and physical activities: participation rates in the 4 weeks before interview by age**

Persons aged 16 and over   *Great Britain: 1996*

Active sports, games and physical activities*	Age							Total	Median age of adult participants
	16-19	20-24	25-29	30-44	45-59	60-69	70 and over		
	Percentage participating in the 4 weeks before interview								
Walking	52	49	45	49	49	45	24	45	43
Any swimming	21	19	20	22	12	9	3	15	36
Keep fit/yoga	20	20	18	16	10	8	3	12	36
Snooker/pool/billiards	39	30	20	11	6	4	2	11	29
Cycling	25	17	13	15	9	6	2	11	36
Weight training	16	14	12	8	2	0	0	6	29
Any soccer	25	14	9	5	1	0	0	5	26
Golf	5	5	4	6	6	4	1	5	42
Running (jogging, etc.)	12	11	8	6	2	0	0	5	31
Tenpin bowls/skittles	12	9	6	4	2	0	0	3	29
Badminton	7	3	3	3	2	1	0	2	34
Tennis	8	3	3	2	2	1	0	2	33
Any bowls	1	0	1	1	2	4	3	2	60
Fishing	2	2	2	2	2	1	0	2	38
Table tennis	6	2	2	2	1	1	0	2	36
Squash	3	2	3	2	1	0	0	1	32
Weight lifting	6	3	2	1	1	0	0	1	27
Horse riding	2	2	2	1	1	0	0	1	35
At least one activity (exc. walking)†	78	70	63	57	40	30	13	46	36
At least one activity†	86	81	77	73	63	55	31	64	40
Base = 100%	*829*	*1039*	*1441*	*4372*	*3686*	*2024*	*2305*	*15696*	

* Includes only activities in which more than 1.0% of all adults participated in the 4 weeks before interview.
† Total includes those activities not separately listed.

Table 13.8 **Sports, games and physical activities: participation rates in the 4 weeks before interview by age and sex**

Persons aged 16 and over   *Great Britain: 1996*

Active sports, games and physical activities*	Age							Total	Median age of adult participants
	16-19	20-24	25-29	30-44	45-59	60-69	70 and over		

Percentage participating in the 4 weeks before interview

Men

Walking	58	58	47	53	52	49	30	49	43
Snooker/pool/billiards	55	45	33	21	12	8	4	20	31
Cycling	37	24	18	19	12	7	4	15	35
Any swimming	18	17	15	20	9	8	3	13	37
Any soccer	47	28	20	11	2	0	0	10	26
Weight training	25	23	19	12	3	0	0	9	29
Golf	8	10	8	11	10	6	3	8	40
Running (jogging, etc.)	14	17	13	11	4	1	0	7	32
Keep fit/yoga	10	10	10	9	5	4	2	7	36
Tenpin bowls/skittles	13	9	6	5	2	0	0	4	30
Fishing	5	4	5	5	3	2	1	3	38
Badminton	7	4	3	5	2	1	0	3	34
Any bowls	1	1	1	1	3	6	4	2	60
Tennis	10	3	3	3	2	1	0	2	33
Table tennis	9	3	3	3	2	1	1	2	36
Squash	4	3	4	4	2	0	0	2	34
Weight lifting	10	4	3	2	1	0	0	2	27
Cricket	8	3	2	2	1	0	0	2	30
Shooting	2	3	2	2	2	1	0	2	38
Self defence	2	4	3	2	0	0	0	1	28
Basketball	14	3	1	1	0	0	0	1	17
Rugby	7	4	2	1	0	0	0	1	23
Climbing	2	2	2	1	1	0	0	1	33
At least one activity (exc. walking)†	87	81	76	68	46	34	18	54	37
At least one activity†	93	90	85	80	68	61	39	71	40
Base = 100%	*418*	*472*	*651*	*1980*	*1729*	*947*	*989*	*7186*	

Women

Walking	45	43	44	45	47	41	19	41	43
Keep fit/yoga	30	28	25	21	14	11	4	17	36
Any swimming	23	21	24	24	14	10	3	17	36
Cycling	14	11	9	12	7	4	1	8	36
Snooker/pool/billiards	24	17	8	3	1	0	0	4	24
Weight training	7	6	6	4	2	0	0	3	30
Tenpin bowls/skittles	10	8	6	4	1	0	0	3	28
Running (jogging, etc.)	9	6	4	3	1	0	0	2	28
Badminton	6	2	3	2	2	1	0	2	33
Tennis	6	2	2	2	1	1	0	2	34
Golf	1	2	1	1	2	2	1	2	48
Horse riding	3	2	3	2	1	0	0	1	34
Any bowls	1	0	1	1	1	3	2	1	59
At least one activity (exc. walking)†	69	60	53	49	34	26	9	38	36
At least one activity†	78	73	70	66	59	51	24	58	40
Base = 100%	*411*	*567*	*790*	*2392*	*1957*	*1077*	*1316*	*8510*	

* Includes only activities in which more than 1.0% of all men or women participated in the 4 weeks before interview.
† Total includes those activities not separately listed.

Table 13.9 **Trends in participation in sports, games and physical activities in the 4 weeks before interview by socio-economic group: 1987, 1990, 1993 and 1996**

Persons aged 16 and over   *Great Britain*

	Year	Socio-economic group*						
		Profess-ional	Employers and managers	Intermediate and junior non-manual	Skilled manual and own account non-professional	Semi-skilled manual and personal service	Unskilled manual	Total†
		Percentage participating in the 4 weeks before interview						
At least one activity (exc walking)	1987	65	52	45	48	34	26	45
	1990	65	53	49	49	38	28	48
	1993	64	53	49	46	36	31	47
	1996	63	52	47	45	37	23	46
At least one activity	1987	78	68	63	62	51	42	61
	1990	79	71	67	66	55	46	65
	1993	82	71	65	63	54	48	64
	1996	80	69	66	63	55	45	64
Base = 100%	*1987*	*705*	*2465*	*6012*	*4051*	*3830*	*1265*	*19529*
	1990	*680*	*2355*	*5666*	*3602*	*3302*	*970*	*17574*
	1993	*708*	*2362*	*5608*	*3486*	*2978*	*1164*	*17552*
	1996	*542*	*2187*	*5091*	*3019*	*2780*	*924*	*15696*

* Socio-economic group is based on the person's current or most recent job.
† Total includes full-time students, members of the Armed Forces, those who have never worked, and those whose job was inadequately described.

Table 13.10 **Sports, games and physical activities: participation rates in the 4 weeks before interview by socio-economic group**

Persons aged 16 and over   *Great Britain: 1996*

Active sports, games and physical activities*	Socio-economic group†						
	Professional	Employers and managers	Intermediate and junior non-manual	Skilled manual and own account non-professional	Semi-skilled manual and personal service	Unskilled manual	Total**
	Percentage participating in the 4 weeks before interview						
Walking	56	48	46	44	39	33	45
Any swimming	23	19	17	11	11	6	15
Keep fit/yoga	14	12	18	7	9	5	12
Snooker/pool/billiards	11	11	8	16	10	7	11
Cycling	19	12	9	11	10	7	11
Weight training	10	5	6	5	3	2	6
Any soccer	5	4	3	6	3	3	5
Golf	11	9	4	5	3	1	5
Running (jogging, etc.)	9	6	4	4	2	2	5
Tenpin bowls/skittles	4	3	4	3	2	1	3
Badminton	3	3	3	1	1	1	2
Tennis	4	3	2	1	1	0	2
Any bowls	1	3	2	2	2	1	2
Fishing	2	2	1	3	2	1	2
Table tennis	5	2	1	1	1	0	2
Squash	5	2	1	1	1	0	1
Weight lifting	1	1	1	1	1	1	1
Horse riding	1	1	1	1	1	0	1
At least one activity (exc. walking)††	63	52	47	45	37	23	46
At least one activity††	80	69	66	63	55	45	64
Base = 100%	*542*	*2187*	*5091*	*3019*	*2780*	*924*	*15696*

* Includes only activities in which more than 1.0% of all adults participated in the 4 weeks before interview.
† Socio-economic group is based on the person's current or most recent job.
** Total includes full-time students, members of the Armed Forces, those who have never worked, and those whose job was inadequately described.
†† Total includes those activities not separately listed.

Table 13.11 **Participation in at least one physical activity in the 4 weeks before interview by socio-economic group and sex: age-standardised**

Persons aged 16 and over   *Great Britain: 1996*

	Professional	Employers and managers	Intermediate and junior non-manual	Skilled manual and own account non-professional	Semi-skilled manual and personal service	Unskilled manual
	Percentage participating in the 4 weeks before interview					
Men						
Observed%	78	72	78	66	66	54
Expected%	70	68	73	69	70	70
Standardised ratio	111*	107*	106*	97*	95*	77*
Base = 100%	*417*	*1472*	*1190*	*2341*	*1034*	*280*
Women						
Observed%	85	62	63	53	48	42
Expected%	65	58	58	55	57	57
Standardised ratio	131*	108*	107*	96*	84*	73*
Base = 100%	*125*	*715*	*3902*	*678*	*1746*	*644*

* Ratio significantly different from 100 (p < 0.05).

Table 13.12 **Participation in at least one physical activity in the 4 weeks before interview by economic activity status and sex: age-standardised**

Persons aged 16 and over   *Great Britain: 1996*

	Working full time	Working part time†	Unemployed	Economically inactive
	Percentage participating in the 4 weeks before interview			
Men				
Observed%	79	82	79	52
Expected%	77	77	80	56
Standardised ratio	102*	106*	99	93*
Base = 100%	*3974*	*495*	*491*	*2226*
Women				
Observed%	69	69	66	45
Expected%	66	64	67	49
Standardised ratio	104*	108*	98	92*
Base = 100%	*2124*	*2086*	*322*	*3979*

* Ratio significantly different from 100 (p < 0.05).
† Includes a small number of cases where hours of work were not known.

Table13.13 **Participation in at least one physical activity in the 4 weeks before interview by household type and sex: age-standardised**

Persons aged 16 and over *Great Britain: 1996*

	One adult only	Two adults only	Three or more adults only	Youngest child aged 0-4	Youngest child aged 5-15
	Percentage participating in the 4 weeks before interview				
Men					
Observed%	63	64	76	79	79
Expected%	64	63	76	81	71
Standardised ratio	98	101	100	98	112*
Base = 100%	*1028*	*2594*	*1396*	*884*	*1284*
Women					
Observed%	41	55	62	64	67
Expected%	42	53	63	68	58
Standardised ratio	98	103	100	94	117*
Base = 100%	*1460*	*2769*	*1374*	*1225*	*1683*

* Ratio significantly different from 100 (p < 0.05).

Table 13.14 **'Top five' sports, games and physical activities: participation in the 4 weeks before interview by region**

Persons aged 16 and over *Great Britain: 1996*

Active sports, games and physical activities	Region													
	North	Yorks and Humberside	North West	East Midlands	West Midlands	East Anglia	Greater London	Outer Metropolitan Area	Outer South East	Total South East	South West	Wales	Scotland	Great Britain
	Percentages participating in the 4 weeks before interview													
Top five sports														
Any walking	41	43	43	44	39	39	43	48	48	46	49	45	50	45
Any swimming	11	13	14	15	14	16	14	17	16	16	18	13	15	15
Keep fit/yoga	11	12	14	10	12	12	14	14	12	13	12	10	12	12
Snooker/pool/billiards	11	11	13	11	11	12	10	11	12	11	10	11	11	11
Cycling	9	11	11	11	9	22	8	12	15	11	15	7	8	11
At least one activity														
(excluding walking)*	41	43	47	44	42	52	45	51	49	48	46	42	46	46
At least one activity*	57	61	63	64	59	67	62	68	67	66	66	63	66	64
Base - 100%	*966*	*1362*	*1739*	*1182*	*1456*	*635*	*1661*	*1518*	*1450*	*4629*	*1433*	*842*	*1452*	*15696*

* Total includes those activities not separately listed.

Table 13.15   **Use of different types of facility by sex**

Persons aged 16 and over   Great Britian 1996

	Men	Women	Total
	Percentage using different types of facility in 4 weeks before interview		
Type of facility			
Indoor mainly used for sport	26	23	24
Indoor other community facility	15	9	12
Indoor/outdoor at home	8	6	7
Outdoor mainly used for sport	18	5	11
Outdoor natural setting	20	9	14
Other - including roads and pathways	10	4	7
Facility belonging to school, college or university	16	14	15
Base = 100%	*7186*	*8510*	*15696*

Table 13.16 **Use of different types of facility by region**

Persons aged 16 and over   Great Britain: 1996

	Region													
	North	Yorks and Humber-side	North West	East Mid-lands	West Mid-lands	East Anglia	Greater London	Outer Metro-politan Area	Outer South East	Total South East	South West	Wales	Scotland	Great Britain
	Percentage using different types of facility in 4 weeks before interview													
Type of facility														
Indoor mainly for sport	21	21	24	26	23	25	25	29	26	26	25	21	25	24
Indoor other community facility	12	12	14	11	10	13	12	12	12	12	12	11	10	12
Indoor/outdoor at home	5	6	9	5	8	8	9	8	8	8	7	6	5	7
Outdoor mainly used for sport	8	10	11	9	9	13	13	14	14	14	11	10	12	11
Outdoor natural setting	12	11	14	13	12	17	11	17	16	14	19	13	14	14
Other - including roads and pathways	5	7	7	7	7	15	6	6	10	7	7	8	5	7
Facility belonging to school, college or university	11	13	16	15	17	15	12	14	17	14	15	18	12	15
Base - 100%	*966*	*1362*	*1739*	*1182*	*1456*	*635*	*1661*	*1518*	*1450*	*4629*	*1433*	*842*	*1452*	*15696*

Table 13.17 **Sports, games and physical activities: percentage of participants* in each activity
(a) who were members of a club for that activity in the 4 weeks before interview
(b) who participated competitively in that activity in the 12 months before interview
(c) who received tuition in that activity in the 12 months before interview**

Participants in each activity aged 16 and over
Great Britain: 1996

Active sports, games and physical activities†	(a)	(b)	(c)	Base = 100%
		Percentages		
Any swimming	11	2	4	2323
Keep fit/yoga	30	3	40	1922
Snooker/pool/billiards	20	11	1	1775
Cycling	2	2	1	1727
Weight training	39	1	26	871
Any soccer	34	43	13	754
Golf	47	42	20	735
Running (jogging etc)	10	8	4	711
Tenpin bowls/skittles	4	8	2	525
Badminton	27	10	9	369
Tennis	30	21	16	317
Any bowls	67	58	9	291
Fishing	30	17	2	265
Table tennis	15	13	5	239
Squash	33	16	8	200
Weight lifting	30	1	26	199
Horse riding	15	27	48	158

* Includes people who had participated in the 4 weeks before interview.
† Includes only activities in which more than 1% of all persons participated in the 4 weeks before interview.

Table 13.18 **Percentage of participants* in any activity by age and sex (a) who were members of a club in the 4 weeks before interview (b) who participated competitively in the 12 months before interview (c) who received tuition in the 12 months before interview**

Table 13.19 **Percentage of participants* in any activity by socio-economic group (a) who were members of a club in the 4 weeks before interview (b) who participated competitively in the 12 months before interview (c) who received tuition in the 12 months before interview**

Participants in any activity aged 16 and over — *Great Britain: 1996*

	Men	Women	Total
(a) Percentage of participants who were members of a club in the 4 weeks before interview			
Age			
16-19	46	17	34
20-24	43	22	33
25-29	38	23	31
30-44	38	24	31
45-59	43	27	36
60-69	48	33	41
70 and over	48	37	43
Total	41	25	34
(b) Percentage of participants who participated competitively in the 12 months before interview			
Age			
16-19	41	14	30
20-24	37	9	24
25-29	33	9	22
30-44	29	7	18
45-59	32	11	22
60-69	32	13	23
70 and over	23	15	20
Total	32	10	22
(c) Percentage of participants who received tuition in the 12 months before interview			
Age			
16-19	39	30	35
20-24	25	25	25
25-29	19	27	23
30-44	18	27	22
45-59	13	28	20
60-69	11	32	21
70 and over	7	19	12
Total	19	27	23
Bases = 100%			
16-19	364	283	647
20-24	381	342	723
25-29	493	421	914
30-44	1339	1164	2503
45-59	799	663	1462
60-69	323	279	602
70 and over	180	124	304
Total	3879	3276	7155

* Includes participants in any activity excluding walking in the 4 weeks before interview

Participants in any activity aged 16 and over — *Great Britain: 1996*

Socio-economic group†	Men	Women	Total
(a) Percentage of participants who were members of a club in the 4 weeks before interview			
Professional	45	36	43
Employers and managers	47	31	42
Intermediate non-manual	41	29	34
Junior non-manual	43	26	30
Skilled manual and own account non-professional	43	27	36
Semi-skilled manual and personal service	33	18	26
Unskilled manual	38	15	25
Total**	41	25	34
(b) Percentage of participants who participated competitively in the 12 months before interview			
Professional	30	6	24
Employers and managers	33	12	27
Intermediate non-manual	32	10	18
Junior non-manual	37	10	16
Skilled manual and own account non-professional	31	10	27
Semi-skilled manual and personal service	24	6	15
Unskilled manual	32	9	19
Total**	32	10	22
(c) Percentage of participants who received tuition in the 12 months before interview			
Professional	20	29	22
Employers and managers	19	34	23
Intermediate non-manual	21	31	27
Junior non-manual	23	28	27
Skilled manual and own account non-professional	13	22	14
Semi-skilled manual and personal service	14	21	17
Unskilled manual	17	17	17
Total**	19	27	23
Bases = 100%			
Professional	255	84	339
Employers and managers	819	320	1139
Intermediate non-manual	415	656	1071
Junior non-manual	308	1029	1337
Skilled manual and own account non-professional	1128	230	1358
Semi-skilled manual and personal service	507	509	1016
Unskilled manual	95	122	217
Total**	3879	3276	7155

* Includes participants in any activity excluding walking in the 4 weeks before interview
† Socio-economic group is based on the person's current or last job.
** Total includes full-time students, members of the Armed Forces, those who have never worked, and those whose job was inadequately described.

227

Table 13.20 **Selected leisure activities: participation rates in the 4 weeks before interview by sex and age**

Persons aged 16 and over   *Great Britain: 1996*

Leisure activities	Age							
	16-19	20-24	25-29	30-44	45-59	60-69	70 and over	Total
	Percentage participating in the 4 weeks before interview							
Men								
Watching TV	99	99	100	99	99	99	98	99
Visiting/entertaining friends or relations	97	98	97	97	95	94	91	95
Listening to radio	93	93	94	93	91	85	78	90
Listening to records/tapes	97	96	94	88	75	67	51	79
Reading books	51	59	57	61	58	60	57	58
Gardening	20	21	36	53	60	68	59	52
DIY	33	40	64	67	64	57	42	58
Dressmaking/needlework/knitting	4	4	2	4	3	3	3	3
Base = 100%	*418*	*472*	*651*	*1980*	*1729*	*947*	*989*	*7186*
Women								
Watching TV	99	98	99	98	99	99	99	99
Visiting/entertaining friends or relations	98	99	99	98	97	96	94	97
Listening to radio	97	95	94	90	86	81	75	87
Listening to records/tapes	99	96	92	90	76	62	42	77
Reading books	74	71	70	71	72	72	66	71
Gardening	10	21	34	50	58	54	40	45
DIY	15	24	23	39	34	21	11	30
Dressmaking/needlework/knitting	16	29	39	37	46	47	36	37
Base = 100%	*412*	*567*	*790*	*2392*	*1957*	*1077*	*1316*	*8511*
Total								
Watching TV	99	98	99	99	99	99	98	99
Visiting/entertaining friends or relations	98	98	98	97	96	95	93	96
Listening to radio	95	94	94	92	88	83	76	88
Listening to records/tapes	98	96	93	89	75	65	46	78
Reading books	63	66	64	66	65	66	62	65
Gardening	15	21	35	52	59	61	48	48
DIY	25	34	50	52	48	38	24	42
Dressmaking/needlework/knitting	9	15	14	22	26	27	22	22
Base = 100%	*830*	*1039*	*1441*	*4372*	*3686*	*2024*	*2305*	*15697*

Table 13.21 **Selected leisure activities: participation rates in the 4 weeks before interview: 1977 to 1996**

Persons aged 16 and over   Great Britain

Leisure activities	1977	1980	1983	1986	1987	1990	1993	1996
	Percentage participating in the 4 weeks before interview							
Watching TV	97	98	98	98	99	99	99	99
Visiting/entertaining friends or relations	91	91	91	94	95	96	96	96
Listening to radio	87	88	87	86	88	89	89	88
Listening to records/tapes	62	64	63	67	73	76	77	78
Reading books	54	57	56	59	60	62	65	65
Gardening	42	43	44	43	46	48	48	48
DIY	35	37	36	39	43	43	42	42
Dressmaking/needlework/knitting	29	28	27	27	27	23	22	22
Base = 100%	23171	22599	19050	19209	19529	17574	17552	15697

Table 13.22 **Selected leisure activities: participation rates in the 4 weeks before interview by socio-economic group and sex**

Persons aged 16 and over   Great Britain: 1996

Leisure activities	Professional	Employers and managers	Intermediate and junior non-manual	Skilled manual and own account non-professional	Semi-skilled manual and personal service	Unskilled manual	Total*
	Percentage participating in the 4 weeks before interview						
Men							
Watching TV	99	99	99	99	98	99	99
Visiting/entertaining friends or relations	95	96	96	95	94	89	95
Listening to radio	94	93	93	88	85	83	90
Listening to records/tapes	84	81	85	75	74	68	79
Reading books	81	69	68	48	49	39	58
Gardening	62	63	51	53	46	43	52
DIY	67	66	59	61	48	41	58
Dressmaking/needlework/knitting	4	4	3	3	3	2	3
Base = 100%	417	1472	1190	2341	1034	280	7186
Women							
Watching TV	98	99	99	100	99	99	99
Visiting/entertaining friends or relations	100	98	97	95	98	96	97
Listening to radio	96	90	90	85	82	78	87
Listening to records/tapes	93	84	80	73	70	64	77
Reading books	91	80	77	63	61	54	71
Gardening	50	55	51	42	42	40	45
DIY	42	36	32	31	27	23	30
Dressmaking/needlework/knitting	30	37	39	40	36	37	37
Base = 100%	125	715	3902	678	1746	644	8511
Total							
Watching TV	99	99	99	99	99	99	99
Visiting/entertaining friends or relations	96	97	97	95	96	94	96
Listening to radio	94	92	91	87	83	79	88
Listening to records/tapes	86	82	81	74	72	65	78
Reading books	83	73	75	51	57	49	65
Gardening	59	61	51	50	43	41	48
DIY	61	56	38	54	35	28	42
Dressmaking/needlework/knitting	10	14	31	11	24	26	22
Base = 100%	542	2187	5092	3019	2780	924	15697

* Total includes full-time students, members of the Armed Forces, persons in inadequately described occupations and those who have never worked.

Table 13.23 **Attendance at leisure classes in the 4 weeks before interview by sex and age: 1983, 1993 and 1996**

Persons aged 16 and over   *Great Britain*

Age	Men			Women			Total		
	1983	**1993**	**1996**	**1983**	**1993**	**1996**	**1983**	**1993**	**1996**
					Percentage attending leisure classes				
16-24	5	8	8	10	12	8	7	10	8
25-34	3	6	5	11	12	10	7	9	8
35-44	3	4	4	10	11	9	7	8	7
45-64	2	4	3	7	11	8	5	8	6
65 and over	2	2	3	3	6	6	3	5	5
Total	3	5	4	8	10	8	5	8	6
Bases = 100%									
16-24	*1692*	*1247*	*890*	*1681*	*1265*	*979*	*3373*	*2512*	*1869*
25-34	*1651*	*1734*	*1322*	*1834*	*1865*	*1615*	*3485*	*3599*	*2937*
35-44	*1700*	*1548*	*1309*	*1690*	*1642*	*1567*	*3390*	*3190*	*2876*
45-64	*2799*	*2569*	*2218*	*3035*	*2741*	*2510*	*5834*	*5310*	*4728*
65 and over	*1590*	*1587*	*1447*	*2366*	*2282*	*1840*	*3956*	*3869*	*3287*
Total	*9432*	*8685*	*7186*	*10606*	*9795*	*8511*	*20038*	*18480*	*15697*

Table 13.24 **Persons attending leisure classes in the 4 weeks before interview by sex and age: 1983, 1993 and 1996**

Persons aged 16 and over attending leisure classes   *Great Britain*

	1983	**1993**	**1996**
	%	%	%
Sex			
Men	26	29	30
Women	74	71	70
Age			
16-24	22	17	15
25-34	23	23	22
35-44	21	18	20
45-64	25	29	28
65 and over	10	13	15
Base = 100%	*1102*	*1388*	*1018*

Table 13.25 **Persons attending leisure classes in the 4 weeks before interview: type of college or organisation running classes by sex of participants: 1983, 1993 and 1996**

Persons aged 16 and over attending leisure classes   *Great Britain*

Type of college/organisation running classes	Men			Women			Total		
	1983	1993	1996	1983	1993	1996	1983	1993	1996
	%	%	%	%	%	%	%	%	%
Local education authority*	47	45	33	48	49	44	48	48	41
College of further education†	11	13	22	6	9	13	7	10	16
University Extra-Mural department	1	5	5	1	3	4	1	4	4
Private class	-	28	19	-	31	18	-	30	18
Other	41	10	24	46	12	23	45	11	23
*Base = 100%**	*278*	*401*	*305*	*790*	*969*	*712*	*1068*	*1370*	*1017*

* Including Evening Institutes and Centres of Adult Education.
† Including technical colleges.
** Percentages may sum to more than 100, as people can attend more than one class.

Table 13.26 **Attendance at leisure classes in the 4 weeks before interview by economic activity status, socio-economic group and sex**

Persons aged 16 and over   *Great Britain: 1996*

Economic activity status and socio-economic group	Men	Women	Total
	Percentage attending leisure classes		
Economic activity status			
Economically active			
Working full time	4	10	6
Working part time	9	10	10
All working*	4	10	7
Unemployed (ILO def)	5	10	7
All economically active	5	10	7
Economically inactive	3	7	6
Socio-economic group			
Non-manual	5	11	9
Manual	3	5	4
Total†	4	8	6
Bases = 100%			
Economically active			
Working full time	*3974*	*2124*	*6098*
Working part time	*424*	*2028*	*2452*
*All working**	*4460*	*4184*	*8644*
Unemployed (ILO def)	*419*	*257*	*676*
All economically active	*4879*	*4441*	*9320*
Economically inactive	*2293*	*4037*	*6330*
Socio-economic group			
Non-manual	*3079*	*4742*	*7821*
Manual	*3655*	*3068*	*6723*
Total†	*7186*	*8511*	*15697*

* Including a few people whose hours of work were not known and those on government schemes.
† Total includes members of the Armed Foces and cases where socio-economic group was not known.

Table 13.27 **Attendance at leisure classes in the 4 weeks before interview by sex and highest qualification level attained**

Persons aged 16-69   *Great Britain: 1996*

Highest qualification level attained*	Men	Women	Total
	Percentage attending leisure classes		
Degree or equivalent	8	20	13
Highest education below			
degree level	5	13	9
Other qualifications	5	10	8
No qualifications	2	4	3
Total	4	9	7
Bases = 100%			
Degree or equivalent	*808*	*592*	*1400*
Higher education below			
degree level	*706*	*670*	*1376*
Other qualifications	*3016*	*3551*	*6567*
No qualifications	*1632*	*2342*	*3974*
Total	*6162*	*7155*	*13317*

* For details of qualification levels see Appendix A.

231

Appendices

Appendix A
Definitions and terms

Activity in the reference week

The reference week is the calendar week ending the Sunday prior to interview. Activities in the reference week are given a priority order, so that people who report more than one activity are classified once only. The order of priority is 'working', followed by the unemployment categories, and these take precedence over the economically inactive categories.

The order of the 'inactive' categories is:

If aged 16-49   - going to school or college

If aged 16-59/64 - permanently unable to work

                    - retired

                    - looking after the home or family

                    - other.

As an activity in the reference week, 'looking after the home or family' is not applied to any person who, in the specified week, was also covered by one of the activities higher in the priority order. There may, therefore, be no-one in the household whose activity in the reference week is described as 'looking after the home or family', or one or more persons in the household may be classified as such.

Acute sickness

See Sickness

Adults

Adults are defined as persons aged 16 or over in all tables except those showing dependent children where single persons aged 16-18 who are in full-time education are counted as dependent children.

Bedroom standard

This concept is used to estimate occupation density by allocating a standard number of bedrooms to each household in accordance with its age/sex/marital status composition and the relationship of the members to one another. A separate bedroom is allocated to each married couple, any other person aged 21 or over, each pair of adolescents aged 10-20 of the same sex, and each pair of children under 10. Any unpaired person aged 10-20 is paired if possible with a child under 10 of the same sex, or, if that is not possible, is given a separate bedroom, as is any unpaired child under 10. This standard is then compared with the actual number of bedrooms (including bedsitters) available for the sole use of the household, and deficiencies or excesses are tabulated. Bedrooms converted to other uses are not counted as available unless they have been denoted as bedrooms by the informants; bedrooms not actually in use are counted unless uninhabitable.

Births

The number of children born to women in successive birth cohorts (by the time they had reached each successive age) includes all liveborn children, regardless of the woman's marital status at the time of the child's birth.

A child is classified as being born outside marriage if the birth occurs more than nine months after the ending of a marriage by separation or widowhood.

Burglary

Analysis is restricted to the 90% of households whose head had been in residence at the current address for at least 12 months and includes burglary with or without loss of goods. Households who were burgled more than once during the reference period are counted only once in the calculation of the burglary rate per 1000 households.

Central heating

Central heating is defined as any system whereby two or more rooms (including kitchens, halls, landings, bathrooms and WCs) are heated from a central source, such as a boiler, a back boiler to an open fire, or the electricity supply. This definition includes a system where the boiler or back boiler heats one room and also supplies the power to heat at least one other room.

Under-floor heating systems, electric air systems, and night storage heaters are included.

Where a household has only one room in the accommodation, it is treated as having central heating if that room is heated from a central source along with other rooms in the house or building.

Chronic sickness

See Sickness

Cohabitation

See Marital Status

Co-ownership or equity sharing schemes

Co-ownership or equity sharing schemes are those where a share in the property is bought by the occupier under an agreement with the housing association. The monthly charges paid for the accommodation include an amount towards the repayment of the collective mortgage on the scheme. The co-owner never becomes the sole owner of the property, but on leaving the scheme a cash sum is usually repaid to the occupier.

Country of birth

Great Britain comprises England, Wales and Scotland; the United Kingdom comprises Great Britain and Northern Ireland; the British Isles comprise the United Kingdom, the Irish Republic, the Channel Islands and the Isle of Man. These and the remainder of the country of birth coding frame are fully described in *Census 1991, Definitions, Great Britain* HMSO (1992).

Dependent children

Dependent children are persons aged under 16, or single persons aged 16 but under 19 and in full-time education.

Doctor consultations

Data on doctor consultations relate to consultations with National Health Service general medical practitioners during the two weeks before interview. Visits to the surgery, home visits, and telephone conversations are included, but contacts only with a receptionist or nurse are excluded.

The average number of consultations per person per year is calculated by multiplying the total number of consultations within the reference period, for any particular group, by 26 (the number of two-week periods in a year) and dividing the product by the total number of persons in the sample in that group.

Drinking: background and methodology

Introduction

Questions about drinking alcohol were first included in the GHS in 1978 and have been repeated in alternate years since then. Prior to 1988, they were asked only of respondents aged 18 and over. Since 1988 the questions have been extended to those aged 16 and 17 who answer them by means of a self-completion questionnaire.

Health effects of drinking alcohol

Sustained excessive consumption of alcohol progressively increases the risk of raised blood pressure and haemorrhagic and subarachnoid stroke, cardiovascular disease (apart from coronary heart disease), and is associated with other medical conditions including various cancers and liver cirrhosis. Excessive drinking is also thought to be associated with increased likelihood of alcohol-related social problems, criminal behaviour and accidents[1].

In December 1995 the Government published these findings in a review of the scientific and medical evidence on the health effects of drinking alcohol[1]. The report set benchmarks for sensible drinking, stating that regular consumption of between three and four units of alcohol a day for men and two and three for women will not accrue significant health risk. However, consistently drinking four or more units a day for men (three or more for women) is not recommended because of the progressive health risk this carries. The review also recognised that alcohol can confer a health benefit, mainly by giving protection from coronary heart disease. This only applies to men over 40 and postmenopausal women and the maximum health advantages can be obtained by drinking between one and two units a day.

The Department of Health's advice on sensible drinking is now based on these daily benchmarks. Revised targets to reflect this new advice are being considered in the context of the Government's new alcohol strategy. In the absence of new targets, the previous recommended weekly maximum levels of 21 units for men and 14 units for women have been retained to provide ready comparability with previous General Household Survey data.

Methodology[2]

Obtaining reliable information about drinking is difficult and in consequence social surveys consistently record lower levels of alcohol consumption than would be expected from data on alcohol sales. In addition to the effect of conscious or unconscious under-reporting of consumption, the amount of alcohol consumed at home is also likely to be underestimated because the quantities drunk are not precisely measured and are likely to be larger than those consumed on licensed premises. Furthermore, there is probably some under-representation of heavy drinkers in survey samples; they may be more difficult to contact or less willing to be interviewed, and there is incomplete coverage of heavy drinkers in surveys like the GHS, which are based on private households and exclude people living rough or in institutions.

In ad hoc surveys of drinking carried out by ONS, respondents are asked to recall all occasions during the previous seven days when they had an alcoholic drink. In addition to helping people to remember their drinking, this method also provides detailed information about drinking habits - where and when people drink, as well as how much. However, it is time-consuming to administer, particularly for heavy drinkers, and is therefore not suitable for the GHS, where drinking is only one of a number of subjects covered in the interview.

The GHS uses an alternative approach, in which respondents are asked how often they have drunk each of five different types of drink in the past year and how much of each they usually drank on any one day. The amount usually consumed is converted into units of alcohol, one unit being approximately equivalent to half a pint of beer, lager or cider, a single measure of spirits, one glass of wine, or one small glass of port, sherry or other fortified wine. Respondents' answers are used to provide an estimate of their alcohol consumption level[3], which is, in effect, their average weekly consumption. Chapter 7 in the GHS 1990 Report compared results from the GHS with those from ad hoc surveys, and in spite of the differences in methodology noted above, the results were generally similar[4].

It should be noted that, because it is based on people's estimates of amounts 'usually drunk on any one day', which is a difficult concept for those with irregular drinking patterns, the GHS alcohol consumption (AC) rating does not give a precise measure of weekly consumption. Further imprecision is introduced because it is based on an estimate of the units of alcohol consumed that is not completely accurate, not least because drinks of the same type - in particular beers and lagers - vary quite widely in their alcohol content[5].

Such errors in estimates of the amounts drunk and also in the frequency of drinking are, however, relatively unimportant for this report since the main aim is to identify broad groups with different levels of consumption - particularly those men who drink more than 21 units per week and women who drink more than 14 units per week.

Some of the tables include estimates of the mean number of units of alcohol consumed per week for groups of sampled individuals. Although not precise, for the reasons described above, this provides an additional summary measure which is useful for making comparisons between groups of respondents with different characteristics - different age groups for example - and is useful for looking at trends over time.

Age-standardisation

Analysis of the relationship between drinking and ill-health is complicated by the fact that both are related to age, but in opposite ways. Heavy drinkers are more likely than light drinkers to be young, but the prevalence of chronic sickness increases markedly (and acute sickness less so) with age. Both these associations with age need to be allowed for if a clear picture is to be obtained of the relationship between drinking and health.

This is achieved by calculating the prevalence of limiting longstanding illness that would be expected at each level of alcohol consumption if age alone had an effect. This is then compared with the observed prevalence, which reflects the effects of both age and alcohol consumption. The observed/expected ratio or standardised ratio is 100 for the sample as a whole. A ratio of more than 100 for a sub-group indicates that the observed prevalence of chronic or acute illness is higher than would be expected on the basis of its age distribution alone and a ratio of less than 100 indicates that is it lower than would be expected on the basis of its age distribution alone.

Notes and references

1   See *Sensible Drinking The Report of an Inter-Departmental Working Group. Department of Health* (1995).

2   The methodology is described in greater detail in Chapter 6 of Foster K et al *General Household Survey 1988*, HMSO (1990).

3   The method used to calculate the alcohol consumption rating is to multiply the number of units of each type of drink 'usually drunk on any one day' by the frequency with which it was drunk, using the factors shown below, and totalling across all drinks.

Multiplying factors for converting drinking frequency and number of units usually consumed on any one day into number of units consumed per week

Drinking frequency	*Multiplying factor*
Almost every day	7.0
5 or 6 days a week	5.5
3 or 4 days a week	3.5
Once or twice a week	1.5
Once or twice a month	0.375 (1.5/4)
Once every couple of months	0.115 (6/52)
Once or twice a year	0.029 (1.5/52)

The number of units of each type of drink usually consumed on any one day is multiplied by the factor corresponding to the frequency with which the drink is consumed. In all except the first category, the factors are averages of the range of frequencies shown in the category. For example, where a drink was consumed '3-4 days a week', the amount drunk was multiplied by 3.5.

The frequency categories and the corresponding multiplying factors used since 1990 are different from those used on the 1988 GHS. Following a review of the drinking section carried out in 1989, it was decided to change the wording of the categories so that they referred clearly to 'days'. Previously there had been some ambiguity as the wording could have been interpreted as referring to days or occasions. The number of categories was also increased to give a more accurate estimate of drinking frequency.

4   See Chapter 7 of Smyth M and Browne F *General Household Survey 1990*, HMSO (1992).
5   See Chapter 8 in Goddard E *Drinking in England and Wales in the late 1980s*, HMSO (1991).

Economic activity

Economically active persons are those over the minimum school-leaving age who were working or unemployed in the week before the week of interview. These persons constitute the labour force.

The definitions of 'working' and 'unemployed' used between 1986 and 1991 differ slightly from those used before 1986. The main differences are in the treatment of young people on Youth Training (YT) and full-time students (FTS).

Since 1989 all those on YT have been classified as 'working'. Between 1985 and 1988 those who were with an employer were classified as working and those at college during the reference week as 'inactive'. In 1984 people on YT or the Youth Opportunities Programme (YOP) were classified according to their own judgement of whether they were working, looking for work or neither during the reference week. In 1983 all people on YOP were classified as 'inactive'.

Since 1986 FTS have been classified as 'working', 'unemployed' or 'inactive' according to their own reports of what they were doing during the reference week. They are excluded from the figures for earlier years.

The definitions of 'unemployed' and 'economically inactive' used since 1991 differ from those used in earlier years. In 1991 the GHS adopted the International Labour Organisation (ILO) definition of unemployment. This classified anyone as unemployed if he or she was out of work and had looked for work in the four weeks before interview, or would have but for temporary sickness or injury, and was available to start work in the two weeks after interview. Otherwise, anyone out of work was classified as economically inactive. In 1994, the definition of 'working' was altered to include unpaid family workers.

The treatment of all categories on the GHS is now in line with that used on the LFS.

See also Unemployed persons; Working persons.

Education
Full-time/Part-time
Past and present education excludes leisure classes (ie those that do not normally lead to an examination or qualification), correspondence courses other than the Open University, and vocational training given by an employer.

For the types of courses classified as full-time or part-time study, see under Students.

Educational status
Prior to 1991, general questions on educational history and qualifications were addressed to respondents aged 16-69, with additional questions on current educational activity being asked of 16-49 year olds. In 1991, the upper limit of the age range for current educational activity was extended to 69. This has had the effect of increasing the proportion of respondents classified as not currently undertaking any formal education and decreased the proportion classified as still at school or studying full time or part time.

Employment
Full-time/Part-time
The general definition of full-time and part-time employment is based on hours worked per week, excluding overtime. Persons who worked 31 hours or more per week are in full-time employment and those who worked 30 hours or less per week are in part-time employment. An exception is made for schoolteachers and lecturers, who are considered to be in full-time employment if they work 26 hours or more per week. From 1989 persons on Government training schemes (YT or ET) were not assigned to full-time or part-time categories even if working with an employer.

Ethnic group
Household members are classified as White, Black Caribbean, Black African, Black other, Indian, Pakistani, Bangla-

deshi, Chinese, or 'none of these groups' by the person answering the Household Schedule.

The 'Black Caribbean' category includes the 'Black Caribbean' and 'Guyanese' groups. In some tables of the report the category 'Black' is used, which includes 'Black African' as well as 'Black Caribbean' and 'Guyanese'.

Family
A family is defined as:

(a) a married or opposite sex cohabiting couple on their own, or
(b) a married or opposite sex cohabiting couple/lone parent and their never-married children, provided these children have no children of their own.

Persons who cannot be allocated to a family as defined above are said to be persons not in the family.

In general, families cannot span more than two generations, ie grandparents and grandchildren cannot belong to the same family. The exception to this is where it is established that the grandparents are responsible for looking after the grandchildren (eg while the parents are abroad).

Adopted and step-children belong to the same family as their adoptive/step-parents. Foster-children, however, are not part of their foster-parents' family since they are not related to their foster-parents.

See also Lone-parent family.

GP Consultations
See Doctor Consultations

Head of household
The head of the household is a member of the household and (in order of precedence) either the husband of the person, or the person, who:

(a) owns the household accommodation, or
(b) is legally responsible for the rent of the accommodation, or
(c) has the accommodation as an emolument or perquisite, or
(d) has the accommodation by virtue of some relationship to the owner in cases where the owner or lessee is not a member of the household.

When two members of a different sex have equal claim, the male is taken as head of household. When two members of the same sex have equal claim, the elder is taken as head of household.

Hospital visits
Inpatient stays
Inpatient data relate to stays overnight or longer (in a twelve month reference period) in NHS or private hospitals. All types of cases are counted, including psychiatric and maternity, except babies born in hospital who are included only if they remained in hospital after their mother was discharged.

Outpatient attendances
Outpatient data relate to attendances (in a reference period of three calendar months) at NHS or private hospitals, other than as an inpatient. No distinction is made between consultative outpatient attendances, casualty attendances, and attendances at ancillary departments.

Day patient
Day patients are defined as patients admitted to a hospital bed during the course of a day or to a day ward where a bed, couch or trolley is available for the patient's use. They are admitted with the intention of receiving care or treatment which can be completed in a few hours so that they do not require to remain in hospital overnight. If a patient admitted as a day patient then stays overnight they are counted as an inpatient.

Household
Household definition: between 1971 and 1980 the definition of a household used in the GHS and in most other surveys carried out by OPCS Social Survey Division was, in summary:

> a group of people who all live regularly at the address ... and who are all catered for, for at least one meal a day, by the same person. (See J Atkinson, *A Handbook for Interviewers*. HMSO, London 1971.)

In 1981 a new definition was adopted, intended to make the survey comparable with the 1981 Census definition of a household. Under the new definition a household is:

> a single person or a group of people who have the address as their only or main residence and who either share one meal a day or share the living accommodation. (See L McCrossan, *A Handbook for Interviewers*. HMSO, London 1991.)

A group of people would not be counted as a household solely on the basis of a shared kitchen or bathroom.

Household membership

Under the 1981 definition, a person is in general regarded as living at the address if he or she (or the informant) considers the address to be his or her main residence. There are, however, certain rules which take priority over this criterion.

(a) Children aged 16 or over who live away from home for purposes of either work or study and come home only for holidays are *not* included at the parental address under any circumstances.

(b) Children of any age away from home in a temporary job and children under 16 at boarding school are *always* included in the parental household.

(c) Anyone who has been away from the address *continuously* for six months or longer is excluded.

(d) Anyone who has been living continuously at the address for six months or longer is included even if he or she has his or her main residence elsewhere.

(e) Addresses used only as second homes are never counted as a main residence.

Household type

There are many ways of grouping or classifying households into household types; most are based on the age, sex and number of household members.

The main classification of household type uses the following categories:

1 adult aged 16-59

2 adults aged 16-59

small family   -   1 or 2 persons aged 16 or over and 1 or 2 persons aged under 16

large family   -   1 or more persons aged 16 or over and 3 or more persons aged under 16, or 3 or more persons aged 16 or over and 2 persons aged under 16

large adult household   -   3 or more persons aged 16 or over, with or without 1 person aged under 16

2 adults, 1 or both aged 60 or over

1 adult aged 60 or over

The term 'family' in this context does not necessarily imply any relationship.

Chapter 2 also uses a modified version of household type which takes account of the age of the youngest household member. 'Small family', 'large family' and 'large adult household' are replaced by the following:

youngest person aged 0-4   -   1 or more persons aged 16 or over and 1 or more persons aged under 5

youngest person aged 5-15   -   1 or more persons aged 16 or over and 1 or more persons aged 5-15

3 or more adults   -   3 or more persons aged 16 or over and no-one aged under 16

The first two categories above are combined in some tables.

In Chapter 2, households are also classified according to the families they contain (see Family for definition), into the following categories:

non-family households containing
- 1 person only
- 2 or more non-family* adults

one family households†
containing
- married couple with dependent children
- married couple with independent children only
- married couple with no children
- lone parent with dependent children
- lone parent with independent children only

households containing two or more families.

Some of the above categories are combined for certain tables and figures.

Income

Usual gross weekly income

The income section was revised and simplified in 1992 so that estimates were accepted as valid responses.

---

* Individuals may, of course, be related without constituting a family. A household consisting of a brother and sister, for example, is a non-family household of two or more non-family adults.

† Other individuals who were not family members may also have been present.

Total income for an individual refers to income at the time of the interview, and is obtained by summing the components of earnings, benefits, pensions, dividends, interest and other regular payments. Prior to 1992, if any component of income was unknown, the value of total gross weekly income was treated as not known. Since 1992, gross weekly income of employees and those on benefits is calculated if interest and dividends are the only components missing.

If the last pay packet/cheque was unusual, for example in including holiday pay in advance or a tax refund, the respondent is asked for usual pay. No account is taken of whether a job is temporary or permanent. Payments made less than weekly are divided by the number of weeks covered to obtain a weekly figure.

Usual gross weekly household income is the sum of usual gross weekly income for all adults in the household. Since 1992, those interviewed by proxy are also included.

Labour force
See Economic activity.

Lone-parent family
A lone-parent family consists of one parent, irrespective of sex, living with his or her never-married dependent children, provided these children have no children of their own.

Married or cohabiting women with dependent children, whose partners are not defined as resident in the household, are not classified as one-parent families because it is known that the majority of them are only temporarily separated from their husbands for a reason that does not imply the breakdown of the marriage (for example, because the husband usually works away from home). (See the GHS 1980 Report p.9 for further details.)

Longstanding conditions and complaints
The GHS collects information about the nature of longstanding illness. Respondents who report a longstanding illness are asked 'What is the matter with you?' and details of the illness or disability are recorded by the interviewers and coded into a number of broad categories. Interviewers are instructed to focus on the symptoms of the illness, rather than the cause, and code what the respondent said was currently the matter without probing for cause. This approach has been used in 1988, 1989, 1994, 1995 and 1996.

The categories used when coding the conditions correspond broadly to the chapter headings of the International Classification of Diseases (ICD). However, the ICD is used mostly for coding conditions and diseases according to cause whereas the GHS coding is based only on the symptoms reported. This gives rise to discrepancies in some areas between the two classifications.

Marriage and cohabitation
From 1971 to 1978 the Family Information section was addressed only to married women aged under 45 who were asked questions on their present marriage and birth expectations. In 1979 the section was expanded to include questions on cohabitation, previous marriages and all live births, and was addressed to all women aged 16-49 except non-married women aged 16 and 17. In 1983 questions on contraception, sterilisation and infertility were introduced. In 1986 the section was extended to cover all women and men aged 16-59.

Marital status
In 1996, for the first time, separate questions have been asked at the beginning of the questionnaire to identify the legal marital status and living arrangements of respondents in the household. The latter includes a category for cohabiting.

Cohabiting
Before 1996, unrelated adults of the opposite sex have been classified as cohabiting if they consider themselves to be living together as a couple. In 1996, this category includes a small number of same sex couples.

Married/non-married
In this dichotomy 'married' generally includes cohabiting and 'non- married' covers those who are single, widowed, separated or divorced and not cohabiting.

Living arrangements (de facto marital status)
In the past, additional information from the Family Information section of the individuals' questionnaire has been used to determine living arrangements (previously known as 'defacto marital status') and the classification has only applied to those aged 16-59 who answer the marital history questions. For this population it only differed from the main marital status for those who revealed in the Family Information section that they were cohabiting rather than having the marital status given at the beginning of the interview. 'Cohabiting' took priority over other categories. For 1996, information on legal marital status and living arrangements, has been taken from the beginning of the interview where both are now asked.

Legal marital status
This classification applies to persons aged 16-59 who answer the marital history questions. Cohabiting people are categorised according to formal marital status. The classification

differs from strict legal marital status in accepting the respondents' opinion of whether their marriage has terminated in separation rather than applying the criterion of legal separation.

Median
See Quantiles.

Pensions
The GHS asks questions about any pension scheme, either occupational or personal, that the respondent belonged to on the date of interview. It is quite possible that some respondents have belonged to an occupational or a personal pension scheme in the past. The GHS measures current membership and not the percentage of respondents who will get an occupational or personal pension when they retire.

Since July 1988, all employees have been given the choice of starting their own personal pension in place of SERPS (State Earnings related Pension Scheme). Previously employees not in an occupational scheme could arrange to pay for a personal pension plan, but they could not leave SERPS.

Some respondents may be contributing to both an occupational and personal pension scheme.

Qualification levels
Degree or equivalent
Higher degrees
First degrees
University diplomas and certificates, qualifications from colleges of technology etc and from professional institutions, of degree standard

Higher education below degree level
Non-graduate teaching qualifications
HNC/HND; City and Guilds Full Technological Certificate; BEC/TEC/BTEC Higher/SCOTECH Higher

University diplomas and certificates, qualifications from colleges of technology etc and from professional institutions, below degree but above GCE 'A' level standard
Nursing qualifications

GCE 'A' level or equivalent
1 or more subjects at GCE 'A' level/AS level/Scottish Certificate of Education (SCE) Higher; Scottish Universities Preliminary Examination (SUPE) Higher; and/or Higher School Certificate; Scottish Leaving Certificate (SLC) Higher; Certificate of Sixth Year Studies City and Guilds Advanced/Final level; ONC/OND; BEC/TEC/BTEC/National/General certificate or diploma

GCSE Grades A-C or equivalent
1 or more subjects at GCE 'O' level (Grades A-C)/GCSE (grades A-C)/CSE Grade 1/SCE Ordinary (Bands A-C); SUPE Lower or Ordinary; and/or School Certificates; SLC Lower City and Guilds Craft/Ordinary level/SCOTVEC

GCSE Grades D-E or equivalent
GCSE (grades D-E)/CSE Grades 2-5/GCE 'O' level (Grades D and E)/SCE Ordinary (Bands D and E);
Clerical and commercial qualifications
Apprenticeship

Foreign and other qualifications
Foreign qualifications (outside UK)
Other qualifications

None
- excludes those who never went to school (omitted from the classification altogether).

The qualification levels do not in all cases correspond to those used in statistics published by the Department for Education.

Quantiles
The quantiles of a distribution, eg of household income, divide it into equal parts.

Median: the median of a distribution divides it into two equal parts. Thus half the households in a distribution of household income have an income higher than the median, and the other half have an income lower than the median.

Quartiles: the quartiles of a distribution divide it into quarters. Thus the upper quartile of a distribution of household income is the level of income that is expected by 25% of the households in the distribution; and 25% of the households have an income less than the lower quartile. It follows that 50% of the households have an income between the upper and lower quartiles.

Relatives in the household
The term 'relative' includes any household member related to the head of household by blood, marriage, or adoption. Foster-children are therefore not regarded as relatives.

Rooms
These are defined as habitable rooms, including (unless otherwise specified) kitchens, whether eaten in or not, but excluding rooms used solely for business purposes, those not usable throughout the year (eg conservatories), and those not normally used for living purposes such as bathrooms, toilets, cloakrooms, store rooms, pantries, cellars and garages.

Sickness
Acute

Acute sickness is defined as restriction of the level of normal activity, because of illness or injury, at any time during the two weeks before interview. Since the two-week reference period covers weekends, normal activities include leisure activities as well as school attendance, going to work, or doing housework. Anyone with a chronic condition that caused additional restriction during the reference period is counted among those with acute sickness.

The average number of restricted activity days per person per year is calculated in the same way as the average number of doctor consultations.

Sickness
Chronic

Information on chronic sickness was obtained from the following two-part question:

'Do you have any long-standing illness, disability or infirmity? By long-standing I mean anything that has troubled you over a period of time or that is likely to affect you over a period of time.

IF YES
Does this illness or disability limit your activities in any way?'

'Long-standing illness' is defined as a positive answer to the first part of the question, and 'limiting long-standing illness' as a positive answer to both parts of the question.

The data collected are based on people's subjective assessment of their health, and therefore changes over time may reflect changes in people's expectations of their health as well as changes in incidence or duration of chronic sickness. In addition, different sub-groups of the population may have varying expectations, activities and capacities of adaptation.

Smoking

Questions about smoking behaviour are currently included on the GHS in alternate years. Since 1974, the questions have been asked of all people aged 16 and over in the household with a self-completion form offered to those aged 16 or 17, where appropriate. It is likely that the GHS understates cigarette consumption and perhaps, to a lesser extent prevalence. This is because the context of the GHS interview, where all members of the family aged 16 and over are interviewed, often together, may affect the reporting of smoking behaviour. The self-completion form is designed to minimise the possible effects of parental disapproval. However, when considering trends in smoking it is assumed that any under-reporting has remained constant throughout the period of the survey. This may not be entirely justified as it is possible that public attitudes to smoking have become more negative over time making it more likely that people will under-report their level of smoking or deny smoking at all.

Socio-economic group

The basic occupational classification used is the Registrar General's socio-economic grouping in *Standard Occupational Classification 1990*, Volume 3 OPCS (HMSO, London 1991), pp 13-14. The majority of tables use a collapsed version of this classification, which is as follows:

Descriptive definition	SEG numbers
Professional	3, 4
Employers and managers	1, 2, 13
Intermediate non-manual	5
Junior non-manual	6
Skilled manual (including foremen and supervisors) and own account non-professional	8, 9, 12, 14
Semi-skilled manual and personal service	7, 10, 15
Unskilled manual	11

In tables showing non-manual/manual socio-economic groups, the non-manual category comprises SEGs 1-6 and 13, the manual category comprises SEGs 7-12, 14 and 15.

For persons aged 16 or over, including full-time students with employment experience, SEG corresponds to their own present job or, for those not currently working, to their last job, regardless of sex or marital status.

Persons whose occupation was inadequately described, the Armed Forces (SEG category 16) and full-time students, are excluded from the totals unless otherwise specified.

Prior to 1992, the socio-economic variable used in a number of tables, particularly in the health, smoking and drinking chapters, classified married or cohabiting couples whose husbands were in the household according to their partner's present (or last) job. Other members of the household were classified according to their own current or last job. It was recognised that there are drawbacks to this classification. First, it has been criticised by some users of GHS as being overtly sexist in classifying women according to a characteristic of their husband or partner. Second, there is an inconsistency in that the classification of other members of the household, e.g. adult children living at home or elderly people living with their children, is based on their own job.

To achieve a more consistent approach and classify all members of the household in the same way, the standard socio-economic variable used in 1992 to reflect living standards was changed to the socio-economic group of the head of household. This will be used in subsequent GHS reports, although for the time being, the old classification will also be used in trend tables so that changes can be monitored on a consistent basis. A classification based on the respondent's own occupation will continue to be used where appropriate.

Sport and leisure activities: methodology

Introduction

The current format of questions about participation in sports and leisure activities has been used in the GHS at roughly three year intervals since 1987. Details are obtained about participation in sports or activities from a prompted list which can be supplemented by the respondent.

New questions on sports participation were introduced in the 1996 GHS. These included the type of facility used for participation in each type of sport and questions on club membership, competitive participation and tuition. These details were not asked for walking, darts or sports not included on the prompted list.

Definition of sports and physical activities

The complete list of sports and physical activities covered by the survey can be found in the questionnaire.

Walking was included only where the walk had been for pleasure and was of 2 miles or more. The question referred to 'a walk or a hike' to indicate that walking for its own sake was of interest. Thus walking as a means of transport would not be included. However, all cycling was included whether it was for pleasure or as a means of transport.

Reference periods

Participation based on two reference periods are presented.

Four-week participation rate: the percentage of people aged 16 and over who took part in an activity in the four weeks before interview.

Since interviewing continues throughout the year, the survey figures represent participation in a four-week period averaged over a year. A reference period of four weeks was adopted in 1973 as being short enough for answers to be reasonably reliable but long enough to be representative of participation and to yield adequate numbers of participants in the main sporting activities.

Twelve-month participation rate: the percentage of people aged 16 and over who took part in an activity in the twelve months before interview.

A twelve-month reference period is useful in obtaining information about activities that occur infrequently. However, recall over such a period may be poor and there is also the risk of overstatement because some respondents may be reluctant to admit that they have not participated in any sports over so long a period. It is not possible from the questions on the survey to measure the extent of any such under- or over-reporting.

Twelve-month rates are likely to be higher than four-week rates because some of those who have participated during the year will not have done so during the four weeks before their interview. This is most likely to occur if the activity is seasonal or attracts infrequent participants.

Frequency of participation

The GHS asks participants about the number of days on which they took part in each activity in the four weeks before interview. In 1996, frequency was not asked for walking. These data are used to calculate two measures of frequency of participation.

Frequency of participation per participant in four weeks: the number of occasions of participation in a sport in the four weeks before interview averaged over the number of participants in that sport.

The number of occasions of participation is equivalent to the total number of days on which a respondent participated in each reported activity. In cases where respondents had participated in an activity more than once on the same day this is counted as a single occasion. This is to avoid difficulties in deciding what to count as separate occasions, for example where heats and finals have taken place on the same day. But if a respondent had taken part in two different activities on the same day this will count as one occasion for each activity.

Frequency of participation per adult per year: the number of occasions of participation in a sport per year averaged over the whole sample of people aged 16 or more.

The number of occasions of participation in an activity in the four-week reference period summed over all participants is multiplied by 13 to give an estimated annual total. This total is then divided by the number of adults interviewed in one year. The measure gives a rough indication of the overall volume of participation in different sports over the year which may be useful as a guide to the level of demand for different kinds of sports facilities.

Age-standardisation
The strong association between participation in physical activity and age needs to be taken into account when investigating the possible relationship between participation and other characteristics of the sample.

This is achieved by calculating the level of participation that would be expected for different sub-groups in the sample if age alone had an effect. This is then compared with the observed level of participation, which reflects the effects of both age and the nature of the sub-group. The observed/expected ratio or standardised ratio is 100 for the sample as a whole. A ratio of more than 100 for a sub-group indicates that the observed level of participation is higher than would be expected on the basis of its age distribution alone and a ratio of less than 100 indicates that is it lower than would be expected on the basis of its age distribution alone.

Step-family
See Family

Students, full-time/part-time
The category of *full-time* student covers all students on full-time and sandwich courses. Students interviewed during a vacation are included, provided they intend to return to full-time study in the following term. Sandwich course students are treated as full-time students regardless of whether they were interviewed during the college or working part of their course. Between 1981 and 1987, full-time students living in institutional accommodation while away were included in tables in the Education chapter.

The treatment of students has undergone certain changes over the period of the survey. Between 1971 and 1976 both sandwich and block-release students were counted as full-time students provided they were interviewed during the college part of their course; if they were interviewed during the working part of their course they were not considered to be students at all.

Before 1973 all nursing training was considered to be purely vocational and was therefore not counted as study. From 1974 to 1979 nursing training was regarded as full-time study, and paramedical training was specifically included in this category from 1978. From 1980 on, in order to bring GHS definitions into line with those used by the Department of Education and Science and the 1981 Census, all nursing and paramedical training has been classified as part-time study.

See also Economic activity; Working persons.

Tenure
From 1981, households who were buying a share in the property from a housing association or co-operative through a shared ownership (equity sharing) or co-ownership scheme are included in the category of owner-occupiers. In earlier years such households were included with those renting from a housing association or co-operative.

Renting from a council includes renting from a local authority or New town corporation or commissions or Scottish Homes (formerly the Scottish Special Housing Association).

Renting from a housing association also includes co-operatives and charitable trusts. It also covers fair rent schemes.

Social sector renters includes households renting from a local authority or New Town corporation or commission or Scottish Homes and those renting from housing associations, co-operatives and charitable trusts.

Private renters include those who rent from a private individual or organisation and those whose accommodation is tied to their job even if the landlord is a local authority, housing association or Housing Action Trust, or if the accommodation is rent free. Squatters are also included in this category.

Unemployed persons
Prior to 1991, the unemployed consisted of those who, in the week before the week of interview, were looking for work, would have looked for work if they had not been temporarily sick, or were waiting to take up a job they had already obtained. In this context temporary sickness refers to illness lasting 28 days or less. These definitions of unemployment apply whether or not the person was registered as unemployed. Unlike the Labour Force Survey (LFS) people who said they were looking for work were counted as unemployed regardless of availability for work and whether they had actively sought work during the previous four weeks.

From 1991 the unemployed consisted of those who were out of work and had looked for work in the four weeks before interview, or would have but for temporary sickness or injury, and were available to start work in the two weeks following the interview.

Working persons

This category includes persons aged 16 or over who, in the week before the week of interview, worked for wages, salary, or other form of cash payment such as commission or tips, for any number of hours. It covers persons absent from work in the reference week because of holiday, sickness, strike, or temporary lay-off, provided they had a job to return to with the same employer. It also includes persons attending an educational establishment during the specified week, if they were paid by their employer while attending it, and people on the Government training schemes.

Persons are excluded if they worked in a voluntary capacity, for expenses only, or only for payment in kind, unless their unpaid work contributed directly to a business, firm, or professional practice owned or operated by a relative.

Full-time students who worked in the reference week have been counted as working since 1986. See Economic activity and Chapter 5 (table footnotes) for changes in the GHS classification of full-time students over time.

Youth Training

People on Youth Training (YT) were classified in 1991 as 'working'. See Economic activity and Chapter 5 (table footnotes) for changes in the GHS classification over time.

Appendix B
Sample Design and Response

The sample design

The most recent change to the sample design of the GHS occurred in 1984 when the Postcode Address File (PAF) replaced the Electoral Registers as the sampling frame.

The GHS uses a two-stage sample design with postcode sectors, which are similar in size to wards, as the Primary Sampling Units (PSUs). From 1986 to 1989 there was provision for rotation of one third of the PSUs each year. The 1995 sample was drawn without using the rotation method.

The sampling selection procedure followed in 1996 was the same as for all years since 1984. Initially postcode sectors were allocated to major strata on the basis of region and area type. The sectors were distributed between 22 such strata. These were created from the UK standard regions by subdividing Wales, Scotland, London and the South East,and then further distinguishing between Metropolitan and non-Metropolitan counties. In Scotland, Glasgow was treated as a District of 'Metropolitan' type.

Within each major stratum, postcode sectors were then stratified according to selected housing and economic indicators available from the 1991 Census. Sectors were initially ranked according to the proportion of households in privately rented accommodation, then divided into two bands containing approximately the same number of households. The PAF includes an indicator of the estimated number of separate units or households at each delivery point (address) and this multi-occupancy count is used to estimate the total number of households.[1] Within each band, sectors were re-ranked according to the proportion of households in local authority accommodation and bands were sub-divided to give four bands of approximately equal size. Finally, within each of these bands, sectors were re-ranked according to the proportion of heads of households in socio-economic groups 1 to 5 or 13.

Major strata were then divided into minor strata of equal size, the number of minor strata per major stratum being proportionate to the size of the major stratum. Since 1984 the frame has been divided into 576 minor strata

Figure A

Percentage renting privately	HIGH		LOW	
Percentage renting from Local Authority	HIGH	LOW	LOW	HIGH
Percentage with HOH in SEG 1-5 or 13	HIGH ↘ LOW	HIGH LOW ↗	HIGH ↘ LOW	HIGH LOW ↗

and one PSU has been selected from each per year. In order, therefore, to minimise the difference between one band and the next, the ranking by the socio-economic group and local authority renting criteria were in the reverse order in consecutive bands, as shown in Figure A.

Until 1994 a supplementary sample of addresses was selected in Scotland to improve estimates in separate analyses for Scotland.

Conversion of addresses to households

Most addresses contain just one private household, a few - such as institutions and purely business addresses[2] - contain no private households, while others contain more than one private household. For addresses containing more than one household, set procedures are laid down in order to give each household one and only one chance of selection.

As the PAF does not give names of occupants of addresses, it is not possible to use the number of different surnames at an address as an indicator of the number of households living there as was done before 1984. A rough guide to the number of households at an address is provided on the PAF by the multi-occupancy (MO) count. The MO count is a fairly accurate indicator in Scotland but is less accurate in England and Wales, so it is used only when sampling at addresses in Scotland.

All addresses in England and Wales, and those in Scotland with an MO count of two or less, are given only one chance of selection for the sample. At such addresses, interviewers interview all the households they find up to a maximum of three. If there are more than three households at the address, the interviewer selects the households for interview by listing all households at the address systematically then making a random choice by referring to a household selection table.

Addresses in Scotland with an MO count of three or more, where the probability that there is more than one household is fairly high, are given as many chances of selection as the value of the MO count. When the interviewer arrives at such an address, he or she checks the actual number of households and interviews a proportion of them according to instructions. The proportion is set originally by the MO count and adjusted according to the number of households actually found, with a maximum of three households being interviewed at any address. The interviewer selects the households for interview by listing all households at the address systematically and making a random choice, as above, by means of a table.

No addresses are deleted from the sample to compensate for the extra interviews that may result from these multi-household addresses but a maximum of four extra interviews per quota of addresses is allowed. Once four extra interviews have been carried out in an interviewer's quota, only the first household selected at each multi-occupancy address is included. As a result of the limits on additional interviews, households in concealed multi-occupied addresses may be slightly under-represented in the GHS sample. The outcome of visits to the addresses selected for the 1996 GHS sample and the resultant number of households interviewed is shown in Table 1.

Table 1 The sample of addresses and households

Great Britain: 1996

Selected addresses	13247
Adjusted sample (extra households)	212
Ineligible addresses: Demolished or derelict Used wholly for business purposes Empty Institutions Other ineligible	1614
No sample selected at address	
Address not traced	
Addresses at which interviews were taken	9178
Total effective sample of households	11845

Data collection

Information for the GHS is collected week by week throughout the year by personal interview. From 1988, the GHS interviewing year was changed from a calendar year to a financial year basis. In 1996 interviews took place from April 1996 to March 1997. In 1994, the survey was carried out for the first time using Computer Assisted Personal Interviewing (CAPI) on laptop computers and BLAISE software. Interviews are sought with all adult members (aged 16 or over) of the sample of private households described above.

On occasion it may prove impossible, despite repeated calls, to contact a particular member of a household in person and, in strictly controlled circumstances, interviewers are permitted to conduct a proxy interview with a near relative who is a member of the same household. In these cases, questions such as those on educational qualifications and income and opinion-type questions are omitted.

Interviewers working on the GHS form part of the overall Social Survey interviewing force and, as such, are recruited only after careful selection procedures after which they take part in a three-day initial training course. Before working on the GHS they attend a briefing and new recruits are always accompanied in the field by a training officer. All interviewers who continue to work on the GHS are observed regularly in the field.

Response

Table 2 shows the quarterly and annual response rates from the 1996 survey. Since the GHS can accept information from partially responding households (ie outcome categories 2a-2c in Table 2) response rates can be measured in a variety of ways.

Partial response can arise for a variety of reasons: some people refuse to answer some questions; others are interviewed by proxy and, as noted above, are not then asked all the questions. Depending on whether or not the various categories of partial response are included, three response rates are calculated.

1 The *minimum* response rate, which accepts only completely co-operating households as responders and treats all partials as non-responders. In 1996 the minimum response rate was 66%.

2 The *maximum* response rate, which accepts all partials as responders. In 1996 this rate was 77%.

3 The *middle* response rate, which accepts some of the partials as responders - that is, it includes households where information is missing for only certain questions (category 2a in Table 2), but does not include those where information is missing altogether for one or more household members (categories 2b and 2c in Table 2). In other words, this middle rate can be thought of as the proportion of the eligible sample of households from whom all or nearly all the information was obtained. This is the rate generally used as the performance index for the survey, and in 1996 it was 76%.

Since 1971, the middle response rate has shown some fluctuation:

	%		%
1971	83	1984	81
1972	81	1985	82
1973	81	1986	84
1974	83	1987	85
1975	84	1988	85
1976	84	1989	84
1977	83	1990	81
1978	82	1991	84
1979	83	1992	83
1980	82	1993	82
1981	84	1994	80
1982	84	1995	80
1983	82	1996	76

Since 1987, following an experiment in 1986, a letter has been sent in advance of an interviewer calling to an address[3]. The letter briefly describes the purpose and nature of the survey and prepares the recipient for a visit by an interviewer. These letters probably resulted in the improvements in middle response rates from 1987 to 1989. The decline in response rate since 1991 is due to an increase in the proportion of households refusing to participate (12% in 1991 rising to 19% in 1996) rather than failure to contact people. A similar decline is being experienced on other ONS surveys and by other survey organisations. The main elements of response and non-response in 1996, and middle response rate figures for each region, are shown in Tables 2 and 3 respectively.

Non-response

In total, 23% of households selected for interview in 1996 were lost to the sample altogether, either because they did not wish to take part (19%) or because they could not be contacted (3%).

A comparison was made of the characteristics recorded on the 1991 Census forms of respondents and non-respondents in the 1991 GHS sample, repeating similar studies made with the help of 1971 and 1981 Census records[4,5]. Results showed that households comprising one adult aged 16-59 or a couple with non-dependent children were under-represented as also were households in London, those living in smaller accommodation

Table 2 **Quarterly and annual response**

Great Britain: 1996

Outcome category	First quarter		Second quarter		Third quarter		Fourth quarter		Year	
	No.	%	No.	%	No.	%	No.	%	No.	%
1 Complete household co-operation	1940	66.2	2060	69.9	1904	64.2	1919	64.0	7823	66.0
2a Non-interview of one or more household members, proxy taken. Partial refusals: all household members co-operated but some sections/questions were refused	314	10.7	296	10.0	290	9.8	275	9.2	1175	9.9
2b Non-contact of one or more household members, no proxy taken	41	1.4	49	1.7	16	0.5	27	0.9	133	1.1
2c Partial refusal: at least one household member refused to be interviewed	5	0.2	3	0.1	16	0.5	23	0.8	47	0.4
3 Whole household refused	501	17.1	436	14.8	555	18.7	590	19.7	2082	17.6
HQ refusal	52	1.8	45	1.5	59	2.0	57	1.9	213	1.8
4 Non-contact of household	78	2.7	60	2.0	128	4.3	106	3.5	372	3.1
Base = 100% **(total effective sample, ie total categories 1-4 plus small data losses)**	2931		2949		2968		2997		11845	
Middle response rate: (codes 1 and 2a as percentage of the effective sample)		76.9		79.9		73.9		73.2		76.0

Table 3 **Regional response rates**

Great Britain: 1996

Region	First quarter %	Rank	Second quarter %	Rank	Third quarter %	Rank	Fourth quarter %	Rank	Year %	Rank
North	78.9	6=	81.4	6	84.2	1	75.1	4	80.0	1
Yorkshire and Humberside	78.9	6=	79.5	9	74.1	7	77.2	3	77.4	6
North West	75.0	9	80.0	8	70.0	9	71.1	9	74.1	10
East Midlands	75.2	8	82.8	2	76.7	6	81.7	1	79.1	3
West Midlands	73.8	10	80.1	7	78.2	5	77.3	2	77.3	7
East Anglia	81.0	2	82.5	3	80.3	3	74.7	5	79.8	2
Greater London	66.1	11	75.4	11	62.3	11	68.6	11	68.2	11
South East (excluding Greater London)	80.4	3	76.8	10	73.6	8	71.1	8	75.4	8
South West	80.1	4	82.4	4	80.7	2	73.0	6	78.9	4
Wales	81.2	1	85.2	1	78.4	4	69.6	10	78.8	5
Scotland	79.3	5	82.2	5	67.7	10	71.7	7	75.3	9
Great Britain	76.9		79.9		73.9		73.2		76.0	

Table 4 **Age comparison of the 1996 GHS and population estimates[†] for mid-1996**

All persons   *Great Britain: 1996*

Age	Males 1996 GHS %	Males Population estimates mid-1996 %	Females 1996 GHS %	Females Population estimates mid-1996 %	Total 1996 GHS %	Total Population estimates mid-1996 %
0 - 4	7.2	6.6	6.8*	6.1	7.0*	6.4
5 - 15	16.2*	14.7	14.8*	13.5	15.5*	14.1
16 - 19	4.8	4.9	4.2*	4.5	4.5	4.7
20 - 24	5.5*	6.7	5.6*	6.2	5.5*	6.4
25 - 29	7.4*	8.1	7.4	7.5	7.4*	7.8
30 - 34	7.5*	8.6	7.6	7.9	7.5*	8.3
35 - 39	7.5	7.5	7.6	7.1	7.5	7.3
40 - 44	6.8	6.6	6.6	6.3	6.7	6.5
45 - 49	6.9	7.2	6.9	6.9	6.9	7.1
50 - 54	6.6*	6.0	5.9	5.8	6.2	5.9
55 - 59	4.8	5.1	5.0	5.0	4.9	5.1
60 - 64	4.9	4.7	4.9	4.7	4.9	4.7
65 - 69	4.5	4.3	4.7	4.7	4.6	4.5
70 - 74	3.8	3.7	4.5	4.5	4.1	4.1
75 and over	5.8*	5.1	7.5*	9.2	6.7*	7.2
Total	48.4	49.1	51.6	51.0	100	100
Base = 100%	*10781*	*28043172*	*11493*	*29094988*	*22274*	*57138160*

* Difference was found to be significant at the 5% level.
† Population estimates include people living in institutional accommodation.

Table 5 Region: a comparison of the 1996 GHS and population estimates for mid-1996

All persons *Great Britain: 1996*

Region	1996 GHS	Population estimates mid-1996
	%	%
England	85.3	85.9
North	6.3	5.4
Yorkshire and Humberside	8.6	8.8
North West	11.3	11.2
East Midlands	7.5	7.2
West Midlands	9.4	9.3
East Anglia	3.9	3.7
Greater London	10.6	12.4
South East (excluding Greater London)	18.7	19.3
South West	8.8	8.5
Wales	5.6	5.1
Scotland	9.1	9.0
Base = 100%	22274	57138160

(with fewer than 4 rooms) and those whose head was born outside the UK. Households containing dependent children were over-represented in the responding sample. More details of the results are given in Appendix C of the 1993 report[6].

Comparison of the 1996 GHS with population estimates for mid-1996

Table 4 compares the age distribution of the 1996 GHS sample with that from population estimates for mid-1996. The comparisons show that the 1996 GHS tended to over-represent children, particularly those aged 5-15, and to under-represent adults in their twenties and early thirties. There were some differences between men and women of the same age. For example, men aged 50-54 were over-represented but women of the same age were not; men aged 75 and over were over-represented whereas women of the same age were under-represented in the sample.

It should be noted that the GHS covers only those people living in private households, whereas population estimates also include those people living in institutional accommodation.

Table 5 shows that the 1996 GHS under-represented people living in the Greater London area, again because of non-response bias. The GHS achieves a lower response in London than elsewhere both because people tend to be harder to contact than in other regions and because of higher refusal rates[6].

Notes and references

1 It is known that the majority of delivery points with a multi-occupancy indicator '2' consist of one private dwelling plus business premises, so these addresses were assumed to contain just one household.

2 Most institutions and business addresses are not listed on the small-user PAF. If an address was found in the field to be non-private (e.g. boarding house containing four or more boarders at the time the interviewer calls), the interviewer was instructed not to take an interview. However, a household member in hospital at the time of interview was included in the sample provided that he or she had not been away from home for more than six months and was expected to return. In this case a proxy interview was taken.

3 Clarke L et al. General Household Survey Advance Letter Experiment. *OPCS Social Survey Division, Survey Methodology Bulletin* No.21, September 1987.

4 Rauta I. A comparison of the census characteristics of respondents and non-respondents to the 1981 General Household Survey (GHS) *Statistical News*, November 1985, No.71.

5 Barnes R and Birch F (1975). The Census as an aid in estimating the characteristics of non-response in the General Household Survey. *OPCS Social Survey Division, New Methodology Series* NM1. (1975)

6 *Foster K et al. General Household Survey 1993.* HMSO 1995. Appendix C

Appendix C
Sampling Error

Tables to this appendix present estimates for sampling errors for some of the main variables used in this report.[1] A wider range of estimates, together with a fuller description of the use of sampling errors, are included in earlier GHS reports.[2,3] As the GHS sample design has remained unchanged since 1984 the results in these earlier reports can be applied to GHS data in subsequent years and can be used to judge the reliability of many of the results described in this report.

Sources of error in surveys

Survey results are subject to various sources of error. The total error in a survey estimate is the difference between the estimate derived from the data collected and the true value for the population. The total error can be divided into two main types: systematic and random error.

Systematic error

Systematic error, or bias, covers those sources of error which will not average to zero over repeats of the survey. Bias may occur, for example, if a certain section of the population is excluded from the sampling frame, because non-respondents to the survey have different characteristics to respondents, or if interviewers or coders systematically influence responses in one way or another. Substantial efforts have been made to avoid systematic errors.

Random error

An important component of random error is sampling error, which is the error that arises because the estimate is based on a survey rather than a full census of the population. The results obtained for any single sample may, by chance, vary from the true values for the population but the variation would be expected to average to zero over a number of repeats of the survey. The amount of variation depends on both the size of the sample and the sample design.

Random error may also be the result of other sources such as variation in respondent's interpretation of the questions, or interviewer or coder variation. Efforts are made to minimise these effects through interviewer and coder training and through pilot work.

Standard error in this appendix is used to refer to the estimate of random error which includes both sampling error and other components of random error at psu level and below.

Confidence intervals

The estimate produced from a sample survey will rarely be identical to the population value, but statistical theory allows us to measure the accuracy of any survey result. The standard error can be estimated from the values obtained for the sample and allows the calculation of confidence intervals which give an indication of the range in which the true population value is likely to fall.

It is common when quoting confidence intervals to refer to the 95% confidence interval around a survey estimate. This is calculated at 1.96 times the standard error on either side of the estimated percentage or mean since, under a normal distribution, 95% of values lie within 1.96 standard errors of the mean value. If it were possible to repeat the survey under the same conditions many times, 95% of these confidence intervals would contain the population value. This does not guarantee that the intervals calculated for any particular sample will contain the population values but, when assessing the results of a single survey, it is usual to assume that there is only a 5% chance that the true population value falls outside the 95% confidence interval calculated for the survey estimate.

The GHS is a multi-stage sample design which involves both clustering and stratification. Clustering can lead to a substantial increase in standard error if the households or individuals within primary sampling units (psus) are relatively homogenous but the psus differ from one another. Stratification tends to reduce standard error and is of most advantage where the stratification factor is related to the characteristics of interest on the survey.

The effect of a complex sample design on the precision of survey estimates is usually quantified by means of the design factor (deft). For any survey estimate, the deft is calculated as the ratio of the standard error allowing for the full complexity of the survey design to the standard error assuming a simple random design. The standard error based on a simple random sample multiplied by the deft gives the standard error of a complex design.

$$se(p) = deft \times se(p)_{srs}$$

Where:

$$se(p)_{srs} = \sqrt{\frac{p(100\text{-}p)}{n}}$$

The formula to measure whether the difference between percentages is likely to be due entirely to sampling error for a complex sample design is:

$$se\ (p_1 - p_2) = \sqrt{deft_1^2 \frac{p_1(100 - p_1)}{n_1} + deft_2^2 \frac{p_2(100 - p_2)}{n_2}}$$

where p_1 and p_2 are observed percentages for the two subsamples and n_1 and n_2 are the subsample sizes. The 95% confidence interval for the difference between two percentages is then given by:

$$(p_1 - p_2) +/- 1.96 \times se\ (p_1 - p_2)$$

If this confidence interval includes zero then the observed difference is considered to be a result of chance variation in the sample. If the interval does not include zero then it is unlikely (less than 5% probability) that the observed difference could have occurred by chance.

Estimating standard errors for other survey measures
The standard errors of survey measures which are not presented in the tables and for sample subgroups may be estimated by applying an appropriate value of deft to the sampling error. The choice of an appropriate value of deft will vary according to whether the basic survey measure is included in the tables. Since most deft values are relatively small (1.1 or less) the absolute effect of adjusting sampling errors to take account of the survey's complex design will be small. In most cases it will result in an increase of less than 10% over the standard error assuming a simple random sample. Whether it is considered necessary to use deft or to use the basic estimates of standard errors assuming a simple random sample is a matter of judgement and depends chiefly on the use to which the survey results are to be put.

Notes and references
1   The estimates of sampling errors for the GHS were obtained by using the 'Epsilon' package which was developed by Social Survey Division of ONS for use on surveys with multi-stage designs.
2   Breeze E. *Report on sampling error*. Series GHS no. 18 OPCS, 1990 HMSO (London).
3   Foster K et al. *General Household Survey 1993*. Series GHS no. 24 OPCS, 1995 HMSO (London).

Table C1 **True standard errors and 95% confidence intervals for age and marital status: 1996**

Base	Characteristic	% (p)	Sample size	Standard error of p	Deft	100 roh	95% confidence interval
	Age						
All males	0-4	7.2	10781	0.27	1.09	1.02	6.6 - 7.7
	5-15	16.2	10781	0.39	1.09	1.04	15.5 - 17.0
	16-44	39.4	10781	0.47	0.99	-0.10	38.4 - 40.3
	45-64	23.2	10781	0.39	0.95	-0.52	22.4 - 24.0
	65-74	8.2	10781	0.27	1.02	0.23	7.7 - 8.7
	75 and over	5.8	10781	0.24	1.01	0.76	5.3 - 6.3
All females	0-4	6.8	11493	0.23	1.00	-0.03	6.4 - 7.3
	5-15	14.8	11493	0.34	1.02	0.17	14.1 - 15.4
	16-44	39.0	11493	0.41	0.90	-0.96	38.2 - 39.8
	45-64	22.7	11493	0.43	1.09	1.02	21.9 - 23.6
	65-74	9.2	11493	0.27	1.01	0.15	8.7 - 9.7
	75 and over	7.5	11493	0.26	1.07	0.66	7.0 - 8.0
	Martial Status						
Men aged 16 and over	Married	60.4	8257	0.60	1.11	1.67	59.2 - 61.5
	Cohabiting	7.5	8257	0.31	1.06	0.99	6.9 - 8.1
	Single	22.4	8257	0.52	1.14	2.32	21.3 - 23.4
	Widowed	4.2	8257	0.24	1.10	1.50	3.8 - 4.8
	Divorced	3.9	8257	0.22	1.05	0.82	3.5 - 4.4
	Separated	1.2	8257	0.15	0.94	-0.76	1.1 - 1.6
Women aged 16 and over	Married	55.3	9007	0.56	1.06	0.85	54.2 - 56.4
	Cohabiting	6.8	9007	0.28	1.07	0.95	6.3 - 7.4
	Single	17.4	9007	0.44	1.09	1.31	16.6 - 18.3
	Widowed	12.3	9007	0.34	0.99	-0.16	11.6 - 13.0
	Divorced	5.5	9007	0.24	1.01	0.12	5.1 - 6.0
	Separated	2.5	9007	0.15	0.94	-0.76	2.2 - 2.8
Adults aged 16 and over							
Men	Working	64.0	8117	0.59	1.12	1.85	62.8 - 65.2
	Unemployed	5.8	8117	0.28	1.10	1.65	5.25 - 6.3
	Economcially inactive	30.1	8117	0.55	1.09	1.48	29.0 - 31.2
Women	Working	49.9	8914	0.56	1.06	0.78	48.8 - 51.0
	Unemployed	3.0	8914	0.18	1.02	0.26	2.6 - 3.4
	Economcially inactive	47.1	8914	0.56	1.06	0.80	46.0 - 48.2

Table C2   **True standard errors and 95% confidence intervals for household type, tenure and burglary: 1996**

Base	Characteristic	% (p)	Sample size	Standard error of p	Deft	100 roh	95% confidence interval
All households	Household type						
	1 adult 16-59	11.3	9158	0.37	1.11	1.50	10.6 - 12.0
	2 adults 16-59	15.4	9158	0.41	1.09	1.30	14.6 - 16.2
	Youngest person aged 0-4	13.2	9158	0.37	1.04	0.50	12.5 - 13.9
	Youngest person aged 5-15	17.2	9158	0.38	0.97	-0.40	16.4 - 17.9
	3 or more adults	10.7	9158	0.35	1.07	1.00	10.0 - 11.3
	2 adults, 1 or both aged 60 or over	16.3	9158	0.40	1.03	0.40	15.5 - 17.0
	1 adult aged 60 or over	16.0	9158	0.41	1.06	0.90	15.2 - 16.8
All households	Tenure						
	Owns outright	25.5	9158	0.51	1.11	1.60	24.5 - 26.5
	Buying with a mortgage	41.4	9158	0.56	1.08	1.20	40.3 - 42.5
	Rents from local authority	19.1	9158	0.53	1.29	4.50	18.0 - 20.1
	Rents from housing association	4.7	9158	0.32	1.43	7.00	4.1 - 5.3
	Private renter (unfurnished)	6.5	9158	0.32	1.23	3.40	5.9 - 7.2
	Private renter (furnished)	2.6	9158	0.21	1.24	3.70	2.2 - 3.1
All households	Burglaries of private households						
Burglary	Households that had been burgled	3.3	9102	0.21	1.13	1.80	2.9 - 3.7

Table C3   **True standard errors and 95% confidence intervals for self-reported illness, cigarette smoking, alcohol consumption and sports participation: 1996**

Base	Characteristic	% (p)	Sample size	Standard error of p	Deft	100 roh	95% confidence interval
All persons	Self-reported illness						
Males	Longstanding illness	33.7	10756	0.54	1.20	2.44	32.6 - 34.8
	Limiting longstanding illness	20.4	10756	0.43	1.11	1.27	19.6 - 21.2
	Restricted activity	14.8	10756	0.41	1.21	2.59	14.0 - 15.6
Females	Longstanding illness	34.8	11471	0.54	1.20	2.40	33.8 - 35.9
	Limiting longstanding illness	22.5	11471	0.45	1.16	1.84	21.6 - 23.4
	Restricted activity	16.4	11471	0.41	1.19	2.24	15.6 - 17.2
	Current cigarette smokers						
Men	"	28.6	7186	0.56	1.05	0.95	27.5 - 29.7
Women	"	27.5	8512	0.56	1.15	2.30	26.4 - 28.6
Cigarette smokers	Mean number of cigarettes smoked per week						
Men		111.4	2044	1.45	1.04	2.68	108.5 - 114.3
Women		96.3	2338	1.13	1.00	0.13	94.1 - 98.6
	Mean units of alcohol drunk per week						
Men		16.0	7169	0.25	1.10	1.50	15.5 - 16.5
Women		63	8496	0.12	1.10	1.60	6.0 - 6.5
All persons	Participation in the 4 weeks before interview						
	Any physical activity	63.7	15696	0.50	1.30	2.66	62.7 - 64.6
Men	Snooker/pool/billiards	19.6	7184	0.53	1.13	2.35	18.6 - 20.63
	Cycling	14.8	7185	0.48	1.14	2.54	13.9 - 15.8
	Swimming	12.8	7186	0.44	1.11	2.11	11.9 - 13.6
	Keep fit/yoga	6.8	7184	0.33	1.11	1.94	6.1 - 7.4
All women	Snooker/pool/billiards	4.3	8510	0.21	0.96	-0.56	3.90 - 4.73
	Cycling	7.8	8511	0.36	1.24	3.99	7.0 - 8.5
	Swimming	16.5	8511	0.47	1.16	2.47	15.6 - 17.4
	Keep fit/yoga	16.9	8511	0.44	1.10	1.34	16.0 - 17.8

Appendix D
General Houshold Survey 1996/97
Household Questionnaire

COMPLETE FOR EACH SAMPLED HOUSEHOLD AT ADDRESS

Areacode	Information already entered
Address	Information already entered
Hhld	Information already entered
IntDate	Date of interview (computed by system)

ALL HOUSEHOLDS

ASK OR RECORD

1 Npersons — How many people normally live in this household?
1..14

2 Nadults — How many people aged 16 or over are normally living in this household?
1..14

3 Nchldren — How many children aged under 16 are there normally living in this household?
0..14

IntroHHB — I'd like to ask a few more questions about the composition of your household. We do this so that we can check that we are covering a cross-section of the population.

HOUSEHOLD INFORMATION

INFORMATION TO BE COLLECTED FOR ALL PERSONS IN ALL HOUSEHOLDS

4 Name — RECORD THE NAME OF HOH/NEXT PERSON'S NAME

REMEMBER THAT WHERE A PROPERTY IS OWNED/RENTED IN THE NAME OF A WOMAN WHO IS MARRIED/COHABITING WITH A MAN, THEN BY DEFINITION, THE MAN IS THE HOH.

(Enter text of at most 15 characters)

5 Sex — Code ...'s sex

Male 1
Female... 2

6 Age — What was your/...'s age last birthday?
0..99

7 Dob — Can you tell me your/...'s date of birth?

(Enter date)

8 Mstat — Are you/Is ...

CODE FIRST THAT APPLIES

Single,that is never married?............... 1

Married and living with husband/wife?.................................. 2
Married and separated from husband/wife?.................................. 3
Divorced? or.. 4
Widowed?... 5

9 Cohabit — **If age 16+ and Mstat = 1,3,4 or 5 and Nadults>1**

(May I just check), are you/is ... living with someone in this household as a couple?

Yes - opposite sex partner................... 1
No.. 2
Yes - same sex partner....................... 3

10 RentOwn — **Ask or record for all persons 16+**

In whose name is the accommodation owned or rented?

CODE WHETHER OR NOT THIS ACCOMMODATION IS OWNED OR RENTED IN THE NAME OF ...

Yes - in his/her name........................... 1
No.. 2

HH1 — I would now like to ask how the people in your household are related to each other.

11 R — Code relationship of ... to ...?

Spouse 1
Cohabitee.. 2
Son/daughter (inc adopted) 3
Step-son/daughter............................... 4
Foster child 5
Son-in-law/daughter-in-law 6
Parent 7
Step-parent 8
Foster parent 9
Parent-in-law 10
Brother/sister (inc adopted) 11
Step-brother/sister.............................. 12
Foster brother/sister 13
Brother/sister-in-law 14
Grand-child... 15
Grand-parent....................................... 16
Other relative 17
Other non-relative 18

ACCOMMODATION TYPE

IntroAcc — The next section looks at the standard of people's housing

All households
12 Haccom — Type of accommodation occupied by this household

CODE FROM OBSERVATION, BUT IF IN DOUBT, ASK INFORMANT

a house or bungalow............................ 1 → Q1
a flat or maisonette.............................. 2 → Q1
a room/rooms...................................... 3 → Q1
other.. 4 → Q1

3 HseTyp　　**If house/bungalow (Haccom=1)**

INTERVIEWER CODE: IS IT ....

detached... 1
semi-detached..................................... 2　⎦→Q19
or terraced/end of terrace.................... 3

4 Built　　**If flat/maisonette (Haccom=2)**

INTERVIEWER CODE: IS IT.....

a purpose built block............................ 1
a converted house/some other
　kind of building................................. 2

5 HasLift　　INTERVIEWER CODE: IS THERE A LIFT?
Yes.. 1⎤→Q18
No.. 2⎦

6 Othaccom　　**If 'other' type of accommodation (Haccom=4)**

INTERVIEWER CODE: IS IT.....

a caravan, mobile home or
　houseboat.. 1　→Q20
some other kind of accommodation
(specify at the next question)............... 2　→Q17

7 XTypAccm　　Please specify type of accommodation

(Enter text of at most 40 characters)　　→Q18

8 Storey　　**If coded 2 or 3 at Haccom or 2 at Othaccom**

What is the floor level of the main living part of the accommodation?

ASK OR RECORD

Basement/semi-basement 1
Ground floor/street level 2
1st floor 3
2nd floor .... 4　→Q19
3rd floor 5
4th to 9th floor 6
10th floor or higher 7

9 DateBlt　　**If NOT coded 1 at Othaccom**

When was this building first built?

PROMPT IF NECESSARY - IF DK CODE YOUR ESTIMATE.

Before 1919....................................... 1
Between 1919 and 1944 2
Between 1945 and 1964 .... 3　→Q20
Between 1965 and 1984 4
1985 or later 5
DK but after 1944 6

0 Bedrooms　　**Ask all households**

Now I would like to ask you about YOUR household's accommodation, EXCLUDING any rooms you may let or sublet.

How many bedrooms do you have, including bedsitting rooms and spare bedrooms?

IF 8 OR MORE, TYPE 8　　　　1..8　→Q21

21 BedCook　　Are any of them used by your household for cooking in - like a bedsitter for example?

Yes.. 1⎤→Q22
No.. 2⎦

22 Kitchen　　(Apart from that), do you have a kitchen, that is a separate room in which you cook?

Yes.. 1　→Q23
No.. 2　→Q26

23 KitSize　　**If Yes (code 1) at Kitchen**

Is the narrowest side of the kitchen less than 6¹/2 ft wide from wall to wall?

Less than 6¹/2 ft................................. 1⎤→Q24
6¹/2 ft or more .... 2⎦

24 KitEat　　Do any of you ever eat meals in it or use it as a sitting room?

Yes.. 1⎤→Q25
No.. 2⎦

25 ShareKit　　**If Yes (code 1) at Kitchen and coded 2-4 at Haccom.**　　　　**Else**　→Q26

Do you share the kitchen with any other household?

Yes.. 1⎤→Q26
No.. 2⎦

26 OthRooms　　**Ask all households**

Apart from the rooms you have already told me about, and not counting bathrooms and toilets, do you have any other rooms?

EXCLUDE GARAGES, UTILITY ROOMS AND ROOMS USED SOLELY FOR BUSINESS

Yes.. 1　→Q27
No.. 2　→Q29

27 WhOthRooms　　**If Yes (code 1) at OthRms**

Which other rooms do you have?

IF THERE IS MORE THAN ONE ROOM CALLED BY THE SAME NAME RECORD IT/THEM AS OTHER AND SPECIFY AT NEXT QUESTION

(Enter at most 5 codes)

Sitting Room 1
Living Room 2
Lounge/through lounge .... 3　→Q29
Dining Room 4
Other (SPECIFY AT
　NEXT QUESTION) .... 5　→Q28

28 XWhRms

Record names of other rooms

(Enter text of at most 150 characters) →Q29

29 CentHeat

Ask all households

Do you have any form of central heating, including electric storage heaters, in your (part of the) accommodation?

CENTRAL HEATING = 2 OR MORE ROOMS, KITCHENS, HALLS, LANDINGS, BATH/WC HEATED FROM ONE CENTRAL SOURCE

Yes .... 1 →Q30
No .... 2 →Q31

30 Fuel

If Yes (code 1) at CentHeat

Which type of fuel does it use?

CODE MAIN METHOD ONLY.

PROBE 'Hot Air' FOR FUEL.

Solid fuel: incl. coal, coke, wood,
    peat 1
Electricity: storage heaters 2
Electricity: other (including oil
    filled radiators) .... 3 →Q31
Gas/calor gas 4
Oil 5
Other 6

CONSUMER DURABLES

IntroDur

Now I'd like to ask you about various household items you may have - this gives us an indication of how living standards are changing

31 TVcol

Ask all households

Does your household have any of the following items in your (part of the) accommodation?

INCLUDE: Items stored or under repair

....Colour TV set?

1 only 1
more than one 2
None 3

32 TVbw

...Black and white TV set?

1 only 1
more than one 2
None 3

33 Satell

...a receiver for satellite television?

Yes 1
No 2

34 Video

...Video recorder?

Yes 1
No 2

35 Freezer

...Deep freezer or fridge freezer?

EXCLUDE: Fridge only
Yes 1
No 2

36 WashMach

...Washing machine?

IF COMBINED WASHING MACHINE AND TUMBLE DRIER, CODE 1 FOR BOTH

Yes 1
No 2

37 Drier

...Tumble drier?

IF COMBINED WASHING MACHINE AND TUMBLE DRIER, CODE 1 FOR BOTH

Yes 1
No 2

38 DishWash

...Dish washer?

Yes 1
No 2

39 MicroWve

...Microwave oven?

Yes 1
No 2

40 Telephon

...Telephone?

SHARED TELEPHONES LOCATED IN PUBLIC HALLWAYS TO BE INCLUDED ONLY IF THIS HOUSEHOLD IS RESPONSIBLE FOR PAYING THE ACCOUNT

INCLUDE: Mobile phones

Yes 1
No 2

41 Cdplay

...Compact disc (CD) player?

Yes 1
No 2

42 Computer

...Home computer?

EXCLUDE: Video games

Yes 1
No .... 2 →Q43

43 Car

Is there a car or van NORMALLY available for private use by you (or any members of your household)?

INCLUDE: ANY PROVIDED BY EMPLOYERS IF NORMALLY AVAILABLE FOR PRIVATE USE BY INFORMANT OR MEMBERS OF THE HOUSEHOLD

EXCLUDE: VEHICLES USED SOLELY FOR
THE CARRIAGE OF GOODS

Yes .... 1 → Q44
No .... 2 → Q45

44 NCars | **If Yes (code 1) at Car**

How many are normally available for use?
1..8 → Q45

TENURE

Introten | Next we look at housing tenure. As you are
probably aware, there have been changes
recently in the numbers of people who rent as
well as in the numbers who own their
accommodation.

45 OwnerTen | **Ask all households**

(May I just check)In whose name is this (HOUSE/
FLAT/ROOM) owned or rented?

IF JOINT HOH and WIFE/COHABITEE and
OTHER PERSON, CODE 3

HOH only 1
WIFE/COHABITEE of HOH
  only .... 2 → Q47
Joint HOH and WIFE/
  COHABITEE 3
Other answers (SPECIFY AT
  NEXT QUESTION .... 8 → Q46

46 XOwnerTn | Specify in whose name this (HOUSE/FLAT/
ROOM) is owned or rented.

(Enter text of at most 30 characters)

47 Ten1 | In which of these ways does this household
occupy this accommodation?

SHOW CARD H2

Own it outright 1
Buying it with the help of a
  mortgage or loan .... 2 → Q54
Pay part rent and part
  mortgage (shared ownership) 3
Rent it .... 4 → Q48
Live here rent-free 5
Squatting .... 6 → Q54

48 Furn | **If 'rents/rentfree' at Ten1 (code 4 or 5)**

Is the accommodation provided:
furnished 1
partly furnished (e.g curtains
  and carpets only) .... 2 → Q49
or unfurnished? 3

49 RentBusn | Are any business premises included in the rent
for this accommodation (in the accommodation
provided)?

INCLUDE: Farm

Yes .... 1 → Q50
No 2

50 RentJob | Does this accommodation go with the present job
of anyone in your household?

Yes .... 1 → Q51
No 2

51 Llord | Who is your landlord?

CODE FIRST THAT APPLIES

the local authority/council/New
  Town Development/Scottish
  Homes?.. 1
a housing association or
  cooperative or charitable
  trust? .... 2 → Q54
employer (organisation) of a
  household member?......................... 3
another organisation?........................... 4 → Q52
relative/friend (before you lived
  here) of household member?. 5 → Q53
employer (individual) of
  household member?......................... 6
another individual private
  landlord?.. 7

52 XLandlrd | **If 'another organisation' at Llord (code 4)**

Who is it rented from? (Who is it provided by?)

(Enter text of no more than 40 characters) → Q54

53 LandLive | **If 'rented from an individual' at Llord (code 5,
6 or 7)**

Does the landlord live in this building?

Yes .... 1 → Q54
No 2

54 ResChek | **Ask of HOH in all households**

How long have you (HOH) lived at this address?

COMPLETE CALENDAR MONTHS/YEARS UP
TO THE END OF THE MONTH PRECEDING
THE INTERVIEW

less than 12 months............................ 1 → Q55
12 months but less than 2 years........... 2
2 years but less than 3 years................ 3
3 years but less than 5 years................ 4 → Q56
5 years but less than 10 years.............. 5
10 years or longer................................ 6

55 ResMths

Ask if informant has lived at this address for less than 12 months (ResChek = 1)

How many months have you (HOH) lived here?

ENTER THE NUMBER OF CALENDAR MONTHS ONLY UP TO THE END OF THE MONTH PRECEDING THE INTERVIEW.

0..11 →, Burglary

BURGLARY

IntroBur

All households
The next section is about burglaries. It is asked so that comparisons can be made between burglaries overall and those reported to the police. It also helps to see whether burglary is increasing or not.

56 BurgA

If informant has lived at address for at least a year (Reschek = 2-6)

During the last twelve months ie since (last 12 complete calendar months) has anybody got into this (HOUSE/FLAT/ROOM) without your permission and stolen or attempted to steal something?

INCLUDE ENTRY UNDER FALSE PRETENCES ONLY IF MENTIONED SPONTANEOUSLY

Yes 1   →Q58
No 2   →Q67

57 BurgB

If informant has lived at address for 1-11 months (ResMths = 1-11)

During the time you (HOH) have lived here (UP TO THE END OF THE MONTH PRECEDING THEINTERVIEW), has anybody got into this (HOUSE/FLAT/ROOM) without your permission and stolen or attempted to steal something?

INCLUDE ENTRY UNDER FALSE PRETENCES ONLY IF MENTIONED SPONTANEOUSLY

Yes 1   →Q58
No 2   →Q67

58 BurgNum

If Yes (code 1) at BurgA or BurgB

How many times has this happened during the last 12 months (the time you (HOH) have lived here)?

1..10   →Q59

Ask for each burglary

59 BurgMon

In what month did the first/second/third burglary occur?

1..12   →Q60

60 BurgYear

In what year did the first/second/third burglary occur?

(Enter year (e.g '96) between 95 & 97)   →Q61

61 Entry

Some burglars get into people's homes by forcing an entry, others get through an unlocked door or window and others get in under false pretences. How did the burglar get into your (HOUSE/FLAT/ROOM)?

Forced entry .... 1⌉
Unlocked door or window .... 2 →Q63
False pretences 3
Burglar didn't get in .... 4⌋
Other (SPECIFY AT NEXT
    QUESTION) 5   →Q62

62 XEntry

Describe other method of entry.

(Enter text of at most 50 characters)   →Q63

63 Stolen

Was anything actually stolen?

Yes 1   →Q64
No 2   →Q66

64 StolnVal

If Yes (code 1) at Stolen

Roughly how much were the stolen goods (and cash) worth in total?

ACCEPT ESTIMATES.

Nothing 1   →Q66
Under £5 .... 2⌉
£5 and under £25 3
£25 and under £50 4
£50 and under £100 5
£100 and under £200 .... 6 →Q65
£200 and under £500 7
£500 and under £1000 8
£1000 and under £2000 9
£2000 and under £5000 10
£5000 or more .... 11⌋

65 Insured

If code 2-11 at StolnVal

Was anything stolen insured?

Yes .... 1⌉
No .... 2⌋ →Q66

66 Reported

For all burglaries

May I just check, was this incident reported to the police?

Yes .... 1⌉
No .... 2⌋ →Q67

MIGRATION

67 ResLen

All persons in all households

(Could I just check) how many years have you/ha (...) lived at this address?

(If under 1, code as 0)   See Q6

68 Nmoves   **If 0-4 years at ResLen**

How many moves have you/has (...) made in the last 5 years, not counting moves between places outside Great Britain?   .. 69

All persons in all households

69 Cob   In what country were you/was (...) born?

England	1
Scotland	2
Wales	3	.Q72
Northern Ireland	4
Channel Islands/Isle of Man	5
Republic of Ireland/Eire	6
European Union countries	7
Other Europe	8
Old Commonwealth	9
India	10
East African New Commonwealth	11
Rest of African Commonwealth	12
Caribbean Commonwealth.	13	.Q71
Mediterranean Commonwealth	14
Far East Commonwealth	15
Remainder Commonwealth	16
Pakistan	17
Bangladesh	18
Africa	19
America	20
Asia-Middle East	21
Rest of Asia and Oceania	22
Answer general but outside UK/EIRE	23
Other (SPECIFY AT NEXT QUESTION)	24	.Q70

70 XCob   In what country were you/was (...) born?

(Enter text of at most 20 characters)   .Q71

71 Arruk   **If 'Other' or 'Eire' (code 6 - 24) at Cob**

In what year did you (...) first arrive in the United Kingdom?

1..97   .Q72

72 FathCob   **All persons in all households**
In what country was your/(...'s) father born?

See codes at Cob

Codes 1-23   .Q74

Code 24   .Q73

73 XFathCob   In what country was your/(...'s) father born?

(Enter text of at most 20 characters)   .Q74

74 MothCob   **All persons in all households**

In what country was your/(...'s) mother born?

See codes at Cob

Codes 1-23   .Q76

Code 24   .Q75

75 XMothCob   In what country was your/(...'s) mother born?

(Enter text of at most 20 characters)   .Q76

76 Origin[*]   **All persons in all households**

To which of the groups listed on this card do you consider you/(...) belong?

SHOW CARD H3

White	1
Black Caribbean	2
Black African	3
Black Other (SPECIFY AT NEXT QUESTION)	4	.Q77
Indian	5
Pakistani	6
Bangladeshi	7
Chinese	8
None of these (SPECIFY AT NEXT QUESTION)	9	.Q77
Not for interviewer use	10

77 XOrigin   **If 'Black Other' or 'None of these' at Origin (code 4 or 9)**

How would you describe the racial or ethnic group to which you/(...) belong?

(Enter text of at most 25 characters)

END OF HOUSEHOLD QUESTIONNAIRE

General Houshold Survey 1996/97
Individual Questionnaire

Area code	Area Number...
Address	Address Number...
Hhld	Household number...
SuppSer	Individual questionnaire number
WhoInt1	Which person(s) do you wish to interview?
	ENTER PERSON NO. OF FIRST PERSON (SECOND PERSON, IF ANY, AT NEXT QUESTION) 1...14
WhoInt2	Which other person do you wish to interview?
	ENTER PERSON NO. OF SECOND PERSON (ENTER ZERO IF ONE PERSON ONLY) 0...14

IntTyp   Code interview with [NAME] as...

Full interview 1
or proxy interview 2
missing, ie non-contact/refusal 3

EMPLOYMENT

All Adults

1 WorklWk1   Did you do any paid work last week - that is in the 7 days ending last Sunday the... - either as an employee or as self-employed?

Yes. .... 1 ⎤
No .... 2 ⎦ ⟶ Q2

2 GovSchem   **Men aged 16-64 and women aged 16-62**

During last week, that is the 7 days ending last SUNDAY were you on any of the following government schemes (including those run by: Training Enterprise Councils (TEC) - England and Wales
Local Enterprise Companies (LEC) - Scotland)

INDIVIDUAL PROMPT

Youth Training(YT)? ONLY ASK
  16-20 YRS .... 1 ⎤
Training for work/Employment
  Training/Employment Action? .... 2 ⎦ ⟶ Q3
Community Action? 3   See
None of these? 4   ⟶ Q4

3 Trn   **If on Youth Training, Employment Action, Employment Training, Training for Work (GovSchem = 1 or 2)**

CODE FIRST THAT APPLIES

Last week were you...
with an employer, or on a
  project providing work experience
  or practical training? 1   See
or at a college or training   ⟶ Q4
  centre?.. 2 ⎦

4 WorklWk2   **If 'no' (code 2) at WorklWk1 (all ages)**

Did you have a job that you were away from last week?

Yes .... 1 ⟶ Q1
No .... 2 ⟶ Q
SPONTANEOUS Waiting to take
  up a new job/business already
  obtained .... 3 ⟶ Q

5 WorklWk3   **If 'no' (code 2) at WorklWk2**

Last week were you ...

CODE FIRST THAT APPLIES

waiting to take up a job you had
  already obtained?.............................. 1 ⟶ Q
looking for work? or............................ 2 ⟶ Q
intending to look for work but
  prevented by temporary sickness or
  injury (CHECK 28 DAYS OR LESS)? 3 ⟶ Q
NONE OF THESE? .... 4 ⟶ Q2

6 LookWork   **If unemployed and looking for work but prevented by temporary sickness or injury (WorklWk3 = 3)**

Thinking of the 4 weeks ending last Sunday the ... ,were you looking for any kind of paid work (or a government training scheme place) at any time in those 4 weeks?

Yes .... 1 ⎤
No .... 2 ⎦ ⟶ Q

7 AbleStrt   **If coded 2 or 3 at WorklWk3**

If a job or a place on a government scheme had been available in the week ending last Sunday the..., would you have been able to start within 2 weeks?

Yes .... 1 ⎤
No .... 2 ⎦ ⟶ Q

8 UnemWtJ1   **If unemployed and waiting to take up a job (WorklWk2 = 3 or WorklWk3 = 1)**

Apart from the job you are waiting to take up, have you ever had a paid job or done any paid work?

Yes .... 1 ⎤
No .... 2 ⎦ ⟶ Q1

All others unemployed (WorkIWk3 = 2 or 3)

9 UnemWtJ2

(May I check), have you ever had a paid job or done any paid work?

Yes .... 1 ⎤
No .... 2 ⎦ - Q10

10 UnempTim

All unemployed last week (WorkIWk3 = 1,2 or 3)

How long altogether have you been out of employment but wanting work in this current period of unemployment, that is, since any time you may have spent on a government scheme, such as YT or ET/Training for Work?

PERIOD = UP TO YESTERDAY

Less than a week .... 1 ⎤
1 week but less than 1 month 2
1 month but less than 3 months 3
3 months but less than 6 months ... 4
6 months but less than 12 months ... 5 ⎬ - See Q11
12 months but less than 2 years 6
2 years but less than 3 years 7
3 years but less than 5 years 8
5 years or more .... 9 ⎦

11 IndD

All economically active except those unemployed who have never worked and are not waiting to take up a job (NOT WorkIWk3 = 4 or UnemWtJ2 = 2)

What does/did the firm/organisation you work(ed) for mainly make or do at the place where you work(ed)?

DESCRIBE FULLY - PROBE MANUFACTURING OR PROCESSING OR DISTRIBUTION ETC. AND MAIN GOODS PRODUCED, MATERIALS USED, WHOLESALE OR RETAIL ETC.

(Enter text at most 80 characters) - Q12

12 IndT

ENTER A TITLE FOR THE INDUSTRY

(Enter text of at most 30 characters) - Q13

13 OccT

What was your (main) job (in the week ending Sunday the xx)?

ENTER JOB TITLE
(Enter text of at most 30 characters) - Q14

14 OccD

What do/did you mainly do in your job?

CHECK SPECIAL QUALIFICATIONS/TRAINING NEEDED TO DO THE JOB
(Enter text of at most 80 characters)

SOCMAIN

Occupation code for main job...100...999

INDMAIN

Industry code for main job........500...999

MAINSEG

Socio-economic group based on main job..0......19

MAINSC

Social class based on main job.0....7

15 Stat

Are/were you working as an employee or were you self-employed?

Employee .... 1 - Q16
Self-employed .... 2 - Q18

16 Manage

If employee (Stat =1)

ASK OR RECORD

Did you have any managerial duties, or were you supervising any other employees?

Manager .... 1 ⎤
Foreman/Supervisor .... 2 ⎬ - Q17
Not Manager/Supervisor .... 3 ⎦

17 NEmplee

How many employees are/were there at the place where you work(ed)?

1 - 2 .... 1 ⎤
3 - 24 2
25-99 3
100 - 499 .... 4 ⎬ - See Q20
500 - 999 5
1000 or more 6
DK, but less than 25 7
DK, but 25 or more .... 8 ⎦
Other (SPECIFY AT NEXT
   QUESTION) .... 9 - Q17a

17a. Xnemplee

If other (code 9) at NEmplee

Specify number of employees

(Enter text of no more than 30 characters) - See Q20

18 Solo

If self-employed (Stat = 2)

ASK OR RECORD

Were you working on your own or did you have employees?
On own/with partner(s) but no
   employees .... 1 - Q19
With employees .... 2 - See Q20

19 SNEmplee

How many people did you employ at the place where you work(ed)?

1 - 5 .... 1 ⎤
6 - 24 2
25 or over. .... 3 ⎬ - See Q20
DK number but has/had
   employees .... 4 ⎦

20 SecndJob

All working (WorklWk1 = 1 or WorklWk2 =1 or GovSchem = 3 or Trn=1)

Last week did you do any other paid work or have any other job or business in addition to the one you have just told me about?

Yes .... 1 → Q21
No 2

21 FtPtWk

In your (main) job were you working.....

Full-time .... 1 → See Q22
or part-time? 2

22 WorkHrs

Employees only (Working AND Stat = 1)

How many hours a week do you usually work (in your (main) job, - please exclude meal breaks and overtime?

INTERVIEWER - EXCLUDE MEAL BREAKS AND ANY PAID OR UNPAID OVERTIME.

(Enter number between 1 and 97) → Q24

23 WorkHrs

Self-employed only (Working AND Stat = 2)

How many hours a week do you usually work in your (main) job, that is excluding meal breaks but including any overtime?

INTERVIEWER - EXCLUDE MEAL BREAKS. INCLUDE ANY OVERTIME. IF WORK PATTERN NOT BASED ON A WEEK, GIVE AVERAGE OVER A FEW MONTHS.
(Enter number between 1 and 97) → Q25

24 JobTime

Employees (main job/government scheme) (Working and Stat = 1)

How long have you been with your present employer (up to yesterday)?

Less than 4 weeks 1
4 weeks but less than 3 months 2
3 months but less than 6 months ... 3
6 months but less than 12 months... 4
12 months but less than 2 years 5   → See Q26
2 years but less than 5 years 6
5 years but less than 10 years 7
10 years or more 8

25 JobTime

Self-employed (main job)(Working and Stat = 2)

How long have you been self employed (up to yesterday)?

Less than 4 weeks 1
4 weeks but less than 3 months 2
3 months but less than 6 months ... 3
6 months but less than 12 months... 4
12 months but less than 2 years 5   → See Q26
2 years but less than 5 years 6
5 years but less than 10 years 7
10 years or more 8

26 BenOff

Men aged 16-69, women aged 16-64 who are not currently on a government scheme GovSchem = 4)

Have you been to an Employment Service local office (formerly an Unemployment Benefit Office) in the last four months for the purpose of claiming allowances or National Insurance contributions?

Yes .... 1 → See Q
No .... 2 → See Q

27 UnBenA

If code 1 at BenOff and working last week (code 1 at WorklWk1 or WorklWk2), else → See Q

Some people who have jobs are also entitled to claim Job Seekers Allowance. So may I just check, were you claiming Job Seekers Allowance in the week ending last Sunday?

Yes .... 1 → See Q
No .... 2 → Q

28 UnBenB

If code 1 at BenOff and not working last week (code 2 at WorklWk2)

So may I just check, were you claiming Job Seekers Allowance (which has recently replaced Unemployment Benefit and Income Support in the week ending last Sunday?

Yes .... 1 → See Q
No .... 2 → Q

29 IncSup

If code 2 at UnBenA or UnBenB

Until recently it was possible to claim income support as an unemployed person. This has now been replaced by income based Job Seekers Allowance. Was your Job Seekers Allowance contributory JSA, income based JSA or both?

BEFORE 14/10/96 ONLY 0
Yes 1
No 2
FROM 14/10/96 3   → Q
Contributory JSA 4
Income based JSA 5
Both 6
Don't know 7

30 NICred

Or were you signed on in order to get credits for National Insurance contributions?

Yes .... 1 → See Q
No 2

31 Activity

All economically inactive (WorklWk3 = 4 and NOT GovSchem = 1, 2 or 3), else Q

CODE FIRST THAT APPLIES

Last week were you:
going to school or college full-time?
(use only if aged 16-49) 1
PERMANENTLY unable to work? → See Q
 (for men 16-64, women 16-62) 2

retired? (for woman, check age stopped
work and use this code only if stopped
when 50 or over) .... 3 ⌉ . See Q33
looking after the home or family?........ 4 ⌋
or were you doing something else?
(SPECIFY AT NEXT QUESTION)... 5 .   Q32

32 Xactivity

Specify what you were doing.

(Enter text of at most 80 characters)   . See Q33

33 WantaJob

**Men aged 16-69 and women aged 16-64 and
Activity = 1,3,4 or 5 or Trn = 2 (at college)**

. Even though you were not looking for work (last
week) would you like to have a regular paid job at
the moment - either a full or part-time job?

Yes .... 1 . Q34
No .... 2 . See Q37

34 NablStrt

If 'yes' at WantaJob (code 1)

If a job (or YT/ET/Training for Workplace) had
been available last week, would you have been
able to start within 2 weeks?

Yes .... 1 ⌉
No .... 2 ⌋ . Q35

35 NlookWrk

Thinking of the 4 weeks ending Sunday (date),
were you looking for paid work (or a YT/ET/
Training for Workplace)at any time in those 4
weeks?

Yes .... 1 ⌉ . Q36
No .... 2 ⌋ . See Q37

36 TimUnemp

If 'yes' at NlookWrk (code 1)

How long altogether have you been out of
employment but wanting work in this current
period of looking for work?

PERIOD = UP TO YESTERDAY

Less than a week .... 1 ⌉
1 week but less than 1 month 2
1 month but less than 3 months 3
3 months but less than 6 months ... 4
6 months but less than 12 months . 5 . See Q37
12 months but less than 2 years 6
2 years but less than 3 years 7
3 years but less than 5 years 8
5 years or more .... 9 ⌋

37 EverWork

**All economically inactive except those retired
(Activity = 3) or Trn = 2 (at college)**

Have you ever had a paid job or done any paid
work?

Yes .... 1 . Q38
No, NEVER WORKED .... 2 . See Q47

38 NIndD

If EverWork NOT 2 (ie have worked)

What did the firm/organisation you worked for
mainly make or do (at the place where you
worked)?

DESCRIBE FULLY - PROBE MANUFACTURING
OR PROCESSING OR DISTRIBUTION ETC.
AND MAIN GOODS PRODUCED, MATERIALS
USED, WHOLESALE OR RETAIL ETC.

(Enter text of at most 80 characters)   . Q39

39 NIndT

ENTER A TITLE FOR THE INDUSTRY

(Enter text of at most 30 characters)   . Q40

40 NOccT

Can you tell me about your **last** job?
What was your job?

ENTER JOB TITLE

(Enter text of at most 40 characters)   . Q41

41 NOccD

What did you mainly do in your job?

CHECK SPECIAL QUALIFICATIONS/TRAINING
NEEDED TO DO THE JOB

(Enter text of at most 80 characters)

SOCLAST Occupation code for last job..100......999

INDLAST   Industry code for last job.......500......999

LASTSEG Socio-economic group based on
last job................................ 0....19

LASTSC   Social class based on last job   0...... 7

42 NStat

Were you working as an employee or were you
self-employed?

Employee .... 1 . Q43
Self-employed .... 2 . Q45

ASK OR RECORD

43 NManage

Employees only (NStat = 1)

Did you have any managerial duties, or were you
supervising any other employees?

Manager .... 1 ⌉
Foreman or supervisor .... 2 . Q44
Not Manager/Supervisor .... 3 ⌋

44 NNEmplee

How many employees were there at the place
where you worked?

1-24 .... 1 ⌉
25-499 .... 2 . See Q47
500 or more .... 3 ⌋

45 NSolo   **Self-employed only (NStat = 2)**

Were you working on your own or did you have employees?

On own/with partner(s) but no
employees 1   → See Q47
With employees 2   →   Q46

46 NSNemple   How many people did you employ at the place where you worked?

1 - 5 1
6 - 24 2   → See Q47
25 or over 3

47 UnPdWk1   **If not in paid work, on a government scheme or away from a job (WorklWk1 = 2 and WorklWk2 = 2 or 3 and GovSchem = 4), else**

Pensions

During the last week, that is in the 7 days ending last Sunday, did you do any unpaid work for any business that you own?

Yes 1   →   Q50
No 2   →   Q48

48 UnPdWk2   **If No at UnPdWk1**

...or that a relative owns?

Yes 1   →   Q49
No 2   → Pensions

49 OwnBusi   **If Yes (code 1) at UnPdWk2**

Was this for a business that is owned by...

spouse/partner 1
or a relative? 2   →   Q50

50 UnPaidHr   **If Yes (code 1) at UnPdWk1 or UnPdWk2**

How many hours unpaid work did you do for that business in the 7 days ending last Sunday?
1..97   →   Q51

51 UIndD   What does the firm/organisation you work for mainly make or do (at the place where you work)?

DESCRIBE FULLY - PROBE MANUFACTURING OR PROCESSING OR DISTRIBUTION ETC. AND MAIN GOODS PRODUCED, MATERIALS USED, WHOLESALE OR RETAIL ETC.

(Enter text of at most 80 characters)   →   Q52

52 UIndT   ENTER A TITLE FOR THE INDUSTRY

(Enter text of at most 30 characters)   →   Q53

53 UOccT   Can you tell me about the unpaid work you were doing?

What is your job?

ENTER JOB TITLE

(Enter text of at most 40 characters)   →   Q5

54 UOccD   What do you mainly do in this job?

CHECK SPECIAL QUALIFICATIONS/TRAINING NEEDED TO DO THE JOB

(Enter text of at most 80 characters)

SOCUPAY   Occupation code for unpaid job100...999

INDLAST   Industry code for unpaid job.... 500...999

55 UManage   Did you have any managerial duties, or were you supervising any other employees?

Manager 1
Foreman/Supervisor 2   →   Q5
Not Manager/Supervisor 3

56 UEmpNo   How many employees were there at the place where you worked?

1 - 24 1
25 or over 2   →   Q5

57 UnPaidHm   Did you do this work mainly:
somewhere quite separate
  from home 1
in different places using home
  as base 2
or in your own home or in the
  same grounds or buildings as   → Pension
  your home? 3
SPONTANEOUSLY ONLY
  ...some days at home, other
  days somewhere quite
  separate from home 4

PENSIONS

PenSec   **THE NEXT SECTION IS ABOUT PENSIONS**

1 PenSchm   **If employee (main job/government scheme)(Trn or WorklWk1 or WorklWk2 = 1 or GovSchem = 3 and Stat = 1)**

(Thinking now of your present job,) some people (will) receive a pension from their employer when they retire, as well as the state pension.

Does your present employer run a pension scheme or superannuation scheme for any employees?

INCLUDE CONTRIBUTORY AND NON-CONTRIBUTORY SCHEMES

Yes 1   →   C
No 2   →   C

2 Eligible

If 'yes' (code 1) at PenSchm

Are you eligible to belong to your employer's pension scheme?

Yes	1	Q3
No..	2	Q5

3 EmPenShm

If 'yes' (code 1) at Eligible

Do you belong to your employer's pension scheme?

Yes	1	
No	2	Q5

4 PSchPoss

If DK at PenSchm or Eligible or EmPenShm

So do you think it's possible that you belong to a pension scheme run by your employer, or do you definitely not belong to one?

Possibly belongs	1	
Definitely not	2	Q5

PersPnt1

If under retirement age and NOT self-employed or other employees or unemployed who have had a job

INTERVIEWER - INTRODUCE IF NECESSARY

Now I would like to ask you about personal pensions (rather than employers' pension schemes).

5 PersPens

Since July 1988, people have been allowed to contract out of the State Earnings Related Pension Scheme (SERPS) and arrange their own pension. The DSS then pays part of the employee's National Insurance contributions into that person's chosen scheme.

Do you at present have any such arrangements?

Yes	1	Q6
No	2	Q8

6 PersCont

If 'Yes' (code 1) at PersPens

Do you make any extra contributions over and above any rebated National Insurance contributions made by the DSS on your behalf?

Yes	1	
No	2	Q7

7 EmpCont

If employee in job last week (NOT WorklWk3 = 1 AND NOT WorklWk2 = 3) and 'yes' at PersPens

Does your employer contribute to the scheme?

Yes.	1	
No	2	Q9

8 EverPers

If 'No' (code 2) or DK at PersPens

Have you ever had any such arrangements?

Yes	1	
No	2	Q9

9 OthPers

All as for PersPnt1

(Apart from the contributions you've already told me about) do you make any other contributions to personal pensions or Retirement Annuities for which the contributions are INCOME TAX DEDUCTIBLE?

Yes	1	
No	2	See Q10

PersPnt2

If Working and Self-employed ((WorklWk1 or WorklWk2 or Trn = 1 or GovSchem = 3) AND Stat = 2)

INTERVIEWER - INTRODUCE IF NECESSARY

Now I would like to ask you about personal pension schemes.

10 SePrsPen

The self-employed may arrange pensions for themselves for which the contributions are INCOME TAX DEDUCTIBLE. These schemes are sometimes called 'self-employed pensions' or 'Section 226 Retirement Annuities' or 'personal pensions'.

Do you at present contribute to one of these schemes?

Yes	1	Movers
No	2	Q11

11 SeEvPers

If 'no' (code 2) at SePrsPen

Have you ever contributed to one of these schemes?

Yes	1	
No	2	Movers

MOVERS OUT OF OWNER OCCUPATION

MoverSec

THE NEXT SECTION IS ABOUT PEOPLE WHO HAVE MOVED FROM OWNED TO RENTED ACCOMMODATION. IT IS NOT ASKED OF EVERYBODY. INTRODUCE WHERE APPROPRIATE.

If accommodation owned (Ten1 = 1, 2 or 3)

1 IntCheck

ARE YOU INTERVIEWING THE HOH, OR SPOUSE OR PARTNER OF HOH?

Yes	1	
No	2	See Q2

If HOH's accommodation is rented (Ten1 = 4,5 or 6) ask all adults, else ask all adults EXCEPT the HOH and wife (IntCheck = 2)

2 Everown
In the last ten years, (that is, since April 1986) have you ever owned your own house or flat?

Yes .... 1 → Q3
No .... 2 → Education

3 OtherOwn
Ask if Everown = 'Yes' (code 1) and there are other adults in the household (NAdults>1)

Did you own this accommodation with someone else in this household?

Yes .... 1 → Q4
No .... 2 → Q6

4 Persono
If Otherown = 'Yes' (code 1)

WRITE IN PERSON NUMBER OF JOINT OWNER
1..14 → Q5

5 IntAlrea
IF THE OTHER JOINT OWNER HAS ALREADY COMPLETED THIS SECTION OF THE INTERVIEW, GO TO THE NEXT SECTION.
IF THE JOINT OWNER IS NOW BEING INTER-VIEWED AS PART OF AN INTERVIEWER PAIR, ASK THIS SECTION OF ONLY ONE PERSON IN THE PAIR.

Joint owner already interviewed . 1 → Education
Joint owner not yet interviewed .. 2
Not sure if joint owner has been → Q6
interviewed 3

6 Ownedadd
Ask if Everown = 'Yes' (code 1) and NOT IntAlrea = 1

RECORD FOR REFERENCE THE ADDRESS OF THE MOST RECENTLY OWNED ACCOMMODATION

(Enter text of at most 20 characters) → Q7

7 RentLA
If code 1 at Everown

Before becoming the owner of (ADDRESS) were you renting it from a local authority or council?

Yes, renting from a LA or council.. 1 → Q8
No, not renting from a LA
or council..................................... 2 → Q9

8 RightTB
Ask if RentLA = 'Yes' (code 1)

Did you buy it under the council's Right to Buy Scheme?

Yes 1
No .... 2 → Q9

9 MBought
Ask all former owners (Everown = 1 and NOT IntAlrea = 1)

In which month did you buy (ADDRESS) or be-come the owner?

ENTER MONTH 1..12 → Q10

10 YrBought
And in which year (did you buy it or become the owner)?

ENTER YEAR 1..97 → Q1

11 MSold
In which month did you leave or sell(ADDRESS)?

CODE EARLIEST DATE
CODE 1-12 FOR MONTHS → Q1
CODE 97 IF STILL OWNS (ADDRESS)

12 YrSold
And in which year (did you leave/sell it)?

ENTER YEAR 1..97 → Q1

13 Whyleft
SHOW CARD A

On this card are some reasons for leaving a house or flat. Please tell me why you left (ADDRESS), choosing your answers from the card.

ENTER AT MOST 6 CODES

Stayed there after a relationship broke
up, but couldn't afford to keep it .. 1
Left after a relationship broke up .. 2
Moved to live with my partner 3
Husband/wife or partner died 4
Sold to avoid mortgage arrears 5
Sold to reduce housing costs 6
In arrears and sold to avoid court . → Q1
action 7
Abandoned it 8
Forced to leave following
court order 9
Lost job or had to give up work 10
Sold to move to a job in a
new area .... 11 → Q1
Planned break between selling old
home and buying a new one 12
Moved to be looked after by
relatives/to sheltered → Q1
accommodation 13
Moved to look after a relative in their
own home 14
Other (Specify) .... 15 → Q1

14 XWhyLeft
If 'other' reason given (Whyleft = 15)

RECORD OTHER REASON

(Enter text of at most 100 characters) → See Q1

15 Empaccom
Ask if reasons at Whyleft include 11 (moved to new job in the area)

(May I just check) Are you now living in accommodation provided by your employer?

Yes 1
No .... 2 → Q1

16 AccomNo
Ask all former owners (Everown = 1 and NOT IntAlrea = 1)

How many different places (eg houses/flats or hotels) did you live in between leaving (ADDRESS) and moving in here?

ENTER NUMBER OF MAIN RESIDENCES
EXCLUDE ANY STAYS OF LESS THAN 4 DAYS
0..99 → Q1

17 AccomTen

SHOW CARD B

Please look at this card and tell me what arrangements you made between leaving (ADDRESS) and moving in here?

(Enter at most 6 codes)

Rented from a Local Authority, New
  Town Corporation or Housing
  Association 1
Rented privately 2
Stayed with relatives or friends 3
Stayed in accommodation provided   - See Q19
  by employer 4
Stayed in a hotel 5
Other .... 6 - Q18

18 XAccomTe

Ask if 'other' arrangements made (AccomTen = 6)

What other arrangements did you make?

(Enter text of at most 50 characters) - See Q19

19 LongTen

If more than one answer to AccomTen,
                          else Q20

SHOW CARD B

Which of these arrangements did you use for the longest time?

(Enter at most 6 codes)

Rented from a Local Authority, New
  Town Corporation or Housing
  Association 1
Rented privately 2
Stayed with relatives or friends 3
Stayed in accommodation provided   - Q20
  by employer 4
Stayed in a hotel 5
Other 6

20 Buyagain

Ask all former owners

Do you think you will eventually buy somewhere again or not?

Yes .... 1 - Q21
No .... 2 - Education

21 Howlong

If Buyagain = 1

How long do you expect it to be before you buy somewhere?

Almost immediately 1
Within a year 2
Within 2 years 3
Within 3 years 4
Within 6 years. .... 5 - Education
Within 10 years 6
In 10 years or more 7
Not sure: can't afford anywhere at
  present 8
Not sure: when I find something
  suitable 9

EDUCATION

EducSec

THE NEXT SECTION IS ABOUT EDUCATION

We will use this information to look at the take-up of further education and at the way qualifications affect the sorts of jobs people get.

All adults

1 EducPres

Are you at present attending any sort of leisure or recreation classes during the day, in the evenings or at weekends?

Yes .... 1 - Q2
No. .... 2 - Q4

2 EdTyp

If 'Yes' (code 1) at EducPres

What type of college or organisation runs these classes?

CODE ALL THAT APPLY

(Enter at most 3 codes)

Evening Institute/Local Education
  Authority/College or Centre of
  Adult Education 1
College of Further Education/
  Technical College .... 2 - Q3
University Extra-Mural
  Department 3
Other - SPECIFY TYPE AND GIVE
NAME AT NEXT QUESTION) 4

3 XEdTyp

Give type and name of college or organisation.

(Enter text of at most 40 characters) - Q4

4 AgeLftSc

All those aged 16-69, else - Sport

How old were you when you left school?
(NOT TECHNICAL COLLEGE)

Never went to school .... 1 - Sport
Still at school .... 98 - Q11
                        1..98 - Q5

5 PresEd

If aged 16-69 and not still at school but has attended school (AgeLftSc NOT 1 or 98)

Apart from leisure classes, and ignoring holidays, are you at present doing any of the types of education shown on this card?

SHOW CARD C

Yes. .... 1 - Q6
No .... 2 - Q7

6 EdNow

If 'yes' (code 1) at PresEd

What are you doing at present?

CODE FIRST THAT APPLIES

Studying at a college on a YT or Employment
  Training (ET) programme .... 1 - Q8

267

Studying at a college or university or polytechnic full-time (INCLUDING SANDWICH COURSE STUDY) 2   → Q11

Training in nursing, physiotherapy, or a similar medical subject 3

Studying at college part-time or on day or block release (INCLUDING COURSES OF UNDER 3 MONTHS) 4   → Q8

Open University course 5

A correspondence course 6

7 FurthrEd

If No, DK or Refusal at PresEd (PresEd = 2, 8 or 9)

I would now like to ask you about any education you may have had since leaving school. Have you ever had any full-time or part-time further education of the types shown on this card?

SHOW CARD C

Yes 1   → Q8
No 2   → Q11

8 LastSch

If coded 1 or 3-6 or DK or Refusal at EdNow or coded 1, DK or Refusal at FurthrEd

Now thinking of your full-time education, what type of school or college did you last attend full-time?
EXCLUDE COURSES OF UNDER 3 MONTHS
RUNNING PROMPT

Was it:
Elementary or secondary school ... 1   → Q11
University 2
Polytechnic (INCLUDE: SCOTTISH CENTRAL INSTITUTIONS) 3   → Q10
Nursing school or teaching hospital 4
Or some other type of college? 5
Other (SPECIFY AT NEXT QUESTION) 6   → Q9

9 XLastSch

Specify other type of school or college

(Enter text of at most 40 characters)   → Q10

10 AgeLftFt

If coded 2-6 at LastSch

How old were you when you left there, or when you finished or stopped your course?
1..97   → Q11

11 QualsB

All adults aged 16-69 (except proxy interviews and those who have never attended school) (NOT AgeLftSc = 1)

SHOW CARD D

Have you passed any examinations of the types listed on this card?

Yes 1   → Q12
No 2   → Q20

12 LevCode1

If 'yes' (code 1) at QualsB

Which ones have you obtained?

(Enter at most 9 codes)

CSE 1   → Q13
GCSE 2   → Q14
GCE 'O' levels 3   → Q15
GCE 'AS' levels. 4   → Q16
GCE 'A' levels 5   → Q17
School certificate or Matric 6   → Q20
Higher School Certificate 7
Scottish exams 8   → Q18
Foreign school exams 9   → Q20

13 CSELev

If CSE (code 1) at LevCode 1

What CSE grade(s) do you have?

(Enter at most 3 codes)

Ungraded or DK grade 1
Grade 1 2   → Q19
Grades 2-5 3

14 GCSELev

If GCSE (code 2) at LevCode 1

What GCSE grade(s) do you have?

(Enter at most 2 codes)

Grades A, B, C 1
Grades D, E, F, G 2   → Q19

15 OLevel

If GCE 'O' Level (code 3) at LevCode 1

What 'O'level grade(s) do you have?

(Enter at most 3 codes)

Obtained before 1975 1
Grades A, B, C 2   → Q19
Grades D,E 3

16 ASLevel

If GCE 'AS' Level (code 4) at LevCode 1

What GCE AS level grade(s) do you have?
(1989 OR LATER)

(Enter at most 3 codes)

Grades A,B 1
Grade C 2   → Q19
Grade D,E 3

17 ALevel

If GCE 'A' Level (code 5) at LevCode 1

What GCE A level grade(s) do you have?

(Enter at most 4 codes)

Grades A,B 1
Grade C 2   → Q19
Grade D,E 3
No grade or don't know grade 4

18 ScotExam

If Scottish Exams (code 8) at LevCode 1

SHOW CARD E

Have you passed any of the exams on this card?

(Enter at most 8 codes)

Scottish Leaving Certificate(lower grade) OR
  Scottish Universities Preliminary
  Exam 1
Scottish Certificate of Education
  Ordinary Grade(before 1973) 2
SCE ordinary grade bands A, B, C3
SCE ordinary grade bands D, E 4
Standard grade level 1-3 .... 5 - Q19
Standard grade level 4,5 6
Standard grade level 6,7 or
  no award 7
SLC/SCE/SUPE at higher grade or
Certificate of Sixth Year Studies ... 8

19 NSub

For each type of exam mentioned at questions 13-18

ASK AFTER EACH TYPE OF EXAM MEN-
TIONED (EXCEPT FOREIGN SCHOOL EXAMS)

In how many subjects at (LEVEL) did you pass?
                                1..20   - Q20

20 QualsC

All adults aged 16-69 (except proxy interviews and those who never attended school)

SHOW CARD F

Do you have any of the qualifications listed on this card or have you passed any of these examinations, whether you are using them or not?

Yes .... 1 - Q21
No .... 2 - Q22

21 LevCode2

If 'yes' (code 1) at QualsC

Which qualifications do you have?
(Enter at most 10 codes)

Recognised trade apprenticeship
  completed 1
Clerical and commercial
  qualifications (eg. typing, shorthand,
  book-keeping, commerce) 2
City and Guilds Certificate - Craft/
  Intermediate/ Ordinary or Part 1 .. 3
City and Guilds Certificate -   - Q22
  Advanced/Final or Part II 4
City and Guilds Certificate - Full
  Technological or Part III 5
BTEC First Award 6
Ordinary National Certificate (ONC)
  or Diploma (OND), BEC/TEC/BTEC
  National/General Certificate or
  Diploma 7

Higher National Certificate (HNC) or
  Diploma, BEC/TEC/BTEC Higher
  Certificate or Higher Diploma 8
SCOTVEC National (1-12 modules) 9   - Q22
SCOTVEC National (13 or more
  modules) 10

22 QualsD

All adults aged 16-69 (except proxy interviews and those who never attended school)

SHOW CARD G

Do you have any of the qualifications listed on this card or have you passed any of these examinations, whether you are using them or not?

Yes... 1 - Q23
No .... 2 - Sport

23 LevCode3

If 'yes' (code 1) at QualsD

Which qualifications do you have?

(Enter at most 9 codes)

Nursing qualifications (eg SEN, SRN,
  SCM, RGN) .... 1 - Sport
Teaching qualifications 2
University Diploma 3
University or CNAA First Degree
  (eg BA, BSc) .... 4 - Q24
University or CNAA Higher Degree
  (eg MSc, PhD) 5
Membership of professional
  institution 6
Other non-school foreign
  qualifications .... 7 - Sport
Any other qualifications not already
  mentioned .... 8 - Q24

24 QualDesc

If 'Teaching' (code 2), 'University' (codes 3-5), Membership (code 6) or 'Other' (code 8) at LevCode3

(TYPE QUALIFICATION) PLEASE GIVE FULL
DETAILS OF ALL QUALIFICATIONS OF THE
ABOVE TYPE, INCLUDING LEVEL AND
MEMBERSHIP STATUS

(Enter text of at most 120 characters) - Q25

25 Award

What was the awarding institution or college?

(Enter text of at most 120 characters) - Q26

26 WhereOb

Where was the qualification obtained?

In the UK 1
or abroad. .... 2 - Q27

27 Degree

If (codes 3-5) 'University' at LevCode 3
What was/were the major subject(s)?

(Enter text of at most 40 characters) - Sport

28 Exam

If LevCode3 = Other (code 8)

Did you have to pass an exam?

Yes. .... 1 ⎤
No. .... 2 ⎦ ▸ Sport

SPORT AND LEISURE

Introsp

THE NEXT SECTION IS ABOUT SPORT AND LEISURE

1 AnyWalks

Ask all (except proxy informants)

In the last twelve months, that is since (....), have you been for a walk or hike of 2 miles or more?

Yes. .... 1 ▸ Q2
No .... 2 ▸ Q3

2 MoWalks

Ask if Anywalks = 1

Now thinking of the 4 weeks ending yesterday, that is since (....), did you go for a walk of 2 miles or more during these 4 weeks?

Yes.. 1 ⎤
No.. 2 ⎦ ▸ Q3

3 AnyYrPA

Ask all (except proxy informants)

SHOW CARD H

On this card is a list of sports and physical activities. Please tell me if you took part in any of them in the last twelve months, that is since (...). Do not count any teaching, coaching or refereeing you may have done.

CODE 42 IF THE RESPONDENT HAS NOT PARTICIPATED IN ANY SPORT
(enter at most 20 codes)

Swimming or diving indoors .... 1 ⎤
Swimming or diving outdoors 2
Cycling 3
Indoor bowls 4
Outdoor (lawn) bowls 5
Tenpin bowling 6
Keepfit, aerobics, yoga, dance
 exercise (INCLUDE EXERCISE
 BIKE) .... 7 ⎥ ▸ Q5
Martial Arts (INCLUDE SELF
 DEFENCE) 8
Weight training (INCLUDE BODY
 BUILDING.) 9
Weightlifting.................................. 10
Gymnastics 11
Snooker, pool, billiards (EXCLUDE
 BAR BILLIARDS) .... 12 ⎦
Darts .... 13 ▸ Q13
Rugby Union or league .... 14 ⎤
American football 15
Football indoors (INCLUDE ⎥ ▸ Q5
 5-A-SIDE) 16
Football outdoors (INCLUDE
 5-A-SIDE) .... 17 ⎦

Gaelic sports .... 18 ⎤
Cricket 19
Hockey (IF ICE, ROLLER OR
STREET HOCKEY EXCLUDE AND
SPECIFY IN 'OTHER' BELOW 20
Netball 21
Tennis 22
Badminton 23
Squash 24
Basketball 25
Table tennis 26
Track and field athletics 27
Jogging,cross country, road running 28
Angling/fishing 29
Yachting or dinghy sailing 30
Canoeing .... 31 ⎥ ▸ Q5
Windsurfing/boardsailing 32
Ice skating (IF ROLLER EXCLUDE
 AND SPECIFY IN 'OTHER'
 BELOW) 33
Curling 34
Golf, pitch and putt, putting (EXCLUDE
 CRAZY/MINIATURE GOLF) 35
Skiing 36
Horse riding (IF POLO EXCLUDE
 AND SPECIFY AT 'OTHER'
 BELOW) 37
Climbing/mountaineering (INCLUDE
 INDOORS) 38
Motor sports 39
Shooting .... 40 ⎦
Other .... 41 ▸ Q4
None of these .... 42 ▸ Q13

4 XothYPA

Please tell me what the other sport(s) or physical activity(s) were?

(Enter text of at most 40 characters) ▸ Q13

5 AnyMoPA

Ask for each sport mentioned at AnyYrPA (except darts (13) and 'other' (41))

Did you take part in (activity) in the past four weeks, that is since (....). Again, please do not count any teaching coaching or refereeing you may have done.

Yes .... 1 ▸ Q6
No .... 2 ▸ Q9

6 NoDays

Ask for each sport participated in during the last 4 weeks (AnyMoPA = 1)

On how many days in the last four weeks have you played/gone(to) (activity).

1..28 ▸ Q7

7 Places

At which of the places on this card have you played (activity) in the last four weeks (that is since ...)?

SHOW CARD I

Indoors at a facility which is **mainly**
 used for sport (e.g sports centre or
 gymnasium or indoor swimming pool
 or commercial leisure facility) ...... 1 ▸ Q8

Indoors at some other location **not
mainly used for sport** (such as a
community centre, village hall or
scout hut) .... 2 ⟶ Q8

Indoors or outdoors at home or
someone else's home................... 3 ⟶ Q9

Outdoors on a court, course, pitch
or playing field (or outdoor
swimming pool) .... 4 ⟶ Q8

Outdoors in a natural setting (such
as the countryside, rivers, lakes
or seaside) .... 5 ⎤
Other - including roads and   ⎟ ⟶ Q9
pathways in towns and cities .... 6 ⎦

8 SchUni

If Places = 1,2 or 4

Do any of these facilities belong to a school,
college or university?

Yes .... 1 ⎤
No .... 2 ⎟ ⟶ Q9
Not sure .... 3 ⎦

9 ClubPa

**For each sport except Darts (13) and Other (41)
at AnyYrPA**

Over the past four weeks have you been a
member of a club, particularly so that you can
play/participate in (activity)?

Yes .... 1 ⟶ Q10
No .... 2 ⟶ Q11

10 TyClub

If ClubPa = 1

What type of club was this?

(ENTER AT MOST 4 CODES)

Health/fitness .... 1 ⎤
Social club (e.g employee clubs,   ⎟
youth clubs) .... 2 ⎟ ⟶ Q11
Sports club .... 3 ⎟
Other .... 4 ⎦

11 Comp

**For each sport except Darts (13) and Other (41)
at AnyYrPA**

Thinking about (activity) have you taken part in
any **organised** competition in (activity) in the **last
twelve months,** that is since (....)?

Yes .... 1 ⎤ ⟶ Q12
No.. .... 2 ⎦

12 Tutor

Over the **past twelve months** have you received
tuition from an instructor or coach to improve
your performance in (activity)?

Yes .... 1 ⎤
No .... 2 ⎟ ⟶ Q13
Not sure .... 3 ⎦

Entertainment

13 Entertn

All adults (except proxy informants)

Now thinking about the four weeks ending
yesterday, could you tell me whether you
have done any of these things in your
leisure time or for entertainment?

14 TV

Watched TV?

Yes .... 1 ⎤
No .... 2 ⎦ ⟶ Q15

15 Radio

Listened to the radio?

Yes. .... 1 ⎤
No .... 2 ⎦ ⟶ Q16

16 Records

Listened to records or tapes?

Yes .... 1 ⎤
No .... 2 ⎦ ⟶ Q17

17 Books

Read books?

Yes .... 1 ⎤
No .... 2 ⎦ ⟶ Q18

18 Visit

Visited friends or relations, or had them
come to see you?

Yes.. 1 ⎤
No .... 2 ⎦ ⟶ Q19

19 Garden

Done any gardening?

Yes .... 1 ⎤
No .... 2 ⎦ ⟶ Q20

20 Sew

Dressmaking, needlework or knitting?

Yes .... 1 ⎤
No .... 2 ⎦ ⟶ Q21

21 DIY

House repairs or do-it-yourself jobs?

Yes.. 1 ⎤
No .... 2 ⎦ ⟶ Health

HEALTH

Quality of Life

HLthSec

Ask all adults except proxy informants

THE NEXT SECTION IS ABOUT HEALTH

IntroQol

For each of the following questions please
look at the card for each topic and say
which statement best describes your own
state of health today.

1 Mobility

SHOW CARD J

I have no problems in walking
about .... 1 ⟶ Q2

I have some problems in
  walking about .... 2 ⌉
I am confined to bed .... 3 ⌋ → Q2

2 SelfCare SHOW CARD K

I have no problems with self care ... 1 ⌉
I have some problems washing or
  dressing myself .... 2 ⌉ → Q3
I am unable to wash or dress
  myself .... 3 ⌋

3 UsualAct SHOW CARD L

I have no problems with performing
  my usual activities. .... 1 ⌉
I have some problems with
  performing my usual activities ...... 2 ⌉ → Q4
I am unable to perform my
  usual activities. .... 3 ⌋

4 PainDisc SHOW CARD M

I have no pain or discomfort............. 1 ⌉
I have moderate pain or
  discomfort.................................... 2 ⌉ → Q5
I have extreme pain or discomfort.. 3 ⌋

5 AnxDep SHOW CARD N

I am not anxious or depressed .... 1 ⌉
I am moderately anxious or
  depressed .... 2 ⌉ → Thermo
I am extremely anxious or
  depressed .... 3 ⌋

Thermo To help people say how good or bad their health
is we have drawn a scale (rather like a
thermometer) on which the best state of health
you can imagine is marked by 100 and the worst
state of health you can imagine is marked by 0.

6 Thermo2 [*] SHOW CARD O

We would like you to indicate on this scale
how good your own health is today, in your
opinion. Please do this by showing me the
point on the scale which indicates how good
or bad your current health is.

RECORD THE POINT ON THE SCALE E.G. IF
MIDWAY BETWEEN 50 AND 60, CODE 55
                        0..100 → General
                                     Health

General Health

1 GenHlth [*] **Ask all (except proxy informants)**

Over the last 12 months would you say your
health has on the whole been good, fairly good,
or not good?

Good .... 1 ⌉
Fairly good .... 2 ⌉ → Q2
Not good .... 3 ⌋

2 Illness [*] **Ask All**

Do you have any long-standing illness, disability
or infirmity? By long-standing I mean anything
that has troubled you over a period of time or that
is likely to affect you over a period of time?

Yes. .... 1 → Q
No .... 2 → Q

3 LMatter [*] **If 'Yes' at Illness (code 1)**

What is the matter with you?

USE NOTEPAD IF ADDITIONAL SPACE
NEEDED

(Enter text of at most 100 characters) → Q

4 LimitAct [*] Does this illness or disability (Do any of these
illnesses or disabilities) limit your activities in any
way?

Yes .... 1 ⌉ → Q
No .... 2 ⌋

5 CutDown [*] **Ask All**

Now I'd like you to think about the 2 weeks
ending yesterday. During those 2 weeks, did you
have to cut down on any of the things you usually
do (about the house/at work or in your free time)
because of (answers at LMatter) or some other
illness or injury?

Yes .... 1 → Q
No .... 2 → Q

6 NDysCutD **If 'Yes' at CutDown (code 1)**

How many days was this in all during these 2
weeks, including Saturdays and Sundays?
                                 1..14 → Q

7 CMatter [*] What was the matter with you?

(Enter text of at most 40 characters) → Q

8 DocTalk **Ask All**

During the 2 weeks ending yesterday, apart from
any visit to a hospital, did you talk to a doctor for
any reason at all, either in person or by
telephone?

EXCLUDE: CONSULTATIONS MADE ON
BEHALF OF CHILDREN UNDER 16 AND
PERSONS OUTSIDE THE HOUSEHOLD

Yes .... 1 → Q
No .... 2 → Q

9 NChats

If 'Yes' (code 1) at DocTalk

How many times did you talk to a doctor in these 2 weeks?

1..9   -   Q10

10 WhsBhlf

For each consultation

On whose behalf was this consultation made?

Informant .... 1 - Q12
Other member of household 16 or
  over .... 2 - Q11

11 ForPerno

If other (code 2) at WhsBhlf

GIVE PERSON NUMBER   1..14 - Q12

12 NHS

For each consultation

Was this consultation ....

under the National Health Service 1
or paid for privately? 2   -   Q13

13 GP

Was the doctor....

RUNNING PROMPT

A GP (ie a family doctor) 1
or a specialis 2   -   Q15
or some other kind of doctor?
   (SPECIFY AT NEXT QUESTION) 3 - Q14

14 XGP

Specify type of doctor.

(Enter text of at most 20 characters)   -   Q15

15 DocWhere

Did you talk to the doctor....

RUNNING PROMPT

by telephone. 1
at your home 2
in the doctor's surgery .... 3 - Q16
at a health centre 4
or elsewhere? 5

16 Presc

Did the doctor give (send) you a prescription?

Yes. 1
No 2   -   Q17

17 OutPatnt

Ask All

During the months of [LAST 3 COMPLETE CALENDAR MONTHS] did you attend as a patient the casualty or outpatient department of a hospital (apart from straightforward ante-or post-natal visits)?

Yes .... 1 - Q18
No .... 2 - Q25

18 NTimes1

If Yes (code 1) at OutPatnt

How many times did you attend in [EARLIEST MONTH IN REFERENCE PERIOD]?

0..31   -   Q19

19 NTimes2

How many times did you attend in [SECOND MONTH IN REFERENCE PERIOD]?

0..31   -   Q20

20 NTimes3

How many times did you attend in [THIRD MONTH IN REFERENCE PERIOD]?

0..31   -   Q21

21 Casualty

Was this visit (Were any of these visits) to the Casualty department or was it (were they all) to some other part of the hospital?

At least one visit to Casualty .... 1 - Q22
No Casualty visits .... 2 .See Q23

22 NCasVis

If went to Casualty (code 1)

So altogether you visited casualty (how many) times?

CHECK OR ASK TOTAL NUMBER OF VISITS TO CASUALTY

1..31   .   Q23

23 PrVists

If some visits not to Casualty (NCasVis<NTimes1 + NTimes2 + NTimes3), else   -   Q25

Was this outpatient visit (were all of your outpatient visits) during [REFERENCE PERIOD] made under the NHS, or was it (were any of them) paid for privately?

All under NHS .... 1 - Q25
At least one paid for privately? ...... 2 - Q24

24 NPrVists

If some private visits (PrVists = 2)

ASK OR RECORD

(May I just check), how many of the visits were paid for privately?

1..31   -   Q25

25 DayPatnt

Ask All

During the last year, that is, since [DATE ONE YEAR AGO], have you been in hospital for treatment as a day patient? A day patient is admitted to a hospital bed or day ward, but doesn't stay in overnight.

Yes. .... 1 - Q26
No .... 2 - Q29

26 NHSPDays

If Yes at DayPatnt (code 1)

How many separate days in hospital have you had as a day patient since [DATE ONE YEAR AGO]?

1..97   -   Q27

27 PrDpTnt — Was this day patient treatment (were all of your day patient treatments) under the NHS, or was it (were any of them) paid for privately?

All under NHS .... 1 ⸱ Q29
At least one paid for privately? ...... 2 ⸱ Q28

28 NPrDpTnt — **If some private and more than one visit (NHSPDays>1 and PrDpTnt = 2)**

ASK OR RECORD

How many of the visits were paid for privately?
1..31 ⸱ Q29

29 InPatnt — **Ask All**

During the last year, that is, since [DATE ONE YEAR AGO], have you been in hospital as an inpatient, overnight or longer?

Yes .... 1 ⸱ Q30
No. .... 2 ⸱ Child Health

30 NStays — **If 'Yes' at InPatnt code 1**

How many separate stays in hospital as an inpatient have you had since [DATE ONE YEAR AGO]?
1..6 ⸱ Q31

31 Nights — **For each stay**

How many nights altogether were you in hospital during your (first/second/...sixth) stay?
1..97 ⸱ Q32

32 NHSTreat — Were you treated under the NHS or were you a private patient on that occasion?

NHS .... 1 ⸱ Child Health
Private patient .... 2 ⸱ Q33

33 PrvStay — **If private (NHSTreat = 2)**

Were you treated in an NHS hospital or in a private one?

NHS hospital .... 1 ⎤ Child
Private hospital .... 2 ⎦ Health

CHILD HEALTH

If children under 16 in household (not asked of proxy informants)

1 Respad — THE NEXT SECTION IS ABOUT CHILD HEALTH

INTERVIEWER - Are either ... or...responsible for any child(ren) in the household?

Yes .... 1 ⸱ Q2
No. .... 2 ⸱ Activity of Daily living

2 Illness [*] — **If Respad = 1**

Now I'd like to ask you about your children under 16.

Do **any** of your children under 16 have any long-standing illness, disability or infirmity? By long-standing I mean anything that has troubled them over a period of time or that is likely to affect them over a period of time.

Yes,(any child) .... 1 ⸱ C
No (all children) .... 2 ⸱ C

3 ChList1 — **If Yes at Illness (code 1)**

Enter from household box the person numbers of those children with long-standing illness, disability or infirmity
⸱ C

4 LMatter [*] — **For each child with a long-standing illness, disability or infirmity**

What is the matter with......?

(Enter text of at most 40 characters) ⸱ C

5 LimitAct [*] — Does this illness or disability (Do any of these illnesses or disabilities) limit ...'s activities in any way?

Yes. .... 1 ⎤
No .... 2 ⎦ ⸱ C

6 CutDown [*] — **All children under 16 (Respad = 1)**

Now I'd like you to think about the 2 weeks ending yesterday. During those 2 weeks, did any of your children have to cut down on any of the things they usually do (at school or in their free time) because of (... or some other) illness or injury?

Yes, (any child) .... 1 ⸱ C
No (all children) .... 2 ⸱ Q

7 ChList2 — **If 'Yes' at CutDown (code 1)**

Enter from household box the person numbers of those children who had to cut down. ⸱ C

8 NDysCutD — **For each child who has had to cut down**

How many days did ... have to cut down in all during these 2 weeks, including Saturdays and Sundays?
1..14 ⸱ C

9 Matter [*] — What was the matter with...?

(Enter text of at most 80 characters) ⸱ Q

10 DocTalk

All children under 16 (Respad = 1)

During the 2 weeks ending yesterday, apart from visits to a hospital, did any of your children under 16 talk to a doctor for any reason at all, or did you or any other member of the household talk to a doctor on their behalf?

INCLUDE TELEPHONE CONSULTATIONS AND CONSULTATIONS MADE ON BEHALF OF CHILDREN

Yes, (any child .... 1 . Q11
No (all children) .... 2 . Q18

11 ChList3

If Yes at DocTalk (code 1)

Enter from household box the person numbers of those children who consulted a doctor. . Q12

12 Nchats

For each child who consulted a doctor

How many times did.... talk to the doctor (or you or any other member of the household consult the doctor on ....'s behalf) in those 2 weeks?
1..4 . Q13

13 NHS

For each consultation

Was this consultation....
under the National Health Service . 1 ⎤ . Q14
or paid for privately? .... 2 ⎦

14 GP

Was the doctor.....

RUNNING PROMPT

a GP (ie a family doctor) .... 1 ⎤ . Q16
or a specialist .... 2 ⎦
or some other kind of doctor? .... 3 . Q15
(SPECIFY AT NEXT QUESTION)

15 XGP

Specify type of doctor.

(Enter text of at most 20 characters) . Q16

16 DocWhere

Did you (or ...) talk to the doctor

RUNNING PROMPT
by telephone .... 1 ⎤
at your home................................. 2 ⎥
in the doctor's surgery................... 3 ⎥ . Q17
at a health centre.......................... 4 ⎥
or elsewhere?............................... 5 ⎦

17 Presc

Did the doctor give (send) ... a prescription?

Yes .... 1 ⎤ . Q18
No .... 2 ⎦

18 OutPatnt

All children under 16 (Respad =1)

During the months of [LAST 3 COMPLETE CALENDAR MONTHS] did any of your children under 16 attend as a patient the casualty or outpatient department of a hospital (apart from straightforward post-natal visits)?

Yes, (any child) .... 1 . Q19
No (all children .... 2 . Q25

19 ChList4

If 'Yes' at OutPatnt (code 1)

Enter from household box the person numbers of those children who attended the casualty or outpatient department of a hospital. . Q20

20 NTimes1

For each child who has been an outpatient

How many times did.... attend in...?
0..97 . Q21

21 NTimes2

How many times did ... attend in ...?
0..97 . Q22

22 NTimes3

How many times did ... attend in ...?
0..97 . Q23

23 Casualty

Was this visit (Were any of these visits) to the Casualty department or was it (were they all) to some other part of the hospital?

At least one visit to Casualty .... 1 . Q24
No Casualty visits .... 2 . Q25

24 NCasVis

If went to Casualty (code 1)

May I just check) how many times did .... go to Casualty altogether?
0..31 . Q25

25 DayPatnt

All children under 16 (Respad=1)

During the last year, that is since [DATE ONE YEAR AGO] have any of your children under 16 been in hospital for treatment as a day patient, ie admitted to a hospital bed or day ward, but not required to remain in hospital overnight?

Yes, (any child)............................. 1 . Q26
No (all children)............................. 2 . Q28

26 ChList5

If Yes at DayPatnt (code 1)

Enter from household box the person numbers of those children who have been in hospital as a day patient. . Q27

27 NHSPDays

For each child who has been a day patient

How many separate days in hospital has.....had as a day patient since [DATE ONE YEAR AGO]?
1..97 . Q28

28 InPatnt

All children under 16 (Respad =1)

During the last year, that is since [DATE ONE YEAR AGO] have any of your children under 16 been in hospital as an inpatient overnight or longer?

EXCLUDE: Births unless baby stayed in hospital after mother had left.

Yes, (any child) .... 1 ⸱ Q29
No (all children) .... 2 ⸱ Activities of
Daily living

29 ChList6

If Yes at InPatnt (code 1)

Enter from household box the person numbers of those children who have been in hospital overnight or longer.   ⸱ Q30

30 NStays

For each child who has been an inpatient

How many separate stays in hospital as an inpatient has ... had since [DATE ONE YEAR AGO]?

1..97   ⸱ Q31

31 Nights

For each stay (up to 6)

How many nights altogether was ... in hospital on the (first/second/... sixth stay)?

1..97 ⸱ Activities of
Daily living

ACTIVITIES OF DAILY LIVING

EldIntro

THE NEXT SECTION ASKS ELDERLY PEOPLE ABOUT HOW WELL THEY MANAGE DIFFERENT ACTIVITIES OF DAILY LIVING.

1 Stairs

All adults aged 65 and over

Do you usually manage to get up and down stairs or steps...

RUNNING PROMPT

on your own .... 1 ⸱ Q2
only with help from someone else .. 2⎤ ⸱ See
or not at all? .... 3⎦ EldInt1

2 StrsEasy[*]

If manages without help (code 1 at Stairs)

Do you find it ...

RUNNING PROMPT

very easy .... 1⎤ ⸱ Q8
fairly easy...................................... 2⎥
fairly difficult or.............................. 3⎥
very difficult to do this on your
   own?.. 4⎦ ⸱ EldInt1

EldInt1

If finds stairs difficult, needs help or cannot manage them at all (codes 2, 3 at Stairs or codes 3, 4 at StrsEasy) else   Q8

Now I'd like to ask about a few tasks that some people may be able to do on their own, while others may need help, or not do them at all.

As I read out each task, I'd like you to look at this card and tell me whether you usually manage to do it on your own, only with help from someone else, or not at all.

3 House

SHOW CARD P

Do you usually manage to get around the house (except for any stairs) ...

RUNNING PROMPT
on your own .... 1⎤
only with help from someone else .. 2⎥ ⸱ C
or not at all? .... 3⎦

4 Toilet

SHOW CARD P

Do you usually manage to get to the toilet ...

RUNNING PROMPT
on your own .... 1⎤
only with help from someone else .. 2⎥ ⸱ C
or not at all? .... 3⎦

5 Bed

SHOW CARD P

Do you usually manage to get in and out of bed

RUNNING PROMPT
on your own................................... 1⎤
only with help from someone else.. 2⎥ ⸱ C
or not at all? .... 3⎦

6 Dress

SHOW CARD P

Do you usually manage to dress and undress yourself ...

RUNNING PROMPT
on your own .... 1⎤
only with help from someone else ..... 2⎥ ⸱ C
or not at all? .... 3⎦

7 Feed

SHOW CARD P

Do you usually manage to feed yourself...

RUNNING PROMPT
on your own .... 1⎤
only with help from someone else .. 2⎥ ⸱ C
or not at all? .... 3⎦

All adults aged 65 and over

8 Bath

SHOW CARD P

Do you usually manage to bath shower or wash all over...

RUNNING PROMPT
on your own, ... 1⎤ ⸱ C
only with help from someone else. ... 2⎥
or not at all? .... 3⎦ ⸱ Q

9 BathEasy[*]

If manages without help (code 1 at Bath)

Do you find it ....

RUNNING PROMPT
very easy .... 1⎤ ⸱ Q
fairly easy .... 2⎥
fairly difficult or .... 3⎥ ⸱ Q
very difficult to do this on your own?.. 4⎦

10 Wash

If finds bathing difficult, needs help or cannot manage at all (codes 2, 3 at Bath or codes 3, 4 at BathEasy)

Do you usually manage to wash your face and hands...

on your own....................................	1	. Q11
only with help from someone else? ...	2	

11 Walk

Ask all adults aged 65 and over

SHOW CARD P

Do you usually manage to go out of doors and walk down the road...

on your own....................................	1	
only with help from someone else ..	2	. Mobility
or not at all?	3	

MOBILITY

IntrMob

Ask all adults

We have already talked a bit about mobility. In this section we are interested in whether people have anything to help them get around, either inside or outside the home.

1 MobDiff[*]

Do you have any difficulty getting about the house/flat without assistance of any kind?

Yes...	1	. Q2
No..	2	. Q4

2 MobAid

If 'yes' (code 1) at MobDiff

What type of assistance do you require?

SHOW CARD Q

CODE ALL THAT APPLY
(Enter at most 4 codes)

Walking aid....................................	1	
Wheelchair....................................	2	. Q4
Assistance from another person.....	3	
Other - SPECIFY...........................	4	. Q3
Can't get about house...................	5	. Q4

3 XMobaid

If 'other' (code 4) at MobAid

Specify other type of assistance.

(Enter text of at most 20 characters)   .   Q4

4 MobOut[*]

Ask all adults

Do you have any difficulty going out of doors and walking down the road without assistance of any kind?

Yes	1	. Q5
No	2	. See Q7

5 Mobbed

If 'yes' (code 1) at MobOut

What type of assistance do you require?

SHOW CARD R

CODE ALL THAT APPLY
(Enter at most 4 codes)

Walking aid	1	
Wheelchair	2	. Q7
Assistance from another person	3	
Other - SPECIFY	4	. Q6
Can't get outside the house	5	. Q7

6 XMobbed

If 'other' (code 4) at Mobbed

What other type of assistance do you require?

(Enter text of at most 40 characters)   .   Q7

7 MobTemp[*]

If needs assistance getting about (MobDiff =1 or MobOut =1)

CODE 1 IF INFORMANT WILL RECOVER AND NO LONGER NEED ASSISTANCE OF ANY KIND

Is this...

A temporary difficulty due to an accident or illness	1	
Or is this likely to be a permanent difficulty?	2	. Q8

8 MobCard

Ask all adults

SHOW CARD S

(Can I just check) Do you have any aids to walking or getting about, either inside or outside your home, such as those shown on this card, including any that you no longer use?

Yes	1	. Q8
No	2	

9 MobNum

If 'yes' (code 1) at MobCard

How many aids to walking do you have?

1..6   .   Q10

10 MobType

For each aid

What is the (first/second etc) type of aid that you have?

RECORD EACH AID MENTIONED AT MOBAID

SHOW CARD S

Walking stick	1	
Crutches	2	. Q12
Walking frame, tripod, zimmer	3	
Trolley (not shopping)	4	

277

Wheelchair - manual .... 5 ⎤
Wheelchair - electric .... 6 ⎥ - Q12
Buggy/scooter .... 7 ⎦
Other - SPECIFY .... 8 - Q11

11 XMobType **If 'other' (code 8) at MobType**

Please describe the 'other' type of aid you use?

(Enter text of at most 30 characters)   - Q12

12 MobWhere **Ask for each aid coded at MobType**

Where did you get the (type of mobility aid) from?

Health/social services .... 1 ⎤
Bought yourself or by spouse
  partner .... 2 ⎥ - Q14
Provided by friend/relative .... 3 ⎥
Voluntary organisation .... 4 ⎦
Other - SPECIFY .... 5 - Q13

13 XMobwher **If 'other' (code 5) at MobWhere**

Specify where you got (mobility aid) from.

(Enter text of at most 30 characters)   - Q14

14 MobPlace **For each aid**

Do you use this (type of mobility aid) for...

RUNNING PROMPT

indoor use only .... 1 - Q16
outdoor use only .... 2 ⎤
indoor and outdoor use? .... 3 ⎦ - Q15
aid not in use .... 4 - Young
                                                          Carers

15 MobWhen **If MobPlace = 2 or 3**

When going out do you use (type of mobility aid) ...

All the time.................................... 1 ⎤
Regularly .... 2 ⎥ - Q16
Occasionally? .... 3 ⎦

16 ChairMan **If MobType = 5,6 (manual or electric wheel chair) and Chair in use (MobPlace = 1,2 or 3)**

Can you manage this wheelchair on your own or do you need someone to help push/control it?

Manage yourself .... 1 ⎤
Always need help .... 2 ⎥ - Young
Sometimes need help .... 3 ⎦ Carers

YOUNG CARERS

1 IntchkYc **Ask all adults where there are young people aged 8-17 in the household, else go to Smoking**

THE NEXT SECTION (YOUNG CARERS) IS ONLY ASKED OF THE HOH OR THEIR SPOUSE/PARTNER. ARE YOU INTERVIEWING THE HOH, OR SPOUSE/PARTNER OF HOH?

Yes .... 1 - Q
No. .... 2 - Smokir

2 IAIreaYc **If 'yes' (code 1) at IntchkYc**

HAS THE YOUNG CARERS SECTION ALREADY BEEN COMPLETED BY THIS PERSON'S SPOUSE/PARTNER?

Yes, (go to next section)................ 1 - Smokir
No, (not yet asked) .... 2 - C

IntroYc **If 'No' (code 2) at IAIreaYc**

The next section is about young people who look after, or help to look after, other members of the household who are sick, handicapped or elderly.

3 DepRes[*] Is there anyone living in this household who is sick, handicapped or elderly?

INTERVIEWER: THIS IS AN OPINION QUESTION BUT CODE 2 IF:
-THE ILLNESS/HANDICAP IS TEMPORARY (E.G. ACUTE SICKNESS, BROKEN LEG OR PREGNANCY)

CODE 3 IF:
-THERE IS A HOUSEHOLD MEMBER AGED 65 OR OVER.
 -YOU HAVE OBSERVED A SICK OR HANDI-CAPPED HOUSEHOLD MEMBER;

Yes. .... 1 - C
Definitely not. .... 2 - Smoki
Possibly (respondent is uncertain)
  (Specify) .... 3 - C

4 AnyYc[*] **Ask if there is, or there possibly is, a person in the household who is sick, elderly or handi-capped (if DepRes = 1 or 3)**

Some young people have extra family responsibilities because they look after someone who is sick, handicapped or elderly.

Do any of the young people in this household, that is (names of young people) look after or give special help to this (these) sick or handicapped (or elderly) person(s)?

INTERVIEWER: OPINION QUESTION BUT CODE 2 (NO) IF YOU ARE TOLD THAT THE ILLNESS/INJURY IS TEMPORARY (EG ACUTE SICKNESS, BROKEN LEG OR PREGNANCY) OR IF THE CARER IS PAID (EG LIVE IN NURSE

Yes. .... 1 - C
No. .... 2 - C
Possibly (respondent uncertain)
  (SPECIFY) .... 3 - C

5 XAnyYC

If 'possibly' (code 3) at AnyYc

Specify why respondent is uncertain.

(Enter text of at most 40 characters)   .   Q7

6 IntAny

Applies if the respondent says there are no young carers in the household (AnyYc = 2)

INTERVIEWER CODE:INTERVIEWER, DO YOU THINK THAT ONE OR MORE OF THESE YOUNG PEOPLE IS ACTUALLY LOOKING AFTER A SICK, HANDICAPPED OR ELDERLY PERSON IN THE HOUSEHOLD, BUT THE RESPONDENT HAS NOT MENTIONED THIS?

Yes - please give details of your
observations, but accept the
answer given   1
No   2   . Smoking

7 NoYC

Ask if there are, or there possibly are, any young people in the household who care for a household member who is sick, elderly or handicapped (AnyYc = 1 or 3)

ASK OR RECORD

How many of the (no.of young people) young people aged 8-17 look after or give special help to someone in the household?

ENTER HOW MANY YOUNG CARERS THERE ARE
                          1..6   .   Q8

8 IntYC

Ask for each young carer

PLEASE ENTER THE PERSON NUMBER OF THE (OLDEST/SECOND OLDEST ETC.) YOUNG CARER.

THE YOUNG PEOPLE IN THIS HOUSEHOLD ARE: (names, ages and person numbers of all young people in the household).
                          1..14   .   Q9

9 NoDep

Does (name) look after or help one sick, handicapped or elderly person or more than one?

ENTER THE NUMBER OF DEPENDANTS (CARED FOR BY (name))
                          1..14   .   Q10

Maintwo

If 3 or more dependants (NoDep>=3)

The next questions relate only to the two dependants that ... helps the most. (only ask about the 2 whom the young person helps most)

10 WhoDep

Ask for each dependant

ENTER THE PERSON NUMBER OF THE (FIRST/SECOND) DEPENDANT. INTER-VIEWER: THE PEOPLE IN THIS HOUSEHOLD ARE:

(names and person numbers of household members).
                          1..14   .   Q11

11 SameDep1

Have you already asked about services etc. for (NAME OF DEPENDANT)?

Yes.   1   .   Q13
No.   2   .   Q12

12 MatDep[*]

If not asked already (SameDep1 NOT 1)

ASK, OR RECORD IF ALREADY MENTIONED BY REPONDENT

May I check, what is the matter with (NAME OF DEPENDANT)?

DO NOT PROBE

(Enter text of at most (50) characters)   .   Q13

13 AffDep

SHOW CARD T

You mentioned earlier what was the matter with (NAME OF DEPENDANT) could I just check how is he/she affected? Is it...

Physically   1
Mentally   2   .   Q15
Both physically and mentally?   3
Other - SPECIFY at next question ...   4   .   Q14

14 XAffdep

If 'other' (code 4) at AffDep

In what way is (NAME OF DEPENDANT) affected?

(Enter text of at most 40 characters)   .   Q15

15 TyHelp

For each dependant of each young carer

What kind of things does (NAME OF YOUNG CARER) usually do for (NAME OF DEPENDANT) over and above what he/she would normally do for someone of this age living with him/her?

SHOW CARD U

CODE ALL TYPES OF HELP THAT APPLY

PROMPT FIRST ITEM AS EXAMPLE

Does (YOUNG CARER) ...
(Enter at most 10 codes)

Help with personal care   1   .   Q17
   (eg dressing, bathing, washing,
   shaving, cutting nails, feeding, using
   the toilet)

Physical help with lifting and
carrying things 2
Physical help with other things 3
(eg with walking, getting up and
down stairs getting into and
out of bed)
Helping with paper work or financial
matters 4
(eg writing letters, sending cards,
filling in forms, dealing with bills,
banking)
Other practical help 5
(eg preparing meals, doing his/her
shopping, laundry, housework,   - Q17
gardening,decoration household
repairs, taking to doctor's or
hospital)
Keeping him/her company 6
(eg sitting with, reading to, talking
to, playing cards or games)
Taking out 7
(eg taking for a walk, taking to see
friends or relatives)
Giving medicines 8
(eg making sure he/she takes pills,
giving injections, changing dressings)
Keeping an eye on him/her to see
he/she is all right? 9
Other help - SPECIFY 10   -   Q16

16 Xtyhelp   In what way does (YOUNG CARER) help
(DEPENDANT)?

(Enter text of at most 40 characters)   -   Q17

17 YCHours   About how long does (NAME OF YOUNG
CARER) spend on average each week looking after
or helping (NAME OF DEPENDANT) - that is doing
the things you've mentioned and including time
when (he/she) needs (NAME OF YOUNG CARER)
just to be there, apart from when (NAME OF
YOUNG CARER) is asleep?

SHOW CARD V

PROMPT AS NECESSARY

USE CODES 8 AND 9 AS A LAST RESORT ONLY

0-4 hours per week 1
5-9 hours per week 2
10-19 hours per week 3
20-34 hours per week 4
35-49 hours per week 5   - See Q19
50-99 hours per week 6
100 hours or more per week 7
varies - under 20 hours 8
varies - 20 hours or more 9
other (SPECIFY - at next question) ... 10   -   Q18

18 XYCHours   Specify how long (CARER) spends looking after
(DEPENDANT) each week.

(Enter text of at most 40 characters)   - See Q19

19 TotHours   **Ask if there is more than one dependant and
after the YCHours has been asked for the
second dependant)   else**   See Q21

Thinking about the total time that (NAME OF
YOUNG CARER) spends caring for both
dependants, about how long altogether does
(NAME OF YOUNG CARER) spend each week
looking after or helping them.

IF ANY TIME RECORDED SEPARATELY
FOR EACH DEPENDANT AT YCHOURS
ACTUALLY OVERLAPS (IE CARER SOME-
TIMES LOOKS AFTER BOTH AT THE SAME
TIME), INCLUDE IT ONLY ONCE IN THIS
WEEKLY TOTAL

SHOW CARD V

USE CODES 8 AND 9 AS A LAST RESORT
ONLY

0-4 hours per week 1
5-9 hours per week 2
10-19 hours per week 3
20-34 hours per week 4
35-49 hours per week 5   - Q21
50-99 hours per week 6
100 hours or more per week 7
Varies - under 20 hours 8
Varies - 20 hours or more 9
Other (SPECIFY - at next question) .. 10   -   Q20

20 XTotHours   Specify how long (CARER) spends looking after
both dependants each week.

(Enter text of at most 40 characters)   - See Q21

21 VisAny   **If not asked already (SameDep1 NOT 1)**

Does (NAME OF DEPENDANT) receive regular
visits at least once a month from any of the
people listed on this card?

SHOW CARD W

(Enter at most 8 codes)

Doctor 1
Community or district nurse 2
Health visitor 3   - See Q23
Social worker 4
Home help 5
Meals on wheels 6
Voluntary worker 7
Other regular professional visitor or
service, or someone but type of visitor
unknown (SPECIFY - at next
question) 8   -   Q22
None of these 9   - See Q23

22 XVisAny   **If 'other' (code 8) at VisAny**

Who else visits (DEPENDANT)?

(Enter text of at most 40 characters)   - See Q23

23 OthCare

For each dependant if not asked already (SameDep NOT 1), else   Q25

Apart from (name of young carer) is there anyone else in the household who also helps to look after (name of dependant/you)?

DO NOT INCLUDE OTHER YOUNG CARERS

Yes - (including if two dependants
  also look after each other) .... 1 - Q24
No .... 2 - Q31

24 NoMore

If 'yes'(code 1) at OthCare

How many people in the household apart from (YOUNG CARER) help look after (DEPENDANT)?

DO NOT INCLUDE OTHER YOUNG CARERS
                                                    1..6 - Q25

25 WhoMore

For each other person in household who helps to care

(FIRST/SECOND etc.) OTHER HOUSEHOLD MEMBER WHO CARES FOR (DEPENDANT)

Who (else) helps look after (DEPENDANT) apart from (FIRST CARER)?

CODE RELATIONSHIP OF (FIRST/SECOND etc.) OTHER CARERS TO (YOUNG CARER) DO NOT INCLUDE OTHER YOUNG CARERS.

mother/step-mother 1
father/step-father 2
grandparent/step-grandparent 3
brother/sister (including   -   Q28
  step/adopted) 4
husband/wife 5
foster brother/sister 6
other relative - please specify .... 7 - Q26
friend in household .... 8 - Q28
other - specify .... 9 - Q27

26 XOthRel

If 'other relative' (code 7) at WhoMore

(FIRST/SECOND etc.) OTHER HOUSEHOLD MEMBER WHO CARES FOR (DEPENDANT)

Specify which other relative helps look after (dependant).

Specify relationship of this other relative to (YOUNG CARER).

(Enter text of at most 40 characters)   -   Q28

27 XWhoMore

If 'other' (code 9) at WhoMore

(FIRST/SECOND etc.) OTHER HOUSEHOLD MEMBER WHO CARES FOR (NAME OF DEPENDANT

Specify which other person helps care for (NAME OF DEPENDANT).

(Enter text of at most 40 characters)   -   Q28

28 MoreYC

For each other person in household who helps to care

(FIRST/SECOND etc.) OTHER HOUSEHOLD MEMBER WHO CARES FOR DEPENDANT

Can I just check, does this person spend more time looking after (NAME OF DEPENDANT) than (NAME OF YOUNG CARER) does)?

Yes 1
No 2   - Q29
Other person(s) spend equal time 3

29 TyOth

(FIRST/SECOND etc.) OTHER HOUSEHOLD MEMBER WHO CARES FOR (DEPENDANT)

What kind of things does this person usually do for (NAME OF DEPENDANT) over and above what he/she would normally do for someone of this age living with him/her?

SHOW CARD U

CODE ALL TYPES OF HELP THAT APPLY

PROMPT FIRST ITEM AS EXAMPLE

Does this person ...
(Enter at most 10 codes)

Help with personal care 1
  (eg dressing, bathing, washing,
  shaving, cutting nails, feeding, using
  the toilet)
Physical help with lifting and carrying
  things 2
Physical help with other things 3
  (eg with walking, getting up and
  down stairs getting into and out
  of bed)
Helping with paper work or financial
  matters 4
  (eg writing letters, sending cards,
  filling in forms, dealing with bills,
  banking)
Other practical help 5   . See Q31
  (eg preparing meals, doing his/her
  shopping, laundry, housework,
  gardening, decoration household
  repairs, taking to doctor's or
  hospital)
Keeping him/her company 6
  (eg sitting with, reading to, talking
  to, playing cards or games)
Taking out 7
  (eg taking for a walk, taking to see
  friends or relatives)
Giving medicines 8
  (eg making sure he/she takes pills,
  giving injections, changing
  dressings)
Keeping an eye on him/her to see
  he/she is all right? 9
Other help - SPECIFY 10   -   Q30

281

30 XTyOth

If 'other' (code 10) at TyOth

(FIRST/SECOND etc.) OTHER HOUSEHOLD MEMBER WHO CARES FOR (DEPENDANT)

In what way does this person help (NAME OF DEPENDANT)?

(Enter text of at most 40 characters) Q31

31 OutHelp

For each dependant if not asked already (SameDep1 NOT 1)

And can I just check, apart from the people already mentioned, is there anyone else outside this household who helps look after (name of dependant), for example, a member of the family outside this household, a friend or some paid helper?

Yes 1 Q32
No .... 2 Smoking

32 NoOuthh

If 'yes' (code 1) at OutHelp

How many people outside the household help looking after (name of dependant)?

(Enter number between 1 and 6) Q33

33 WhoOuth

For each person outside the household who helps care

(FIRST/SECOND etc) OTHER NON-HOUSE-HOLD MEMBER WHO CARES FOR DEPENDANT)

Who outside the household helps look after (NAME OF DEPENDANT)?

CODE RELATIONSHIP OF (FIRST/SECOND ETC) OTHER CARER TO (NAME OF YOUNG CARER)

mother/step-mother 1
father/step-father 2
grandparent/step-grandparent 3
   brother/sister (including Q36
step/adopted) 4
husband/wife 5
foster brother/sister 6
other relative - please specify 7 Q34
friend in household 8 Q36
other - specify 9 Q35

34 XOthRelO

If 'other relative' (code 7) at WhoOuth

(FIRST/SECOND ETC.) NON-HOUSEHOLD MEMBER WHO CARES FOR (NAME OF DEPENDANT)

Specify relationship to (YOUNG CARER) of this other relative who helps look after (NAME OF DEPENDANT).

(Enter at most 40 characters) Q36

35 XWhoOuth

If 'other non-household member' (code 9) at WhoOuth

(FIRST/SECOND ETC) NON-HOUSEHOLD MEMBER WHO CARES FOR (NAME OF DEPENDANT)

Specify relationship to (YOUNG CARER) of which other person who helps care for (NAME OF DEPENDANT)

(Enter text of at most 40 characters) Q3

36 MoreOuth

For each person outside the household who helps care

(FIRST/SECOND etc.) NON-HOUSEHOLD MEMBER WHO CARES FOR (DEPENDANT)

Can I just check, does this person spend more time looking after (NAME OF DEPENDANT) than (NAME OF YOUNG CARER) does?

Yes 1
No 2 Q3
Others spend equal time 3

37 TYOthoh

(FIRST/SECOND etc.) NON-HOUSEHOLD MEMBER WHO CARES FOR (NAME OF DEPENDANT)

What kind of things does this person usually do for (NAME OF DEPENDANT)?

(Enter text of at most 40 characters)

SHOW CARD U

CODE ALL TYPES OF HELP THAT APPLY.

PROMPT FIRST ITEM AS EXAMPLE.

Help with personal care 1
(eg dressing, bathing, washing,
  shaving, cutting nails, feeding, using
  the toilet)
Physical help with lifting and carrying
  things 2
Physical help with other things 3
  (eg with walking, getting up and down
  stairs getting into and out of bed)
Helping with paper work or financial ..
  matters 4
  (eg writing letters, sending cards,
  filling in forms, dealing with bills, banking)
Other practical help 5
  (eg preparing meals, doing his/her Smoki
  shopping,laundry, housework, gardening,
  decoration household repairs, taking to
  doctor's or hospital)
Keeping him/her company 6
  (eg sitting with, reading to, talking to,
  playing cards or games)
Taking out 7
  (eg taking for a walk, taking to see
  friends or relatives)
Giving medicines 8
  (eg making sure he/she takes pills,
  giving injections, changing dressings)
Keeping an eye on him/her to see he/she
  is all right? 9
Other help - SPECIFY 10 Q3

38 XTyothoh If 'Other' (code10) at XTyothoh

(FIRST/SECOND ETC.) NON-HOUSEHOLD
MEMBER WHO CARES FOR (NAME OF
DEPENDANT)

In what way does this person help (NAME OF
DEPENDANT)?

(Enter text of at most 40 characters)   ▸ Smoking

SMOKING

SmkIntro **All adults (except proxy informants)**

The next section consists of a series of questions
about smoking.
(Not asked of proxy respondents)

1 SelfCom1 **All 16 and 17 year olds**

INFORMANT IS AGED 16 OR 17 - OFFER
SELF-COMPLETION FORM AND ENTER CODE

Informant accepted self-completion .... 1 ▸ Q2
Informant refused self-completion ...... 2 ▸ Drinking
Data now to be keyed by interviewer ..... 3 ▸ Q2

2 SmokEver **All adults aged 18 or over or if SelfCom1 = 3**

Have you ever smoked a cigarette, a cigar,
or a pipe?

Yes .... 1 ▸ Q3
No .... 2 ▸ Drinking

3 CigNow **If respondent has ever smoked (SmokEver = 1)**

Do you smoke cigarettes at all nowadays?

Yes .... 1 ▸ Q4
No .... 2 ▸ Q13

4 QtyWkEnd **If respondent smokes cigarettes now (CigNow = 1)**

About how many cigarettes a day do you usually
smoke at weekends?

IF LESS THAN 1, ENTER 0   0..97 ▸ Q5

5 QtyWkDay About how many cigarettes a day do you usually
smoke on weekdays?

IF LESS THAN 1, ENTER 0   0..97 ▸ Q6

6 CigType Do you mainly smoke.....

RUNNING PROMPT

filter-tipped cigarettes .... 1 ⎤ ▸ Q7
or plain or untipped cigarettes .... 2 ⎦
or hand-rolled cigarettes? .... 3 ▸ Q10

7 CigDesc **If cigarette types include plain or filter
cigarettes (CigType includes 1 or 2)**

Which brand of cigarette do you usually smoke?

GIVE 1) FULL BRAND NAME;
2) SIZE, eg King, luxury, regular;
3) whether filter-tipped or plain

(Enter text of at most 60 characters) ▸ Q8

8 Brand1 Is coding of brand to be done now, or later?

CODE THE BRAND IN THE INTERVIEW IF
POSSIBLE

Now .... 1 ▸ Q9
Later .... 2 ▸ Q10

9 CigBrand **If Brand1 = Now (code 1)**

Review cigarette details, & assign 3-digit code
from CARD X.

IF NOT ON LIST, CODE AS 997.
1..997 ▸ Q10

10 NoSmoke[*] **All who currently smoke cigarettes (CigNow = 1)**

How easy or difficult would you find it to
go without smoking for a whole day? Would
you find it ...

RUNNING PROMPT

Very easy .... 1 ⎤
Fairly easy .... 2 ⎥ ▸ Q11
Fairly difficult or .... 3 ⎥
Very difficult? .... 4 ⎦

11 GiveUp[*] **Would you like to give up smoking altogether?**

Yes .... 1 ⎤ ▸ Q12
No .... 2 ⎦

12 FirstCig How soon after waking do you usually smoke
your first cigarette of the day?

PROMPT AS NECESSARY

Less than 5 minutes. .... 1 ⎤
5-14 minutes .... 2 ⎥
15-29 minutes .... 3 ⎥ ▸ Q16
30 minutes but less than 1 hour .... 4 ⎥
1 hour but less than 2 hours.......... 5 ⎥
2 hours or more .... 6 ⎦

13 CigEver **All who do not smoke cigarettes now but have
smoked a cigarette or cigar or pipe (SmokEver = 1)
and (CigNow NOT 1)**

Have you ever smoked cigarettes regularly?

Yes .... 1 ▸ Q14
No .... 2 ▸ Q17

283

14 CigUsed

If CigEver = Yes (code 1)

About how many cigarettes did you smoke IN A DAY when you smoked them regularly?

IF LESS THAN 1, ENTER 0   0..97   ▸ Q15

15 CigStop

How long ago did you stop smoking cigarettes regularly?

PROMPT AS NECESSARY

Less than 6 months ago	1
6 months but less than a year ago	2
1 year but less than 2 years ago	3
2 years but less than 5 years ago	4
5 years but less than 10 years ago ...	5
10 years or more ago	6

▸ Q16

16 CigAge

All who have ever smoked cigarettes (CigNow = 1) or (CigEver = 1)

How old were you when you started to smoke cigarettes regularly?

SPONTANEOUS: NEVER SMOKED CIGARETTES REGULARLY - CODE 0   0..97   ▸ Q17

17 CigarReg

Do you smoke at least one cigar of any kind per month nowadays?

Yes	1	▸ Q18
No	2	▸ Q19

18 CigarsWk

About how many cigars do you usually smoke in a week?

IF LESS THAN 1, ENTER 0   0..97   ▸ See Q20

19 CigarEvr

Have you ever regularly smoked at least one cigar of any kind per month?

Yes	1	▸ See Q20
No	2	

20 PipeNow

Men only - others go to Drinking

Do you smoke a pipe at all nowadays?

Yes	1	▸ Drinking
No	2	▸ Q21

21 PipEver

Have you ever smoked a pipe regularly?

Yes	1	▸ Drinking
No	2	

DRINKING

DrkInto

All adults (except proxy informants)

The next section consists of a series of questions about drinking.
(Not asked of proxy respondents)

1 Selfcom2

(INFORMANT IS AGED 16 OR 17) OFFER SELF-COMPLETION FORM (TO RESPONDENT) AND ENTER CODE

Interviewer asked section	1	
Informant accepted self-completion .	2	▸ Q2
Data now keyed by interviewer	3	

2 DrinkNow

Do you ever drink alcohol nowadays, including drinks you brew or make at home?

Yes	1	▸ Q9
No	2	▸ Q3

3 DrinkAny

If respondent says they do not drink nowadays (DrinkNow = 2)

Could I just check, does that mean you never have alcoholic drink nowadays, or do you have an alcohol drink very occasionally, perhaps fo medicinal purpc or on special occasions like Christmas or New Yea

Very occasionally	1	▸ Q9
Never	2	▸ Q4

4 TeeTotal

If respondent says they never drink (DrinkAny =

Have you always been a non-drinker, or did you stop drinking for some reason?

Always a non-drinker	1	▸ Q5
Used to drink but stopped	2	▸ Q7

5 NonDrink[*]

If the informant has always been a non-drinker (TeeTotal=1)

What would you say is the main reason you have always been a non-drinker?

Religious reasons	1
Don't like it	2
Parent's advice/influence	3
Health reasons	4
Can't afford it	5

▸ Family Information

Other (SPECIFY AT NEXT QUESTION)	6	▸ Q6

6 XNonDrnk

If respondent gives an 'other' reason for not drinking (NonDrink = 6)

Specify reason.

(Enter text of at most 40 characters)   ▸ Family Information

7 StopDrin [*]

If the informant used to drink but has stopped (TeeTotal=2)

What would you say was the main reason you stopped drinking?

Religious reasons	1
Don't like it	2
Parent's advice/influence.	3
Health reasons	4
Can't afford it	5

▸ Family Information

Other (SPECIFY AT NEXT QUESTION)	6	▸ Q8

8 XStopDrk **If the respondent has given an 'other' reason for not drinking (StopDrin = 6)**

Specify reason.

(Enter text of at most 40 characters) . Family Information

9 DrinkAmt[*] **If the respondent drinks at all nowadays (DrinkNow = 1) or (DrinkAny = 1)**

I'm going to read out a few descriptions about the amounts of alcohol people drink, and I'd like you to say which one fits you best. Would you say you:

RUNNING PROMPT

hardly drink at all 1
drink a little 2
drink a moderate amount .... 3 . Q10
drink quite a lot 4
or drink heavily? 5

10 Shandy SHOW CARD Y

How often have you had a drink of...SHANDY (exclude bottles/cans) during the last 12 months, that is since (date last year)?

Almost every day 1
5 or 6 days a week 2
3 or 4 days a week .... 3 . Q11
once or twice a week 4
once or twice a month 5
once every couple of months. 6
once or twice a year 7
not at all in last 12 months .... 8 . Q13

11 ShandyAm **If drank shandy at all this year (Shandy = 1 - 7)**

How much ....SHANDY (exclude bottles/cans) have you usually drunk on any one day during the last 12 months, that is since (date last year)?

ENTER NO. OF HALF-PINTS, OR CODE 97 AND SPECIFY AT NEXT QUESTION.
1..97 . Q12

12 XShndyAm **If ShandyAm = 97**

Specify amount of ...SHANDY (exclude bottles/cans) usually drunk on any one day during the last 12 months, that is since (date last year)?

EXCLUDE:ANY NON-ALCOHOLIC DRINK, ANY LOW-ALCOHOLIC DRINKS

(Enter text of at most 20 characters) . Q13

13 Beer **If the respondent drinks at all nowadays (DrinkNow = 1) or (DrinkAny = 1)**

SHOW CARD Y
How often have you had a drink of..... BEER, LAGER, STOUT, CIDER during the last 12 months, that is since (date last year)?

EXCLUDE:ANY NON-ALCOHOLIC DRINK, ANY LOW-ALCOHOLIC DRINKS

Almost every day 1
5 or 6 days a week 2
3 or 4 days a week .... 3 . Q14
once or twice a week 4
once or twice a month 5
once every couple of months 6
once or twice a year 7
not at all in last 12 months .... 8 . Q16

14 BeerAm **If drank beer at all this year (Beer = 1 - 7)**

Other than cans or bottles, how many HALF PINTS of ....BEER,LAGER,STOUT,CIDER have you usually drunk on any one day during the last 12 months, that is since (date last year)?

ENTER NO. OF HALF PINTS
PROBE WHETHER CANS OR BOTTLES ARE DRUNK

If bottles, cans (or cannot specify in half pints) CODE 97
1..97 . See Q15

15 XBeerAm **If BeerAm = 97**

Specify amount of..(bottles, cans etc or other on any one day during the last 12 months, that is since (date last year)?

(Enter text of at most 20 characters) . Q16

16 Spirit **If the respondent drinks at all nowadays (DrinkNow = 1) or (DrinkAny = 1)**

SHOW CARD Y

How often have you had a drink of ..... SPIRITS OR LIQUEURS (eg gin, whisky, rum, brandy, vodka, advocaat) during the last 12 months, that is since (date last year)?

EXCLUDE:ANY NON-ALCOHOLIC DRINK, ANY LOW-ALCOHOLIC DRINKS

Almost every day 1
5 or 6 days a week 2
3 or 4 days a week .... 3 . Q17
Once or twice a week 4
Once or twice a month 5
Once every couple of months 6
Once or twice a year 7
Not at all in last 12 months .... 8 . Q19

17 SpiritAm **If drank spirits at all this year (Spirit = 1 - 7)**

How much ....SPIRITS OR LIQUEURS (eg gin, whisky, rum, brandy, vodka, advocaat) have you usually drunk on any one day during the last 12 months, that is since (date last year)?

ENTER NO. OF SINGLES, OR CODE 97 AND
SPECIFY AT NEXT QUESTION.

(COUNT DOUBLES AS 2 SINGLES)...
1..97 . See Q18

18 XSpirtAm   **If SpiritAm = 97**

Specify amount of....SPIRITS OR LIQUEURS (eg
gin, whisky, rum, brandy, vodka, advocaat) usually
drunk on any one day during the last 12 months,
that is since date last year?

(Enter text of at most 20 characters) . Q19

19 Sherry   **If the respondent drinks at all nowadays
(DrinkNow = 1) or (DrinkAny = 1)**

SHOW CARD Y

How often have you had a drink of .....SHERRY OR
MARTINI (including port, vermouth, cinzano,
dubonnet) during the last 12 months, that is since
(date last year)?

EXCLUDE:ANY NON-ALCOHOLIC DRINK,
ANY LOW-ALCOHOLIC D

Almost every day	1
5 or 6 days a week	2
3 or 4 days a week	3
Once or twice a week	4
Once or twice a month	5
Once every couple of months	6
Once or twice a year	7
Not at all in last 12 months	8

. Q20 (1-7), Q22 (8)

20 SherryAm   **If drank sherry at all this year (Sherry = 1 - 7)**

How much ....SHERRY OR MARTINI (including
port, vermouth, cinzano, dubonnet) have you
usually drunk on any one day during the last 12
months, that is since (date last year)?

ENTER NO. OF SMALL GLASSES, OR CODE
97 AND SPECIFY AT NEXT QUESTION.
1..97 . See Q21

21 XSheryAm   **If SherryAm = 97**

Specify amount of....SHERRY OR MARTINI
(including port, vermouth, cinzano, dubonnet)
usually drunk on any one day during the last 12
months, that is since (date last year)?

(Enter text of at most 20 characters) . Q22

22 Wine   **If the respondent drinks at all nowadays
(DrinkNow = 1) or (DrinkAny = 1)**

SHOW CARD Y

How often have you had a drink of .....WINE (inc.
babycham,champagne) during the last 12 months,
that is since (date last year)?

EXCLUDE:ANY NON-ALCOHOLIC DRINK, ANY
LOW-ALCOHOLIC DRINKS

Almost every day.	1
5 or 6 days a week	2
3 or 4 days a week	3
Once or twice a week	4
Once or twice a month	5
Once every couple of months	6
Once or twice a year	7
Not at all in last 12 months	8

. Q23 (1-7), Q25 (8)

23 WineAm   **If drank wine at all last year (Wine = 1 - 7)**

How much ....WINE (inc. babycham,champagne) have
you usually drunk on any one day during the last 12
months, that is since (date last year)?

ENTER NO. OF GLASSES, OR CODE 97 AND
SPECIFY AT NEXT QUESTION.
1..97 . See Q24

24 XWineAm   **If WineAm = 97**

Specify amount of....WINE (inc. babycham,champagne)
usually drunk on any one day during the last 12
months, that is since (date last year)?

(Enter text of at most 20 characters) . Q25

25 IfOther   **If the respondent drinks at all nowadays
(DrinkNow = 1) or (DrinkAny = 1)**

Have you had any other alcoholic drinks during
thelast 12 months, that is since (date last year)?

EXCLUDE:ANY NON-ALCOHOLIC DRINK, ANY
LOW-ALCOHOLIC DRINKS

Yes	1	Q26
No	2	Q29

26 OtherDr   **If drinks an 'other' drink (IfOther = 1)**

Please specify other drink(s)

(Enter text of at most 40 characters) . Q27

27 OtherD   SHOW CARD Y

How often have you had a drink of ..... (other drink)
during the last 12 months, that is since (date last
year)?

Almost every day	1
5 or 6 days a week	2
3 or 4 days a week	3
once or twice a week	4
once or twice a month	5
once every couple of months	6
once or twice a year	7
not at all in last 12 months	8

. Q28 (1-7), Q29 (8)

28 OtherAm   How much of .... (other drink) have you usually drunk on any one day during the last 12 months, that is since (date last year)?

ENTER AMOUNT...   ▸ Q29
(Enter text of at most 20 characters)

29 DrOften[*]   **If the respondent drinks at all nowadays (DrinkNow = 1) or (DrinkAny = 1)**
(Thinking now about all kinds of drinks) how often have you had an alcoholic drink of any kind during the last 12 months?

SHOW CARD Y

Almost every day	1
5 or 6 days a week	2
3 or 4 days a week	3
once or twice a week	4
once or twice a month	5
once every couple of months	6
once or twice a year	7
not at all in last 12 month	8

▸ Q30

30 DHAmount[*]   You may know that the Department of Health and the medical profession recommend that people should drink no more than a certain amount of alcohol each a week. Do you think you usually drink more or less than the recommended amount?

More	1	See
Less	2	▸ Family
Recommended amount	3	Information

FAMILY INFORMATION

FamIntro   THE NEXT SECTION CONSISTS OF A SERIES OF QUESTIONS ABOUT FAMILY INFORMATION
(Not asked of proxy respondents)

To all aged 16-59

1 SlMar   **If single or same sex cohabiting**

Have you ever been legally married?

Yes	1
No	2

▸ Q5

2 ChkFIA   **If not single or same sex cohabiting**

INTERVIEWER CODE: -

Informant is married or cohabiting but their partner is NOT a household member	1	▸ Q3
Everyone else	2	▸ Q5

3 HusbAway   **If married/cohabiting, but partner not a household member**

Is your husband, wife or partner absent because he/she usually works away from home, or for some other reason?

Usually works away (include Armed Forces, Merchant Navy)...	1	▸ Q5
Marriage broken down	2	
Some other reason (SPECIFY AT NEXT QUESTION)	3	▸ Q4

4 XHusbAwy   **If 'other' at HusbAway (code 3)**
Specify reason.

(Enter text of at most 30 characters)   ▸ Q5

5 SelfCom3   OFFER (COLOUR)SELF-COMPLETION FORM TO RESPONDENT AND ENTER CODE

Interviewer asked section	1	
Informant accepted self-completion	2	▸ See Q6
Data now being keyed by interviewer	3	
Interpreter aged under 16 - section not asked	4	▸ Income

FaminfSG   Variable computed in the BLAISE program used in derived variables.

Women:

Married: Self-completion	1
Married: I/viewer administered	2
Cohabiting: Self-completion	3
Cohabiting: I/viewer administered	4
Never married: Self-completion	5
Never married: I/viewer administered.	6
Wid,div,sep: Self-completion	7
Wid,div,sep: I/viewer administered.	8

Men:

Married: Self-completion	9
Married: I/viewer administered	10
Cohabiting: Self-completion	11
Cohabiting: I/viewer administered	12
Never married: Self-completion	13
Never married: I/viewer administered...	14
Wid,div,sep: Self-completion	15
Wid,div,sep: I/viewer administered	16

6 WhereWed   **To married men and women (MStat = 2)**

Thinking of your present marriage, did you get married with a religious ceremony of some kind, or at a register office, or are you simply living together as a couple?

Religious ceremony of some kind	1	
Register Office	2	▸ Q8
Religious ceremony and register office	3	
Living together as a couple	4	▸ Q9

287

To widowed, divorced or separated men and women (MStat=3,4 or 5 OR SLMar = 1)

7 WhereWed — Thinking or your most recent marriage, did you get married with a religious ceremony of some kind, or at a register office, or were you simply living together as a couple?

Religious ceremony of
  some kind .... 1 ⎤
Register office. .... 2 ⎥ → Q8
Religious ceremony and
  register office .... 3 ⎦
Living together as a couple .... 4 → Q9

8 NumMar — **If coded 1-3 at WhereWed**

How many times have you been legally married?

(NUMBER INCLUDING PRESENT MARRIAGE)
                              1..7 → Q14

9 ClMon — **Cohabiting men and women (exc. couples now separated and same sex couples) (cohabit = 1 OR (WhereWed = 4 and MStat = 2))**

When did you and your partner start living together as a couple?
                              1..12 → Q10

10 ClYr — ENTER YEAR   0..97 → Q11

11 ClPrtMar — Has your partner ever been married, that is legally married?

Yes .... 1 ⎤ → Q12
No .... 2 ⎦

12 ClMar — **Cohabiting (and ex-cohabiting) men and women (Cohabit = 1 or WhereWed = 4)**

Have you yourself ever been legally married?

Yes .... 1 → Q13
No .... 2 → Q32

13 ClNumMar — **If 'yes' (code 1) at ClMar**

How many times have you been legally married altogether?
                              1..7 → Q14

MarrInt — **To all who are, or have been legally married (NumMar or ClNumMar>=1)**

THE NEXT SCREEN CONSISTS OF A TABLE OF MARRIAGES FOR (...). PLEASE ENTER DETAILS OF MARRIAGES STARTING WITH THE EARLIEST AND ENDING WITH THE CURRENT OR MOST RECENT

14 MonMar — **For each marriage**

What month and year were you married?

ENTER MONTH   1..12 → Q15

15 YrMar — ENTER YEAR   0..97 → Q1

16 LvTgthr — Before getting married did you and your husband/wife live together as a couple?

Yes .... 1 → Q1
No .... 2 → Q1

17 MonLvTg — **If 'yes' at LvTgthr (code 1)**

What month and year did you start living together?

ENTER MONTH   1..12 → Q1

18 YrLvTg — ENTER YEAR   0..97 → Q1

19 PartMar — **All who are or have been legally married**

Had your husband/wife been legally married before?

Yes .... 1 ⎤ → Q2
No .... 2 ⎦

20 Current — **For last marriage entered**

INTERVIEWER - IS THIS MARRIAGE CURRENT OR HAS IT ENDED?

Current .... 1 → Q3
Ended .... 2 → Q2

21 HowEnded — **If marriage ended (code 2 at Current or marriage number less than total marriages)**

Did your marriage end in ...

death .... 1 → Q2
divorce .... 2 ⎤ → Q2
or separation? .... 3 ⎦

22 MonDie — **If marriage ended in death (HowEnded = 1)**

What month and year did your husband/wife die?

ENTER MONTH   1..12 → Q2

23 YrDie — ENTER YEAR   0..97 → Q28

24 MonSep — **If marriage ended in divorce or separation (HowEnded = 2 or 3)**

What month and year did you stop living together?

ENTER MONTH   1..12 → Q2

25 YrSep — ENTER YEAR   0..97 → See Q

26 MonDiv — **If marriage ended in divorce (HowEnded = 2)**

What month and year was your decree absolute granted?

ENTER MONTH   1..12 → Q

27 YrDiv   ENTER YEAR   1..97 . Q28a

28a Tgthr1   **To widowed, divorced, separated or single men and women**

INTERVIEWER: ARE THERE ADULTS OF THE OPPOSITE SEX IN THE HOUSEHOLD AND UNRELATED TO THE RESPONDENT?

Yes .... 1 . Q28
No .... 2 . Q32

28 Tgthr2   **Ask where there is an unrelated adult of the opposite sex in the household who is not married or cohabiting.(Tgthr1 = 1)**

Introduce as necessary.

(As you know, some couples live together without actually getting married, either because they cannot get married for some reason, or because they prefer not to get married.)

Are you currently living with someone as a couple?

Yes .... 1 . Q29
No .... 2 . Q32

29 StrtMon   **If 'yes' at Tgthr2**

When did you and your partner start living together as a couple?

ENTER MONTH.   1..12 . Q30

30 StrtYr   ...AND YEAR.   0..96 . Q32

31 CPartMar   Has your partner ever been married, that is legally married?

Yes 1
No .... 2 . Q32

32 Children   **All adults aged 16-59**

INTERVIEWER: DOES THIS PERSON HAVE ANY CHILDREN IN THE HOUSEHOLD (IN-CLUDES ADULTS AND/OR STEP OR FOSTER CHILDREN)?

Yes .... 1 . Q33
No .... 2 -See Q39

33 StpChld2   **If Children = 1**

(The next questions are about the family.)

Have you any step (foster or adopted) children (of any age) living with you?

Yes .... 1 . Q34
No .... 2 -See Q39

34 NumStep   **If stpchld2 = 1**

How many step, foster, or adopted children have you living with you altogether?
    1..7 . Q35

StepInt   THE NEXT SCREEN CONSISTS OF A TABLE FOR THE STEP-CHILDREN (AND ADOPTED AND FOSTER-CHILDREN) OF (...).

PLEASE ENTER DETAILS FOR EACH CHILD

35 StpersNo   **For each stepchild**

ENTER PERSON NUMBER(S) OF THE CHILD (INCLUDES ADULT CHILDREN).
    1..20 . Q36

36 StepType   ENTER CODE FOR:

Step 1
Foste .... 2 . Q37
Adopted 3

37 StLivMon   DATE STARTED LIVING WITH INFORMANT

ENTER MONTH: 1..12 . Q38

38 StLivYr   ... YEAR: 1..97 - See Q39

39 Baby   **All women aged 16-59**

ASK OR CODE

EXCLUDE ANY STILLBORN. INCLUDE ANY WHO ONLY LIVED FOR A SHORT TIME.

Have you ever had a baby?

Yes .... 1 . Q40
No .... 2 - See Q45

40 NumBaby   **If 'yes' at Baby**

EXCLUDE ANY STILLBORN

How many children have you given birth to, including any who are not living here and any who may have died since birth?
    1..20 . Q41

BirthInt   THE NEXT SCREEN CONSISTS OF A TABLE OF CHILDREN TO WHOM (...) HAS GIVEN BIRTH

PLEASE ENTER DETAILS FOR EACH CHILD.

41 BirthMon   **For each child**

Date of birth.

ENTER MONTH: AS A GUIDE, THE MONTH OF BIRTH OF EACH HOUSEHOLD MEMBER IS LISTED BELOW.

(Ignore the 0 codes)   1..12 . Q42

289

42 BirthYr

AND YEAR OF BIRTH: AS A GUIDE THE YEAR OF BIRTH OF EACH HOUSEHOLD MEMBER IS LISTED BELOW.

(Ignore the 0 codes)　　　　0..97　→　Q43

43 BirthSex

Sex of child

Male .... 1 ⎤
Female .... 2 ⎦ → Q44

44 ChldLive

Is child living with informant?

Yes .... 1 ⎤
No, lives elsewhere .... 2 ⎥ → See
No, deceased .... 3 ⎦ Q45

45 Pregnant

All women aged 16-49

(May I just check), are you pregnant now?

Yes .... 1 ⎤
No/unsure .... 2 ⎦ → Q46

46 MoreChld [*]

Do you think that you will have any (more) children (after the one you are expecting)? Could you choose your answers from this card.

SHOW CARD Z

Yes .... 1 ⎤
Probably yes .... 2 ⎥ → Q48
Probably not .... 3 ⎥
No .... 4 ⎦ → Income

47 ProbMore [*]

If 'DK' at MoreChld

On the whole, do you think...

You will probably have any/more
  children .... 1 → Q48
Or you will probably not have any/more
  children? .... 2 → Income

48 TotChld [*]

If coded 1 or 2 at MoreChld or 1 at ProbMore

(Can I just check, you have.... children still alive). How many children do you think you will have born to you in all [including those you have had already (who are still alive) (and the one you are expecting)]?

1..14　→　Q49

49 NextAge [*]

How old do you think you will be when you have your first/next baby (after the one you are expecting)?

1..97　→ Income

INCOME

IncomSec

THE FINAL SECTION IS ABOUT INCOME

This is a topic that affects all the other areas we've been talking about. We're interested in income from benefit, employment and investments.

1 StatBenE

All adults (except proxy informants)

SHOW CARD AA

Would you please look at this card and tell me whether you are receiving any of the state benefits listed on it?

INCLUDE ET, TRAINING FOR WORK AND EA ALLOWANCE

NB: USE CODE 7 ONLY IF INFORMANT REFUSES ALL INCOME QUESTIONS

Yes receiving benefits - code at next
  question. .... 1 → Q2
No, not receiving any .... 2 → Q4
Refused whole income section .... 7 → Q60

2 StatBnM

If 'yes' (code 1) at StatBenE

SHOW CARD AA: RECORD BENEFITS RECEIVED

CODE ALL THAT APPLY
(Enter at most 5 codes)

Child benefit (including one parent
  benefit) .... 1 ⎤
Income support .... 2 ⎥
NI retirement pension or old age
  pension .... 3 ⎥
Unemployment benefit .... 4 ⎥ → Q3
NI Incapacity benefit,NI sickness
  benefit, or Invalidity benefit .... 5 ⎥
Disability living allowance .... 6 ⎥
Severe disablement allowance .... 7 ⎥
Job Seeker's Allowance .... 8 ⎦

3 StatBnAm

In total how much do you receive from these benefits per week?

0.01..999.97　→　Q4

4 CardBenE

All (except proxy informants)

SHOW CARD BB

Here is a second card on benefits. Are you receiving any of the benefits listed on this card?

EXCLUDE HOUSING BENEFIT

Yes receiving benefits - code at next
  question .... 1 → Q5
No, not receiving any .... 2 → Q8

5 CardBnM

If 'yes' (code 1) at CardBenE

SHOW CARD BB

Record benefits received.

CODE ALL THAT APPLY
(Enter at most 5 codes)

Family credit .... 1 ⎤
Widow's pension or war widow's
  pension .... 2 ⎥ → Q7
Any other state widow's benefits (eg
  widowed mother's allowance) ... 3 ⎦

	War disablement pension	4 ⌉	
	Industrial disablement pension	5	
	Attendance allowance	6	- Q7
	Invalid care allowance	7	
	Disability working allowance	8 ⌋	
	Any other type of benefit (SPECIFY AT NEXT QUESTION)	9	- Q6

6 XCrdBnM   Specify type of benefit.   - Q7

7 CardBnAm   In total how much do you receive from these benefits per week?

0.01..999.97   - Q8

8 OthSourc   **All (except proxy informants)**

SHOW CARD CC

Would you please look at this card and tell me whether you are receiving any regular payment of the kinds listed on it?

Yes, receiving benefits - code at next
question 1   - Q9
No, not receiving any 2   - Q12

9 OthSrcM   **If 'yes' (code 1) at OthSourc**

SHOW CARD CC: RECORD PAYMENTS RECEIVED

CODE ALL THAT APPLY
(Enter at most 4 codes)

Occupational pensions from former
  employer(s) .... 1 ⌉
Occupational pensions from a
  spouse's former employer(s) 2
Private pensions or annuities 3   - Q10
Regular redundancy payments from
  former employer(s) 4
Government Training Schemes, YT
  allowance on course .... 5 ⌋

10 OthNetAm   In total how much do you receive each month from all these sources AFTER tax is deducted? (ie NET)

DO NOT PROBE MONTH. ACCEPT CALEN-DAR MONTH OR 4 WEEKLY.

0.01..99999.97   - Q11

11 OthGrsAm   In total how much do you receive each month from all these sources before tax is deducted? (ie GROSS)

DO NOT PROBE MONTH. ACCEPT CALEN-DAR MONTH OR 4 WEEKLY.

0.01..99999.97   - Q12

12 ReglrPay   **All (except proxy informants)**

SHOW CARD DD

Now would you look at this card and tell me whether you are receiving any regular payments of the kind listed on it?

Yes receiving benefits - code at next
question 1   - Q13
No, not receiving any. 2   - Q15

13 ReglrPM   **If 'yes' (code 1) at ReglrPay**

SHOW CARD DD: RECORD TYPES OF PAYMENT RECEIVED

CODE ALL THAT APPLY

Educational grant .... 1 ⌉
Regular payments from friends or
  relatives outside the household .. 2   - Q14
Rent from property or subletting... 3
Maintenance, alimony or separation
  allowance .... 4 ⌋

14 ReglrpAm   In total how much do you receive from these each month?

0.01..99999.97   - Q15

15 PyPeriod   **If Employed, else**   - Q28

How long a period does your wage/salary usually cover?

One week .... 1 ⌉
Two weeks 2
Three weeks 3
Four weeks 4
Calendar month 5   - Q16
Three months 6
Six months 7
One year 8
Other period (SPECIFY) .... 9 ⌋
Family worker -no pay received ... 10   - See Q37

16 TakeHome   **If coded 1-9 at PyPeriod**

How much is your usual take home pay per [period at PyPeriod] after all deductions?

0.00..99999.97   - See Q17

17 TakHmEst   **If DK at TakeHome, else**   - Q18

SHOW CARD EE

Would you look at this card and estimate your usual take home pay per [period at PyPeriod] after all deductions.

1..30   - Q18

18 PayeAm   **If coded 1-9 at PyPeriod**

How much is usually deducted for income tax and National Insurance per [period at PyPeriod]?

0.00..99999.97   - See Q19

19 PayeEst   **If DK at PayeAm**

SHOW CARD EE

Would you look at this card and estimate how much is usually deducted for income tax and National Insurance?

1..30   - Q20

291

20 GrossAm

If coded 1-9 at PyPeriod

How much are your usual gross earnings per [period at PyPeriod] before any deductions?

0.01..99999.97 → See Q21

21 GrossEst

If DK at GrossAm, else → Q22

SHOW CARD EE

Would you look at this card and estimate your usual gross earnings per [period at PyPeriod] before any deductions?

1..30 → Q22

22 PaySlip

If coded 1-9 at PyPeriod

INTERVIEWER - CODE WHETHER PAYSLIP WAS CONSULTED.

Pay slip consulted .... 1 → Q23
Pay slip not consulted .... 2 → Q24

23 IntPySlp

If Code 1 at PaySlip

WAS PAY SLIP CONSULTED BY INTER-VIEWER?

Yes .... 1 ⎤
No.. 2 ⎦ → Q24

24 PayBonus

All employees except Unpaid Family Workers (PyPeriod NOT 10)

In your present job, have you received an occasional addition to pay in the last 12 months, that is since [DATE ONE YEAR AGO] such as a Christmas bonus or a quarterly bonus?

EXCLUDE SHARES AND VOUCHERS

Yes .... 1 → Q25
No.. 2 → See Q37

25 HowBonus

If 'yes' at PayBonus

Was the bonus or commission paid....

RUNNING PROMPT

after tax was deducted (net). .... 1 → Q26
or before tax was deducted
   (gross) .... 2 → Q27
or some before and some after?. . 3 → Q26

26 NetBonus

If coded 1 or 3 or DK at HowBonus

What was the total amount you received in the last 12 months after tax was deducted (ie net)?
0.01..99999.97 → See Q27

27 GrsBonus

If coded 2 or 3 at HowBonus
What was the total amount you received in the last 12 months before tax was deducted (ie gross)?

0.01..99999.97 → See Q37

28 LongSelf

If Self-employed less than 12 months (Stat = 2 AND Jobtime = 1 to 4), else → Q33

How long have you been self-employed?

ENTER MONTHS 1..11 → Q29

29 GrsPrLTY

How much did you earn before tax but after deductions of any expenses and wages since becoming self-employed?

IF NOTHING OR MADE A LOSS, ENTER ZERO
0.00..999999.97 → Q30

30 PrLTYEst

SHOW CARD EE

Would you look at this card and estimate the amount that you expect to earn before tax but after deductions of any expenses and wages in the first full 12 months that you will have been self-employed, that is up to the end of (month) next?
0..30 → Q31

31 SInsLTY

Do you pay a National Insurance contribution?

Yes .... 1 → Q32
No.. 2 → See Q37

32 SIAmLTY

If 'yes' (code 1) at SinsLTY

How much National Insurance contribution have you paid in the ....months that you have been self-employed?
0.01..9999.97 → See Q37

33 GrsPrft

If Self-employed 12 months or more (STAT = 2 AND JobTime>4 or DK)

How much did you earn in the last tax year, before tax but after deduction of any expenses or wages?

IF NOTHING OR MADE A LOSS, ENTER ZERO
0.00..999999.97 → See Q34

34 PrftEst

If DK at GrsPrft

SHOW CARD EE

Would you look at this card and estimate the amount that you earned in the last tax year, before tax but after the deduction of any expenses or wages?
0..30 → Q35

35 SENatIns

Do you pay a National Insurance contribution?

Yes .... 1 → Q36
No.. 2 → See Q37

36 SENatAm

If 'yes' (code 1) at SENatIns

How much National Insurance have you paid in the last 12 months (that is since...), relating to your self-employment?
0.01..9999.97 → See Q37

37 SecJob2

If no mention of Second Job previously (SecndJob NOT 1), else   .   Q44

Do you earn any money (from a second job), from odd jobs or from work that you do from time to time (apart from your main job)?

PROMPT AS NECESSARY & INCLUDE BABYSITTING, MAIL ORDER AGENT, POOLS AGENT, ETC

Yes .... 1 . Q38
No .... 2 . Q44

38 SjReg

If has Second Job (SecJob2 or SecndJob = 1)

(You told me that you had a second job last week)

Is that a job you do:

regularly each week .... 1 ⎤ . Q40
or from time to time? .... 2 ⎦
or other (SPECIFY AT NEXT
   QUESTION) .... 3 . Q39

39 XSjReg

Please specify.

(Enter text of at most 40 characters)   .   Q40

40 SjEmplee

In that job do you work as an employee or are you self-employed?

employee .... 1 . See Q41
self-employed .... 2 . See Q43

41 SjNetAm

If Employee in second job regularly each week (SjReg = 1 AND SjEmplee = 1)

In the last month, how much did you earn from your second/occasional job(s) after deductions for tax and National Insurance (ie net)?
              0.01..99999.97   .   Q42

42 SjGrsAm

In the last month, how much did you earn from your second/occasional job(s) before deductions for tax and National Insurance (ie gross)?
              0.01..99999.97   .   Q44

43 SjPrfGrs

If Self-employed, or employee in second job but NOT regularly each week (NOT (SjReg = 1 AND SjEmplee = 1))

In the last 12 months, that is, since [DATE ONE YEAR AGO] how much have you earned from this work, before deducting income tax, and National Insurance contributions, (and money drawn for your own use but after deducting all business expenses)?

IF MADE NO PROFIT ENTER 0
              0.00..99999.97   .   Q44

44 IncTax

Ask All (except proxy informants)

During the last 12 months, that is, since [DATE ONE YEAR AGO] have you paid any tax direct to the Inland Revenue?

Yes .... 1 . Q45
No .... 2 . Q46

45 IncTaxAm

If 'yes' (code 1) at IncTax

How much income tax did you pay direct to the Inland Revenue?
              0.01..99999.97   .   Q46

46 PEP

Adults aged 18 or over (except proxy informants)

There is a scheme called a Personal Equity Plan or PEP which gives people tax relief if they invest in shares or unit trusts. Do you have a personal equity plan at present?

Yes .... 1 . Q47
No .... 2 . Q49

47 PepTypm

If 'yes' (code 1) at PEP

Is this...

RUNNING PROMPT

CODE ALL THAT APPLY
(Enter at most 3 codes)

a Unit Trust only plan .... 1 ⎤ . Q49
a Single Company plan .... 2 ⎦
or some other type of plan? (SPECIFY
   AT NEXT QUESTION) .... 3 . Q48

48 XPepTyp

Specify type of PEP

(Enter text of at most 20 characters)   .   Q49

49 Accounts

All (except proxy informants)

SHOW CARD FF

Do you currently have an account or investments or have you had an account or investments during the last 12 months, such as those listed on this card?

Yes .... 1 . Q50
No .... 2 . Q56

50 AccTypM

If 'yes' (code 1) at Accounts

SHOW CARD FF

Which of these types of accounts or investments do you have?

CODE ALL THAT APPLY
(Enter at most 11 codes)

Bank Account .... 1 ⎤
Building Society Account 2
Post Office Savings Account 3
National Savings Bonds 4
National Savings Certificates. 5   . Q52
TESSAs. 6
Government gilt-edged stock 7
Bonds, debentures
  (exc. premium bonds) 8
Dividends from shares 9
Dividends from unit trusts .... 10 ⎦
Other (specify at next question) ... 11 . Q51

51 XAccTyp | Specify type of account or investment.

(Enter text of at most 30 characters)   .   Q52

InVInt | THE NEXT SCREEN CONSISTS OF A TABLE OF THE ACCOUNTS & INVESTMENTS OF (...).

52 IntDiv | **For each investment**

Have you received or been credited with any interest (or dividends) on this investment/account in the last 12 months (that is since...)?

Yes .... 1 → Q53
No .... 2 → Q56

53 IntDivNG | **If 'yes' (code 1) at IntDiv**

Was the interest or dividend on this account/ investment paid gross or net of income tax?

Gross .... 1 ⎤
Net .... 2 ⎦ → Q54

54 IntDivAm | How much interest did you yourself receive or were you credited with in the last 12 months (that is since...)?

IF A JOINT ACCOUNT DIVIDE THE INTEREST BETWEEN THE TWO PARTIES
      0.01..99999.97 → See Q55

55 IntDvEst | **If DK amount**
INTERVIEWER - IF INFORMANT DOES NOT KNOW AMOUNT, SHOW CARD GG AND ASK THEM TO ESTIMATE
      1..10 → Q56

56 OthRgPay | **All (except proxy informants)**

And finally, apart from anything you have already mentioned, are you receiving any regular payment from any other organisation or source in the last 12 months (that is since...)?

SPECIFY DETAILS AT NEXT QUESTION

EXCLUDE BENEFITS NO LONGER RECEIVED

Yes .... 1 → Q57
No .... 2 → Q60

57 OthRgPy | **If 'yes' (code 1) at OthRgPay**

Specify details of other regular payments since ...

(Enter text of at most 60 characters)   .   Q58

58 XOthRgPAm | How much have you received in the last 12 months?
      0.01..99999.97 → Q60

59 NtIncEst | **If Proxy informant**

I would now like to ask you about the income of (...) Please could you look at this card and estimate the total net income, that is after deduction of tax, National Insurance and any expenses (...) brings into the household in a year from all sources (benefits, employment, investments etc.).

ENTER CODE FROM CARD EE
      1..30

60 FollowUp | **All (except proxy informants)**

If we want to contact you about any future survey, would it be all right if we called on you again?

Yes, it would be all right
(UNCONDITIONAL 1
No, (UNCONDITIONAL) 2
Yes, (WITH CONDITIONS/
QUALIFICATIONS: SPECIFY
AT NEXT QUESTION .... 3 → Q61

61 XFollowUp | State the conditions.

(Enter text of at most 100 characters)

END OF INDIVIDUAL QUESTIONNAIRE

Appendix E
Summary of main topics included in the GHS questionnaires 1971 to 1996

ACTIVITIES ON SCHOOL PREMISES

Whether attended any event/activity
on school premises in last 12 months

Whether activities organised by school or
parent teacher's association

Type of activity attended (if not organised
by school/parent teacher's association),
number of times attended and whether
attended a day or evening class

BURGLARIES AND THEFTS FROM PRIVATE HOUSEHOLDS

Incidence of burglaries in the
12 months before interview — **1972-73,**

Value of stolen goods and whether — **1979-80,**
insured — **1985-86,**

Whether incident was reported — **1991, 1993, 1996**
to the police

Reasons for not reporting to the police — **1972-73,
1979-80, 1985-86**

Incidence of attempted burglary in the — **1985-86**
12 months before interview

BUS TRAVEL — 1982

Frequency of use of buses in the six months
before interview

Physical and other difficulties using buses

Reasons for not using buses

CAREER OPPORTUNITIES — 1972

Attitudes towards careers in the Armed Forces
and the Police Force

Whether ever been in one of the Armed Forces

CAR OWNERSHIP

Number of cars or vans, if any, available to the
household for private use — **1971-96**

In whose name (person or firm) each car/van
was registered — **1980, 1992-93**

Driving licences and private motoring — 1980

Whether held current licence for driving a car
or van, and for how long full licence held

Whether non-licence holders (aged 17-70) intended
to apply for a licence (again), and reasons for
not having done so or for not intending to do so

1984 Frequency of use, for private motoring, of
car/van available to the household

If household car/van not available, or not used for
private motoring in the year before interview:
- whether used any car/van for private motoring in
that year
- whether drove a car, van, lorry, or bus in the
course of work in that year

COLOUR AND COUNTRY OF BIRTH

Colour, assessment of persons seen* — **1971-92**

Country of birth
of adults and their parents — **1971-96**
of children — **1979-96**

Year of entry to UK
adults — **1971-96**
children — **1979-96**

Ethnic origin — **1983-96**

DRINKING

Rating of drinking behaviour according to
quantity - frequency (QF) index based
on reported alcohol consumption in the — **1978, 1980,**
12 months before interview — **1982, 1984**

Rating of drinking behaviour according — **1986, 1988, 1990,**
to alcohol consumption (AC) rating — **1992, 1994, 1996**

Personal rating of own drinking — **1978, 1980, 1982**
behaviour — **1984, 1986, 1988, 1990, 1992, 1994, 1996**

Whether think drinking/smoking — **1978, 1980, 1982,**
can damage health — **1984, 1986, 1988, 1990**

Whether non-drinkers have always been
non-drinkers or used to drink but — **1992, 1994,**
stopped, and reasons — **1996**

Whether drink more or less than the
recommended sensible amount

EDUCATION

Current education

Current education status — **1971-96**

Type of educational establishment currently attended
- by adults aged under 50 — **1971-81, 1984-90**
- by adults aged under 70 — **1991-96**
- by children aged 5-15 — **1971-77**

* *Including children*

295

Qualification/examination aimed at	**1971, 1974-76**

Expected date of completion of full-time
   education
Whether intend to do any paid work while   **1971-76**
   still in full-time education, and if so when

Whether currently attending any leisure or
   recreation classes   **1973-78, 1981, 1983, 1993-96**

Past education
Age on leaving school   **1972-96**
Age on leaving last place of full-time education
Type of educational establishment last attended
   full time   **1971-96**
Qualifications obtained

Pre-school children (aged under 5)
Whether currently attending nursery/primary school,
   day nursery, playgroup, creche etc   **1971-79, 1986**
Frequency of attendance   **1979, 1986**

Whether received regular day care from person
   other than parents, and for how many hours
   per week
Whether working mothers would have to stop   **1979**
   work if existing arrangements for the care of
   their children were no longer available, or
   whether they could make other care
   arrangements

Child care (for children aged 0-11)   **1991**
Whether uses any child care arrangements
Frequency of use and cost
Whether employer contributes towards cost,
   and if so, the amount

Job training
Whether currently doing a trade apprenticeship   **1971-84**

Identification of persons seriously thinking of
   taking a course of training or education for a
   particular type of job, with some details of
   the course and the source of any financial
   support   **1973-74**

Students in institutional accommodation   **1981-87**
Estimate of numbers of full-time students at
   university or college living away from home in
   institutional accommodation, and therefore
   excluded from the GHS sample

EMPLOYMENT
Those currently working
Main job - occupation and industry
       - employee/self employed   **1971-96**
Subsidiary - occupation and industry   **1971-78, 1980-84**
   job   - employee/self employed   **1987-91**

Last job   - occupation and industry   **1986**
       - employee/self employed
Whether present job was obtained through
   a government scheme   **1989-92**

Youth Opportunities Programme Schemes   **1982-84**
- identification of young persons aged 16-18
   receiving training or work experience through
   the Youth Opportunities Programme or Youth
   Training Scheme

Youth Training Scheme   **1985-95**
- identification of young persons aged 16-19
   who were on the YTS and whether they were
   working with an employer or at college or
   training school

Journey time to work   **1971-76, 1978**

Usual number of hours worked per week
   (excluding overtime)   **1971-96**
Hours of paid/unpaid overtime usually
   worked per week   **1973-83**

Usual number of days worked per week   **1973, 1979-84**
Number of days worked in reference week   **1977-78**

Length of time with present employer/present
   spell of self-employment   **1971-96**

Whether self-employed during the previous
   12 months   **1986-91**

Number of changes of employer in
   12 months before interview   **1971-76, 1979-91**

Number of new employee jobs started
   in 12 months before interview   **1977-78, 1983-91**

Source of hearing about present job
   started in 12 months before interview   **1971-77, 1980-84**
Source of hearing about all jobs started
   in 12 months before interview   **1974-77, 1980-84**

Whether paid by employer when sick   **1971-76, 1979-81**

296

Whether employer is in the public/private
  sector   **1983, 1985, 1987**

Trade Union and Staff Association membership   **1983**

Whether people work all or part of the time at home,
  reasons for doing so, whether employer makes any
  financial contribution to expenses of working at
  home, equipment provided by employer   **1993**

Whether does any unpaid work for members of the
  family and if so, for whom, number of hours a
  week, type of work and where   **1993-95**

Whether has ever been a company director   **1987**

Type of National Insurance contribution paid by:
- married and widowed women
    aged 16 or over   **1972-79**
    aged 16-59   **1980**
- married, widowed, and separated women
    aged 16-59   **1981-82**
    aged 20-59   **1983**

Level of satisfaction with present job as a whole **1971-83**
Level of satisfaction with specific aspects of
  present job   **1974-83**
Whether thinking of leaving present employer, and
  if so why   **1971-76**

Whether signed on at an Unemployment
  Benefit Office in the reference week, either
  to claim benefit or to receive National
  Insurance credits   **1984-90, 1994-96**

Absence from work in the reference week
- reasons for absence   **1971-72, 1974-84**
- length of period of absence   **1971-72,1974-80, 1984**
- number of working days off last week   **1981-84**
- whether absent because of illness or
  accident, and length of absence   **1973**
- whether in receipt of National Insurance
  sickness benefit (and supplementary
  allowance) for the absence   **1971-76**

Sickness absence in the four weeks before
  interview   **1981-84**
Sickness absence in the 3 months before interview **1992**
Whether registered as unemployed in the reference
  week (if had worked less than full week)   **1977-82**

Unemployment experience in 12 months
  before interview   **1975-77, 1983-84**

Economic activity status 12 months before
  interview and, if economically inactive then,
  reasons for (re-)entering the labour force   **1979-81**

Economic activity status 12 months before
  interview, including whether a full-time student
  and working   **1982-91**

Whether in employment prior to present job,   **1986**
  and if so
    - whether that job was full/part time
    - reasons for leaving

Whether on any government schemes   **1985-96**

Usual job of father
- of all persons aged 16 or over   **1971-76**
- of persons aged 16-49 in full-time or part-
  time education   **1977-78**
- of all persons aged 16-49   **1979-89**
- of all persons aged 16-59   **1989-92**

Those currently unemployed
Most recent job - occupation and industry   **1971-96**
                 - employee/self-employed

Whether most recent job was obtained through
  a government scheme   **1989-92**
Whether has ever had a paid job   **1986-96**
Whether has ever worked for an employer
  as part of a government scheme   **1989-91**
Whether registered as unemployed in the
  reference week   **1971-83**
Methods of seeking work in the reference week

Whether signed on at an Unemployment
  Benefit Office in the reference week, either
  to claim benefit or to receive National
  Insurance credits   **1984-90, 1994-96**

Whether looking for full or part-time work   **1983**

Whether taking part in either the Youth Training
  Scheme or the Youth Opportunities Programme
  last week   **1984**

Whether last job was organised through the Youth
  Opportunities Programme (persons aged 16-19)   **1982**

297

For those who in the reference week were looking
    for work
- would they have been able to start within
    2 weeks if a job had been available   **1991-96**

For those who in the reference week were waiting
    to take up a new job already obtained:
    - would they have started that job in the
      reference week if it had been available then,
      or would they have chosen to wait   **1977-82**
    - when was the new job obtained and when did
      they expect to start it   **1979**

Whether paid unemployment benefit (and
    supplementary allowance) for reference week   **1971-74**

When last worked and reasons for
    stopping work   **1971-73, 1974-79, 1986**
Reasons for leaving last job   **1981-82, 1986**
Whether last job was full/part time   **1986**
Length of current spell of unemployment   **1974-96**
Unemployment experience in 12 months
    before interview   **1975-77, 1983-84**

Economic activity status 12 months before
    interview and, if economically inactive then,
    reasons for (re-)entering the labour force   **1979-81**

Economic activity status 12 months before
    interview, including whether a full-time
    student and working   **1982-91**

Number of new employee jobs started in
    12 months before interview   **1977, 1982-91**
Source of hearing about all jobs started in
    12 months before interview   **1982-84**

Whether on any government schemes   **1985-96**

Whether does any unpaid work for members of the
    family and if so, for whom, number of hours a
    week, type of work and where   **1993-96**

Whether has ever been a company director   **1987**

Type of National Insurance contribution paid in the
    preceding two completed tax years by:
    - married, widowed, and separated women
      aged 20-59, who were not working
      in the week before interview   **1982-83**

Usual job of father
- of all persons aged 16 or over   **1971-76**
- of persons aged 16-49 in full-time or part-
   time education   **1977-78**
- of all persons aged 16-49   **1979-88**
- of all persons aged 16-59   **1989-92**

The economically inactive
Major activity in the reference week
Last job - occupation and industry   **1971-96**
       - employee/self-employed

Usual job (of retired persons)
- occupation and industry   **1973-76, 1979-88**
- employee/self-employed

When finished last job   **1971-73, 1977-78, 1986**
Reasons for stopping work   **1971-73, 1978-82, 1986**

Whether registered as unemployed in the
    reference week   **1972-83**
Whether signed on at an Unemployment
    Benefit Office in the reference week, either
    to claim benefit or to receive National
    Insurance credits   **1984-90, 1994-96**
Whether paid unemployment benefit (and
    supplementary allowance) for reference week   **1972-74**

Whether would like a regular paid job, whether
    looking for work, and if a job had been
    available would they have been able to start
    within 2 weeks   **1991-96**
Length of time currently out of employment   **1993-96**

Main reason for not looking for work   **1986-87**
Whether would like regular paid job   **1986-87**
Whether has ever had a paid job   **1986-96**
Whether has had a paid job in last 12 months   **1987-91**
Whether has ever worked for an employer as
    part of a government scheme   **1989-91**
Whether has had a paid job in previous 3 years   **1986**
Whether last job was full/part time   **1986**

Unemployment experience in 12 months   **1975-77,**
    before interview   **1983-84**

Economic activity status 12 months before
    interview (persons aged 16-69)   **1980-81**

Economic activity status 12 months before
    interview including whether a full-time
    student and working   **1982-91**

Number of new employee jobs started in 12 months before interview	**1977, 1984-91**
Source of hearing about all jobs started in 12 months before interview	**1977**
Whether on any government schemes	**1985-96**
Whether does any unpaid work for members of the family and if so, for whom, number of hours a week, type of work and where	**1993-96**
Whether has ever been a company director	**1987**

Type of National Insurance contribution paid in the preceding two completed tax years by:
- married, widowed, and separated women aged 20-59, who were not working in the week before interview   **1982**

Future work intentions, including whether would seek work earlier if satisfactory arrangements could be made for looking after children   **1971-76**

Usual job of father
- of all persons aged 16 or over   **1971-76**
- of persons aged 16-49 in full-time or part-time education   **1977-78**
- of all persons aged 16-49   **1979-88**
- of all persons aged 16-59   **1989-92**

FAMILY INFORMATION/FERTILITY
Marriage, cohabitation and childbirth

Marital history	**1979-96**
Date of present marriage	**1971-78**
Whether first marriage	**1974-78**

Expected family size:
     at time of present marriage
     at time of interview
Whether woman thinks she has completed her family
Age when most recent baby was born   **1971-78**
Age when expects to have last baby
Date of birth and sex of each child born in present marriage

Date of birth and sex of all liveborn children and whether they live with mother	**1979-96**
Where children under 16, not living with mother, are currently living	**1979**
Where children under 19, not living with mother, are currently living	**1982**

Date of birth of step, foster, and adopted children living in the household, and how long they have lived there	**1979-87, 1989-96**
Whether women think they will have any (more) children, how many in all, and age at which they think will have their first/ next baby	**1979-96**
Current cohabitation	**1979-96**
Cohabitation before current or most recent marriage	**1979, 1981-88**
Cohabitation before all marriages	**1989-96**

Contraception and sterilisation

Whether woman/partner has been sterilised for contraceptive reason	**1983-84**
Details of sterilisation operations	**1986-87**
Whether woman/partner has had other sterilising operation	**1989,1991,1993, 1995**
Details of any reversal of sterilisation operations	**1983-84, 1986-87**
Current use of contraception/reason for not using contraception	**1983, 1986, 1989, 1991, 1993, 1995**
Previous usual method of contraception	**1989, 1991, 1993, 1995**
Use of contraception in the previous 12 months	**1989**
Use of contraception in previous 2 years	**1991, 1993, 1995**
Use of emergency contraception in previous 2 years	**1993, 1995**
Whether woman/partner would have difficulties in having (more) children Reasons for difficulties and whether consulted a doctor about difficulties in getting pregnant	**1983-84 1986-87, 1989 1991,1993, 1995**

FORESTS

Whether ever visits forests or woodland areas, facilities visitors would like to see there	**1987**

HEALTH
Chronic sickness (long-standing illness or disability)

Prevalence of long-standing illness or disability*	**1971-76, 1979-96**
Causes of the illness or disability*	**1971-75**
When the illness or disability started*	**1971**
Type of illness or disability	**1988-89, 1994-96**

Including children

Prevalence of limiting long-standing
   illness or disability*   **1972-76, 1979-96**

When it started to limit activities and whether
   housebound or bedfast because of it*   **1972-76**

**Acute sickness (restricted activity in a two-
week reference period)**
Prevalence and duration of restricted
   activity*   **1971-76, 1979-96**

Causes of restricted activity*   **1971-75**
Number of days in bed and number of days of
   (certificated) absence from work/school*   **1971-76**
Help from people outside household with
   housework or shopping   **1971-74**

**Health in general in the 12 months before
interview**   **1977-96**

Chronic health problems   **1977-78**
Prevalence of chronic health problems
Constant effects of chronic health problems
   (eg taking things easy, using prescribed/non-
   prescribed medication, watching diet, taking
   account of weather)

Contact with health services in 12 months before
   interview because of chronic health problems

Effect of chronic health problems in the 14 days
   before interview (eg resting more than usual,
   using prescribed/non-prescribed medication,
   changing eating or drinking habits, cutting
   down on activities, consulting GP, seeking
   advice from other persons)

**Short-term health problems (in the 14 days
before interview)**   **1977-78**
Prevalence of short-term health problems
Effects of short-term health problems in the 14
   days before interview

GP consultations
Consultations in the two weeks before interview:
   number of consultations*
   NHS or private*
   type of doctor*   **1971-96**
   site of consultation*

   cause of consultation*   **1971-75**

whether consulted because something was the
   matter, or for some other reason*   **1981**

whether consultation about reported long-   **1983-84,**
   standing illness or restricted activity*   **1986-87**

whether was given a prescription*   **1981-96**
whether was referred to hospital*   **1981-85, 1988-90**
whether was given National Insurance   **1981-85**
   medical certificate

Access to GPs: **1977**
   whether own doctor worked alone or with other
   doctors
   whether could usually see doctor of own
   choice at surgery
   most recent consultation at surgery:
   - when it took place
   - NHS or private
   - by appointment or not
   - how far ahead appointment made
   - time spent waiting at surgery
   - attitudes towards waiting time for
      appointment, waiting time at surgery, and
      length of consultation

Outpatient (OP) attendances
Attendances at hospital OP departments in a three-
   month reference period:
      number of attendances*   **1971-96**
      NHS or private   **1973-76, 1982-83, 1985-87, 1995-96**
      nature of complaint causing attendance*   **1974-76**
      whether claimed for under private
      medical insurance   **1982-83, 1987, 1995**
      number of casualty visits*   **1995-96**

Appointments with OP departments: **1973-76**
   whether had (or was waiting for) an
   appointment* how long ago since told
   appointment would be made*

Day patient visits
Number of separate days in hospital as a
   day patient in the last year*   **1992-96**
   whether NHS or private   **1995-96**

Inpatient spells
Spells in hospital as an inpatient in a three-
   month reference period:
      number and length of spells*   **1971-76**
      NHS or private patient*   **1973-75**

* Including children

Stays in hospital as an inpatient in a 12-month
   reference period:

number of stays*	**1982-96**
number of nights on each stay*	**1992-96**
NHS or private patient	**1982-83, 1985-87, 1995-96**
whether claimed for under private	
medical insurance	**1982-83, 1987**

Whether on waiting list for admission to
   hospital and length of time on list*   **1973-76**

Mobility aids   **1993, 1996**

Whether has any difficulty getting about without
   assistance, and if so, what help is needed,
   whether the problem is temporary or
   permanent, the number and types of walking
   aids, and who supplied them

Accidents   **1987-89**

Accidents in the three-month reference period
   that resulted in seeing a GP or going to a hospital:
      whether saw GP or went to hospital or did both
         and in the last case, which first*
      type of accident and where occurred*
      whether occurred during sport*
      whether occurred during working hours*
      time off work as a result of accident
      whether went to hospital A & E Department
         (Casualty) or other part of hospital*
      whether stayed in hospital overnight as a
         result of accident, and if so how many nights*

Accidents at home   **1981, 1984**

Accidents at home, in a three-month reference period,
   that resulted in seeing a GP or going to hospital:
      whether saw GP or went to hospital or did both
         and, in the last case, which first*
      whether went to hospital A & E Department
         (Casualty) or other part of hospital*

Health and personal social services

Use of various services:

- by adults and children	**1971-76**
- by persons aged 60 or over	**1979**
- by persons aged 65 or over	**1980-85, 1991,1994**

Elderly persons

Whether any relatives living nearby:

- persons aged 60 or over	**1979-80**
- persons aged 65 or over	**1994**

Persons aged 65 or over:

- whether need help in getting about	**1980, 1985.**
inside the house and outside, and	**1991, 1994,**
with a range of personal and	**1996**
household tasks	
- if help is needed, who usually helps	**1980, 1985**
- frequency of social contacts with	**1991, 1994**
relatives and friends	

Informal carers   **1985, 1990, 1995**

Whether looks after a sick, handicapped or elderly
   person in same or other household, nature of care
   provided and time spent, whether help received
   from other people or statutory services

Reasons for not receiving help from statutory	
services	**1995**
Whether dependent receives respite care	**1995**

Informal carers aged 8-17   **1996**

- whether looks after a sick, handicapped or
   elderly person in the same household, nature of
   care provided and time spent, whether help
   received from other people or statutory services

Sight and hearing

Difficulty with sight and whether wears glasses
   or contact lenses:

- persons aged 16 or over	**1977-79, 1981-82**
- persons aged 65 or over	**1980, 1985, 1987, 1991, 1994**

Whether wears glasses or contact lenses*	
Whether obtained new glasses in previous	**1987,**
12 months and number of pairs*	**1990-1994**
Whether had a sight test in previous	
12 months*	
Whether sight test was NHS or private	**1990-94**
Whether sight test was paid for by informant	
or employer, provided free by optician, or	
covered by insurance	**1991-94**
Whether obtained any ready made reading	
glasses in the previous 12 months	**1992-94**

Types of contact lens worn, and whether	
obtained through NHS or privately	
Reasons for trying contact lenses	**1982**
Reasons stopped wearing contact lenses	
Care of contact lenses	

* *Including children*

Difficulty with hearing and whether wears an aid:
- persons aged 16 or over   **1977-79, 1981, 1992, 1995**
- persons aged 65 or over   **1980, 1985, 1991, 1994**

Types of hearing aid worn, and whether
    obtained through NHS or privately   **1979**
Reasons for not wearing an aid   **1979, 1992, 1995**
Whether hearing aid was obtained through NHS
    or bought privately, and if bought privately,
    the reason(s)   **1992, 1995**

Tinnitus (sensation of noise in the ears or head)
Prevalence of tinnitus, frequency and duration of
    symptoms, whether ever consulted a doctor
    about it   **1981**

Dental health
Whether has any natural teeth   **1983, 1985, 1987,**
    1989, 1991, 1993, 1995

To those aged under 18, how long ago since
    last visit to the dentist, and whether registered
    with a dentist*   **1993, 1995**
How long ago since last visit to the dentist*
Treatment received*   **1983**

Whether goes to the dentist for check-ups,   **1983, 1985,**
    or only when having trouble with teeth*   **1987, 1989,**
    1991, 1993, 1995

Medicine-taking   **4th qtr.1972, 1973**
Medicines taken in the seven days before
    interview:
- categories of medicine
- patterns of consumption of analgesics

Private medical insurance   **1982-83, 1986-87, 1995**
Whether covered by private medical insurance
    and, if so:
- whether policy holder or dependant on
      someone else's policy*
- whether subscription paid by employer

Whether covered by private medical
    insurance in the last 12 months   **1987**
Whether company director's private medical
    insurance subscription is paid for by the
    company of which he is a director   **1987, 1995**

HOUSEHOLD COMPOSITION
Age*, sex*, marital status of household
    members   **1971-96**
Relationship to head of household*
Family unit(s)
Housewife   **1971-80**

HOUSING (see also MIGRATION)
Present accommodation: amenities
Length of residence at present address*
Age of building
Type of accommodation   **1971-96**
Number of rooms and number of bedrooms
Whether have separate kitchen
Bath/WC: sole use, shared, none   **1971-90**
WC: inside or outside the accommodation

Installation/replacement of bath or WC
Cost of improvements made to the   **1971-76**
    accommodation

Floor level of main accommodation   **1973-96**
Whether there is a lift

Tenure
Whether present home is owned or rented   **1971-96**
Whether in co-ownership housing association
    scheme   **1981-95**

Change of tenure on divorce or remarriage   **1991-93**

Housing history of local authority tenants and
    owner occupiers who had become owners in
    the previous five years   **1985-86**

Whether ever rented from a local authority,
    and if so, whether bought that accommodation,
    source of finance, whether have since moved
    and distance moved   **1991-93**

Owner occupiers:
- in whose name the property is owned   **1978-96**
- whether property is owned outright or being
      bought with a mortgage or loan   **1971-96**
- how outright owners originally acquired
      their home   **1978-80, 1982-83, 1985-86**
- source of mortgage or loan   **1978-80, 1982-86, 1992-93**
- whether currently using present home as
      security for a (second) mortgage or loan
      of any kind, and if so, details   **1980-82, 1992-93**

* Including children

- whether owner occupiers with a mortgage
  have taken out a remortgage on their
  present home, and if so, details   **1985-87, 1992-93**
- whether recent owner occupiers had previously
  rented this accommodation and, if so,
  from whom and for how long   **1981-82, 1985-86**
- whether had rented present accommodation
  before deciding to buy   **1992-93**
- whether previous accommodation was owned
  and if so, details of the sale   **1992-93**

Renters:
- from whom the accommodation is rented   **1971-96**
- whether landlord lives in the same
  building   **1971-72, 1975-76, 1979-96**
- whether have considered buying present
  home and, if not why not   **1980-89**
- tenure preference   **1985-88**
- whether previously owned/buying
  accommodation and reasons for leaving   **1995-96**

Local authority renters:
- whether expect to move soon, and if so
  whether expect to rent or buy
- whether expect to buy present home   **1990-91**
- landlord preference
- awareness of Tenants' Choice Scheme

Housing costs

Gross value   **1971-86**
Net rateable value ⎤ Scotland   **1971-86**
Yearly rate poundage ⎦ only   **1972-86**

Type of mortgage   **1972-77, 1979, 1981, 1984-86**
Current mortgage payments   **1972-77, 1979, 1981, 1984**
Purchase price of present home, amount of
  mortgage or loan and date mortgage
  started   **1985-86, 1992-93**
Current rent ⎤
Amount of any rent rebate/allowance ⎬   **1972-77,**
  and/or rate rebate received ⎦   **1979, 1981**
Whether in receipt of housing benefit   **1985-95**

Method of obtaining mortgage tax relief   **1984**

Central heating and fuel use

Whether have central heating   **1971-96**
Type of fuel used for central heating   **1978-92**
Type of fuel mainly used for central heating   **1993-96**
Type of fuel mainly used for room heating   **1978-81,**
  in winter   **1983, 1985**

Consumer durables

Possession of various consumer
  durables   **1972-76, 1978-96**
Possession of a telephone   **1972-76, 1979-96**
Possession of a mobile telephone: **1992**
- number available for use
- in whose name each is owned or rented
- whether fitted in a car or van

Deep frying   **1986**

Whether does any deep frying, frequency and
  methods used

HOUSING SATISFACTION

Overall level of satisfaction with present
  accommodation   **1978, 1988, 1990**
Reasons for dissatisfaction ⎤
Satisfaction with specified aspects of
  accommodation   ⎬ **1978**
Troublesome features ⎦
Housing preferences   **1978, 1987, 1988**
Satisfaction with landlord   **1990**

INCOME
Income over 12 months before interview
Gross earnings as employee, from self-
  employment ⎤
Income from state benefits, investments,
  and other sources   ⎬ **1971-78**
Number of weeks for which income
  received from each source ⎦

Whether currently receiving income from each
  source   **1974-78**

Current income
Current earnings (gross, take-home, usual) as
  employee, from self-employment, and from
  second or occasional jobs ⎤

          ⎬ **1979-96**

Current income from state benefits,
  occupational pensions (own or husband's),
  rents, savings and investments, and any
  other regular sources ⎦

Current income from maintenance, alimony
  or separation allowance   **1981-96**

Financial help received from former husband
   towards household bills   **1982-83**

INHERITANCE   **1995**

Number, type, value and dates of
   inheritances received
Details of property inheritance

LEISURE

Holidays away from home in the four   **1973, 1977,**
   weeks before interview: **1980, 1983, 1986**
     length of holiday
     countries visited (in UK)

Leisure activities in the four weeks before   **1973, 1977**
   interview: **1980, 1983**
     types of activity   **1986**
     number of days on which engaged in each activity
     whether activity done while away on holiday

Sports activities in the four weeks and year   **1987, 1990,**
   before interview: **1993, 1996**
   - number of days on which engaged in each sport
   - where activities took place   **1996**
   - whether member of a sports club

Arts and entertainments, museums, galleries,   **1987**
   historic buildings:
   - whether visited in the 4 weeks before interview
   - number of days on which visited

Social activities and hobbies in the   **1973, 1977, 1980**
   four weeks before interview   **1983, 1986, 1987,**
                       1990, 1993, 1996

LIBRARIES   **1987**

Whether visited a public library in the
   4 weeks before interview:
   - number of visits
   - library services used

LONG-DISTANCE TRAVEL   **1971-72**

Number of long-distance journeys made in
   the 14 days before interview
Starting and finishing points of journeys
Type of transport used for longest part of journeys
Main purpose of journeys
Number of people travelled with

MIGRATION
Past movement

Length of residence at previous address*   **1971-77**

Previous accommodation:
   - tenure   **1971-73, 1978-80**
   - household composition   **1971**
   - number of rooms
   - bath/WC: sole use, shared, none
   - WC: inside or outside accommodation

Reasons for moving from previous address   **1971-77**

Number of moves in last five years*   **1971-77, 1979-96**

Potential movement

Identification of households containing
   persons who are currently thinking   **1971-78,**
   of moving*   **1980-81,**
Whether will be moving as whole   **1983**
   household or splitting up*
Reasons for moving   **1971-76,1978, 1980-81**
Proposed future tenure   **1980-81, 1983**
Actions taken to find somewhere to   **1971-76, 1980-81**
   live
Whether had experienced difficulties
   - in finding somewhere else to live
   - in raising a mortgage/loan or in finding   **1980-81**
   a deposit

Frustrated potential movement

Identification of households containing
   persons who, though not currently
   thinking of moving, had seriously
   thought of doing so in the   **1974-76, 1980,**
   two years before interview*   **1983**
Whether would have moved as whole
   household or would have split up*

Proposed tenure   **1974-76, 1980**
Reasons for deciding not to move   **1974-76, 1980, 1983**
Whether decision not to move was
   connected with rise in house prices   **1974-76, 1980**
Whether reasons for thinking about moving
   were work-related   **1983**

Whether had experienced difficulties in raising
   a mortgage/loan or in finding a deposit   **1980**

* *Including children*

304

PENSIONS

Whether covered by	**1971-76, 1979, 1982-83,**
employer's pension scheme	**1985, 1987-96**
Whether the scheme is contributory, reasons for	
not belonging to the scheme	**1971-76, 1979, 1982-83,**
	1985, 1987
Whether ever belonged to present	
employer's pension scheme	**1985, 1987**
Length of time in present employer's	
pension scheme	
Whether transferred any previous pension rights	**1983,**
to present employer's pension scheme	**1985,**
Whether in receipt of a pension from a previous	**1987**
employer, and if so, at what age they first drew it	
Whether ever belonged to a previous employer's	
pension scheme	
Length of time in last employer's pension	
scheme and in last job	**1985**
Whether retained any pension rights from any	**1971-76**
previous employer	**1979, 1982-83, 1985, 1987**
Whether pays Additional Voluntary	
Contributions into employer's pension scheme	**1987**
Whether currently belongs to a personal pension	
scheme and whether employer contributes	**1991-96**
Whether has ever contributed towards	
a personal pension	**1987-96**
Date the personal pension was taken out	**1989-90**
Whether belonged to an employer's pension	**1989-90**
scheme during the 6 months prior to taking	
out a personal pension	
Whether makes any other income tax deductible	
pension contributions	**1993-96**
Whether receiving an occupational pension,	
and if so, how many	
Age first drew occupational pension and	
whether this was earlier or later than the	**1990**
usual age	
Reasons for drawing the pension early or late,	
and whether the amount of pension was affected	

SHARE OWNERSHIP

Whether owns any shares	**1987-88**
Whether shares are owned solely or	
jointly with spouse	**1987**
Whether shares owned are in employer's	
company	**1987-88**
Whether has a Personal Equity Plan	**1988**

SMOKING

Cigarette smoking

Prevalence of cigarette smoking	**1972-76, 1978, 1980,**
	1982, 1984, 1986, 1988, 1990, 1992, 1994,1996
Current cigarette smokers	
number of cigarettes	**1972-76, 1978, 1980,**
smoked per day	**1982, 1984, 1986, 1988,**
type of cigarette smoked	**1990, 1992, 1994, 1996**
mainly	
usual brand of cigarette smoked	**1984, 1986, 1988,**
	1990, 1992, 1994, 1996
age when started to smoke	**1988, 1990, 1992,**
cigarettes regularly	**1994, 1996**
whether would find it difficult to	
not smoke for a day	
whether would like to give up	**1992, 1994, 1996**
smoking altogether	
when is the first cigarette of the	
day smoked	

Regular cigarette smokers:
- age when started smoking cigarettes	**1972-73**
regularly	

Occasional cigarette smokers:
- whether ever smoked cigarettes regularly	
- age when started to smoke cigarettes	
regularly	
- number smoked per day when	
smoking regularly	**1972-73**
- how long ago stopped smoking cigarettes	
regularly	

Current non-smokers	
whether ever smoked	**1972-76, 1978, 1980, 1982,**
cigarettes regularly	**1984, 1986, 1988, 1990, 1992,**
	1994, 1996
age when started to smoke	
cigarettes regularly	**1972-73,**
number smoked per day when	**1980, 1982,**
smoking regularly	**1984, 1986, 1988,**
how long ago stopped smoking	**1990, 1992, 1994,**
cigarettes regularly	**1996**

Cigar smoking

Prevalence of cigar smoking	**1972-76, 1978, 1980,**
	1982, 1984, 1986, 1988, 1990, 1992, 1994, 1996

Current cigar smokers

   number of cigars smoked

     per week   **1988, 1990, 1992, 1994, 1996**

   number of cigars smoked per month   } **1972-73**

   type of cigar smoked

   age when started to smoke cigars regularly   **1972**

Current non-smokers

   whether ever smoked cigars

     regularly   **1972-76, 1978, 1980, 1982, 1984, 1986,**

                        1988, 1990, 1992, 1994, 1996

   age when started to smoke cigars regularly   } **1972**

   how long ago stopped smoking cigars regularly

Pipe smoking

Prevalence of pipe smoking among males   **1972, 1978,**

              1986, 1988, 1990, 1992, 1994, 1996

Current pipe smokers

   amount of tobacco smoked per week   **1972-75**

   age when started to smoke a pipe regularly   **1972**

Current non-smokers

   whether ever smoked a pipe regularly   **1972-76, 1978,**

              1986, 1988, 1990, 1992, 1994, 1996

   age when started to smoke a pipe regularly   } **1972**

   how long ago stopped smoking a pipe regularly

TRAINING

Whether received any job training in the previous

   4 weeks, and if so: **1987-89**

   - the type of training   **1987-89**

   - hours spent in last 4 weeks

   - whether paid by employer while training

   - whether compulsory   **1987**

   - reasons for doing training

VOLUNTARY WORK

Whether did any voluntary work in the   **1981, 1987,**

   12 months before interview and, if so: **1992**

   - what kind of work, whether also done

      in the last 4 weeks, and amount of

      time spent   **1981, 1987, 1992**

   - whether done regularly or from time to time   **1981**

   - on how many days   **1987, 1992**

   - number of hours spent   **1992**

   - whether any organisation was involved   **1981**

   - which organisations were involved   **1987, 1992**

   - whether the organisation was a trade union

      or political party   **1987**

   - who mainly benefited from the work   **1981**

Appendix F
List of tables

Previous Volumes in the GHS Series

General Household Survey:
Introductory report
  Origin and development of the survey -
Population - Housing - Employment -
Education - Health

HMSO 1973

General Household Survey 1972
  Population - Household theft -
Housing - Employment - Education -
Health - Medicine-taking - Smoking -
Sampling error

HMSO 1975

General Household Survey 1973
  Population - Housing - Employment -
Leisure - Education - Health -
Medicine-taking - Smoking

HMSO 1976

General Household Survey 1974
  Population - Housing and migration -
Employment - Education - Health -
Smoking

HMSO 1977

General Household Survey 1975
  Population - Housing and migration -
Employment - Education - Health -
Smoking

HMSO 1978

General Household Survey 1976
  Trends 1971 to 1976 - Population -
Housing and migration - Employment -
Education - Health - Smoking -
Sampling error

HMSO 1978

General Household Survey 1977
  Population - Housing and migration -
Employment - Education - Health -
Leisure

HMSO 1979

General Household Survey 1978
  Population - Housing and migration -
Housing satisfaction - Employment -
Education - Health - Smoking,
drinking, and health

HMSO 1980

General Household Survey 1979
  Population - Housing - Burglaries
and thefts from private households -
Employment - Education - Health -
Family information - Income

HMSO 1981

General Household Survey 1980
  Population - Housing and household
mobility - Burglaries and thefts from
private households - Employment -
Education - Health - Smoking -
Drinking - Elderly people in private
households

HMSO 1982

General Household Survey 1981
  Population - Housing - Employment -
Education - Health - The prevalence
of tinnitus - Voluntary work

HMSO 1983

General Household Survey 1982
  Population - Marriage and fertility -
Housing - Employment - Education -
Health - Smoking - Drinking - Cigarette
smoking, drinking and health - Bus
travel - Non-government users of the
GHS

HMSO 1984

General Household Survey 1983
  Population - Marriage and fertility -
Contraception, sterilisation and
infertility - Housing - Employment -
Education - Health - Leisure

HMSO 1985

General Household Survey 1984
  Population - Marital history, fertility
and sterilisation - Housing -
Employment - Education - Health -
GP consultations in relation to
need for health care - Cigarette
smoking: 1972 to 1984 - Drinking

HMSO 1986

General Household Survey 1985
  Population - Marital status
and cohabitation - Housing -
Employment - Education -
Health

HMSO 1987

315

General Household Survey 1985 HMSO 1988
Supplement A: Informal carers
by Hazel Green

General Household Survey 1986 HMSO 1989
  Population - Marriage and
  fertility - Contraception, sterilisation
  and infertility - Housing -
  Burglary - Employment -
  Education - Health - Smoking -
  Elderly people in private households
  1985 - Leisure

General Household Survey 1986 HMSO 1989
Supplement A: Drinking
by Hazel Green

General Household Survey HMSO 1990
Report on sampling error
Based on 1985 and 1986 data
by Elizabeth Breeze

General Household Survey 1987 HMSO 1989
  People, households and families -
  Housing - Health - Sterilisation and
  infertility - Entertainments, libraries,
  forests - Occupational pension scheme
  coverage - Share ownership - Employment -
  Education - Family information and fertility

General Household Survey 1987 HMSO 1990
Supplement A: Voluntary work
by Jil Matheson

General Household Survey 1987 HMSO 1991
Supplement B: Participation in sport
by Jil Matheson

General Household Survey 1988 HMSO 1990
by Kate Foster, Amanda Wilmot and
Joy Dobbs
  People, households and families -
  Family information and fertility - Health -
  Smoking - Drinking - Education -
  Share-ownership - Employment -
  Occupational and personal pensions -
  Housing

General Household Survey 1989 HMSO 1991
by Elizabeth Breeze, Gill Trevor and
Amanda Wilmot
  People, households and families -

Employment and pension schemes -
Health - Accidents - Marriages and
cohabitation - Fertility and contraception -
Housing

General Household Survey 1990 HMSO 1992
by Malcolm Smyth and Fiona Browne
  People, households and families -
  Housing - Occupational pension scheme
  coverage and receipt of occupational
  pensions - Health - Smoking - Drinking -
  Sport, physical activities and entertainment

General Household Survey: OPCS 1992
Carers in 1990
  OPCS Monitor SS 92/2

General Household Survey 1991 HMSO 1993
by Ann Bridgwood and David Savage
  People, households and families -
  Housing - Burglaries in private households -
  Employment - Occupational and personal
  pension scheme coverage - Childcare -
  Health - Contraception - Education -
  Family information

General Household Survey 1991 HMSO 1994
Supplement A: People aged 65 and over
by Eileen Goddard and David Savage

General Household Survey 1992 HMSO 1994
by Margaret Thomas, Eileen Goddard,
Mary Hickman and Paul Hunter
  People, families and households -
  Health - Smoking - Drinking - Occupational
  and personal pension scheme coverage -
  Employment - Education - Family
  Information - Housing

General Household Survey 1992 HMSO 1994
Supplement A: Voluntary work
by Eileen Goddard

General Household Survey 1993 HMSO 1995
by Kate Foster, Beverley Jackson,
Margaret Thomas, Paul Hunter, Nikki Bennett
  People, families and households -
  Housing - Burglaries in private households -
  Employment - Health - Contraception -
  Sport and leisure activities - Family
  Information - Education - Pensions

Living in Britain
Preliminary results from the 1994
General Household Survey

HMSO 1995

Living in Britain
Results from the 1994
General Houshold Survey
by Nikki Bennett, Lindsey Jarvis,
Olwen Rowlands, Nicola Singleton,
Lucy Haselden
   Housholds, families and people- Health -
   Smoking - Drinking - Elderly people in
   private households - Employment -
   Pensions - Family information -
   Education - Housing

HMSO 1996

Living in Britain
Preliminary results from the 1995
General Household Survey

The Stationery Office 1996

Living in Britain
Results from the 1995
General Houshold Survey
by Olwen Rowlands, Nicola Singleton,
Joanne Maher, Vanessa Higgins
   Housholds, families and people- Housing
   and consumer durables - Employment -
   Pensions - Education - Health - Private
   medical insurance - Dental health -
   Hearing - Contraception - Family information

The Stationery Office 1997

Living in Britain
Preliminary results from the 1996
General Household Survey

The Stationery Office 1997